Home Plans

Murray Armor

J.M. Dent

Originally published as *Home Plans for the 80s* in 1983.
Second edition 1984.
Third edition 1985.
Fourth edition 1988.
Fifth edition 1992.

Published in the United Kingdom by
J.M. DENT & SONS LTD
Orion House
5 Upper St Martin's Lane
London WC2H 9EA

ISBN 0 460 86083 6

ACKNOWLEDGEMENTS

Cover by: Terry Whitworth
Drawings by: Derrick Spence.
Design pages co-ordinator: Richard Cartledge
With many others whose work has been acknowledged
in the text or privately.

Typeset in Souvenir by Spooner Graphics, London NW5

Contents

Introduction

Having a new home built to a design that you yourself have chosen is one of the most popular ambitions in the world, and for thousands of people every year it is a dream which comes true. Individual building plots are easier to come by these days than they have been for many years. The Banks and Building Societies are in competition to lend money for new houses, and are much more flexible in the ways in which they will do this. The recession in the building industry means that both builders and sub-contractors are enthusiastic about working for private clients. If you have always wanted to build to your very own design, now is the time to do it.

To take advantage of this and build on your own land you will have to make many decisions, and you will have to plan and manage the whole thing in a very careful way. Making the right decision depends on your analysis of many different factors, but the aim of everyone building for themselves is the same. Invariably your new home has to be *a very good investment,* and *exactly the home you want to live in* and building it has to be a cheerful and stress-free business.

Achieving these aims is not difficult, but the whole business has to be handled properly, and this needs a very clear understanding of how the system works, and of the options open to you.

Home Plans is set out in a way to give you all the information that you will need to make the right decisions, and to make your own dreams come true. The options explained and the advice given are based on day-to-day experience with thousands of people who have built on their own land. All the designs shown have been built, often with modifications to suit individual clients. Some of them have been built literally hundreds of times.

Later in this book you will find details of how the plans can be obtained, and details are given of other services which you will find useful. At the very end is a list of organisations and firms that can give specialised help in many ways. We hope all of this will be useful to the readers for whom this book was written — those who dream of a new home and intend to make their dreams come true.

A new home— The essentials

So you are looking at designs for a new home. If you are just looking, dreaming dreams perhaps, or looking for ideas to help you choose what sort of house you should buy from a builder, then this is a book to be dipped into whenever it interests, and it has lots to say. On the other hand, if you are really hoping to build on your own land, then you have got to read it in a very different way. You have to sort out the dreams from reality, and to do this you have to look hard at three essentials.

First of all, you need to consider designs in relation to your financial situation. You know what you can afford to spend, and now you have to work out what you can build within your budget.

Secondly, you have to think about your dream house as an investment, and to make sure that what you will pay for it will be more than covered by its market value. You will want it to increase in value in step with house values generally, and hopefully ahead of them.

Thirdly, you have to think about your home being exactly the building that you want to live in, suiting your own life-style, with the appearance and the atmosphere that you want.

If you have already got a site, or there is a site which you are thinking of buying, then you can look at all of this in relation to that site. You will be able to identify a narrow range of options, and then make firm decisions. If you have not got a site, and are reading this book to help you to know what is both possible and practicable when you look at building plots for sale, then it is even more important to understand the basis of the decisions which you will have to make in due course.

Sad to say, many of the decisions will be made for you by others. The planners will decide whether your new home can be built at all, and if they agree then they must approve every detail of its appearance and materials. The Building Regulations will often control where you put the building on the site, and will determine many details of its construction. The cost of services — water, gas, electricity and road access — and involvement with other legal obligations can be a major factor in choosing a design. All of these constraints and legal requirements are dealt with in a separate chapter and it is vital to realise the importance of all of them.

The cost of a new home is dealt with on pages 2 to 8. Here you will find repeated references to 'costs per sq.ft' and this is a concept that has just got to be understood if you are to get anywhere. Average cost per sq.ft. multiplied by the number of sq.ft. in a design, gives a very rough indication of total cost. This can be related to your budget costs, and doing this is the essential first step in deciding what you can afford, and what is out of the question.

The whole business of design, and how best to analyse your own requirements, is discussed in the next chapter. This deals with concepts — with changing styles in design, with styles that will date and those that are less likely to, and with the relationship between design features and costs. Other specialist chapters deal with the materials and the fittings which give the home its feel and character.

The 300 pages of home plans include designs to meet almost every situation in a wide variety of styles and materials. Plans are available for all of them as they are illustrated, and they can also be supplied with modifications and alterations within the original design concept. These standards plans are also of great use in deciding what features you may want in a design that has to be specially drawn to suit your own particular requirements. However before you consider a special design of your own remember that all of the standard homes have been built and all of their designs were drawn to be cost effective. They are all capable of being built in a straightforward way using standard building industry techniques. Twenty of the designs are by Prestoplan Limited, and are specifically for timber frame construction. Timber frames are discussed at length in a later chapter, and if required most of our three hundred can be built in this way.

Finally, the chapter 'Making it all happen' is concerned with just that, and describes how a design on our pages can become a real home. This usually takes between 6 months and a year; 2 to 4 months obtaining planning consent and dealing with legal matters, and 4 to 6 months building. Sometimes things move more quickly, but rarely does a new house built on a fixed price basis take longer — and you *must* deal in fixed prices in this age of inflation. All the advice in the book is written lightly, because you simply must read it all if you want to build, and a more formal style would not encourage you to do so! It is based on experience with over 2000 new homes built on the owner's own sites. All of them got their dream homes — as does virtually everyone who actually makes a start. If you decide to build for yourself then your planning of the project involves so many others — Building Society Managers, the Bank, Planners, Building Inspectors, builders, the N.H.B.C., Inspecting Architects and so on — that they all have a vested interest in seeing the job through. Once you wind up the machine it starts rolling and will carry on right to the end. And at the end you will not only have your dream home, you will also have had a lot of fun. Good luck.

What will it cost?

Long before you are able to consider the actual cost of the particular house or bungalow that you want to build you will need to know the approximate cost of the sort of home that you have in mind. This is essential to enable you to know the size of property which you can afford, and the sort of designs which you should consider. These figures which you need are expressed in costs per sq.ft. This requires some further explanation.

For most technical and legal purposes the floor area of a building is not the overall area, but is the 'area enclosed by the internal faces of the external walls'. It is at least 10% less than the area obtained by multiplying together the outside measurements, which is called the plinth area. The diagram explains this. In this book all areas are the strict legal areas, but in some publications it is the overall areas, or plinth areas that are quoted. Obviously costs per sq. ft. of plinth areas are significantly less, so that care must be taken in comparing figures from different sources. For a two storey building the areas of the two floors are added together.

Any general figures for costs per sq.ft. depend on three factors. These are:

What you build

How you build

Where and when you build

How these factors affect your costs is dealt with on the following pages.

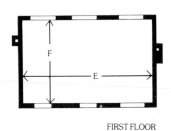

FIRST FLOOR

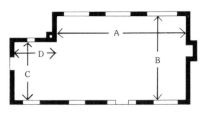

GROUND FLOOR

The area of a dwelling is the total floor area enclosed by the internal faces of the external wall.

$(A \times B) + (C \times D) + (E \times F) = $ *total area for the plan above. which is for the house on the right.*

SIZE RELATED TO HOUSING TYPE

Up to 700 sq. ft. — Holiday chalets and 1 or 2 bedroomed old people's bungalows only.

700 to 800 sq. ft. — Smallest possible 3 bedroom semi-detached houses. Small 2 bedroom bungalows.

800 to 900 sq. ft. — Small 3 bedroom bungalows with integral lounge/dining rooms and compact kitchen. 2 bedroom bungalows with larger kitchens or a separate dining room. Most estate built 3 bedroom semi-detached houses.

Around 1000 sq. ft. — Large 3 bedroom semi-detached houses. 3 bedroom detached houses. Small 4 bedroom houses. 4 bedroom bungalows with integral lounge/dining room. 3 bedroom bungalows with separate dining room or large kitchen. Luxury two bedroom bungalows.

Around 1300 sq. ft. — 3 or 4 bedroom detached houses and bungalows with the possibility of a small study, or second bathroom, or a utility room.

Around 1600 sq. ft. — 4 bedroom houses, or bungalows with 2 bathrooms, large lounges, small studies, utility rooms.

Around 2000 sq. ft. — Large 4 or 5 bedroom houses and bungalows.

Above. A house of 2090 square feet built in Herefordshire.

Middle. A house of 1670 square feet.

Bottom. A bungalow of 1100 square feet with a double garage.

WHAT YOU BUILD

The costs per sq.ft. for both bungalows and houses are much the same provided that the buildings have straight-forward foundations, and that you can avoid expensive roofing materials.

The key element in costs is the roof — how it is built and how it is tiled. Any arrangement to put rooms in the roof, as in dormer bungalows, or in many traditional style house designs, inevitably adds to costs. The most cost effective roofs are built from factory made trussed rafters. These are wholly supported by external walls, and although they provide useful attic space for storage and water tanks they do not provide any room for living accommodation. A dormer bungalow with rooms in the roof needs traditional purlin construction, and in most circumstances this costs significantly more than a trussed rafter roof.

Dormer bungalows are unpopular with the planners and generally out of fashion, but gable window features in two storey designs are very much part of today's cottage style. It is often possible to build these using trussed rafters. The diagrams explain this. Wherever possible all designs in this book use trussed rafters.

The span of the roof is an important cost factor, with the optimum distance about 25 ft. Any span over 30 ft. involves increased construction costs, and any spans under 20 ft. are disproportionately expensive. The pitch, or angle of the slope of the roof, affects the cost by increasing the area to be tiled, and above 35° this becomes significant. However, the most important

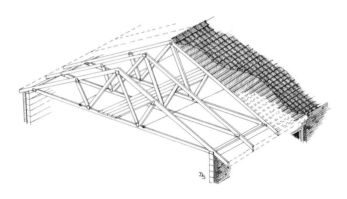

Trussed rafter roof — easily erected, cost effective, limited space for storage.

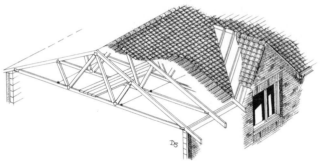

Gable feature in a trussed rafter roof requires that the window head is below the eaves.

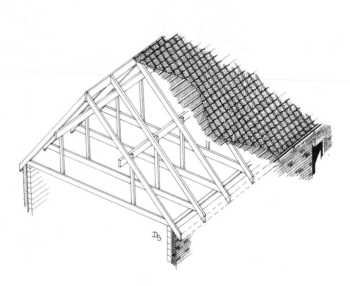

Traditional purlin roof — plenty of room but expensive to construct.

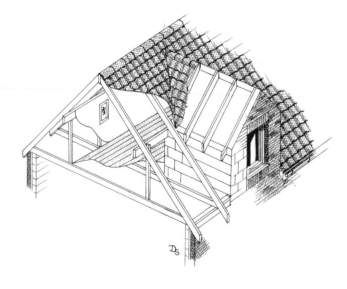

Gable window in a traditional roof can be set at any height.

factor in roof costs is the roofing material.

95% of all new roofs are tiled with concrete inter-locking tiles, and these are available in a wide variety of shapes and colours. Some are indistinguishable from natural clay tiles. In certain areas the planners may insist on other roofing materials, and these can add enormously to costs. Clay tiles, traditional plain tiles whether concrete or clay, and either real or artificial slates are all very significantly more expensive. Some of these materials require rafters to be set closely together to support their weight, and add 50% to the cost of the roof timbers. All this is discussed further in the chapter on roof tiles; at this stage the thing to remember is that any movement away from concrete inter-locking tiles will cost a lot of money. How much?

One example: the 'Carlton' design shown below costs about £3000 more to build when roofed with concrete plain tiles than when it is built with inter-locking pantiles.

Below the roof your costs will be determined by two things — the fixtures and fittings you choose, and the shape and materials of the shell. Fixtures and fittings — kitchens, bathrooms, doors, fireplaces, flooring etc — are up to you. Our average costs are based on fittings appropriate to the size of the dwelling — luxury kitchens in large homes, economy kitchens in small homes. The economies of scale when building large properties tend to be balanced by the more expensive fittings and fixtures put into them, so average costs do not vary much with size.

The Carlton bungalow, which costs £3000 more to roof if using one concrete tile than another. This is considerably more than the extra cost of putting it on a reinforced raft foundations. Many clients are unnecessarily concerned at the cost of special foundations but ignore the greater expense of any special tiles required by the planners.

A house has a smaller roof than a bungalow for the same floor area, so the effect of expensive tiles on houses is less significant in terms of cost per sq. ft.

The cost of building the walls depends on a number of factors, and whether or not you use a timber frame is irrelevant compared with the cost of the outer skin. Our average costs are based on this being in wire-cut facing bricks, or in blocks for a rendered finish, or in a good quality artificial stone. Natural stone, especially with stone surrounds for windows, will add significantly to costs — although not as much as expensive roof materials. There are no general price guidelines for stone; everything depends on local prices and who you can get to lay it in a way that will do it justice. If everything else about a property is right, then building it in real stone is an investment as it should add significantly to the value of the property. The same is true of building in hand made bricks, but in practice those who build in real stone, or in hand made or reclaimed bricks, do so at the insistence of the planners, and rarely from choice. All of this is discussed at length later.

External joinery can be the usual painted softwood, or stained softwood which adds nothing to cost and a great deal to character, or hardwood. Hardwood windows, windowboards, door frames and doors add about £800 to the cost of a medium sized home. They should add far more than that to its value, and hardwood joinery is now the choice of the majority of those who build for themselves. Aluminium and plastic windows are principally used in the refurbishing of old buildings, and are not used to any significant extent in new housing. Their day may come, but it has not arrived yet. They are very expensive. All this is discussed elsewhere in the chapter on joinery.

The design of the superstructure of a building has an effect on costs that relates mainly to the way it affects the area of external walling involved. The diagram explains this. Ceiling spans over 14'6" bring problems for your architect, as do galleries, large stairwells, and projecting balconies, but these features are usually found in large houses where they have less effect on costs per square foot than in smaller properties.

Below the superstructure are the foundations, defined as the part of the building where you pour your money into the ground, never to be seen again. Do not worry about the 'best' foundations for any situation; Building Regulations are so strict and so concerned with the worst possible circumstances that any foundations approved at the Town Hall will be more than adequate for their purpose. All that you have to do is to make sure that the work is in accordance with the drawing. Fortunately the Building Inspector will also make this his concern, but he will not help you to meet the cost of his enthusiasms. Before you agree to any special foundation arrangements always make sure they are obligatory and not just a suggestion, and look at the full cost implications.

Most new houses are built on standard strip foundations with solid floors. This involves digging trenches under the walls, pouring a 9" layer of concrete in the bottom, building up from this to just above ground level, and then laying a concrete floor. There are alternatives for different sites but all of them cost money. These are shown opposite in order of descending cost.

2 small two bedroom bungalows and one had 30% more walling to be paid for than the other.

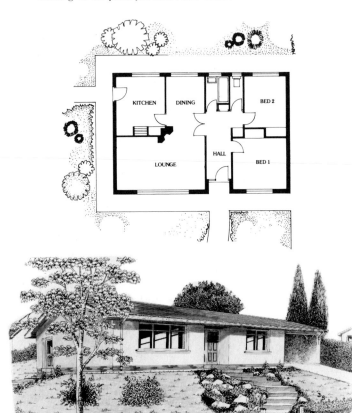

Piling. Building a modern home on deep piles driven into the ground can cost £3 a sq.ft. or more by the time you have paid for the test bore holes, engineer's designs and the work itself. It is a way of being able to build on very bad ground indeed, and is often cost effective when the land was cheap to start with, or when the value of the finished home will be high.

Underbuilding. Building a garage under the home, or building a home into a hillside to give a series of split levels, is definitely not cost effective and should be avoided if you are very concerned with cost and have acceptable alternatives. Developers and those concerned with the building industry often build in this way very cheaply, but will rarely tender competitive prices to do this for others. It is invariably cheaper to carve out a plateau from a hill, or to build one up and then to build from the level base. On the other hand, multilevel buildings do look very nice from outside. Whether they will suit your living pattern is another matter.

Raft Foundations. In mining areas or on soft land the authorities may require you to build on a raft, which is simply a slab of reinforced concrete that sits just under the surface taking the whole weight of the building. This is rarely as expensive as you fear it will be, and is unlikely to add more than £1 a sq.ft.to the costs —often less.

Trench Fill Foundations. This is a technique for filling your foundation trenches to the top with concrete, and avoiding foundation brickwork altogether. In rural areas where bricklayers' travelling costs are significant and where a concrete truck can get all around the foundations this approach may even save money.

Reinforced Strip Foundations. If the authorities are concerned about the ground on which you are building and are making noises about a raft, then ask if reinforced strip foundations might be acceptable. You will need a civil engineer to specify the reinforcing mesh to be put in the concrete, and to provide design calculations for this, but his fees plus the cost of the work may be significantly less than the alternative.

Suspended Floors. There are only two reasons for having suspended floors. Firstly if you like a suspended wooden floor, believing it to be kinder to your arthritis, or giving a better spring to the floor when you have disco parties, then go ahead and pay for it. It will cost less than £1 a sq.ft. The other reason for having it is that you may have more than 2'6" of fill to be put into your foundations between ground level and floor level. If this is the case the N.H.B.C. will insist on a suspended floor, and although the building regulations do not require it, it is a good thing anyway. It can be either a wooden floor or a reinforced concrete floor; the latter may be marginally cheaper.

Service Connections. Finally, the total cost of your new home will also depend on what you have to pay for service connections. The cost of getting water, gas and electricity to the site are really part of your site costs, but have to be considered carefully just the same. Most serviced plots have got these utilities conveniently to hand, and only connection fees and service trenches have to be considered. Isolated plots in the country are a different matter.

All our costs quoted allow for the average cost of making drain connections on serviced plots, or for the installation of a septic tank on isolated sites. Surprisingly, septic tanks cost very little more than a drain connection.

So much for the cost of what you build.

HOW YOU BUILD

There are two ways in which those building a new home on their own land arrange to have the building work done. The majority — perhaps 75% — engage a builder to take the whole job as a single contract, with an N.H.B.C. certificate on the finished property at the end of it all. The others manage the job themselves using sub-contactors, and the popularity of this approach is growing. In Milton Keynes for instance, where the new town authority releases hundreds of serviced plots a year for sale to private individuals, most of them build in this way. There is rarely a middle road; the idea of having a builder to put up the shell and then taking the job on from there yourself is attractive, but it does not often happen. Building using sub-contractors gives very real cost savings, and also very real responsibilities, problems and panics to be dealt with. All this is discussed further in a later chapter, but as the cost saving can be 20% or more the approach that you adopt does affect your budget costs. If in doubt use a builder. The self-build movement is for those with abundant self-confidence.

WHERE AND WHEN YOU BUILD

We are all used to regional variations in the market values of homes in different parts of the country, and accept as a fact of life that a house in Surrey will cost twice as much as the same home in Humberside. Land prices account for much of this. What is more difficult to understand is that building costs will also vary, although not to the same extent. Why this should be so is an interesting subject for an argument over a pint of beer, but such debate will not detract from the fact that you will have to pay more to build on your own land in some areas than in others. Generally speaking it will cost up to £2 a sq.ft. over the average to build in a high cost housing area.

In rural areas costs are usually lower, but you may have to pay more than the average if the site is remote and the workmen's travelling costs are significant. This is particularly true in the South West and parts of West Wales. On the other hand, a surprisingly large number of those who build already have local contacts or are very good at making them, and find the bargains.

Any cost of building for yourself, and indeed the ease with which you can interest a builder in quoting for a job on your own land, depends on the state of trade in the building industry. At present it is very depressed, and builders are anxious to quote for any sort of work. In the 70's when the housing market was firmer, builders were less enthusiastic about one-off jobs. Whether these conditions will return is a mute point, but it is important always to look at up-to-date costs and to keep in mind the possibility of an upturn in home sales. If this happens it will be more difficult and more expensive to build on your own site, but also the value of the home you build will escalate quickly, and the differential between cost and value will improve.

One of the best ways of getting reliable up-to-date costs is to look at the figures quoted by the companies who provide a package service for individual sites. Both the firms concerned with traditional construction and those selling a timber-frame service will quote realistic prices, and if you make sure that these are for the finished job, including the services and the access, then they are an excellent guide to what you should expect to pay. Design & Materials Limited publish case histories giving the plans, photos and the actual costs of a recently completed job every month, and these are available through Plan Sales Services to anyone sending a stamped addressed envelope. They are concerned with both the contract costs of those who build using sub-contractors in all parts of the country. The costs shown here are based on an analysis of these case histories and on other real experience.

Spring 1992 national average costs for single and two storey homes to D & M standard designs, built on single sites by individual clients, on straight-forward foundations, including fittings and fixtures appropriate to the size of the property, central heating, double glazing, connection to drains or septic tank, garage, short length of drive, no landscaping.

When built by an established N.H.B.C. builder, working from his offices following an invitation to tender, formal contract.
— from £38 to £46 per sq. ft.

When built by a reputable small builder, N.H.B.C. registered, working from his home, usually himself a tradesman, following an informal approach and contract should be established by exchange of letters.
— £32 to £39 per sq. ft.

When built by competent private individual on a direct labour basis, using sub-contractors, without providing any labour himself.
— from £28 to £37 per sq. ft.

Self-build housing, individuals or housing associations, typically over 50% of the labour provided by the individual or the association.
— sometimes below £24 per sq. ft.

The average figures quoted remain remarkably consistent, irrespective of the size of the building. The more expensive fittings in larger properties are balanced by savings consequent on the economies of scale.

FACTORS WHICH WILL KEEP DOWN COSTS

Use of concrete inter-locking tiles.
Cost effective walling materials.
Trussed rafter roofs with spans of between 24 ft. and 28 ft.
Care taken that any special design features are arranged in the most economical way.
Building on a level plinth.
Building using strip foundations and level floors.

FACTORS WHICH WILL INCREASE COSTS

Unusually expensive fixtures and fittings.
Roofing material other than inter-locking concrete tiles, especially on steep pitches.
Natural stone or hand-made brick walling (but this may be a good investment).
Building other than on a level site.
Complex designs which increase the area of external walling, and involve complex roof shapes.
Dormer roofs, especially dormer bungalows.
Special foundation arrangements.

Choosing a design

Typical design used for both rural and suburban housing in the '60s.

Having considered the size of your home that will suit your finances, the constraints of your site, and bearing in mind the probable requirements of the planners, you can move to the business of choosing between designs. This involves the appearance and style of the building, and the number, size and arrangement of the rooms which it will contain.

The external appearance of homes built in Britain in the last sixty years has varied enormously, and until very recently there has been a marked distinction between the *avant garde* homes that are featured in the text books as being the influential designs of their decade, and what was actually being built. The architecturally significant homes of the thirties had flat roofs, architectural use of glass, rounded corners and a German name — the Bauhaus style. They were about as different from the mock Tudor homes that the developers were actually building as they could be. Then came the War, and after it both the theorists and the developers wanted a change. In the fifties and sixties, architects were seeking to express the essentials of function in bricks and mortar, stripping away unnecessary decoration and contrived features. At the same time the less aesthetically aware were opting for homes with simple (and cheap) shapes, and with low pitch roofs and picture windows (as in Hollywood films). Later in this period contrasting panels of timber and plastic became almost obligatory.

New rural housing today, built to look 100 years old.

With the first oil crisis in 1972, came the concern for smaller windows and 'boxier designs'; the fashionable few built Georgian houses in Regency proportions, while the developers simply put Georgian windows into their same old boxes. Enter the Georgian style executive residence.

Meanwhile something was happening at the Town Hall. The reorganisation of local government in 1974 gave planners throughout the country a chance to see that they got their own way in the brand new authorities. In the old District Councils the planners had always been new boys, upstarts from the fifties, lacking the weight of those who had administered finance, housing or sewerage since the nineteenth century. In the new councils they could establish themselves — and they did. County design guides were produced, setting out clearly and unambiguously exactly what could expect to be approved, and what could not. Whether, as some maintained, it was never Parliament's intention that the Planning Acts should be used to exercise this sort of control is irrelevant; the design guides were published and have had a far reaching effect on our low density housing.

Perhaps it is fortunate that they were drawn up when there was no coherent establishment style for new homes, for in the absence of anything better they reached back to the early nineteenth century and everywhere looked for the essential features of the local

New suburban housing today, with a design that looks back to the 1930s.

cottages of that era. In Nottinghamshire, farm houses used to have gable roofs with steep pitches, so hipped roofs and low pitched roofs were forbidden. Essex cottages once had black boarded gables and dark stained joinery; these features became essential to speculators' developments in Basildon. Nowhere in 1830 had builders stuck panels of contrasting materials below windows to make their houses look pretty, and this fashion of the sixties came to an abrupt halt. Window design also changed as is discussed and illustrated in the chapter on joinery later. Even more far reaching, complex shapes and involved roof lines were introduced to give 'interest' to a design, sponsored by architects who had been urging simple shapes and functional structures only fifteen years before.

It was all fascinating, especially to the big developers who had to find whole ranges of new designs to replace their old ones that had lasted since the fifties. Look at a Wimpey estate of 1960, and a Wimpey estate today, and, if you prefer today's house designs, you will feel it

fortunate that those who bought the older homes have disguised them with such splendid front gardens.

Architects protested vigorously against the idea of any design guide at all, but mindful of a frightening fall-off in commissions due to the recession they hastily climbed on the band wagon and became pedantically involved in the minutiæ of the regional styles. By 1980 the *avant garde* and popular taste had met up. Both were concerned that building shapes should be as complex as finances would permit, with careful use of natural looking material, and with small windows that were conveniently energy saving as well as being traditional. Within two years this led to contrived traditional features added as ornaments, and even to the re-emergence of pseudo Tudor styles and half-timbered houses with herringbone brick infill. Within one generation our whole approach to house styles had undergone a total revolution. We have arrived at post modernism and the eighties, still the style of the nineties.

What is the relevance of this history lesson to the

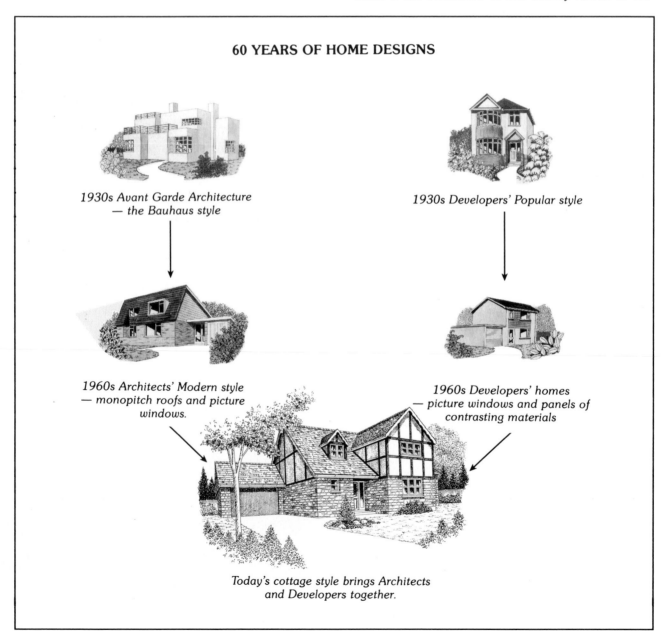

60 YEARS OF HOME DESIGNS

1930s Avant Garde Architecture — the Bauhaus style

1930s Developers' Popular style

1960s Architects' Modern style — monopitch roofs and picture windows.

1960s Developers' homes — picture windows and panels of contrasting materials

Today's cottage style brings Architects and Developers together.

reader who wants to build a new home today? For one thing, it must surely reassure him that today's style is likely to be with us for a long time. There is no alternative on the horizon, and there is widespread public disillusion with the modern architecture which it has replaced. Because it is traditional it suits our growing interest in conservation. All of this can only be a very good thing.

In all his drawings in this book Derrick Spence has shown homes in the styles that are likely to be generally acceptable to the planners in the sort of settings in which they are illustrated. However, you must remember that there are wide regional variations in planning policy, and particularly in the way in which bungalows are regarded. It is generally true that in most areas the planners would like to reduce the proportion of single storey homes that are approved. Planning authorities also differ in the extent to which accepted regional styles are insisted on in areas where there is a preponderance of existing buildings in other styles.

What will happen if you do not like the design guide recommendations for your new home? Except in conservation areas and other places of particular importance, the planners will often back down, or at least negotiate, on their imposition of many design features, and if they will not, formal planning appeals on these issues are often successful. On the other hand, a formal planning appeal is a lengthy process, and by the time you are discussing design details you are usually locked into a tight programme and cannot spare the time to appeal. Another consideration is that the cottage style is here to stay, and that if your home is to be the best possible investment, then like all other investments from Unit Trusts to jewellery, it should be a good fashionable example of its type.

The top end of the scale — a large farmhouse in Nottingham-shire built on a commanding site on a large arable farm. A building of this size is usually treated by the planners as an architectural unit on its own, and is less likely to have to conform to strict design guide standards.

Architect — Dennis E. Wilburn R.I.B.A.

So much for the external appearance of your home; now for the arrangement of the living space inside the building. If you wish you can simply leaf through the design pages and make a note of the plans which particularly appeal to you, but if you are actually choosing a new home let us urge you to find the time to analyse your wants before you get involved with individual designs. Start with the front door. Do you feel that front doors are important, and should be a key feature in the view of the front of the building as in a typical Georgian style house? Or are they not really important — as in many fifties style houses? Front doors lead into a hall. If you can build only 1500 sq.ft. within your budget, then do you want to use 150 of them on an imposing hall that is a room in its own right, with space for furniture, or do you want the minimum size hall and to use the area saved elsewhere? Or do you want

Do not get too involved with design details without having a clear idea of the atmosphere which you hope to give your new home.

a hall at all, and would you like a dining room in the centre of the house to give access to other rooms as in so many American designs?

A whole list of these different concepts of how we like to arrange the accommodation in our homes is shown opposite. Please answer the questions and establish your requirements in concept before considering the plans — it really is the right way round to do things. Whatever your requirements, today's cottage style, with

HOUSE/BUNGALOW LAYOUT
DESIGN CHECK LIST

Front Entrance

Do you think an impressive front entrance should be a key feature of the house?
Or just take its place in the front elevation?

Front Porch

Is this required? Is a storm porch required to draught-proof the hall when the door is opened?

Front Hall

Is it important that the hall should convey the whole feeling of the house as soon as you step inside? Or is it just a space between other rooms?
What furniture do you want in the hall? How essential is a cloaks cupboard?
Do you prefer a glazed or solid front door?

Lounge

Lounge or lounge/dining room? Is the feel to be of an enclosed room, with no more window than to provide a view, or is the preference for a large area of glazing with the room relating to the garden or patio outside? Are patio windows required?
Is a fireplace required? If not perhaps a dummy fireplace? If so, a feature fireplace or a classical small fireplace? If a feature fireplace, should this have a vertical feel, to the ceiling, or be a full wall feature, or have an extended mantel to provide shelving?
If you are having a lounge-dining room, is some form of room divider or natural break between the two parts of the room preferable?

Does the lounge/dining room need a door to the kitchen or just a hatch?
In general terms, do you like 'L' shaped lounge/dining rooms?

Dining Room

Maximum number to sit at table?
Door or hatch to kitchen?
Is a built-in sideboard acceptable to save space?

Kitchen

Will the family eat in the kitchen?
At a breakfast bar or table?
How many?
What major appliances are required in this room?
Is a structural larder required?
Is an Aga or similar solid fuel cooker required?

Utility Room

Need this be any more than a large porch?
What appliances are required in it?
What storage space?
A w.c. adjacent to the back door (useful in rural areas)?

Bathroom

One bathroom or two? If two, is one to be en suite with the master bedroom?
Fittings in bathrooms—bath? basin? w.c.? bidet? separate shower?
Airing cupboard in bathroom, or can it be elsewhere?

W.C.

Where?—in bathroom(s)? in cloakroom or hall? at back entrance?
Basins—in which w.c.'s?
Cloaks cupboard—in a cloakroom which is also a w.c., or would you save space by having hooks and rails actually in the cloakroom itself, not enclosed in a separate cupboard?

Bedrooms

How many double, how many single?
Is the master bedroom to be as generous as possible at the expense of the others?
Is provision to be made for built-in furniture?

Study

Is this to be significant room, or very small with just room for a desk and filing cabinet?
Does it need built-in shelving, or cupboards?
Will it double as an occasional bedroom, and thus require room for a divan?

Garage

Integral with the house with a communicating door to the utility room or kitchen, or separate?
How many cars?
Plus extra room for garden tools etc.?

Central Heating

What type of central heating system is envisaged?

Future

Is there any possibility of future extensions or alterations to suit changed family circumstances?

complex shapes and involved roof lines, makes special arrangements and alterations a lot easier than they were when everything had to be accommodated in a more simple shape. Most things are possible if the site and your finances permit, and while you will have to accept the advice of your architect or designer about how you achieve your ambition, if you are paying the bill it is your prerogative to say exactly what your ambition is.

We hope you will find one of our plans that exactly suits your living pattern, your site, and the whim of the planning officer; but you will probably want to make changes, and the best way of advising us is given at the end of the book. However, before sharpening your pencil you may find the following notes useful. They are based on a great deal of experience of dealing with clients' requests for alterations to standard plans.

POINTS TO BEAR IN MIND

* Beware of adding windows to give more light and more views; you usually end up with nowhere to put your furniture.

* Try to keep windows a minimum of 2'3" from the corners of the building. This ensures the strength of the structure. If you want a corner window you will have to pay for some way of reinforcing the corner walls.

* Look at the way that the architect has put windows symmetrically in the building, and beware of damaging this symmetry. In general a ground floor window is balanced by a first floor window of the same width. Not essential, but think about it.

* Regulations require that the main windows in a lounge, living room, dayroom, study and bedroom must be 12' from any boundary. Fire regulations limit the total area of doors and windows in all walls near to a boundary. You can have 60. sq ft. of openings in a wall 3'3" from the boundary, but only 10 sq. ft. if you move in to 3'0". You need professional advice on this.

* All rooms have to have opening lights to the windows up to a total of 5% of the floor area of the room. Patio doors count as windows if they also have trickle ventilators.

* Bathrooms and lavatories can be built without any windows, as long as they have fan assisted ventilation via ducts in the roof, but even if you like this it is a bad re-sale feature.

* Stairs are subject to dozens of regulations and cannot be moved about with impunity. Try to leave the stairs where they are. Above all try to avoid plans for two storey houses with no stairs at all. Every few years some authority or other builds council houses with this interesting feature, to the delight of the popular press.

* A W.C. cannot open into a kitchen or living room. The W.C. should lead into a 'ventilated lobby' which is a hall, landing or utility room.

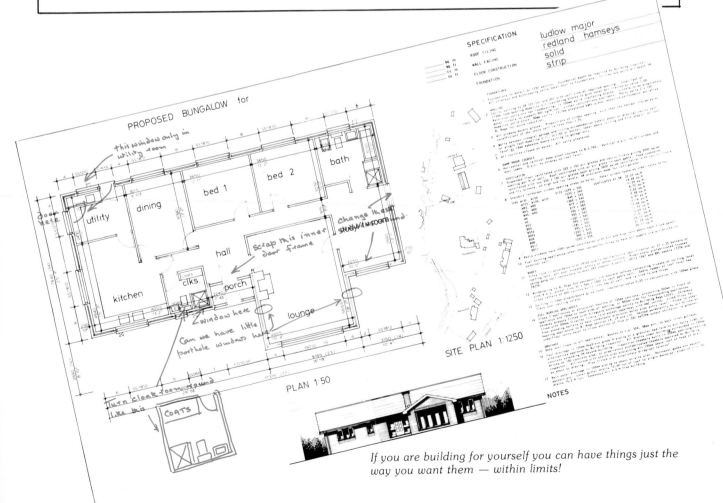

If you are building for yourself you can have things just the way you want them — within limits!

GARAGES

A garage for the car is part of our image of a dream home. This concept is so firmly rooted in our idea of what is right that it is worth looking at the argument against having a garage, as it is rarely realised how easily this can help a budget problem.

A garage usually accommodates a car and an assortment of garden tools. The car will not deteriorate if left standing in the open, although it will be colder to get into on a winter morning. The garden tools can go in a garden shed at the bottom of the garden, easily disguised with a vigorous evergreen climber. Thus the only reason for a garage is to conform to a dream image that is based on pride in one's automobile, and a desire to be seen to cherish it. However illogical this is, the great majority of people build a garage!

In spite of this you may wish to consider whether you would rather have two extra rooms instead of an integral garage, or perhaps a huge landscaped patio with a barbecue pit and pergola instead of a detached garage. Another option is to build the concrete slab for the garage foundation but to do no more until the new home is finished and you are sure you have the funds to build the home for the car. Until then the car will not come to any harm parked outside.

The pros and cons of detached versus integral garages are equally worth considering. If you have a narrow site you may not have much choice, but if this is not the case, then consider the factors in the box below.

As a compromise you may wish to consider a carport. If so, it is important that it is properly designed, with solid piers and a deep fascia so that it relates properly to the main building. This is never easy, and today's homes are less well suited to carports than the ranch style homes popular a few years ago.

DETACHED VERSUS INTEGRAL GARAGES

* A detached garage can be positioned in relation to a house or bungalow so that the group of two buildings look better than a single dwelling with an integral garage. A link wall can add to this effect.

* A detached garage is cheaper to build than an integral garage, as it does not require complex foundations, a fireproof ceiling, or other expensive features.

* A detached garage can be built after the house or bungalow is built, or when it is approaching completion. If you are uncertain whether you can afford it you may find this useful.

* It is more expensive to put a water tap, electricity, or an outside W.C. into a detached garage than it it is into a integral garage.

* An integral garage provides somewhere to put a central heating boiler, or an extra freezer, and in many ways tends to be useful simply because it is part of the main building.

* An overwhelming advantage of an integral garage to the elderly or infirm is the opportunity to get in and out of the car 'out of the weather'.

Bricks

Today's cottage style housing, in a way, rediscovered brick. Its concern with houses that have complex shapes, with emphasis on architectural details, and with subtle use of colour and texture in materials encouraged brickmakers to widen the range of bricks available, and gave an opportunity for bricklayers to bring craft bricklaying back to house building. In the sixties and seventies brickwork in most housing was very dull, with bricks laid in the simplest possible way as a foil to contrasting panels of other materials. Brickwork features and special bricks were rarely used. Since then we have seen a brickwork revolution, and facing bricks are back in all their full range of shapes, colours and textures. This chapter is to help you in choosing both the brick and the style of brickwork for your new home.

First of all, keep in mind the traditional use of bricks in your local area. In much of the country brick is the traditional premier walling material, and the type and colour of the bricks used, and the way in which they are laid, is part of the local architectural tradition. You will invariable find that the planners are very keen to maintain this tradition. On the other hand, if the dominant walling material locally is stone, or perhaps a rendered finish, it is equally important to see what use is made of bricks in existing brick buildings, and what is the usual choice of bricks to blend happily with the other materials. A choice of bricks that is very distinctive and quite different from the local brickwork style will rarely be acceptable at the planning office except in some urban situations.

Today's bricks — a wide range of colours and face textures, most of them with a rustic feel.

Butterley Smooth Red bricks for the soldier course and gable window surrounds provide a pleasing contrast to the Butterley Wentworth mixture bricks used for this house in Northern Ireland.

16

Virtually every planning consent has a condition reading 'samples of walling material shall be submitted and approved before construction commences'. Whether you handle this yourself, or whether someone deals with this for you, the choice of the brick that you submit will normally be yours, and you will want advice on making your decision. If the planners decide to press alternatives on you, then it is even more important to know what you are discussing with them and where to go for further help.

As an alternative to this, in a particularly sensitive situation such as a conservation area, the planners may actually specify the bricks they require. You can argue, but are unlikely to win. In this case ask them to give you a sample!

Bricks are given trade names by manufacturers, such as Butterley Muirfield Mixture, where Butterley are the manufacturers, and Muirfield Mixture is one of their trade names. To the ordinary person this means nothing, but somewhere in the manufacturer's leaflet you should find a clue to which of a number of types the bricks belong. All bricks are available in a selection of colours and textures, but it is the type of brick that dictates the price. These prices vary enormously, and this is always a major consideration. The average 1000 sq.ft. bungalow needs about 7,000 bricks, and the average 1600 sq.ft house about 12,000. As brick prices can vary by £300 per thousand it is essential to know the cost of what you are discussing, and also to keep in mind that haulage costs form a significant part of the delivered price. However, price is not the only consideration.

All bricks made today have to meet very strict standards for both strength and durability and are suitable for all normal domestic uses. There are special standards for bricks that are to be used in special situations, such as cills, copings and some retaining walls. If plans for your new home have been professionally prepared then they will specify the type and class of brick that is to be used, and any divergence from this will quickly attract the attention of both the Building Inspector and the N.H.B.C. Inspector. Advice on this is readily available from the brick manufacturers, who can best advise you if you send them a print of your drawings.

BRICKS AND BRICKWORK

Having considered the different types of brick, it is important to appreciate the distinction between the colours which are available, and the textures. Two bricks of the same colour, but with different textures, can be very different in appearance. If you add another variable by using coloured mortar, the differences are emphasised. The colours of clay facing bricks are determined by the inherent colour of the fired clay, additions to the clay body to give through colours, surface effects given by the application of stained sands — which are rendered colour fast during firing — and variations in the firing conditions. Special textures may be given to the bricks in a wide variety of ways, or sometimes they are simply left smooth.

Such a variety of colours and textures is now available that it would be cumbersome to list them all here. A choice between them must be a personal judgement.

Finally, how on earth do you choose between them? One of the best ways is to find a builders' merchant with a brick library — a term for a display of representative bricks which are available. Usually these bricks are displayed in panels and choosing between them is easier than when looking at a single brick. Alternatively, write to the facing brick manufacturer for details of their clay facing bricks and delivered prices.

Choosing bricks from samples is always an interesting business. Make sure you view them in natural light if possible, and if you are looking at sample panels consider the effect of

the mortar colour. Ideally confirm your choice by looking at a building in the brick which you want to use.

Butterley Jubilee Mixture

Butterley Desford Old English Russet.

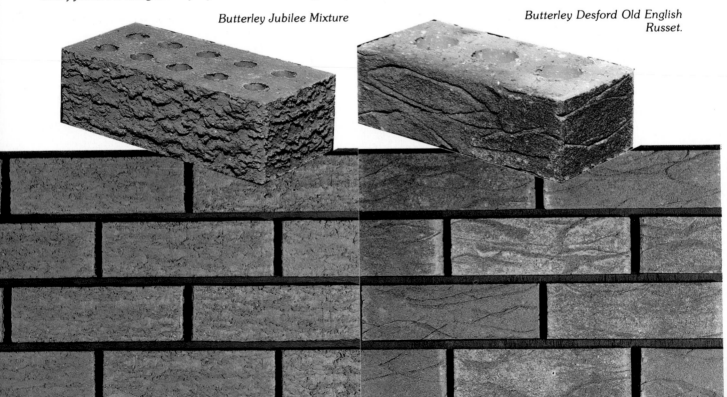

TYPES OF BRICKS

Fletton Bricks are also called LBC bricks, after the name of the only company which manufactures them. They are made from deposits of London clay, require little fuel to bake them, and as a result they are the cheapest clay bricks available. They are not very strong, but meet all the requirements for building above damp course. Fletton bricks are widely used in the Home Counties, and may be specifically required by planners in certain areas. Elsewhere they tend to be used in budget housing only. The price, ex works, for this type of brick is about £130 per thousand.

Wirecut Facing Bricks are made by a continuous extrusion process which enables the physical properties of the brick to be closely controlled, and are available to any standard required. A typical ex works price for Butterley facing bricks is £227 per thousand for Jubilee Mixture. The range of colours and textures is very wide indeed, and these are the bricks usually used in new houses built by individuals on their own sites unless there are special considerations.

Stock Bricks are a traditional type of brick found in certain parts of the country. They have an irregular shape and the colour and surface texture is distinctive.

Handmades are bricks which are literally made by hand. They have a distinctive appearance with a folded face known as the smile — see the photo below — and are always made from the very best of clays with super colours. Very much the thing for prestige housing. An average price is between £350 and £400 per thousand.

Secondhand Bricks are widely used in certain areas of Cheshire, East Anglia and Sussex where they may be required by the Planners. If you are buying secondhand bricks it is essential to get all you want for a job from the same source at the same time, otherwise they may not all match. It is unwise to make firm arrangements to buy secondhand bricks without consulting the builder or the bricklayer who is actually going to lay them. The cost of these bricks can vary enormously — and so can the quality.

Because of these problems a few manufacturers now make simulated secondhand bricks — new bricks with the physical characteristics and colourings of reclaimed bricks but the advantage of guaranteed quality and unlimited supply. Butterley Claughton Manor Victorian Mixture is a typical brick of this sort, and currently costs £178 per thousand, ex works.

Commons are bricks which are to be covered up by plaster or otherwise concealed, so that they do not need to have an attractive appearance. Always take advice on the suitability of Commons for the purpose to which you intend to put them. The cost of Common bricks is usually about £80 per thousand.

Engineering Bricks are high quality bricks which are used for foundations, retaining walls and other situations where strength and resistance to water are important.

Concrete Bricks, Sandlime Bricks, Calcium Silicate Bricks are not made from clay at all. They are used for housing in some areas, but it is a good idea to inspect them in a finished building rather than to choose from a catalogue or samples.

Butterley Sandringham Handmade

Butterley Jacobean Blue-Red

Butterley Canterbury Multi Stock bricks complement the half timbering on this house in Staffordshire.

Butterley Tudor Golden Russet bricks were used for this imposing house in Dorset.

BRICKWORK IS MORE THAN THE BRICK

A brick building takes its character from:
* The bricks.
* The bond or pattern in which they are laid.
* The colour of the mortar in the mortar joint.
* The use of brickwork features in the design.

The choice of bricks, and approval of brick features is something that may have to be settled with the planners, but the way in which the bricks are laid is largely going to depend on your builder or his bricklayer. Modern cottage style designs give many opportunities for the

Brick features are back — what a good thing!

man who will lay your bricks to show off his craft skills, and if you take an interest in this you will be surprised how flattered he will be, and what a keen interest he will take in doing a good job for you. There are many patterns of brickwork, known as bonds, which were in general use until cavity walls came into use fifty years ago. The cavity requires that bricks are now laid in stretcher bond, which is dull, but the monotony of this can be relieved in various different ways. Brick pillars and landscaping features do not usually have a cavity, and the old bonds can be used. Soldier courses and other features can be used in cavity walls, and brick cills give a great deal of character to any building. Corbelled eaves at gable ends look well, and are a traditional feature in many parts of the country.

In addition to this, talk to the builder about the colour of the mortar. This normally depends on the sand used — most builder's merchants have a choice of grey, red or yellow sand, and each gives its own colour to the mortar made with it. Artificial colours are available for mixing with mortar if required, although great care should be taken with this. The mortar joint itself can be either recessed or flushed, or pointed in a variety of styles. Consideration of all of this is beyond the scope of this book, but what we do want to get across is the need to get the bricklayer interested in the job he is doing on your home, and the best way to start is to ask him to build a sample panel using the actual bricks that you are going to use. Give him half a chance and he will be demonstrating bonds and pointings until the pubs open, and then continue his lecture in the public bar. Once you have got your key building craftsman as interested as this, you can be pretty sure of getting the best job for miles around.

Above: 'Squint' bricks used to form the window cill. These particular ones are from Butterley's Caernarvon works.

BRICK FEATURES IN WALLING

Brick features in cavity walls have to conform to building regulations, and cannot be as uninhibited as when used in landscaping or for internal feature walls. The cavity must be left unobstructed, and recognised bond used to maintain the strength of the panel. However, there are far more options than is often realised. Generally speaking any brickwork feature that is in the same brick as the main area of walling and which is properly proportioned in relation to the building as a whole will enhance the appearance of the property. If well done it will help to lift it right out of one class of building into another — and that means out of one level of investment up to another.

Butterley handmade Golden Russet bricks were used for the walling for this feature courtyard.

Choose bricks for landscape features with the same care that you use when you choose them for a fireplace. The Jacobean bricks used for this barbecue were ordered with a matching plaque made by the brick manufacturer, and were chosen to complement the Land End paver bricks.

Fireplaces made with Butterley handmade bricks. The manufacturers will help with plans and kits for these indoor features.

The Butterley handmade bricks used on this new home in Nottinghamshire help it to look as if it has stood for a century.

The use of bricks for internal feature walls is increasing. They project their own character wherever they are used, so you must make sure that they will suit the furniture and the general decor, carpets and curtains that you will choose for the room. Besides feature fireplaces, internal brickwork is often used for halls, stairwells and kitchens. Usually hand made bricks are chosen.

The major brick companies will provide advice on all aspects of using bricks, from making suggestions on appropriate bricks that need planning requirements in any particular part of the country, to designing retaining walls and providing the structural calculations for them. In particular they will advise on the use of bricks for window surrounds, decorative brickwork at eaves, arches and garden walling that are part of the renaissance of ornamental brickwork in the nineties. If you send them copies of your plans with your enquiry (*not the originals*) you will help them to be specific in the advice they will give to you.

Material for this chapter and all the photographs were provided by Butterley Brick Limited. Their bricks are available from works throughout the country, and Butterley freely give expert advice and help in choosing bricks for a new home. Contact them at Butterley Brick Limited, Wellington Street, Ripley, Derby. Tel: 0703 570570.

Building in stone

A decision to build a new home in stone, or to have stone features as a significant element in the design, immediately involves you in making a whole list of decisions about the right stone to use, and the best way to use it. The right decisions will result in a house that is a show piece, and it is well worthwhile going to a great deal of trouble to look at all the options and to get the best advice.

First of all, any use of stone has to be in the local architectural style. Stone is used in different ways in different parts of the country, and invariably the way in which it is used reflects the characteristics of the local stone itself. Where it is easily worked to give a smooth finish, this finish to the walling is often an essential part of the character of local buildings, and the use of stone with a rough finish is incongruous. Some stone has a pronounced grain to it, rather like the grain in wood, and is always laid with the grain horizontal. In areas where this is traditional one can perhaps use other stone that is not typical of the area so long as it is laid with the long edge of every block horizontal. To do otherwise is to make the building stand out like a sore thumb, when the essence of any stone construction is that it should be seen to be a natural part of the landscape. Every area where stone is the traditional walling material has its own rules of this sort, and you will have to take care that you follow them. The planners themselves will give advice, as will your own architect or builder. Often the man who is selling you the stone will be the most help of all.

Stone is used in new buildings in two ways — as the walling material for the whole of the shell of the structure, or just for ornamental features. This latter use is now declining, and stone panels below windows, stone chimneys in brick bungalows, and stone gables are not nearly as common as they were in the '60s and '70s. On the other hand, during the 1980s the use of stone for the whole building has increased, and continues to do so, as part of the general move to natural materials and traditional design. This often involves designing the building to suit the actual stone to be used. Yorkshire gritstone with rocky face needs to be used in wide panels to give a massively solid feel to the structure, while Bath stone that is worked to a fine face can be used for narrow piers and delicate window surrounds. If your site is in a conservation area or if there are special design considerations then all of this has to be given very careful thought indeed.

Having considered the need for a design that suits the material, there are four aspects of any use of stone which have to be taken into account; the colour, the surface texture, the way it is laid, and the use of traditional features or 'dressings'. Each of these requires separate consideration.

Colour. Stone comes in a wide variety of colours, from warm Cotswold shades to the severe greys of the north. Often the choice of shade will be dictated by the planners, but if there is a choice it is important to guard against simply choosing the prettiest colour among the samples, and to consider the look of the building as a whole. This involves visualising the new home in its setting, and keeping in mind the colour of the roofing material that is to be used. Beware of non-traditional shades and keep very well clear of mixes of colours unless there is a local style that has quoins or window surrounds of a different shade to the rest of the walling. That is not to say you shouldn't consider using 'weathered' shades of reconstructed stone where darker tones are added to the base colour to give an appearance of time-aged stone. This is particularly useful in situations where new buildings are built close to older ones, helping to make the two blend visually. Mortar joints must always match the colour of the stone itself, and the brickwork technique of using a contrasting mortar to give a special effect should never be used.

Surface Finishes. The surface texture on stone walling can have as much effect on the overall appearance of the building as the colour. Faces vary from smooth to very rough and uneven, and all have special names — ashlar, tooled, chisel dressed, rough hewn etc, and different quarries and manufacturers have their own names for the different surfaces. Again, take local advice and make up your mind after looking at finished buildings rather than small samples. The same applies to different ways of pointing the mortar joints.

Features. Features in stonework such as quoins, window surrounds, and corbels once had a specific structural role in the building, but are now really ornamental. None of them are essential to ensure that the building will not fall down, but when used in the proper way they give a splendid air of 'being right' to a new house, and are definitely something to have if costs permit. The special blocks of stone used for features are called dressings or fittings, and a whole range of them are illustrated opposite.

Laying Stone. Building in stone is a very different business from laying bricks. Most stone used for new houses is either laid in a completely random way, or else used in irregular courses, and yet it has to be a coherent element in an integrated design. If a window has to be set at a certain height then the mason has to ensure that the pattern of stonework reaches this height as a natural break. The more irregular the pattern in which the stone is being used, the more important this is, because the effect of random walling depends on the regular use of large stones or jumpers. If these are missing near a window or doorway the whole wall will look wrong. If you are using coursed stone, remember traditional

walling of this sort depends for its effect on the courses being of different heights, and the balance between the courses is critical.

Achieving the right effect with natural stone is a job for a mason, who often has to cut or 'dress' the stone to size. Reconstituted stone is more easily laid, and is supplied in mixes of blocks to set proportions which suit the walling style required. Both quarries and reconstituted stone manufacturers have leaflets which show the styles of walling for which their stone is suitable.

Whoever is laying your stone will have a clear idea of the way that he is using it — make sure this matches your own ideas as well. Discuss the jointing and the different types of pointing, and jump in your car and go off for an hour with him to look at other stonework that he has built. It may be worthwhile getting him to spend half a day building you a panel of sample walling — indeed, the planners may ask for this. The home that he is to build for you will last hundreds of years; if you are building it in stone then do not grudge the time to make sure the use of the stone is exactly as you wish it.

Architectural feature stonework, or 'dressings' are part of traditional stone construction, and are available to match most types of walling stone. The illustration shows the whole building in Bradstone reconstructed stone, and the dressings used are as follows:

1–Plinth course. 2–Quoins. 3–Porch surround. 4–Traditional window surround without label moulding. 5–Label moulding used as a string course. 6–Coping. 7–Traditional window surround with label moulding. 8–Kneelers. 9–Gable coping or water tabling. 10–Apex stone. 11–Traditional chimney coping. 12–Conventional chimney coping.

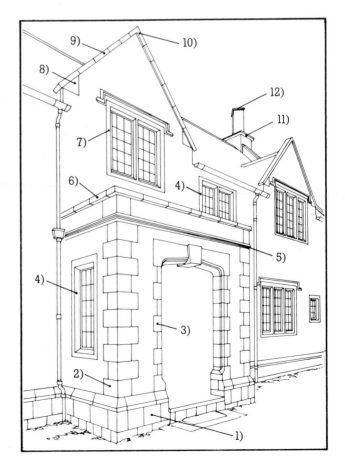

STONE LANDSCAPING

Stone built houses have a traditional feel to them, and invariably this is very important to their owners. It is most important not to detract from this atmosphere by using alien or aggressively modern materials for land-scaping. Concrete paths, cheap paving slabs or modern screen walling can easily spoil the appearance of a stone home, and all landscaping features should be given as much consideration as the design of the house itself. This involves careful thought about the scale of the features as well as about the materials.

Courtyards and patios in particular should be large enough to give the house or bungalow a perspective, and to spread it visually. A small patio often looks like an outsize door mat, and gives a doll's house effect when it should help to make the whole building more impressive. The same is true of steps and balustrading, especially when they lead to a front entrance. All of this is a subject on its own. In this book we simply emphasise that it is an important subject, and that if you are building a new home in stone it is worthwhile making a modest investment to provide stone land-scape features to give it the best possible setting. The market for stone in landscaping is very important to both quarries and artificial stone manufacturers, and they will all advise on matching landscaping material which they have available.

Reconstituted stone paving need not look 'new'. Bradstone Wetherdale (above) and Octavian/Old Wetherdale (below) all capture the appeal of natural materials.

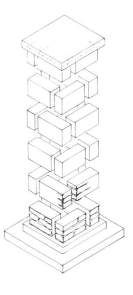

Sundials such as this are easy to build. It is essential, however, to build them on a properly constructed foundation.

STONE AND YOUR BUDGET

All this mention of stone has so far avoided the question of cost. What does it cost to build in stone, and how will this suit your budget? The answer is that you have a very wide choice indeed, and, as with everything else, you will get the value that you pay for.

Building in natural stone is at the very top end of the market. The right house in hand dressed local stone, provided it is the right design and the right site, leads the field in value. For a four bedroomed detached house the cost will probably start at £5000 more than building in any other material, and it can be much more. Part of this is the cost of the stone itself, part is attributable to the high wastage of material when using real stone, and the rest to the premium cost of employing a stone mason. The results should be worth it, and it is certainly worthwhile obtaining the very best advice and workmen to make sure that you get what you are paying for.

With this level of costs it is not surprising that the majority of those who build in natural stone do so because this is a condition of their planning consents, and for no other reason. Most home builders who start off with an interest in using stone from a local quarry find that their budget will stretch to two extra rooms if they change their minds and use a reconstructed stone.

Reconstituted stone is defined in the relevant British Standard Specification as 'manufactured from cement and natural aggregates for use in a manner similar to natural building stone'. It comes in two types, split stone and cast stone and is used just as brick for the outer skin of normal cavity wall construction. It is also commonly used for the outer skin to timber frame houses.

As the name implies, split stone is formed by splitting concrete made from ground natural stone which results in a rock-like surface profile with a granular texture and consistent colour. A guillotined stone look is the initial result of the splitting process and in this form the walling blocks suit certain applications. More frequently the blocks are 'rough faced' in a secondary process which rounds off the sharp edges.

Blocks are available in size ranges which allow either random or coursed stone walls to be built and with Countrystone, for instance, the face texture is carried round one end so that there is continuity where returns show at door and window openings. Should there be a need to shorten a block and expose the cut face there is no problem as the texture and colour is consistent throughout.

Without being an exact replica of natural stone, split stone has much of its appeal visually and with the use of quoins and architectural dressings such as windows and door surrounds, will provide a home of individual character. As far as cost is concerned, split stone can be cheaper than facing bricks but there are regional variations.

A more sophisticated replica of natural stone, cast stone goes to some lengths to recreate its natural counterpart. The essential characteristics of natural stone are largely colour, texture and size — each of these dictated mainly by nature in the way local stone types were formed and consequently how they can be worked by stone masons.

Using natural aggregates and cement, cast stone is made in moulds taken from actual stone masters. There are a number of masters (and moulds) for each individual block size to avoid obvious repetition of profile.

Probably the best known and most developed range is Bradstone made by ECC Building Products at three

Above. Bradstone walling and matching window dressings.

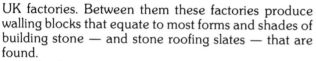

Left: A new house built in ECC Countrystone.

Something of the subtlety of the shades in which Bradstone can be made is seen in the photograph above.

UK factories. Between them these factories produce walling blocks that equate to most forms and shades of building stone — and stone roofing slates — that are found.

While there are some particularly sensitive areas where planners will only accept natural stone, Bradstone is widely seen in areas of outstanding natural beauty. This is simply because most people cannot tell the difference between Bradstone and natural stone. Planning consent will often specify exactly the style and colour to be used and even the factory of origin.

Another option in your choice of stone is to use reclaimed material from an old building. This is a pratical proposition in some circumstances, but it is important to make a cynical appraisal of the old stone available before basing your whole budget on its use. The best person to advise you about this is almost certainly the mason who will be handling it for you, and he should be asked to confirm the proportion of the old stone that is sound, whether or not he is likely to get the total quantity that you require from the amount available, the cost of re-dressing it to give both the face and the bed (or thickness) that you require, and the labour cost of building your own home in this rather difficult material. After consideration of all this the usual decision is that the old stone will be used for garden walling only! However, if you go ahead it is most important to work out exactly how much re-dressed stone you will require, with a 25% allowance for wastage, and to have this quantity dressed and stacked ready for use before you start building. In this way you will avoid the risk of running out of stone which cannot be matched from elsewhere.

BUILDING IN STONE — YOUR COST OPTIONS.

Typical costs of a square metre of walling stone, ex-quarry or ex-works, in September 1992

Dressed stone. 4″ on bed — material for building the outer skin of the walls.

Cotswold Stone, quarry in Wiltshire, £95 plus.
York Stone, quarry at Otley, from £30 to £50.
Forest of Dean Stone, local quarries, £35 plus.

Split faced artificial stone

Countrystone walling, £10.60 per square metre.

Moulded reconstructed stone

Bradstone traditional walling, £16.10 per square metre.

Photographs for this chapter were provided by ECC Building Products Ltd. of Okus, Swindon, SN1 4JJ, manufacturers of Bradstone and Countrystone. Attractive colour leaflets for their full range of products are available from them at the address above, and their sales representatives will be pleased to call to advise on the use of their materials for a new home in any part of the country.

Pavers

One of the more interesting developments in the modern use of traditional materials in recent years has been the return of clay pavers, sometimes called paving bricks, for roads, drives and paths to new homes. The name 'paver' is correct, and manufacturers discourage the term 'paving bricks' because pavers have different physical qualities from ordinary bricks, and are made to meet appropriate standards for their use.

The reason for this popularity is linked with the whole ethos of post modernistic architecture, with its concern for natural materials, attractive detailing and the move away from stark functionalism. Natural clay pavers provide an opportunity to build paths and drives in a whole range of subtle colours, in a wide choice of patterns and with a variety of surface textures. They can set off a building in a way that tarmac or concrete can never equal, and like all natural materials will mellow and get more attractive as the years go by.

Pavers can be laid in two different ways, described as rigid jointed paving and flexible paving. The former is the way in which they have been used for many years, and it involved bedding them with mortar onto a concrete base. More recently, following continental practice, flexible paving has been gaining in popularity in Britain for all types of application providing significant cost benefits. This technique involves a consolidated sub base of suitable material covered with 50mm of sharp sand. The pavers are laid in the pattern required on the sand and are settled into it using a special vibrator. There is no cement involved, avoiding unsightly splashing, and providing that the surface is kerbed to give adequate edge restraint and the sub base is properly compacted, the resulting surface is fully the equal of hot rolled asphalt.

There is a very wide range of pavers available, and when making your choice you should consider the other materials to be used on the site, and particularly the walling bricks for both the house and for garden walls and features. Not only the colour should be considered but also the surface texture and the pattern in which the pavers are to be laid. Flexible paving will enable you to use pavers with chamfered edges, and this helps with drainage in bad weather and gives you yet another choice of a distinctive look to the surface.

As with all building materials, pavers are best chosen from samples, Butterley sales offices throughout the country have them on display, and it is worth making a special trip to make sure that you choose the right pavers to surface your new drive — remember that they will be there for the whole of the next century.

The patterns in which paver bricks are used are just as important as the bond used in brickwork walling. A selection are shown on this page, taken from a Butterley Paver leaflet.

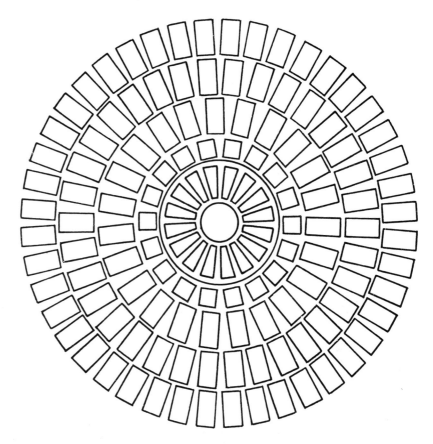

1. Stretcher Bond – a simple pattern often used to emphasise a particular route or to improve run-off from minimum fall areas.

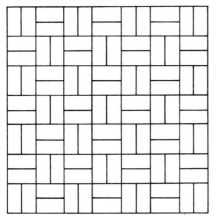

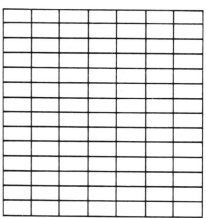

2. Basket Weave – a very adaptable pattern which gives a good interlocking static pattern and also offers many variations.

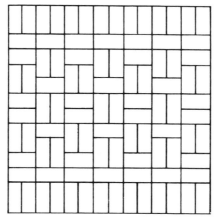

3. Herringbone – a very popular pattern which provides a secure interlock, and is ideal for areas where vehicular traffic is intended.

Material for this chapter and all the photographs were provided by Butterley Brick Limited. Their bricks are available from works throughout the country, and Butterley freely give expert advice and help in choosing bricks for a new home. Contact them at Butterley Brick Limited, Wellington Street, Ripley, Derby. Tel: 0773 43661.

Roofs

As far as the home-buyer is concerned the roof of a new house is simply something that has to support the tiles that he has chosen, is expected to give no trouble of any sort, and provides storage for odds and ends. Someone building his own home will want to know a little more, and it is useful to understand the basic design options, and costs, involved in getting a roof over your head.

There are two types of roofs with which you may be involved — purlin roofs and trussed rafter roofs. Other sorts of roofs that you may read about belong to the history books. A choice between them depends on many factors, and you may not have the option as the design of the house that you have chosen may dictate the sort of roof involved.

A trussed rafter roof is based on the use of factory made trusses, delivered to the site as complete units and manhandled up onto the wall plate, which is a length of timber which rests on the top of the inner leaf of the side walls of the building. Provided that the wall plate is level and the building has been built square, a trussed rafter roof will fit together like a jigsaw puzzle, and a complex structure can be fixed and ready for the tilers in only two or three working days.

A purlin roof is different in many ways, with the whole roof built on site. Instead of individual roof trusses, each taking its share of the weight of the roof tiles as it stands right across the building, the traditional rafters rest on massive purlins that run parallel to the wall plate, and which are themselves built into gable walls. Constructing a roof in this way demands very specific skills, and joiners who have the experience to build a good purlin roof with a level ridge and really flat sides are not easy to find. Purlin and trussed rafter roofs are illustrated on page 4.

Until fairly recently it was usual to build purlin roofs from timber purchased in a local timber yard, but new and complex building regulation requirements now make it usual to buy all types of roofs from a specialist supplier. These companies supply the complex design calculations that will be required by the Local Authority and provide certificates that all the timber used has been stress graded. They will arrange for preservative treatment of the timber if this is wanted. All the components are sent in one load, including galvanised steel items like truss shoes and joist hangers. They will do this for either trussed rafters or purlin roofs, and will also deal with the complex situation when the design requires that one part of the roof uses trussed rafters with another part in purlin construction.

To get building approval for a roof on even the simplest structure it is necessary to demonstrate that it is designed to meet a bewildering variety of circumstances. The roof has to be able to support the weight of the tiles or slates that you intend to use, together with a huge safety margin to cover the activities of the tilers or anyone else walking on the roof, like your T.V. aerial installer. It has to support the maximum weight of snow that experience has shown is likely to pile up on it. It has to resist the worst gales ever recorded in your local area, and for this the country is divided up into areas with different exposure ratings. Inside the roof the ceiling joists have to support your water tank, which is very heavy, as well as your electrician when he is installing the wiring. He may or may not be as heavy as the water tank, but he will certainly want to drill holes in the roof timbers for the wiring, and his friend the plumber will want to notch the timbers for pipes. As the activities of this pair are unpredictable, the whole roof has to be designed to permit them to do their worst to it anywhere. Design calculations are required for all of this, and these days are usually provided as computer print outs.

Add to this the possible need for preservative treatment to your own requirements, and insecticide treatment to meet special regulations in certain parts of the country, called 'Longhorn beetle areas', and you will begin to understand that this is a very complex subject. If a builder is quoting for your new house it is certainly a good idea to ask who is supplying the roof, to ask whether the timber is stress-graded, and to discuss if you wish it to be preservative treated. If you are managing your own building operation you should put the whole business in the hands of a specialist supplier at an early stage.

Often you will find that you have little opportunity to choose between trussed rafter and purlin construction, as the design will suit either the one system or the other. If you do have the choice then you will find that when you add together material costs and labour costs, the trussed rafters have a total package advantage. Besides this, trussed rafters help to ensure a first class job as all the trusses are made under controlled conditions in a factory. Certainly it is reassuring to know that every joint has been properly made, and does not depend on someone remembering to hammer in the right number of nails while perched 30 ft up in the air in a strong wind.

Architects are often asked to arrange for a new home to be built so that it is possible to 'put a room in the roof' at a future date. It is not usually realised exactly what this means in terms of costs, and the restraints that it places on design. A room set in a roof involves up-rating the ceiling joists from 4 x 2 timber to 8 x 2 timber to carry the new floor load, providing support from below for these joists as appropriate, designing for a staircase opening to be framed in the ceiling at a later date, and, above all, using a system of roof construction that will give a clear space for the room itself. This will require that either all or part of the roof is built using purlins, or else that elaborate and expensive attic trusses are used. Your roof specialist will be delighted to supply all the additional material for this, but the cost is significant, and it is a considerable undertaking.

There is rather more space available in the ordinary trussed rafter roof than may be realised, and although the ceiling ties will not support any significant weight, they are so over-designed to take occasional loads that they will cope with the suitcases, folding prams, unwanted presents and everything else that is usually found in a loft. Recent windbracing regulations require a boarded walkway through the trusses from gable to gable, and this serves very well as a decking for your storage area.

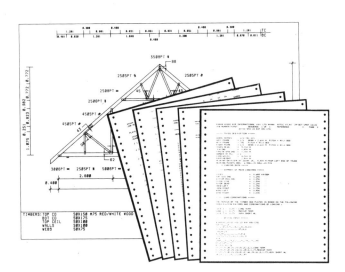

Even a simple roof like the one above has dozens of components; wall plate, trusses, binders, bracing, ladders, barges, fascias etc. etc. All this is bext bought from a roof specialist who will supply both the roof materials and also all the schedules and calculations that you will need. The documentation on the left is for a roof supplied by Hy Arnold Ltd., who provide a service for new homes throughout the country. Write to them for details at Hy Arnold (Trussed Rafters) Ltd, Holton Heath Trading Park, Poole, Dorset BH16 6LE. Telephone: (0202) 623777, Fax. (0202) 632064. or Hy Arnold (Castleford) Ltd., Carr Wood Road, Glasshoughton, Castleford, West Yorkshire WF10 4PS. Telephone: (0977) 554220, Fax. (0977) 513017.

Tiles and Slates

The appearance of the roof of a building is an essential part of the character of the structure as a whole. As today's traditional style houses involve us in ever steeper roof pitches, so the area of roof which we see from the ground level increases and its importance as a feature increases with it. This has very important implications for those who are building a new home, and before you start looking at samples and colour charts it is worthwhile looking at the overall picture.

First of all, tiles and slate of all types which are used on new buildings today are made to standards that will ensure that they will last a lifetime or longer, and will keep out any extremes of weather provided they are fixed properly. No worries here. As far as anyone building a new home is concerned the criteria are costs, appearance and what the Planners say. A realistic view of this avoids confusion, the facts to be considered are as follows.

'Traditional' roofing materials are the ideal choice for traditional building. Unfortunately the market for them is so small that at times they are not widely available, and the price is usually very high, both of the materials and the labour to fix them. Because of this they are only used when cost is not an important consideration, or where the planners insist that traditional slates or clay tiles should be used. As with natural stone, the home builder on a fixed budget will find that using traditional material for his roof will take him right out of one level of costs into another, and that if he can use concrete tiles instead, then the saving will pay for a larger home with an extra bedroom. As a result he invariably chooses concrete tiles.

Concrete tiles suffer from their name, which is a pity as a hundred years of expertise has gone into making sure that they look nothing like concrete! They are technically superior to most traditional tiles and slates, can be more securely fixed, and are used on lighter and more cost effective roof structures. Most of them lock together, which determines the spacing, and they are quickly and easily laid. Research over the years has led to standards which enable one manufacturer — Redland — to guarantee their performance for 100 years. They are used for over 90% of new housing, and modern tiles can match traditional tiles in appearance so perfectly that only an expert can tell the difference.

Tiles and slates are also used in cladding walls, and tile hung walls are a most important feature of the domestic architecture of S.E. England and E. Anglia. All that is said about roofing tiles applies to wall tiles, and again concrete tiles have virtually taken over from traditional material.

For this reason the following pages are mainly concerned with concrete tiles, but in order to relate them to the clay tiles which they match so closely, and the different sorts of slate, and so that the reader can understand what the planners may talk about, it is first necessary to look at the range of traditional roofing materials. This is not an exhaustive list, and there are regional specialities which vary from Norfolk Reed to Westmoreland Slate. However, if you think that you may use these materials you have a very special situation and need special advice.

Traditional tiling materials which you are likely to come up against are:

Clay Tiles. Generally of two types, small plain tiles about 8"x5", and larger curved pantiles. Modern clay tiles are machine made and lack the irregularities of the old handmade tiles, although some companies now offer tiles which mimic the old handmade tiles — combining authentic looks with precision manufacture. Although modern clay tiles appear virtually identical to concrete tiles when on a roof, planners may well insist on the traditional material in certain areas.

Welsh Slate. High cost and limited availability largely prevent its use. However, a real alternative to natural slate does now exist. The Redland Cumbrian Slate is composed of two-thirds natural slate dust mixed with tough resins: the result is a lightweight, interlocking slate, with a thin leading edge and rivened surface — virtually indistinguishable from the real thing. Fibre cement and concrete products on the market tend to be smooth, flat and grey — designed to give a roof the suggestion of slate — but there is no serious comparison. If you want to build in Wales you may have to use natural slate or a quality slate alternative such as Redland Cumbrian, but discuss the possible alternatives with your architect or designer.

Stone Slates. The cost of using any form of stone slate is very high indeed. The genuine material is almost prohibitively expensive, and the various artificial stone slates merely very expensive. Both are heavy and require specially designed roofs. If you are lucky enough to have a site in an area where the Planners will insist on stone slate, such as parts of the Cotswolds or the Lake District, then the finished value of your house will balance the cost. If you do have any choice, then examine all the cost implications with care.

Secondhand Tiles and Slates. As with old hand-made bricks, there is a market in second-hand tiles and slates, and these are often advertised in magazines concerned with rural interests. This is something which always attracts those who are building in the country, and it can be a very good way of getting a genuinely traditional roof. It can also be a disaster.

If you want to use second-hand slates or tiles then get the best advice about the actual tiles that interest you, and if possible have a reputable tiling contractor buy and fix them for you. Above all make sure that you get enough sound tiles to finish the roof, as it is possible to find that you are short a couple of hundred tiles which cannot be found anywhere else!

Tiling in the Home Counties style. Plain tiles used for the vertical cladding, under a Redland Regent tile roof..

ROOF TILES — COSTS

To illustrate the tremendous variation in the cost of using different types of tiles and slates, and the implication of increasing the roof pitch, we look at the cost of a roof for our 'Blyth' house.

This is our most popular house design, and has been built with roof pitches varying from 22° to 40°. These are the roof and tiling costs in the Home Counties for this house in mid 1992, with the work carried out on a supply and fix basis, including roof trusses, under-slating felt and roof battens, all the tiles, but excluding the chimney and step flashings. The price differentials include allowances for the extra roof timbers for the heavier materials.

STANDARD COSTS WITH ROOF PITCH 35°

Concrete interlocking tiles £5250
Traditional Welsh slate £11600
Asbestos cement slates £11300
Clay pantiles £7250
Concrete plain tiles £8600
Artificial stone slabs (diminishing
courses) £13000

Blyth Design House

CHOOSING TILES OR SLATES

Modern roofing materials are available in a very wide range of styles and shades. As in all domestic architecture, recent years have seen a move away from formal geometric shapes and simple colours back to traditional shapes, subtle and mixed colours, and greater use of special feature tiles. The best way to choose tiles or slates is on roofs, and the manufacturers' representatives are always able to show you the sort of tile that interests you on the sort of roof that you intend to build. These descriptions of some of the more popular tiles and slates from the Redland range are to help you identify what you will be seeing.

The tiles and slates illustrated on Pages 38 and 39 are, clockwise from the bottom of this page, Rosemary clay plain tiles, Redland mottled plain concrete tiles on a roof, the same tiles in close up, Redland Grovebury double pantiles, and the new Redland Cumbrian slates. All Redland tiles and slates are available in a wide variety of different colours, and it is wise to seek the assistance of the manufacturer's field staff when making a choice.

Trough valley tiles used between two slopes of Redland Grovebury double pantiles. You should get expert advice on whether to use a lead valley or valley tiles.

Special valley tiles used with Redland plain tiles. In 1985 the whole range of Redland tiles were awarded the British Standard Kitemark, the first roof tiles to receive this distinction.

Above is a ridge tile flue vent. A flue from a small gas appliance can discharge through an inconspicuous vent of this sort, saving the cost of a chimney.

Building Regulations require that roof spaces are ventilated. Your tiler can handle this for you using this Redvent eaves ventilation system which now has an Agrément Certificate.

If you are taking an interest in the tiling on your new home you will have to learn the language. The top of the roof is the ridge, the valley between the two different planes of the roof is not surprisingly called the valley, and special tiles are used for both the ridge and the valley as seen in the photographs. You can also get special ventilation tiles and gas fire flue vents that fit on to the roof ridge. An alternative to valley tiles at low pitches may be a lead valley. If your architect has left you in any doubt about whether valley tiles or a lead valley should be used, then consult the manufacturer's representative.

The bottom edge of a roof is usually finished with a fascia board which carries the gutters. The soffit is the 'ceiling' under the overhang behind the fascia. The side edge of the roof is the verge. Until recently most verges were either hidden behind a barge board, or finished with mortar pointing, but now new cloaked verge tile systems give a maintenance free verge and are well worth considering.

Vertical tile hanging is usually handled by the same tiling contractor who deals with the roof. The choice of tile for vertical tile hanging is critical; it must be chosen at the time that you choose the roof tiles, and must complement the colour, style and texture of the roof tile.

Special cloaked verged tiles are now available, giving a more secure and maintenance free installation than the old pointed verges.

Tiling a roof is not only physically demanding and dangerous: it is also a very exact science.

LAYING TILES

A roof of Redland tiles carries a 100 year guarantee on the tiles themselves, but they must be laid to manufacturer's recommendations. Roof tiling is skilled work, and the country is divided into four different exposure zones with different ways of fixing tiles in each zone to suit wind speeds and other factors.

The work of the roof tiler includes fastening under slating felt and the wooden battens to which the tiles are fixed. Here again the standards are precise, and have to be followed. Tiling work on a new home built on an individual site is best specified by reference to the manufacturer's recommendations, as these set standards that exceed statutory requirements and are very easily understood. The manufacturer's field staff will also keep in touch with work on site in their local areas, and will advise any problems.

Material and photographs for this chapter were provided by Redland Roof Tiles Limited of Redland House, Reigate, Surrey. Their telephone number is 0737 242488 and the company is always pleased to give advice and supply literature to anyone interested in tiling a new home.

Windows

We expect rather a lot from windows. They must provide daylight, ventilation, a view of the outside world, and are an essential element in architectural style. They must be openable, yet keep out wind and rain. They must reduce unwanted noise. They must be safe to operate and must be easily cleaned. They must do all these things at an economic cost. The windows that you choose for a new home — or which the planners permit you to choose — will play a major part in the appearance and character of the building. Some idea of how important this is can be seen in these illustrations.

There is a bewildering range of window options in various materials. In this feature we look at the choice of windows with which you are most likely to be concerned if you are building on a plot of your own. Most building plots sold to individuals are in rural or suburban areas where planners are expecting designs to conform to the traditional local style. Window design is a matter where they impose their views very strongly, and most county design guides emphasise the need for windows which have what they call 'a vertical emphasis'. This requires that individual casements should be taller than they are wide, often without any small top hung ventilators. Most of the plans in this book are illustrated with windows of this sort.

There are some parts of the country where there are not such strict rules, particularly in Wales and in the South West, and a wider choice of windows can be used in most urban areas. It is always interesting to look at the sort of windows being installed in new housing under construction on individual plots near to where you hope to build, and ask at the planning office if you want specific advice on windows considered suitable in a particular situation.

When choosing windows for a new home you have first to consider the style that is appropriate, then the materials from which the windows will be made, the hinges and catches which you want them to have, and finally you must make sure that they are well made and will do a good job.

To start with design. As we have seen the planners will be much involved with your choice, and since April 1982 there has been another constraint. New building regulations concerned with insulation standards limit the windows in a new home to 12% of the wall area if single glazed, 24% if double glazed, and 36% if triple glazed. The effect of this is to ensure that virtually all new homes will be double glazed using sealed units — and the windows must be designed to suit them.

The main styles of windows for you to consider are shown overleaf. The notes reflect experience with those building for themselves rather than the views of either the architectural establishment or the manufacturers. Windows are available in all these styles in various finishes with a wide variety of fittings, and on a later page we look at these fittings in detail.

This timber frame house by Prestoplan owes much of its character to its carefully chosen joinery.

Bay window

Picture window

Sash window

Pivot window

Casement Windows. Any windows with a vertical emphasis. These are the fashionable windows today, usually double glazed and increasingly fitted with elaborate continental style hinges and sophisticated draught-proofing. They may be fitted with one central horizontal rail and called 'Town and Country windows' or cottage windows.

Ejma. Builders call this an Ejma style window, and they are to be found in most houses built between the twenties and the mid-seventies. Now rarely seen in new housing, simply because the small opening top light which spoils the symmetry is out of fashion and is unpopular with planners.

Landscape. Fixed bottom lights and opening top lights. Popular in the sixties and seventies when they went with ranch style homes with low pitch roofs.

Sash Windows. Traditional windows for period homes, and the only choice for a Georgian style house if cost is not a major consideration. Modern sash windows have spiral springs instead of weights, and are surprisingly reasonably priced.

Georgian Windows. More properly called full-bar windows. The popularity of these windows in the late 1970s was the first evidence of the move away from picture windows back to a cottage style. Not now generally used in new housing as difficult to glaze using sealed units.

Pivot Windows. The popularity of these windows with architects is matched by their unpopularity with house-holders. Great for tearing curtains when opened roughly. Windows of the same shape are now available with other hinge systems which have overcome this difficulty. Reversible projecting sash or twin windows are

Casement window

Patio door

Bow window

Landscape window

Circular window

Georgian window

Ejma window

now preferred by most designers.

Picture Windows. Fashionable until recently, now criticised as providing goldfish bowl living. Problems with both Planners and Building Regulations.

Patio Doors. Architecturally impossible to integrate successfully into a traditionally styled home, but the convenience and householder appeal of patio doors outweighs all other considerations and they are here to stay. The way in which they provide a link between outdoors and indoors is the modern equivalent of the Victorian conservatory — and, like the conservatory, they have to be considered as features in their own right. All patio windows should be double glazed. Hardwood patio doors are now available.

French Windows. The predecessors of patio doors — less convenient but more attractive. When fitted with full-bar glazing they can be very elegant but have hundreds of window corners to be cleaned. Difficult to draught-proof successfully, and costly to maintain.

Bay Windows. A bay window is a splendid addition to any large room when considered from inside the house, but is difficult to incorporate into a modern exterior unless the shape of the building is already fairly complex or the structure is very large.

Bow Windows. Bow windows give character to a room from inside, but are difficult to fit into an overall design unless a number of bow windows are part of the whole design. As with bay windows, it is essential that the house is designed for these features, and that they are not 'stuck on' as an afterthought.

Circular Windows. Can be used to great effect to light a hall, or as features in a gable where they will also light the attic.

French window

The overwhelming majority of new homes are built with wooden joinery, and although aluminium and plastic windows are widely promoted their use in new housing is very limited.

With wood windows you have a choice of hardwood or softwood. Hardwood windows will add £500 to £1000 to the cost of a new home by the time you have paid for matching windowboards, but they also lift the property out of one value bracket straight into another. In this way they are a first class investment — if you can afford them. They give their own distinctive style to a property, which may take some time getting used to as we tend to expect a view through a window to be surrounded by a white painted frame. However, contrary to some fears, they do not make a room seem dark.

Hardwood windows are very durable, and virtually maintenance free, requiring only a wipe with Sadolin or similar preservative every year. Most that are available in standard ranges are made in Luan or Philippines Mahogany, or else in slightly more expensive Brazilian Mahogany. Although special windows can be made to order, if you stick to standard ranges you will save a lot on cost and usually get a quicker and more reliable delivery.

Softwood windows are now made from timber that is preservative treated, and have an indefinite life. They are increasingly available in decorative water repellant priming which gives the option of either painting or staining. Stained finishes are very popular with the

Modern reflex hinges permit the outside of this window to be cleaned from inside the room, and when closed they hold the casement tightly into a sophisticated modern weatherseal.

A single horizontal glazing bar like this is the distinguishing feature of a cottage window, and the gentle curve on the window head makes it a 'swept cottage window'.

This is a reversible top hung window which can be opened without disturbing curtains or blinds. It is completely reversible so that the outside can be cleaned from inside the room.

planners and reduce maintenance costs. However, remember that this finish usually looks best under a stained roof facia, and has to be considered in relation to the whole house style.

FITTINGS
Until recently all windows were fitted with butt hinges and cheap simple window stays and latches. We have lagged far behind the rest of Europe in this, and at last we are catching up with new modern fittings that are much more attractive. These really do make sense, and add very little to the cost of a new home.

Firstly hinges. Remember that you intend to clean your windows, and that there is no reason why you should not clean the outside surface from inside the house. Reflex type hinge systems make this possible, and usually incorporate friction pads of some sort to hold the window in any position required without having to secure it with a window stay. The extra cost over butt hinges is quite modest. The biggest advantage is that the last part of the movement when the window is shut is not a pivoting aciton, and all edges of the casement tighten into the frame together. This enables draught seals to be fitted to the frame to the best advantage.

This elegant deep arch casement window is usually supplied factory glazed. When considering your choice of windows remember that you can decide which should be the opening casements, and whether they open on the left or the right can be very important when you move in.

'Turn and tilt' hinges are more elaborate, and enable a window to be opened in two ways. Firstly the sash tilts inwards, hinged from the bottom rail, to provide draught free ventilation. Secondly it can be opened inwards on vertical hinges, so that the outside of the glass can be cleaned easily. Although they involve special machining of the window frames and are fairly expensive, there is no doubt they will grow in popularity.

Window catches need to fulfil three roles: to look attractive, to be as secure as possible, and to provide trickle ventilation. As with hinges, we have lagged far behind other countries in this, and are only just beginning to realise that an expensive window in an expensive home deserves more than a cheap and nasty latch. Many modern latches incorporate security latches.

Trickle ventilation or night vents can be fitted to most windows by manufacturers as optional extras. They incorporate fly screens, but otherwise it is hard to know what they offer that a two position latch does not. They certainly do not improve the appearance of the joinery to which they are fitted, but there are situations in which they are useful, particularly in windy areas where draughts can be a nuisance.

The ever popular Georgian window can only be single glazed, has dozens of corners to clean, but is the first choice for many home owners.

All the windows are from the John Carr range.

Hardwood patio doors are becoming very popular. Doors of the size illustrated can cost from £500 to £700 depending on the specification, and you do not have to buy a separate sub frame. For this you can expect 20mm double glazing units in safety glass, elaborate ventilation arrangements, security locking and stainless steel tracks and working parts. This Carr Ledbury door is also available with arched window heads.

PATIO WINDOWS

Patio windows are an anachronism in a traditional cottage style home, but are certainly here to stay. The essential with a patio window is to relate it to a paved area outside that is large enough to balance the whole effect. The paved area should be at least half the wall area of the side of the house above it. If this is not possible then some other way of arranging the landscaping to do the same thing is most important.

Until recently the majority of patio windows were aluminium, usually fitted in hardwood frames. The popularity of hardwood joinery in recent years has led to the introduction of reasonably priced hardwood patio windows, and these are likely to become progressively more popular as a result of our concern with traditional materials. There are wide price ranges in patio windows, and, as with much else, you get what you pay for. The cheaper patio windows are made for replacing french windows in old houses, and are inappropriate to new homes. Choose from the middle or top of the range offered by a reputable manufacturer, and if the window does not run absolutely smoothly or is not completely draught-proof then complain vigorously. The problem is invariably with the installation.

In an earlier chapter it was explained that a room must have windows that open to provide ventilation to a total of 5% of the floor area. Patio windows can

contribute to this total only if there is a minimum of 15 sq. ins.of other ventilation provided, and if there is not another ordinary window in the room this means the patio window has to be fitted with a trickle ventilator. The design of these can vary from unobtrusive to very ugly; ask to see a sample and do not rely on a catalogue.

The photographs used in this chapter were provided by the John Carr Group, whose wide range of windows, patio doors and other joinery is particularly well suited to custom designed individual homes. They have very attractive literature on their products, which is obtainable from their main stockists who are Malden Timber, with branches throughout the country. An up-to-date catalogue and list of branch addresses where John Carr joinery can be inspected and where advice on joinery is generally readily available can be obtained from Malden Timber, Malden House, Radlett Road, Park Street, St Albans or telephone 0727 73337.

The Weldon Aluminium patio door from John Carr. Illustrated here with a coloured finish, this is a typical modern unit with safety glass double glazing, security catches and an adjustable ventilator. A door like this will cost about £250, with another £70 for the wooden sub frame.

A hinged 'patio door' in hardwood. The popularity of patio doors over French windows has led to a demand for traditional hinged doors that have the appearance, insulation and security of a patio door. The outcome is this John Carr Gloucester door, which is priced at under £500.

Doors

Doors are important. The front door is usually the focal point of the front elevation of the building, and the internal doors are the part of your home that you actually touch more than any other. Yet in spite of this importance, their share of the total building cost is very small, and the expense of moving from run-of-the-mill doors to something rather special is quite small.

What is involved? A front door, a back door and eight interior doors to the standard generally used by a developer of desirable executive residences cost about £350. If you care to double this figure for your own home, you can get doors that are better made, with a better finish, and with a far wider range of styles to

choose from. However, as usual, let us look at some facts before examining what is on offer.

There are three categories of doors in new housing: exterior doors, interior doors and fire doors. Exterior doors have to keep out the weather, must offer security from intruders, and need a finish that will stand up to extremes of sun and rain. Interior doors have to open and close discreetly, and must maintain their shape however high you turn up the central heating. Fire doors have to resist a blaze for half an hour and yet must look like any other door. All of them have to be attractive in appearance. These different categories are best considered separately.

A solid panelled door like this is a must for giving the right feel to your front entrance. Make sure that is is British made, and expect to pay up to £130 . Well worth it.

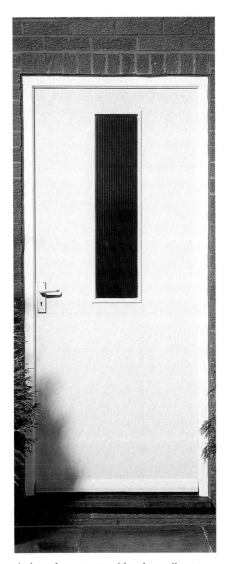

A door for painting like this will cost about £40.

Stable doors are becoming very popular, and will cost about £65.

A glazed door like this in either hardwood or softwood can cost about £40 to £60.

EXTERIOR DOORS

By exterior doors we mean both front and back doors: both have to meet the same standards. They are usually slightly larger than interior doors, and also thicker. For the last ten years the manufacturers have been changing over from imperial to metric standards, and virtually all ranges of doors are available to both modules. Doors for new construction should really be metric, with imperial doors kept for renovations. Little attention is paid to this, and with lots of imperial doors going into new buildings so presumably both ranges will be with us indefinitely. The usual sizes are 6′9″ high by 2′9″ wide, or the slightly differently proportioned metric 2040 x 826. However, there are doors in many other stock sizes, including double doors. Virtually all are 1¾″ or 46mm thick. All of them are inherently weatherproof if made to British standards — but they should always be hung with protection at the head of the door, a weather board and a window bar at the bottom, and draught seals in the rebates. If they are in a porch this may not be necessary, but if the rain can reach your door ensure that it has all the protection you can give it.

The security which a door offers is mainly provided by the locks and any alarms fitted to it, but these are no better than the provision made for fixing them by the door manufacturer. Generally speaking the more you pay for a door, the larger and more solid the lock blocks will be, and doors at the very top of the market are sometimes drilled for elaborate three point locking systems and may incorporate a sheet of metal.

It is the appearance of the door which usually dictates a choice, and for a front door your consideration of this starts by looking at the way in which the hall gets its light. Glazed front doors were very popular until recently, either on their own in small houses, or in a frame with a storey height side-light in larger properties. Frequently there was no other glazed area in the hall or landing. Today it is more usual to have solid front doors, with a window elsewhere in the hall. The side panel is only retained where it is a key architectural feature in its own right or where there simply isn't room for a window. Your choice in this is really a part of your decision about the style of the whole house. Some options are above. The photos are John Carr doors, with January 1988 costs.

INTERIOR DOORS

Interior doors are usually smaller and slimmer than exterior doors, and the usual sizes are 6′6″ × 2′6″ and 2040 × 726mm. The standard thicknesses are generally 1⅜″ or 40mm, but other thicknesses are available. Having an internal door that is a little thicker than the standard is a good way to get a 'quality' feel to things in a new home, but you must make sure than it will fit the rebate depth of your door casings.

Pairs of internal doors are growing in popularity, and the standard combined widths of pairs of doors are 3′10″ or 4′6″. The latter look better. If you want a pair of doors discuss whether they should be rebated where they meet, or not, and whether you want them hung on two-way hinges.

If there is any likelihood of a disabled person using your home, it's worth considering fitting 3′ wide doors where appropriate. These are much more easily negotiated by wheelchairs.

Glazed double doors between rooms make the home seem larger, and can help to lighten a dark hall.

FIRE DOORS

As already explained, firedoors are doors that offer half an hour's protection from a blaze on the other side. They are required by Building Regulations to be installed between garages and living accommodation, and in various other special situations. Your architect will have marked your drawings to show the openings where you are obliged to use them. They are very solidly built, a minimum of 46mm thick and are often used in place of ordinary interior doors where something better than usual is required. Fire doors are available in most styles, but are not usually glazed. If they are, Building Regulations require ugly wired glass to be used in them.

Samples from batches of fire doors are regularly tested in the side of a furnace, and they really do work. Some people prefer them for bedroom doors because of this. If you wish to do so make sure that door casings are fitted in your bedroom wall to suit the thicker fire doors.

DOORSETS

A doorset is a door complete with its frame, hinges and latch, all factory assembled, and usually packed in a cardboard box. If it is an external door it comes complete with the weather bar and security lock, and often three point security locks are fitted.

This is certainly the best possible way of getting a door that fits exactly, that is properly hung, and that has the accessories that the manufacturer intended for it. It costs more than buying the components separately, but this is recouped by the saving in site labour, provided that your builder takes advantage of this in the way that is intended.

Doorsets are either supplied for the frames or casings to be built in first in the conventional way, with the pre-fitted doors popped in later, or else the whole doorset is put into a prepared opening at the last stages of finishing off the house. Whichever system is used, it is essential that the recommended fixing arrangements are made, and that both doors and frames are well protected on site. Doorsets are growing in popularity, and if you are having a new home built to your own requirements, with the high standards of site super-vision that usually goes with this, then it is certainly a good thing to do to discuss using doorsets with your builder. They are available in all of the ranges that have been shown.

The photographs used in this chapter were provided by the John Carr Group, who manufacture a wide range of doors of all types in all price ranges. They have most attractive and informative literature on their products, which is obtainable from their main stockists who are Malden Timber, with branches throughout the country. An up-to-date catalogue and list of branch addresses where John Carr doors can be inspected and where advice on choosing a door is available can be obtained from Malden Timber, Malden House, Radlett Road, Park Street, St Albans or telephone 0727 73337.

The classic panelled door is now available in every price range, and adds enormously to the elegance of today's new homes.

DO'S AND DON'TS ON DOORS

*   Avoid very cheap imported doors, especially cheap solid panel doors from the Far East, unless you regard them as simply an item of short term decor to be quickly replaced.
*   Have your carpenter drill the door frame or door casing for any burglar alarm wires before the door is hung, otherwise the electrician will have to chop out for them later.
*   Follow manufacturers' recommendations for treating the external doors, and do not use polyurethane varnish.
*   Do not plan to use door knobs on glazed doors. These doors have narrow stiles which require special narrow locks or latches, and your fingers will catch the casing if you fit a knob on one of these locks. Use a lever handle.
*   If you plan to have thick ceramic tiles or deep carpets under your doors, insist that the door casings are fitted to suit, as trimming too much off the bottom of the door may spoil the proportions.
*   Before cutting a hole for a letter plate in your new front door consider whether you should not build a letter slot into the wall, with a hardwood liner and appropriate fittings. Letter boxes like this look very attractive, and most doors look better without a letter plate.

Garage Doors

If your new house is to have an integral garage it is likely that the garage door will be the largest feature on the front of the building, bigger than the front door or any of the windows. It is also the part of the home that is looked at as a car travels up the drive, and it will probably open and shut at least a thousand times a year. In spite of this, the choice of the garage door in a new home is often left to the builder, and the various options are frequently ignored by home owners who will be meticulous in the choice of the door handle for the guest bedroom. Garage doors deserve more consideration than this.

Incidentally, in spite of its importance, a garage door is probably the cheapest element in the walls in terms of unit cost. This will probably be only half as much per sq. ft. as the front door, and only a third as much as any window, although it will be more prominent than either. If you are building a detached garage the door is likely to account for less than 5% of the total cost, and yet it will certainly be the dominant feature of the whole structure. With this importance/cost ratio it is well worth giving careful consideration to buying the best door that fits your total budget, and ensuring that it suits your new home and your life style in every way.

Unless you are involved in a special situation it is certain that you will be buying an up and over garage door. These have no place in our architectural heritage, but their convenience outweighs all other considerations, and it is now very unusual indeed for the old side hung garage doors to be used in a new building. A further development is the growing popularity of electrically operated doors, which are opened and closed either by pushing a button, or using a small radio transmitter. There are different ways in which up and over doors are set in the door opening, different ways in which they work, and different styles in different price ranges. As with so much else, it is important to consider all your options.

First, size. It is generally desirable that the garage door should not be any wider than is necessary for the car or cars to pass through, and this is usually taken as 7ft for a single door, or 14ft for a double door, although other sizes are available. This leads to the issue of whether a garage for two cars should have one large double door, or a pair of single doors, and here again there are various factors to consider. There is no doubt that two doors with a brick or stone pillar between them look better than a double door, and help the whole building to look more up-market. In fact, two 7ft doors are unlikely to cost as much as one 14ft door in the same style, and if there are bedrooms over the garage, or a complex roof, then the arrangements for the ceiling joists will be a lot easier and cheaper if the pillar is available. It is possible that this will save you enough to enable you to have two expensive electric doors instead of a cheaper double one. Your decision will probably depend on the overall width of your garage: a single 14ft door can serve a garage with a minimum width of

Henderson garage doors in mahogany, cedar, steel and ABS plastics. The photo opposite shows Doric canopy doors.

about 16ft, while with a central pillar a width of 17ft 6ins is required. This extra 18ins may be critical to your frontage; if not, the choice is yours, and you will probably find a pair of doors is a better buy.

If the door or doors are for a garage that is integral with the dwelling, the height of the garage door is normally set by the need for the top of the garage door frame to line up with the top of the ground floor windows.

Another factor is a Building Regulation requirement that there should be a step down into the garage from the floor level in the house, intended to make sure that leaking petrol from the car cannot run into the living accommodation. Again, there is the need to have a 3ins slope on the floor from the back of the garage to the front to let rain water dripping from the car drain away. Putting all of this together means that most garage doors for integral garages are 7ft high, with a 3ins top rail to the frame giving an overall opening height of 7ft 3ins. This suits adjacent windows and door frames that

are set with the heads 6ft 9ins above floor level. Garage doors at other heights are available.

If you are building a detached garage then it is the garage door height that will control the dimensions of the building, instead of vice versa, and it is usual to choose a door that is rather lower, often 6ft 6ins, to give better proportions.

Architects are often asked to arrange for a garage door to be large enough for a caravan. Beware: this is rarely a success with an integral garage, and a detached garage for a caravan tends to be so large that it is out of proportion with the house. Keeping a caravan on an ordinary sized building plot is always a problem, and hiding it behind a jumbo sized garage door is rarely a satisfactory solution.

Having decided on the size of your garage doors you can also choose where they should be set in the door opening. This can be at the front, which will give an extra 9 ins of room in the garage, or at the back of the opening which will look far more distinguished. If the width of the garage is critical you can even set them back behind the door opening, as shown in the sketch on the following page.

DOOR GEAR SYSTEMS

The next consideration is the type of mechanism to open the door. This is called door gear, and there are a number of different systems.

Canopy Doors open so that part of the door projects forward of the building as shown on the sketch. All the mechanism is on the door frame, and there are no tracks of any sort in the garage. These doors are easily fixed in wooden frames, and they are cheaper than the alternatives. Their disadvantage is that although they are easy to operate they do not move as smoothly as tracked doors, and the projecting canopy may not be considered attractive.

Canopy doors are available up to 14ft wide. There are electric operator systems to suit some of them, but it is preferable to choose a tracked door if you want an operator.

Framed Canopy Doors. These come in a metal frame, so that they can be fixed directly into or behind the brickwork openings. Of course they can also be used with wood frames. The advantage is the ease with which they are installed. In all other respects they are like other canopy doors except that they are not available in the double sizes.

Horizontally Tracked Doors. These doors pull right back inside the building when they are open, and when open are supported on high level horizontal tracks which are either suspended from the garage ceiling, or fixed to the side walls. This system enables doors to move more smoothly than is possible with canopy systems, and is particularly well suited to electric operators. This sort of door is available through a wide range of prices, and doors in wood or fibreglass have to be of this type because of their weight. Incidentally, this weight is all taken by the springs in the door gear when the door is moving, and as far as the person opening and closing the door is concerned the only difference between a heavy door and a light one is that the former will move more smoothly and positively. There is no brute strength required at all, although a high wind can present problems with double doors in exposed positions.

Henderson Double Doric Door

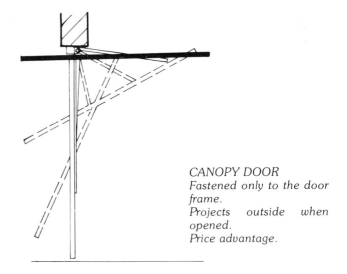

CANOPY DOOR
Fastened only to the door frame.
Projects outside when opened.
Price advantage.

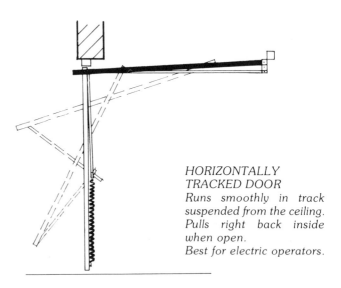

HORIZONTALLY TRACKED DOOR
Runs smoothly in track suspended from the ceiling.
Pulls right back inside when open.
Best for electric operators.

POSITIONING A GARAGE DOOR

Door fixed forward in the reveal increases the space in the garage.

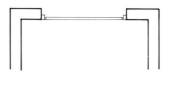

Door set back in the reveal looks more distinguished.

Door set behind the reveal suits a minimum garage width.

ELECTRIC OPERATORS

Electric Operators can be fitted to most garage doors which run on horizontal tracks, and are available for some canopy doors. As a general rule it is obviously preferable that you should get an operator that is marketed by a door manufacturer for his own doors, especially as many operators are imported and the back up and spares service may be limited.

Now there is need for a word of warning about garage door operators. Of all domestic gadgets they are the most addictive, and once you have lived with a garage door opener there is little chance of you ever being able to live without one. The cost, complete with a portable radio controller, is about the same as a good quality single door. The effect on your morale when you come home in the rain and the door opens and the lights go on at the touch of a button while you are still in the car is incalculable. Another button on the wall in the garage closes the door and after a delay the gadget turns off the lights. It is all as reliable as any other domestic appliance, and if anything does go wrong it is easily fixed. In the USA they are taken for granted, and they are steadily growing in popularity in this country. Incidentally, their cost in real terms is going down quickly: in 1970 the author's Henderson operators for his two garage doors cost £200 each: they would cost much the same in today's devalued currency. They work as well as the day they were installed.

The modern controllers for electric operators are radio units, operated on a special frequency allocated by the G.P.O. The range is about 30yds, and they are meant to be carried in the glove compartment of your car. To open the door you pick up the controller, point it at the door through the window, and press the button. However, there is a more polished alternative which is not advertised by the manufacturers.

All these controllers operate on frequencies which require them to have ferrite rod aerials, and if these are within an inch or so of any other metal it will induce a frequency shift. Indeed, you can move the frequency of your controller up and down by putting either a steel rod or a brass rod up against it. Thus the advice is to hold the controller in your hand, which ensures that it will be at least a couple of inches from any metal. Now if you are gadget-minded you will find that an extension lead is easily fitted to the switch, and the controller can then be mounted behind the radiator grill of your car provided that it is fastened on a thick wooden mounting block and some arrangement is made to ensure that it keeps dry. Your garage door can then be opened by touching a spare switch on the facia, which gives great dignity to the whole proceeding. If you understand all this, then you can arrange it easily. If not, ignore it.

Having looked at all the different engineering options, the final decision on what you buy concerns the appearance of the doors, and this is probably the most important of the choices. The essential thing to do is to look at all the alternatives, and not simply to choose one of the popular models in stock at your local Builders' Merchant. After three decades of selling plain and uninteresting doors to suit the functional and uninteresting house designs of the '50s and '60s, manufacturers have brought out the new ranges of doors in a wide choice of materials. Some are shown in the photographs in this chapter, but your selection is best made by getting the makers' catalogue and looking at all the options. There are not many comprehensive displays of garage doors about — they are too large for this — so this is one item you will probably choose from a catalogue. You can get the catalogue from a manufacturer, who will send you a list of stockists, and you can then insist that the stockist makes arrangements to show you the model that you want. Above all, do not leave the choice to your builder.

GARAGE DOORS — TYPICAL COSTS

Single doors 7' x 7'; double doors are 14' x 7'

Canopy doors
Without a frame: Single doors in galvanised steel with a colour coat, from £111.
Double doors in aluminium, from £343.
With a frame: Single doors £138.
Double doors are not generally available.

Steel or aluminium panel doors with a horizontal track system
Without a frame: Single doors £161.
Double doors: £466.
With a frame: Single doors £188.
Double doors are not generally available.

Top of the market doors in wood (cedar), ABS plastics or glass reinforced plastic
Single doors from £276.
Double doors from £728.

Electric operator with radio control system
Complete, for single or double doors, £293.

All the doors featured in this chapter are by P.C. Henderson Limited, of Romford, Essex, RM3 8LU. Details of their full range of garage doors and accessories, including a folder of leaflets on their new range of garage doors to suit today's new house styles, are available from them by return of post. They have stockists in all parts of the country.

Stairs

Now that houses are being designed to look interesting and pretty, instead of being simply functional and well proportioned, the staircase as a feature in its own right is coming back into fashion. It is necessarily a focal point in the whole building, and is often the first thing that a visitor sees when he enters the front door. The opportunity to make sure that it reflects the feel and character of the home should not be overlooked, and discussing the staircase with your architect is as important as discussing the size of the rooms or the type of windows that you want. The photographs in this chapter show what the right staircase can do for your hall. If you want to arrange for your stairs in your new house to be as attractive as the photos, you will first have to be capable of describing what you want, and consequently to know a little of the possibilities. Here goes.

An attractive staircase gains its effect equally from two things: the basic design and shape, and the materials and the finish which is given to them. Starting with the design, stair manufacturers report that there is a fast growing demand for stairways with two or three flights, using landings and winder stairs. This requires a stair well, with its own balustrade on the upper floor, and increasingly this is elaborated to form a gallery above the hall. Even in its simplest form, a stairway with quarter or half landings adds enormously to the interest in the hall, and a half landing that is generous enough in size to have its own piece of furniture, perhaps with its own window, becomes a key feature in the whole house. To many elderly people it is even more important as somewhere to stop and catch their breath half way up to the first floor.

A straight flight does not offer these opportunities, but these days it can be 'dressed up' in many ways, perhaps with a wide curtail step at the bottom, and a carefully chosen balustrade. Bullnose steps are also popular. These traditional options were very unusual only five years ago: now they are right back in fashion and likely to stay there.

Whichever sort of stairway you particularly like, it is important to realise that it has to be allowed for in the basic design of the house, and you cannot leave your decision until a later stage, as with your kitchen and bathroom. It is also virtually impossible to alter the position or shape of a staircase once the house design is settled. One reason for this is the large number of regulations which affect stairways, all of which have to be complied with. To start with, there have to be specific clear spaces allowed for at the top and bottom of flights, so that you do not open a door and step straight out down the stairs. Then all the steps have to be of equal height, and a minimum width — which is 3ft. The height, or rise of each step may not exceed 8ins. The overall angle of the flight must not exceed 42 degrees, and at all points there must be minimum head room of 6ft 7ins. Add to this the general requirement that your stairs have to start off from a convenient position in the hall, and end up in a sensible position on the first floor landing, while the stairs themselves have to be securely fastened into

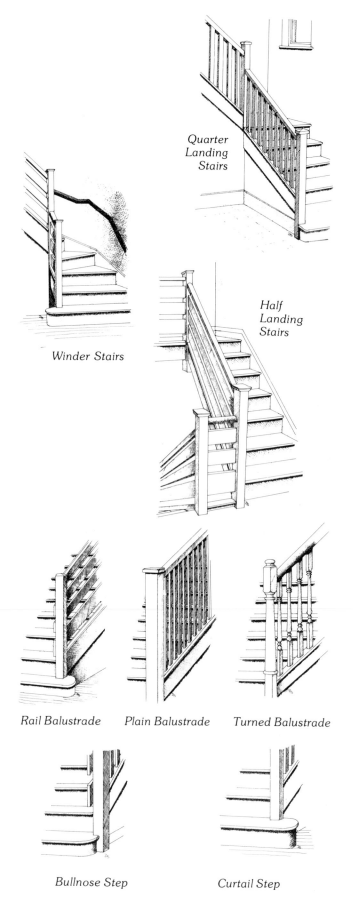

Quarter Landing Stairs

Winder Stairs

Half Landing Stairs

Rail Balustrade   *Plain Balustrade*   *Turned Balustrade*

Bullnose Step   *Curtail Step*

Quarter Landing Stair in Parana Pine by Boulton & Paul. The current cost of this staircase is £570. Note the matching apron around the edge of the stair well.

the fabric of the building. These are not the only technical requirements, but perhaps they are enough to emphasise how important your stairs are in the basic design of the structure.

All these Building Regulations are very necessary, and they are joined by others which are rather more contentious. Most of them are concerned with safety. All stairs should have hand rails on both sides, although this regulation is often ignored, and there are minimum heights for balustrades, both at the side of the stairs and around the stair well. A further requirement which was introduced in 1976 is that no gap in the stairs or in the balustrade may permit the passage of a 4″ diameter ball. This effectively banned many popular designs of open tread stairs, and is a major constraint on the design of the balustrades. The reason was to stop children using stairs as a climbing frame: this at a time when climbing frames looking very like open tread stairs were a feature of every adventure playground. One result of this particular regulation was to hasten the move back to traditional Victorian style balustrades with vertical balusters.

The key element in any staircase is the string, which is the massive sloping piece of timber which carries the weight of the staircase at the side. This is one of the most important pieces of wood in the house, and it is on view for all to see, unlike other structural members such as floor joists and rafters which are hidden away. It is elaborately housed out on its inner edge to take the treads and risers, and is itself usually recessed into the

newel posts. Stairs to be painted should have the string in parana pine, and this straight grain timber can also be varnished to give a Scandinavian look. Hardwood stairs usually have the string in either mahogany or an African hardwood, and the treads are always of the same material as the string. The risers, which are the pieces of vertical timber between the steps, are usually of laminated timber, with a laminate on the outer face to match the treads.

There are a number of patterns of open tread stairs which have been designed to meet the 4″ ball Building Regulation, and these are usually made in hardwood, or if they are in parana pine they are stained and varnished.

Balustrades should be chosen carefully to match the stairs themselves, and also to suit your own ideas for the decor and feel of the home. Whatever style you choose, a good general rule is to make sure that the newels are as large as practicable. These are the big posts which are at the end of each run of railing, and the more substantial they are, the more impressive your staircase will be. If the balustrade is carried on around the stairwell at first floor level it is important to consider how the edge of the well is finished. Ideally it should have a timber lining to match the stairs, which is called an apron, and there should be a nosing above it to retain the carpet. This is the sort of detail which makes all the difference to the appearance of the finished job.

Finally, there are two ways of ordering a staircase. Either it can be made to suit the exact dimensions shown on the drawings, in which case there need not be any personal contact with the manufacturer, or else the stair well is measured by the manufacturer's represent-ative and the staircase is made to fit. As it is not unusual for a house to gain an inch or more on the dimensions on the drawings as it is built, the latter procedure is preferable if it can be arranged. The staircases shown in the photo-graph are all by Boulton & Paul, who will send their local man to measure your new home for its stairs wherever you live, just as soon as the first floor joists are in position. The stairs are delivered three weeks later. This gives a useful opportunity to discuss all the options available, and is probably the best way to get exactly what you want, knowing that it will fit exactly as it ought.

Winder stairs like this from Boulton & Paul will cost £287.

WHAT WILL YOUR STAIRS COST?

A straight flight in parana pine will cost about
£130

A simple balustrade and handrails in softwood to suit may cost as little as £35

Parana pine stairs with a quarter landing and a balustrade that returns around the stairwell will cost about £450

For hardwood — double the above figures

For hardwood stairs to be a key feature in the house and the envy of your neighbours — allow £1250

Compared with what you will spend in the kitchen, your stairs are the best bargain in the house!

These open stairs in a straight flight cost £470 at January 1988 prices.

The photographs used in this chapter are of stairs by Boulton & Paul Limited. Their staircases are made at their Melton Mowbray factory, and are distributed nationally. Full details from Boulton & Paul Stair Advice Centre, Kings Road, Melton Mowbray LE13 1QJ, or phone 0664-64111 and ask for extension 600.

BALUSTRADING

Of all the changes in house design in the last decade, none has been more dramatic than the emphasis which is now given to stairs and stairwell balustrades. Beautiful balustrading was a feature of Georgian and Victorian homes, but for some reason it was all lost in the early years of this century and replaced with the plainest and dullest ways of fencing in the stairs. At the same time the cult of functionalism in architecture often reduced halls and landings to little more than passageways. The return to traditional values in the last few years has restored the hall to being a room in its own right, and the stairs are invariably a focal point that give a feel and character to the home as soon as you walk in through the door.

The character comes from the use of traditional balustrading components — newels, spindles, turns and so on — and their re-introduction is largely the work of one firm, Richard Burbidge of Oswestry, who have harnessed computers to traditional woodturning lathes to reproduce the work of Georgian and Victorian craftsmen at practicable costs. Their balustrades are used by leading staircase manufacturers, builders, joiners and D.I.Y. enthusiasts and can be fitted to any stairs, old or new.

A choice of balustrading involves deciding on both the finish and the style that you want, not in isolation, but in relation to the character that you want to give your hallway. The first consideration is whether your stairs are to be painted, left with a natural wood finish, or built with a polished handrail above painted balusters. This will probably depend on your choice of doors for the house, and you can have your balustrade in mahogany or hemlock to give the finish that you require.

Next you need to consider the design of the balustrading. The spindle balusters are turned in a variety of patterns with names that evoke the periods in which they were first seen — Georgian, Victorian, Old Colonial, and so on — and all can be used in different ways. They come in various diameters and heights to give different styles, and there are newel bases and turnings available to suit all of them, including half newels for use against a wall. All this is complemented by handrails and handrail components with all of the classical staircase features — goosenecks, volutes, ramps, turns and so on. The difference between the eighteenth and nineteenth century originals and today's Burbidge staircases is that a Victorian cabinet maker would take a month to make a flight of stairs while Burbidge components are quickly and effectively assembled in a day using concealed fixing brackets.

As with so many other details of fixtures for a new home, it is important to make sure that the choices are your own, and are not made for you. Do not settle for a specification that reads 'spindle balustrades'; instead send for a brochure and look at all the styles and all the options. There are so many alternatives that it is unlikely that you will be able to see them all at your local timber stockist or D.I.Y. store, but the stockist can certainly get you the necessary components in any style you choose.

A brochure giving the full range of Burbidge staircase parts can be obtained from Richard Burbidge Ltd, Oswestry, Shropshire SY11 1HZ or telephone them on 0691 655131.

Burbidge balustrading turns this simple staircase into a focal point in the hall.

Glass

Glass plays a key role in the appearance of a house — windows, french windows, patio doors and glazed doors. This glass, in one form or another, accounts for between 3% and 5% of the total building cost. It lets in all the daylight, and lets out between 15% and 35% of the heat depending on the attention that you have paid to insulation. As such, it merits rather more consideration than it is usually given, for we generally take it for granted. There is more to glass than you think.

Making glass is a very old technology, and when our ancestors, who first of all learned to make bottles, had discovered how to make glass in sheet form, it had a profound effect on all architecture. It facilitated the development of stained glass windows as focal points in our cathedrals, and the whole of classical Georgian architecture is an exercise in balancing the proportions of windows that could be larger than ever before because of advances in glass making. In this century we have seen the picture window craze of the '50s and '60s demonstrated in every housing estate with its concept of linking the inside with the garden. The occupiers inconsiderately thwarted this ideal by filling the windows with net curtains to avoid what they thought was goldfish bowl living, until the energy crisis and the County Design Guides combined to restrict window sizes in the '70s. The glass makers, seeing the total area of glazing in homes decreasing, reacted by devising a wider range of glazing options to give even more ways of filling the window space in your walls. In these pages we look at what they offer. All the illustrations are from Pikington Glass, who are a British firm and are the world's leaders in glass technology. Besides making glass from raw materials they also process it into double glazing units, toughened glass, doors etc as well as supplying most others who make glass products.

There are various ways in which you should consider the glass for a new home. Firstly, we must think about heat loss, the pros and cons of double and triple glazing, and special glass to control energy loss or energy gain. Secondly, we must look at the safety aspects of glazing, and at the new regulations to improve safety standards. Finally, there is the aesthetic use of the glass surface. Patterned glass is now available in a huge range of styles, many of them very discreet and complementary to all styles of decor. Patterned glass may be used in many situations besides the bathroom windows, such as glass screens between rooms, glass doors, clerestory lights and other ways of borrowing light from one room to illuminate another.

All these aspects of a choice of glass for a new home are linked, and the choices are generally complementary rather than alternatives. You can order a double glazing unit with a tinted solar control glass, with a low emissivity coating, — and you can specify that it should be toughened or laminated. Costs of the options are discussed later, but first we look at all the alternatives.

GLASS AND ENERGY

The control of the flow of energy through the glass in a window has to be considered in two ways. One is the heating effect of direct sunlight, which in a modern well insulated house can make a room uncomfortably hot. The other is the loss of heat through a glazed surface from the inside of a building to the outside. These two circumstances are quite different, as the heat gain from sunlight comes from the energy in the sun's rays, while the loss of heat from a warm room through a window is mainly due to the warm air in the room warming one surface of the glazing, and the glazing itself losing heat to the outside. Because of this, the techniques for keeping heat out are quite different from those for keeping it in.

DOUBLE AND TRIPLE GLAZING

Virtually everyone building a new home for themselves fits sealed double glazing units in their windows. Provided that the windows are made to be double glazed the cost is not exorbitant, and is far less than the sort of double glazing costs quoted to those who want to improve the insulation of an existing house. There is little to choose between the units made by any of the leading manufacturers, most of which carry a five year guarantee.

The actual saving in heat loss, and the financial advantages of this, are not as high as the tone of double glazing advertising may lead you to expect. What is probably more important is the amenity value of being able to stand near to a window in bad weather without feeling 'the cold striking through', and the reduction in condensation. However, all is irrelevant beside the fact that everyone now expects a new home to be double glazed, and it will certainly not be a good investment if it does not have this feature.

In addition to this, building regulations require that all windows should be double glazed when the area of window opening in a dwelling is over 12%, and should be triple glazed if the area exceeds 24%.

There are many misconceptions about double glazing, and it is useful to refute some of the fallacies. Double glazing as installed in new homes refers to sealed units with the gap filled with dry sterilized air. Double glazing units have never had a vacuum between the glass surfaces, although some special units may be gas filled. All of today's units have seals formed by aluminium spacers set in mastic, as the technology for this has killed off earlier glass-to-glass and bonded metal systems which were not commercially viable. 'Double glazing' provided by separate removable sashes is usually sold to those who are updating insulation standards in existing houses, although it is sometimes used with full bar or Georgian windows in new homes. The term is also used for Scandinavian double sash windows, which tend to be very expensive.

This leads on to consideration of the width of the cavity in a double glazing unit, which is the subject that receives a great deal of attention in the manufacturers' leaflets. The standard cavity is 6mm wide. A wider cavity will give an improvement in the performance of the unit, but this is probably irrelevant in the context of overall heat loss from the dwelling when it is considered against the appearance of the wider units. Units with a 6mm cavity look very much like single glazing. The narrow spacers at the edge are not noticeable. The wider spacers of 12mm or 25mm units are much more obtrusive, and this can be distracting, especially with hardwood windows. It is most important to consider this carefully before making a choice, especially as the wider units may require expensive specially made joinery, as do triple glazed windows.

Double glazing units can have a very useful secondary value in providing sound insulation, and this can be important near airports or on busy roads.

A few years ago, the double glazing market was beset with cowboy manufacturers, but most of them have now moved on to less competitive fields. Even so, it is worthwhile always ensuring that units are from a reputable maker and carry the kite mark. Some units 'fail', usually by the seal breaking and permitting condensation in the cavity, or by developing thermal cracks. These cracks have a distinctive shape, quite unlike impact damage cracks. Problems of this sort are rare, and if they do happen it will be in the first two years. All reputable manufacturers give a five year guarantee and deal promptly with troubles of this sort.

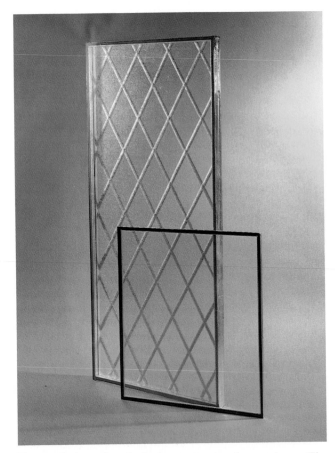

Two sealed insulated glazing units are shown above. The larger leaded light is triple glazed, and glazing of this sort is obligatory when the window area of the building comprises more than 24% of the wall surface area. The standard double glazing unit shown with it is mandatory when the figure is 12%.

Patio windows combining double glazing to keep heat in with solar control glass to keep direct sunlight out.

It is extremely important that double glazing units are fixed properly in their frames, and that the frames themselves suit the selected units. It is not uncommon to find that units chosen at a late stage in the construction of a home will not fit in the windows which have already been built in.

Double glazing units to be fitted in wood frames are bead glazed, which means that they are held in the frame by a strip of wood instead of by putty. All unit manufacturers issue detailed instructions on the techniques and materials to be used for bead glazing, and these are not simple. Typically the wood has to be sealed with a sealer, units are bedded on plastic bedding blocks, with plastic spacers against the side of the reveals, all set in a non-setting butyl mastic, and the bead pointed off with a different gun applied mastic. This is often skimped — it is worthwhile making sure it is not.

ANTISUN GLASS

The amount of heat energy which passes through a window as sunlight can be controlled by using an Antisun solar control glass. Clear glass lets the sunlight pass through it with about a 15% loss of energy. Antisun glass absorbs more of the heat energy, warming up in the process. It then re-radiates this heat both into the room, and also back outside. It takes a moment's thought to appreciate the implications of this concept, but the net effect is to reduce the amount of heat energy passing through the window from 85% to 65%. This reduction is enough to prevent a room becoming uncomfortably hot in our climate.

Antisun glass is tinted, as it is the pigment in the colours which absorbs the energy, and it is available in grey, bronze or green. Bronze is by far the most popular colour, and in ordinary housing it is commonly used for large south facing windows. It is particularly popular with those who have antique furniture or valuable carpets which should be protected from direct sunlight. Window surrounds for these windows are sometimes given a bronze finish to match.

This solar control glass should not be confused with the reflective glass often used for the same purpose in large commercial buildings. It does not look like a mirror from the outside, and the illustration above is a pretty accurate representation of its appearance from the inside.

Incidentally, double glazing in itself has little effect on the heating effect of sunlight, and by providing better insulation to the room it makes it more likely that an uncomfortable temperature will be reached. Antisun glass can be used in double glazing units, to give a combined solar control and thermal insulation unit.

ENERGY SAVING GLASS

A new energy saving glass has been developed by Pilkingtons called Pilkington K Glass and is destined to have a far reaching effect on the glazing scene. Pilkington K Glass has a special coating on one side which is virtually invisible and which acts as a one way mirror to radiate heat. A window that is losing heat from inside the building to the outside is transmitting a significant part of it by radiation. Pilkington K Glass reflects this heat back into the room, whilst at the same time permitting heat from the sun to enter the room with little additional hindrance. In general terms the effect of using double glazing units incorporating Pilkington K Glass is to give it the insulating value of triple glazing making your rooms more comfortable and enabling the central heating thermostat to be turned down. In fact, for every 1°C reduction on the thermostat setting, heating bills can be cut by 7p in the pound.

Pilkington K Glass gives triple glazing performance in a double glazing unit.

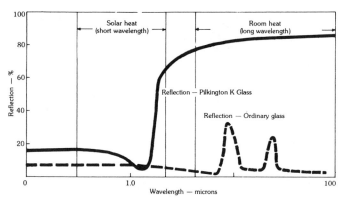

HOW IT WORKS

Ordinary glass lets radiated room heat out through the window. Pilkington K Glass reflects most of it back into the room. The graph shows how both Pilkington K Glass and ordinary glass pass short wavelength solar radiation. Long wave radiation of room heat is also passed outside by ordinary glass, while Pilkington K Glass reflects 80% of it back into the room.

SAFETY GLASS

In recent years a great deal of attention has been paid to hazards of glass in the home, and to the horrific injuries which can be caused through falling through a large area of glazing. As a result, there is a new British Standard, BS 6262, which is concerned with the thickness and type of glass which should be specified in certain situations. BS 6262 is not mandatory yet, although it is possible that it will become so before long. However, it is possible that anyone who ignores it could be held liable for neglect in some circumstances, and obviously the new standard should be followed.

It requires that fully glazed doors, including patio doors, french windows, and other doors where the glazing takes up most of the area, should be glazed in an appropriate safety glass. This also applies to any area of glazing that looks like a door, or to any other un-protected glazing which reaches to below 800mm (31") from the ground. Safety glass is also required for any glazing in a bath or shower screen, or anywhere else near a wet or slippery surface.

Safety glass in this context refers to safety from impact and is of two types, toughened and laminated (it should be noted that wire glass is a fire safety glass). Your glazier or glass merchant will be able to advise on the appropriate use for each sort, and clear, patterned, solar control or low emissivity glasses such as Pilkington K Glass are all available in toughened or laminated form.

PATTERNED GLASS

All recent advances in glass technology have been based on float glass, which is made by floating molten glass on a surface of molten tin, giving a flawless sheet of any required thickness. This is the basis of today's window glass, double glazing units, toughened glass, and of all the special glasses.

The glass still seen in old properties with minor surface blemishes which cause distortions is called sheet glass, and is now only used for greenhouses. However, this antique effect is sometimes considered desirable in older properties, and Minster patterned is available to meet this need as its soft, stippled texture is ideal for staining and leading to create a warm, welcoming look to any home.

Minster, one of the traditional Heritage group of patterns, is just one of a wide range of patterned glasses which can be used in a variety of ways to transform the home either decoratively or as a practical solution to the need for privacy. Patterned glasses are produced with varying degrees of obscuration and are grouped according to the decorative effect — a pastoral pattern such as Mayflower gives the impression of spring flowers all the year round and also gives a high degree of privacy whereas Strata from the Classical collection gives a feeling of elegant regency stripes, but has a lesser level of privacy.

In addition to room dividers and screens for internal decoration, patterned glasses can be made up into double glazing units and, since the textured surface is actually inside the double glazing unit, the window or door panel is much easier to clean. In fact, a double glazing unit with a patterned glass plus the energy-saving Pilkington K Glass is ideal for glazing in a bathroom where privacy and maximum warmth is a necessity.

Four patterns of obscure glass below are, starting clockwise with the glass adjacent to the page number, Minster, Mayflower, Strata and Taffeta.

GLAZING INSIDE THE HOUSE

The use of glazing inside a house is a very personal choice, as any area of glass other than the glass in the windows will tend to determine the feel of the room concerned. Glass is often used in this way because this is exactly the effect the owner requires, but it may also be used to provide 'borrowed light' to illuminate a dark corner, or to bring daylight into a passage, landing or room that lacks natural light. The use of decorative glazing or mirrors in a purely decorative role is beyond the scope of this book, but the techniques of employing borrowed light require consideration at the time that a home is designed.

The most popular way of lighting a dark passage is with lights above doors which are fixed in storey height door casings. This is simple, as the casings are a stock merchants' item, are inexpensive and look conventional. It is often worthwhile glazing them with double glazing units to provide sound insulation.

Glazed doors can vary from traditional 'pattern 10' doors with a heavy wood surround, available from every door manufacturer, to all-glass doors obtained from glass merchants which come complete with handles and hinges fixed directly to the glass. Both should be in toughened glass of an appropriate thickness, and the pattern and colour used is all-important. Glass doors sometimes have a pictorial etching rather than a pattern — very much a matter of one's personal taste.

Alternatives to using glazed doors for borrowed light are glazed screens, or high level sceens called clerestory lights. These always seem to be associated with displays of indoor plants, and this usually improves them enormously. Consider double glazing to clerestory lights if they are in a bedroom wall.

Mirrors can be used to lighten a room, in which case the whole room will have to be furnished to suit them. Again this is very effective when done properly. Remember, mirrors can be made to fairly large sizes, and if consideration is given to them before the plasterer starts work it is possible to make provision for them to be recessed into a wall.

COMPARATIVE COSTS OF USING DIFFERENT TYPES OF GLASS

Cost of glazing for a frame of 1 square metre. Retail prices typical in 1992.

4mm clear float glass	£12.74
6mm clear float glass (a lot stronger)	£21.11
Standard double glazing unit, 6mm cavity, clear glass	£30.90
Standard double glazing unit 12mm cavity, clear glass	£30.90
Double glazing unit with bronze Antisun glass	£49.40
Laminated float glass	£31.17
Laminated double glazing unit, 6mm cavity	£85.10
Obscure glass, Cotswold, 4mm	£14.71
Obscure double glazing unit, 6 mm cavity, Cotswold	£36.00

Clerestory light   *Storey height door casing*

Staccato, another pattern from the Pilkington Glass Classical Collection.

Conservatories glazed with Pilkington K Energy Saving Glass.

CONSERVATORIES

Once upon a time a conservatory was a grand appendage to every prosperous home. It offered a striking and usually elegant change of atmosphere from the main part of the house, as well as an opportunity to grow exotic plants. Then, perhaps because the conservatory was so typical of aspects of Victorian and Edwardian lifestyle which had become so unfashionable, they disappeared from the design scene altogether.

Now they are back, partly due to the wheel of fashion turning, and partly because they can contribute significantly to energy saving. They can add enormously to the look of a house from the outside, and can give an impression of space and elegance to the rooms to which they form a natural extension. However, this effect will only be achieved if the conservatory is properly designed and seen to enhance the appearance of the house from the outside. There also has to be a commitment to furnishing it in an appropriate way. If it is built in an inappropriate style or is used as somewhere to store garden furniture and childrens' toys it will detract from the prestige and value of a new property, so if you are considering a conservatory it is important to give careful thought to the design, and to whether or not you intend to make the best use of it. You cannot shut the door on an untidy conservatory as you can shut the door to a spare room. If what you really want is somewhere to keep the garden furniture, consider a summer house instead.

The role of a conservatory in energy saving can be very significant, and save enough heat to make a useful contribution to the heating bill for the entire house. A visit to the low energy park at Milton Keynes, or any energy saving exhibition, will make it clear how important conservatories are to designs for homes having the lowest possible heating cost, how practical they are, and how attractive they can look.

However, designing an energy efficient conservatory for a new house is a complex business. It must be considered at the design concept stage, and cannot be dealt with as an afterthought. The appearance, utility and cost will all require careful consideration. As with every other aspect of the design of a new home, this is best handled by getting hold of all the information generally available on the subject, and learning enough about it to know what questions to ask the professionals. There are a number of books on the subject, and the Glass and Glazing Federation have a useful guidebook and a number of relevant information sheets which you can obtain by writing to them at 44-48 Borough High Street, London SE1 1XB. The phone number is 071-403-7177, and they will send you copies without charge. The Conservatory Association publish a booklet 'A Touch of Glass' which you can obtain by writing to them at 2nd floor, Godwin House, George Street, Huntingdon, Cambs, PE18 6BU. The telephone number is 0480-458278, and again it is free of charge. ·

Visits to conservatory centres may be misleading, as the displays are of conservatories to meet the mass market, which is for add-on units for existing homes. However, they will help when you are considering matters such as sill heights, the difference in feel between a conservatory with single doors and double doors, etc. etc. Grander conservatories are advertised in the quality Sunday papers, and particularly in magazines like Country Living or Homes & Gardens. When you have a clear idea of what you want, you will then have the choice of either buying a proprietary unit from a national manufacturer, or of having a conservatory made for you by a local specialist firm, or having it built as an integral part of your house by your own builder or sub-contractors. This latter course is not to be recommended unless the builder or sub-contractor concerned has a track record of building conservatories, and you have been to see some of them.

Those concerned with safety advise that there are 30,000 accidents involving areas of vertical glazing each year, many of them invloving children. As a result of this new regulations for the use of glass in new dwellings were promulgated as Section N1 of the Building Regulations in 1991. These require that safety glass should be used at low levels in areas of vertical glazing, and this invariably results in a decision to use safety glass throughout. The new regulations apply only to areas of vertical glazing. It is now usual to have conservatory roofs glazed in polycarbonate, and any proposal to use glass overhead should be discussed carefully with the professionals.

Temperature control in a conservatory is a matter of striking the right balance between the type of glazing used and the ventilation provided. This will depend on whether the structure is south facing or on a north wall, on its dimensions, particularly the height, and on the use to be made of it, particularly in the winter. There is a choice to be made between single and double glazing, and the new types of thermal glass described elsewhere are often appropriate. It may be necessary to arrange special roof insulation with automatically opening vents. Some of these are electrically operated, but others are self-contained.

Whatever you decide to do, it is a good idea to make use of the advisory service of the Glass and Glazing Federation. You can send them your detailed drawings together with a note on the use that you intend to make of the conservatory round the year, and they will recommend appropriate types of glass and ventilation requirements. Their qualified engineers who handle this have unique and specialist experience which is at your disposal free of any charge.

Much of the material and photographs for this chapter were provided by Pilkington Glass. They publish a very wide range of attractive and informative leaflets on all aspects of choosing glass for a new home, and these should be available from any glass merchant. Merchants should also have samples of all the types of glass described in this chapter, but in case of any difficulty write to Pilkington Glass Limited, Prescot Road, St. Helens, WA10 3TT.

Kitchens

How many times have you been in a friend's kitchen and wondered just why there was no work surface next to the cooker on which to place a saucepan? How many times have you inherited a kitchen when you have moved house and wondered why the waste bin was at the farthest point possible from the sink? How many times have you thought 'I could do better'? If you are building your own home you have an opportunity to do just that. For many couples, and most wives, this is the most challenging part of the whole business of building a new house or bungalow.

First of all, before considering either layouts or designs of kitchen units you will have to decide how big a kitchen you need. Kitchens in today's house designs range from the smallest practicable 'cooks' workshops' to traditional farmhouse kitchens to suit a lifestyle where everyone at home spends the whole day in the kitchen and the family only move into the parlour in the evening. Between the two is the functional kitchen that includes a small table and four chairs for informal family meals. Make sure that you get the size of kitchen that you need, and then you can set about furnishing it.

Next, what character are you going to give your kitchen? Your choice of fittings will determine this —the old world charm of oak, the farmhouse appeal of pine, the functional, clinical lines of white, the warmth of textures, the high-tech appeal of primary colours. Keep in mind the basic requirement that your kitchen has to complement the character of your house. In particular, if the kitchen is to be open plan with another room it must be complementary to the decor of that room; nothing looks worse than a classical lounge with a back drop of modern, brightly coloured kitchen units. Decide on a character for the kitchen, and stick to it.

This character must follow through all the details, and these are very important. Door handles, light fittings, pelmets, even the design of the bread board can either enhance or detract from the overall effect.

Once you know how big a kitchen you have to furnish, and the character that you wish to give to it, you can start considering how you plan the layout. As this planning involves shuffling the position of kitchen units, let us look at their general characteristics and think about your own preferences before getting down to details.

Farmhouse kitchen

'Cooks workshop' kitchen

Family kitchen. Decide what size and style of kitchen you need before considering the details of the layout.

Opposite: Spring Ram Contracts' New England kitchen

Spring Ram Contracts' Country Harmony kitchen shown here in Maize

Spring Ram Contracts' Vermont kitchen shown here in Medium Oak.

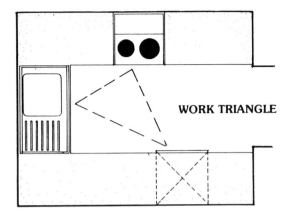

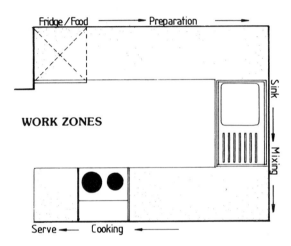

Typical kitchen plans showing the work triangle and work zones.

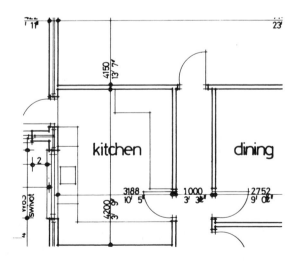

This kitchen plan is taken from a building regulation application drawing. The layout is purely notional, but you should stick to the sink position shown. Otherwise there are no mandatory building regulation requirements for kitchens, although the N.H.B.C. have storage and layout standards. All electrical work is to meet relevant safety regulations.

Don't try to put your ultimate kitchen layout on your Building Regulation plans — keep your options open!

Having considered all of this you can get down to the actual kitchen planning. There is no shortage of books on this subject, and many suppliers offer a design service although most housewives have their own strong views on the subject. Whatever your own opinions — and if you are planning your own home you should get the kitchen *you* want — remember that all kitchen design theory revolves around the work triangle. The three corners of this triangle are the fridge, sink and cooker; and the sides should total more than 4M and less than 7M. This ensures that there is sufficient space around appliances and work surfaces, and avoids too much walking.

Once the work triangle is established the kitchen falls into natural 'zones', each with its own storage and work top space. The proportions of each zone should depend on your own lifestyle.

Bathrooms

Modern bathrooms arrived when central heating enabled a whole house to be heated to a comfortable temperature. That was twenty-five years ago. Before then, the bathroom was the Cinderella of the home. It was often cold, and consequently neglected. When central heating made the bathroom as comfortable a room to enter as any other, the stage was set for a design revolution.

People realised that the bathroom had not only been neglected in general, but that over decades little change had taken place in the design of the basic requirements — the baths, washbasins, and W.Cs.

Manufacturers realised this too, and the demand for the bathroom to become a really live, integral part of the home encouraged great advances in the range of bathroom fittings, the way in which they worked, and their appearance. Bathroom technology and bathroom design was expected to equal the standards of modern kitchens and other rooms. The photographs show how effectively this has been done.

With the wide range of both functional and decorative bathroom fittings now available it is important to *plan* the bathroom in a new home, and not simply to buy a bathroom suite and then choose tiles to match. Look carefully at the best of what is on offer, and remember that the bathroom has only just come of age. Make your selection from the designs of the '80s rather than looking back to the styles used in older homes. The three basics of bath, basin and W.C. have now been joined by matching bidets, showers, sophisticated taps and mixers, co-ordinated surrounds, special tiling, soft floor covering and feature lighting. If a modern kitchen is chosen to be an attractive and efficient working area, a modern bathroom should be chosen to be a luxurious and efficient place to relax and be invigorated. This means considering the bathroom as an entity, and the best place to do this is in a supplier's showroom.

Baths are now available in many designs, shapes and sizes, and there is a continuing move away from iron baths to those in acrylic material which soak up far less heat and can be moulded into a wide range of interesting shapes. Corner baths offer one of the cheapest ways of providing a touch of super-luxury living to your home, as do the whirlpool baths which are now available.

Basins, whether on pedestals or built into vanity units, bidets, water closets and shower trays have not changed appreciably in design concept over the years, but what a change in design detail! One of the greatest improvements is in the way in which the taps and other controls are now co-ordinated into the design as a whole, and not stuck on as an afterthought.

It is taps and other 'water terminals' which are undergoing the biggest changes at the present time. Simple 'cold' and 'hot' taps are being overtaken by sophisticated mixer units with washerless controls. This means the end of dripping taps, no more stains from the drips, and does away with the chore of changing

Michelangelo suite in Whisper Grey from Ideal Standard.

washers. It also means that a single lever is all that has to be moved to obtain water at a pre-set temperature, with all that this offers to the elderly or to a mother bathing small children.

It is unfortunate that many bathroom displays at exhibitions in building centres seem to concentrate on layouts for large bathrooms, which is not very helpful to those looking for ideas for modern en suite bathrooms for new homes. This is because the largest market for the exhibitors is with those who are up-grading bathrooms in older houses, and the displays are geared to this. Do not imagine from this that the best in design is essentially for the large bathroom — the compact installation had just as much to gain from modern trends and modern design, and there is plenty that is designed with space saving in mind.

Manufacturers of bathroom products keep up with the trends in colour, and even lead the fashion moves. One example is the introduction of three delicate shades, whisper pink, whisper blue, and whisper green by Ideal Standard. These were introduced at the same time as Pilkington launched two matching ranges of tiles called Tones and Echoes. White taps and shower controls from Ideal Standard complete this two company 'whisper tones' bathroom concept.

New decor and colour options are now available with Ideal-Standard's Brasilia Patterns. Illustrated is the Geneva pattern.

Above left. This Dualux basin mixer tap has a new colour finish which is becoming very popular.

Above right. Modern shower controls give constant water temperatures whatever the pressure. This is the Ideal-blend unit, which has ceramic disc seals which are unaffected by the hardest water.

Left. Ideal-Standard's Tulip suite offers top design for small sized bathrooms.

All the bathrooms illustrated here are by Ideal Standard, whose brochures are a useful source of ideas. Full details and a list of stockists can be obtained from Ideal Standard Ltd., P.O. Box 60, Hull HU5 4JE.

Insulation

There is no need to emphasise the importance of insulation in houses or bungalows to be built today; this is widely understood and many of those planning for a new home are in some ways almost too concerned with this. The features on the subject in every home interest magazine are mainly concerned with insulation in existing houses; since April 1982 all new homes have had to have new standards of built-in insulation, and these standards are so high that any additional expense on extra insulation is most unlikely to be cost effective.

The idea that you can have more than enough insulation often seems heretical to the housewife who is brain washed by a hundred features on the radio, or her husband who has read as many articles in D.I.Y. magazines, but there is a limit. This comes when no further expenditure is going to be cost effective, and when the level of insulation requires special precautions against condensation, or that you adopt an unusual lifestyle. We read of experimental houses that are so well insulated that they are kept warm with the heat from the electric light bulbs. All well and good — but how long do you think they take to warm up when children leave the door open? The 1982 insulation standards strike a balance between energy saving, ordinary living patterns, and worthwhile investment that should not be ignored lightly. If you decide to have any higher standards of insulation you should try to get first hand reports of what is involved, and should not rely on press features. Few low energy experimental homes are fun to live in, or are a long term unqualified success; their importance is as experiments.

Another point to keep in mind when considering all of this is that with the 1982 insulation levels no expenditure on insulation is likely to save as much money as turning the central heating thermostat down by two or three degrees. The most cost effective further investment is on thermal underwear, not on insulating the building.

Of course, all of this assumes that you also are concerned about having the best sort of central heating and central heating controls. This is dealt with in a separate chapter. As far as insulation is concerned, there are five separate areas of potential heat loss which you should recognise.

WALLS

In traditional construction the 1982 insulating standards are usually met by having an inner skin of 4″ insulating blocks and additional insulation in the cavity. In a new home you can arrange this in any way you wish, and there are obvious advantages in using an insulating system that retains the cavity air space and which does not fill it completely. This is invariably done by increasing the cavity width to 3″ and having a 1″ slab of insulating material fastened against the inner skin with special wall ties. If you want even more insulation than is required to meet the standard you use a 2″ slab of insulation. This arrangement gives the best of both worlds — insulation plus a clear cavity to keep out any threat of damp.

In timber frame construction the insulation is provided by a special quilt set into the frame, and invariably exceeds the required standard. This is dealt with at length in the chapter on timber frame homes. There are other ways of insulating walls in both traditional and timber frame homes, but they are not in general use in new construction.

DRAUGHT PROOFING

All windows and doors in modern homes should take advantage of the new sophisticated draught proofing seals which are now available, and ideally these should be built into the windows when they are manufactured, and not stuck on afterwards. Windows of this sort are usually called high performance windows. The specifications for all designs in this book are for High Performance windows.

ROOF

Mandatory standards are met by a 4" quilt of glass fibre. There are various other ways of providing the required insulation, but they are unusual. The quilt is usually laid between the ceiling ties and is available in either 24" or 16" widths to suit the usual rafter spacings.

This insulation is usually exposed to view in the roof space, and if you want to increase the thickness you can do so at any time. Another way of improving the level of roof insulation, which can only be arranged when the home is being built, is to specify foil backed plaster board. This provides significant extra insulation at very modest cost.

When the design involves a sloping ceiling just under the tiles, as in many purlin roof designs, the insulation specified between the plaster board and the tiles is most important, as it cannot be seen once it is installed. Make sure it is put there!

FLOORS

Current requirements for ordinary detached homes do not require normal floors to be insulated. If you want to stop heat loss down into the foundations this can be arranged quite easily, but you must make up your mind about this at an early stage so that details can be given in your Building Regulation application.

Solid floors are often insulated by having a layer of insulation below the concrete slab. This can be put below the full area of the building, or can be installed around the perimeter of the structure only.

Suspended floors used to be specially insulated by having a glass fibre quilt between the floor boards and the joists, but this is now being overtaken by the use of insulated flooring board. These can also be used on solid floors, and in some ways this is much easier than putting insulation under the floor slab.

Whichever way you may decide to install floor insulation it is essential to work to the material manufacturer's instructions to ensure that you avoid damp and condensation problems.

DOUBLE GLAZING

Heat goes out through windows, and double glazing is now virtually standard in all new homes. This is because it has become an accepted amenity; the actual regulations say that single glazing is acceptable provided it does not form more than 12% of an external wall; double glazing is acceptable up to 24%, and then triple glazing should be used. There is unlikely to be any advantage to be gained in moving to triple glazing other than to comply with the regulations. 'Double glazing' in new homes means sealed units fitted in windows which are designed for them. There are other approaches to this, but they are unusual and should be considered by inspecting a house in which they are fitted, and not by looking at catalogues or advertisements.

There is much more about double glazing in the chapter on glass.

VENTILATION AND CONDENSATION

Modern homes with high standards of insulation and effective draught proofing offer more opportunities for condensation to be a nuisance than draughty buildings to earlier standards. Since 1982 new standards of roof ventilation have been obligatory which helps to offset this. However, it remains important to remember that your draughtproofing has done away with uncontrolled ventilation, and that you must provide controlled ventilation via your opening windows and extractor fans. This is particularly important in a new home that is still drying out. The N.H.B.C. has an excellent booklet about this.

Heating

The decision on how you heat a new home has to be made at the design stage, as there are different structural requirements for different heating systems, and the details have to be given in your Buildings Regulations application. The choice that you make will depend on three factors: your appraisal of future fuel costs and availability, your own personal preferences for the sort of installation you want in your new home, and on your assessment of how your choice will affect the resale value of property.

There are lots of facts to consider. In the last twenty years oil has moved from being the cheapest and most popular way of heating a large detached house to being the most expensive. Underfloor heating systems have been popular, but have dropped out of fashion. The undoubted economic advantages of gas are balanced by uncertainties about its future price and the certainty that North Sea supplies may start to run out in the next decade. Harnessing natural energy, like solar energy, seems as far away as ever. We have been waiting for cheap electricity from nuclear energy for 30 years, and there is no sign of it yet. Let us look at the real options open to you today.

There are two basic decisions to be made: how your rooms are going to be heated, and what fuel you are going to use.

There is little doubt that most of us choose to heat a room from a specific identifiable heat source — from a fire, or from radiators that throw out heat which you detect as you approach them. Systems based on circulating warm air, or on warming the whole of the floor, walls or ceiling, have never been popular for any length of time. Perhaps we were moulded in our attitudes by our ancestors who sat round wood fires, or it may be a popular prejudice. The fact remains that the overwhelming majority of home owners who are able to exercise any choice in the matter want localized heat sources, and this means open fires and radiators.

Choosing anything else may affect how sought after a home is when it is offered for resale, and thus affects its investment potential. Whether this is important or not depends on your own circumstances.

An open fire will burn coal or a smokeless fuel, or it may be a gas fire. There is a wider choice of ways of heating your radiators — oil, gas, solid fuel or electricity.

Oil is convenient and expensive, while gas is convenient and relatively inexpensive, but the cost of both these fuels is artificial, dictated by government fuel price policies and taxation arrangements. Supplies of both are running out, and it is hard to imagine that governments will move from taxing these fuels to subsidising them. This leaves coal, which is plentiful. Its cost reflects wage rates in this country, and so it is unlikely to increase in price ahead of inflation as oil and gas have done.

Coal is a major source of energy for power stations, and electricity is now such an essential part of our lives that its availability and price stability can be taken for granted. If you are building a house now, it seems inevitable that for most of its life through the next century and beyond it will be heated by coal, either directly, or by coal converted to electricity. In this chapter we look at solid fuel heating, using coal in a direct way, and in the next chapter discuss heat pumps which use electrical energy derived from coal in a far more complex way.

Today's fires — a huge choice of styles all with modern efficiency.

Cog

Esse Dragon

Bell "Hole in the middle"

Above: Welcome's 'Lomond' fireplace. Below: Van Delft, design 330.

FIREPLACES AND FIRES

The fireplace is usually the focal point in a room. Where it is situated determines the positioning of the furniture, and its style must suit the feel that you intend the room to have. It would be nice if a choice could be postponed until the house is built so that you can stand in the room and gauge exactly what you think will look best. Unfortunately this is not possible, as the hearth has to be allowed for in the foundations, and the chimney is not easily added afterwards.

First let us consider fireplaces, which frame the fire and provide its character. As it is not a structural element in the building your choice is very wide. On the previous page we illustrate a 'hole in the wall' fireplace in a modern style, contrasted with a free standing fire in surround that looks back in design concept to inglenooks in period homes. On the facing page are two architectural fire surrounds by Richard Burbidge Limited, one with a Victorian style grate and the other with a modern fire. This particular style is now very fashionable, and one reason for this is that it reintroduces a vertical emphasis, with the fireplace taller than it is wide. Fireplaces with a horizontal emphasis arrived in the 50's with the ranch style homes, low pitch roofs and picture windows. They lasted longer than these other American design features, but are now giving way to the traditional British way of framing a fire, and Burbidges have a wide range of them with an excellent catalogue. Their address is on page 62.

Now let us consider the chimney. You may wish it to be a key feature in the external appearance of your home, or you may want it to be just discreetly part of the roof. You may wish it to carry more than one flue, so that it serves a fire in the lounge and perhaps also an Aga-type cooker in the kitchen. If the latter, then it will probably have to be an inside-wall. Corner fireplaces and imaginative island fireplaces are gaining in popularity, but are only possible if they suit a practicable chimney arrangement. Besides the position of the chimney, you have to consider whether its thickness is to be taken up in a chimney breast inside the room, or whether this should be outside, in which case it becomes an architectural feature. If your home is to have more than one chimney, their relationship to each other in the roof line is important. Thus you need to make your decisions at design concept stage, and to do this you will want to give consideration to the actual fireplace which is going to determine the position of the chimney above it.

If you are heating your domestic hot water with a back boiler you will need to use an immersion heater in the summer, and to do this economically means having a large tank and electricity on an 'Economy 7' tariff. The alternatives are to link your back boiler with a system using another boiler, or to have a solid fuel kitchen stove which has its own back boiler. In the country the latter alternative is very popular.

The next thing to consider is the fuel that you want to burn. One third of all households in Britain are in smokeless zones, but these are generally in large cities where few new homes are being built. In these areas you have to use smokeless fuel, but most people burn ordinary house coal in open fires if they have any choice. Closed room heaters have to be used with smokeless fuel.

Burning logs has a mystique of its own, and there are those who happily spend every Sunday with a chain saw cutting up their fuel for the following week. As a spare time activity this is slightly more hazardous than jogging, and the benefits are equally personal and intangible. If this is your scene you should remember that either your supply of timber or your enthusiasm may not last, and it is important that your fire or stove is a multi-fuel appliance so that you can burn coal as well. This is also an important factor when considering the resale potential of the house.

Finally there are a growing number of advanced fires on the market with special air circulation arrangements or other features which give them a very high output, or which enable them to stay in for a very long time. Some of these are gaining an excellent reputation, but it is important to ensure that any appliance that you buy is approved by the Solid Fuel Advisory Service, and to satisfy yourself that spares are likely to be available in the future. The question of the availability of spares is also important if you are considering an imported fire.

In recent years there has been a huge increase in the range of fireplaces available, and if you are prepared to pay as much for a fireplace as you will pay for a three piece suite the choice is very wide. You can have an inglenook fireplace with an iron fire-back cast in genuine 19th century mould, or you can have a free standing stainless steel fire which looks as if it has escaped from a museum of modern art. Between the two there are classical Adam style fires and mantels, stone and tile fireplaces in the style of the 1930s, fires built in feature walls of brick or stone, 'hole in the wall' fires designed to appear to be set in a frame, and specially built fireplaces that are linked with bookshelves, a T.V. shelf, or anything else you wish. The choice is entirely yours.

With the exception of the inglenook and modern free standing fires, all these fireplaces can be fitted with efficient modern back boilers. With the relatively cheap control systems now available, the output from the back of a fire can be used to heat your domestic water, to heat some or all of your radiators, or can be linked into a larger heating system based on a separate boiler elsewhere. Whether this is worth doing depends on the use you intend to make of the fire. If it will usually only be lit in the evening then there is little advantage in a back boiler. If it will be in constant use all winter then a back boiler is essential to get full value from your fuel. The possibility of getting the most out of the back boiler may be the key factor in your choice of an appliance.

A back boiler can be obtained for almost any type of fire, and will provide all the domestic hot water that a family is ever likely to require. Many fires can also be fitted with high output back boilers, which will heat the water and up to five or six radiators. If you want more output than this you have to opt for a room heater. Room heaters have all the advantages of open fires except that they don't look like an open fire. However useful they may be, your final choice will probably depend on how you rate their appearance, and most people either like them a lot, or hate them. Certainly there are plenty to consider in many different styles.

Burbidge architectural fire surround with a modern fire and marble surround.

Another Burbidge fireplace in a similar style to the one above with a traditional Victorian cast iron grate and floral tile surround.

SOLID FUEL BOILERS

Solid fuel boilers have changed far more than fireplaces in the last few years, and are now far less demanding and far more controllable than they used to be. A typical solid fuel boiler for a medium sized detached house burns anthracite grains which feed themselves into the firebox from a hopper. You need only fill the hopper once a day, when the only other attention required is to pull a lever to transfer the ash into an ashbox. This only needs to be emptied once a week. Boilers of this sort are compact, attractively styled, and will heat all but the largest homes. They will remain alight for a whole weekend if you are away, but if you are going to leave them alone for a longer period, you will either have to arrange for a neighbour to call to look after things, or let your boiler go out. For really large houses there are fully automatic boilers with automatic stokers and electric ignition, but these systems are not practicable for units of less than 70kW.

All solid fuel boilers have the sort of controls that were originally developed for oil and gas boilers, with room thermostats, zone controls, and all the time clocks and programming arrangements that you can possibly want. As previously described, linking a boiler with the back boiler of an open fire in the same house is perfectly practicable, although the Solid Fuel Advisory Service emphasise that this cannot be done casually, and prefer to advise on this sort of installation.

You will have to choose the position for your boiler to suit the chimney that it requires, and it usually goes in the kitchen or utility room. Avoid putting the boiler in a garage. To do so is not against building regulations, but it is inherently unsafe due to the risk of petrol leaking from a car.

A modern programmer and thermostatic radiator valves are essential to a modern heating system.

Above: The Dunsley Condor a striking modern room heater with a high output boiler.

Left: Modern solid fuel boiler. This one is by Trianco.

Solid fuel cooking stoves are becoming very fashionable, particularly among gourmet cooks. They are economical to run, last for ever, and will give you all the hot water you can ever want. Some models will also heat your radiators.

These stoves are by Rayburn (top) and Franco-Belge (below).

VENTILATION AND CHIMNEYS

All fires consume large quantities of air, and this helps avoid condensation in the house. Unfortunately if they don't get the air they need they will not perform as intended. Some manufacturers avoid this risk by designing fires to have their own air supply under the floor, with an air intake pipe leading to an air grate in an outside wall. Others have to have some other provision made and this is something about which a S.F.A.S. authorised dealer will be able to advise you. An inadequate air supply is a common cause of chimney smoking — which leads to consideration to the whole business of smoking fires.

A fire that refuses to draw or which lets smoke blow back into the room is the worst possible advertisement for solid fuel heating, and the S.F.A.S. will go to great pains to advise and help anyone who meets this problem. They have a first class booklet on the subject called *Curing Chimney Troubles* which is a great deal better than all the folk-lore about smoking chimneys that you will be told in the pub.

There are only three reasons why a fire will smoke: either it is not getting enough air, or the design of the fire and the chimney do not suit each other, or your chimney is affected by the slope of a hill, large trees, or a neighbouring building which causes the air pressure above the chimney to be higher than the air pressure at the bottom. There are solutions to all these problems, although it can take some time to find the right one. If this sounds discouraging, remember that only a tiny proportion of those with solid fuel heating ever meet this difficulty.

However, if you are buying an unusual fire it is worth while making sure that it is S.F.A.S approved, and try to arrange for the supplier to install it on the basis that he is responsible for ensuring that it works as intended. Most suppliers will do this.

A well designed chimney can add a lot to the appearance of a new home.

STORING SOLID FUEL

If you are building a new home where you are using either coal or smokeless fuel it is important to give consideration to where and how it is stored. A carefully designed home, built with carefully chosen material, is not improved by putting a concrete coal bunker at the back door. Unless the storage arrangements have been carefully thought out, bringing in the coal will be unnecessarily tedious.

One satisfactory way of dealing with this is to invest in enough cheap plastic coal hods to hold a week's supply of fuel. These can all be filled at the weekend, and then stored somewhere convenient ready for use. An arrangement of this sort can justify a coal bunker being further from the house. The bunker itself should be large enough to hold at least a ton of coal, and more if you wish to take advantage of some summer offers. If you intend to use two separate fuels you will have to double up on this.

As a general rule build your coal store from the same materials that were used in the house, make it look solid with 9″ walls, and take the opportunity to combine it with some other amenity — a dustbin screen perhaps, or a garden cold frame. A sloping floor will allow moisture to drain and make it easier for the coal to be moved to the front.

A coal bunker need not be an eyesore.

Material for this feature was provided by the Solid Fuel Advisory Service, which has sixty local offices available to give help and advice on all aspects of solid fuel heating. Addresses are found in all telephone directories, or write to S.F.A.S., Hobart House, Grosvenor Place, London SW1X 7AX.

There is a wide range of illustrated leaflets available from the Solid Fuel Advisory Service, and you can usually get these from authorised appliance dealers.

Electricity

Twentieth century living depends on electricity, and our own life styles are increasingly tied around a bewildering variety of gadgets which need a convenient wall socket. Today's luxury novelty is tomorrow's essential appliance, and almost certainly it is fitted with a 13 amp plug. This chapter is about the provision that must be made for these plugs, and for all the other ways in which electricity is used in the home.

The private individual who is having a building erected to his own requirements has an opportunity to determine exactly where and how electricity will be made available for both his present and his future requirements. The cost of making provision for every imaginable future need is very little if the necessary work is done when the house is being built. Arranging for additional wiring at a later date is invariably expensive and presents problems with decor. There are NHBC regulations setting out the minimum number of lighting points and plug sockets, but they have been unchanged for many years and are not now appropriate to the average household. In spite of this, it is the required minimum provision that will be provided unless the householder makes it quite clear that something better is required. The way to do this is set out later; first of all it is important to look at the options.

The earliest use of electricity in the home in the 1890s was for lighting, and a pendant lamp fitting in the middle of the room was the usual approach. As far as many builders are concerned it is also their present approach, but a visit to any lighting centre will show how many other options there are. Which do you think right for your new home? The answer is all of them. A lighting point costs under £10 whether it is for a wall light, pendant light, spot lamp, concealed lighting, display

lighting, or anything else, and it is there for ever. Fashions in lighting change, and making provisions for the changes is most important. A few years ago it was common for curtains to patio windows to be lit by fluorescent tubes behind the pelmets but today, curtains are likely to be hung on poles. Pelmets will certainly be in and out of fashion several times in the lifetime of the house. A lighting outlet to suit pelmet lighting over an important window is always there when it is wanted. The same is true of wall lights and lights over pictures. The question to ask is not "how do I intend to light this room?", but rather "what are the ways in which this room can be lit?" — and then to make provision for all of them.

The same approach is even more important when considering sockets for appliances, from food mixers to fairy lights for the Christmas tree. It does not matter that you do not need them now: the electrician will fit the outlet box with a blanking off plate that can be changed for a socket when it is required — and required it will be during the lifetime of the building. Until recently all this was slightly inhibited by the uninspiring style of standard socket outlets and light switches. Today there is a wide range of styles of outlets with matching switches, indicators, dimmers, shaver outlets etc., including the telephone and TV aerial sockets. These can be chosen to suit the decor of the room, to be changed at will, as they all fit the same outlet boxes in the wall.

The two photographs below are from MK Electrics and illustrate two different ranges of light switches to suit different rooms. Changing from one range to the other takes an electrician only a few minutes as all MK fittings use the same British standard outlet boxes.

ELECTRICITY IN THE GARDEN

One area in which it is important to look at trends in housing is in the use of electricity outdoors. This can be as security lighting, or to provide outlets for the use of electrical appliances in the garden, or for garden lighting as an element of landscaping. Security lighting is by far the most interesting of these, aided by two recent developments. The first is the introduction of new low energy bulbs with exceptionally long lives and very low electricity consumption, matched with the availability of sophisticated automatic switches that involve timelocks, daylight sensors or proximity switches that turn on a floodlight when they detect an intruder. This type of lighting is frequently linked to an alarm system, and is often considered more of a deterrent than the usual bells. Sad as it may be, there is no doubt that security lights will be standard fittings in a few years' time, and even if they are inappropriate now, it is important that the wiring and switches are there when they will be required.

Security lighting is invariably 230 volts, requiring special weatherproof fittings. Other outdoor use of electricity can be either at mains voltage or at safe low voltages. The latter is obviously preferable for ornamental garden lighting, pumps for garden pools, etc., while 230 volts are necessary for barbecue accessories, garden tools and other adjuncts of outdoor living. Arrangements for all of this can be made very easily at modest cost with complete safety when a house is under construction — ad hoc arrangements of trailing leads made at a later date will be dangerous and inconvenient.

A flood-lit house is inviting to the family and visitors alike, but is definitely uninviting to the burglar, while garden lighting gives a new dimension to landscaping. Garden lights are Nightglow units from Hozelock-Ash of Haddenham, Aylesbury, Bucks.

ELECTRICAL SAFETY

To most people electricity is safe because of the fuse box, which they know is there to protect them from electric shocks and to stop the house catching fire. So far so good, but unfortunately there is a limit to how well fuses can do this, and to their ability to keep pace with the pressure put on electrical wiring by our ever increasing use of electricity in the home. If you are planning a new home this needs further consideration.

A fuse is a piece of very thin wire that will melt and break an electrical circuit if the wiring is over-loaded. It protects against simple faults, but it does not detect potential faults before they become serious, or offer complete protection against all risks. In particular, fuses do not give any help to a person in contact with live parts of an electrical appliance who gets a shock when current flows through their body to earth. In fact, the majority of electrical fires are started by currents earthing, and this cannot be controlled by a fuse. Simple fuses are no longer part of today's technology, and something better is required.

That 'something better' is a modern distributor board fitted with miniature and residual current breakers. This jargon is better described as a sentry system, and the best known (and British made) system is called the MK Sentry. This continuously monitors the electrical wiring in a house and detects the slightest abnormality from wrongly connected or damaged equipment, or other problems. If it detects a fault it turns off a switch so quickly that it is almost impossible to get a serious shock or have any risk of fire. A row of these switches cover different parts of the wiring in the house, just as with the old fuse boards. If they turn off the current they can be simply turned on again by the householder after unplugging the offending appliance. This is far less trouble than repairing a fuse, and avoids the hazards of fuses being fitted with the wrong sort of fuse wire. As an added safeguard the Sentry system has a test button which simulates a fault in the wiring so that you can see the switches turn off automatically.

All electrical installations in new homes have to be made to exacting standards, and before the meters are installed the electricity board carry out simple tests on the wiring. However, the specification for the equipment to be installed is up to the specifier — who is the householder or the architect. There is no doubt at all about what it should be — a sentry system with all the fittings throughout the house from the same manufacturer.

MK electrical protection — wall socket.

MK electrical protection — distributor board.

SPECIFICATION FOR AN ELECTRICAL INSTALLATION

There are two ways to specify an electrical installation in a new home. The first is to decide exactly what you want while looking at the plans, and either to mark up the drawings with what you require or else to get your architect to do it for you. You can then get a firm quotation for the work involved, and this becomes part of the contract for the construction of the property.

A more flexible approach, and usually a better way of arranging things, is to obtain a quotation for the NHBC standard requirements for an electrical installation. This is quite arbitrary, and may be unrealistic: it does not matter as it provides an excellent starting point providing that you also obtain a fixed price quotation for each additional lighting point, switch, and socket outlet required. Electricians are well used to quoting in this way. When the house is roofed and the internal partition walls are built up you then go round your new home with the electrician and a piece of chalk. Mark up the actual positions of all the switches etc., that you require. In this way you will be able to stand in the rooms and decide exactly what you want, and where it is to be. This procedure enables you to make the decision — with the advice of the electrician — and you can be sure that you will get exactly what you require. When doing this give special consideration to the height of switches, to which side of the door they are required, the height of socket outlets, any special consideration for disabled persons, and remember to plan for the year 2000 as well as for tomorrow.

The way in which this can be arranged is seen in the appropriate sections of the standard P.S.S. specification which are reproduced opposite. Note that it calls for a sentry system, and requires that fittings from one manufacturer are used right through the house. The manufacturer should be detailed by name to avoid the use of cheap foreign fittings which may not comply with the required British standard, and which also may not be available in the future if the style of the switch plates is to be changed.

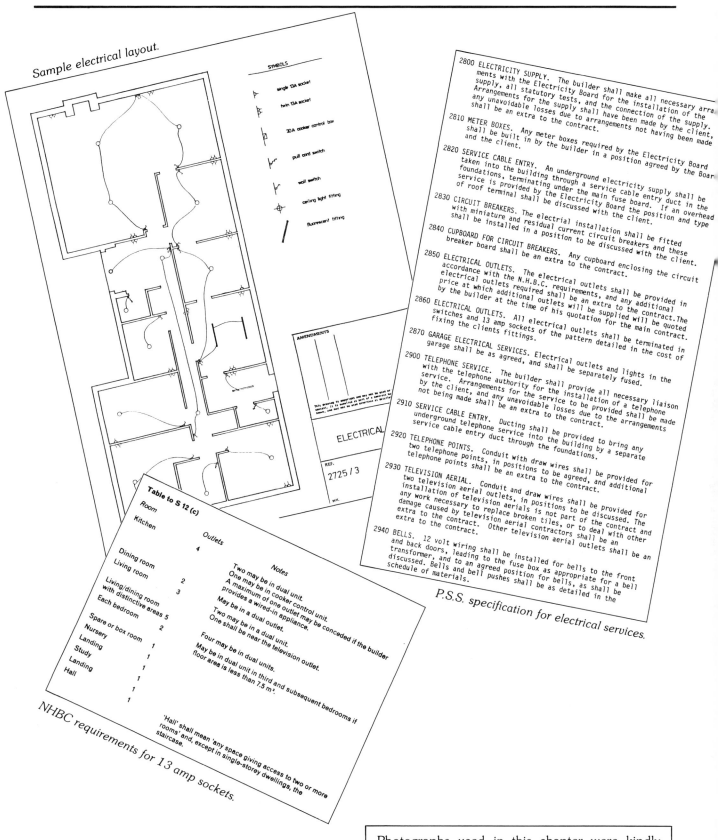

Sample electrical layout.

SYMBOLS

- single 13A socket
- twin 13A socket
- 30 A cooker control box
- pull cord switch
- wall switch
- ceiling light fitting
- fluorescent fitting

AMENDMENTS

ELECTRICAL

REF.

2725 / 3

P.S.S. specification for electrical services.

2800 ELECTRICITY SUPPLY. The builder shall make all necessary arrangements with the Electricity Board for the installation of the supply, all statutory tests, and the connection of the supply. Arrangements for the supply shall have been made by the client, any unavoidable losses due to arrangements not having been made shall be an extra to the contract.

2810 METER BOXES. Any meter boxes required by the Electricity Board shall be built in by the builder in a position agreed by the Board and the client.

2820 SERVICE CABLE ENTRY. An underground electricity supply shall be taken into the building through a service cable entry duct in the foundations, terminating under the main fuse board. If an overhead service is provided by the Electricity Board the position and type of roof terminal shall be discussed with the client.

2830 CIRCUIT BREAKERS. The electrial installation shall be fitted with miniature and residual current circuit breakers and these shall be installed in a position to be discussed with the client.

2840 CUPBOARD FOR CIRCUIT BREAKERS. Any cupboard enclosing the circuit breaker board shall be an extra to the contract.

2850 ELECTRICAL OUTLETS. The electrical outlets shall be provided in accordance with the N.H.B.C. requirements, and any additional electrical outlets required shall be an extra to the contract. The price at which additional outlets will be supplied will be quoted by the builder at the time of his quotation for the main contract.

2860 ELECTRICAL OUTLETS. All electrical outlets shall be terminated in switches and 13 amp sockets of the pattern detailed in the cost of fixing the clients fittings.

2870 GARAGE ELECTRICAL SERVICES. Electrical outlets and lights in the garage shall be as agreed, and shall be separately fused.

2900 TELEPHONE SERVICE. The builder shall provide all necessary liaison with the telephone authority for the installation of a telephone service. Arrangements for the service to be provided shall be made by the client, and any unavoidable losses due to the arrangements not being made shall be an extra to the contract.

2910 SERVICE CABLE ENTRY. Ducting shall be provided to bring any underground telephone service into the building by a separate service cable entry duct through the foundations.

2920 TELEPHONE POINTS. Conduit with draw wires shall be provided for two telephone points, in positions to be agreed, and additional telephone points shall be an extra to the contract.

2930 TELEVISION AERIAL. Conduit and draw wires shall be provided for two television aerial outlets, in positions to be discussed. The installation of television aerials is not part of the contract and any work necessary to replace broken tiles, or to deal with other damage caused by television aerial contractors shall be an extra to the contract. Other television aerial outlets shall be an extra to the contract.

2940 BELLS. 12 volt wiring shall be installed for bells to the front and back doors, leading to the fuse box as appropriate for a bell transformer, and to an agreed position for bells, as shall be discussed. Bells and bell pushes shall be as detailed in the schedule of materials.

Table to S 12 (c)

Room	Outlets	Notes
Kitchen	4	
Dining room	2	Two may be in dual unit.
Living room	3	One may be in cooker control unit. A maximum of one outlet may be concealed if the builder provides a wired-in appliance.
Living/dining room with distinctive areas	5	May be in a dual outlet.
Each bedroom	2	Two may be in a dual outlet. One may be near the television outlet.
Spare or box room	1	
Nursery	1	Four may be in dual units.
Landing	1	May be in dual unit in third and subsequent bedrooms if floor area is less than 7.5 m².
Study	1	
Landing	1	
Hall	1	

'Hall' shall mean 'any space giving access to two or more rooms' and, except in single-storey dwellings, the staircase.

NHBC requirements for 13 amp sockets.

How are you going to build?

The fundamental differences between the various ways of building a new home are the different levels of your involvement with the building process, from simply handing the whole job over to someone who is going to make it all happen for you, through to providing all the drive and management to get everything done yourself. These are the choices.

USING AN ARCHITECT

The Rolls Royce way of having a new home built is to use an architect in private practice who specialises in individual houses. He will handle everything for you, and though you can tell him that you want him to arrange to use one of our designs, you will probably find that he will prefer to draw up his own design. He will find you a builder, prepare the contract for you to sign, supervise the work, and approve the bills before sending them on to you to pay. He will be concerned to see you get full value for money, but he does operate at the top end of the market. His fees will be around 10% of the cost of the building, plus expenses. If this is for you, then it is essential to make sure you explain exactly what your budget is, and to make it clear that the job must be completed within this figure.

USING A DESIGN CONSULTANT

A look at a typical local authority planning register will show just how many planning applications are made by design consultants. They are not subject to the control of the R.I.B.A. or the Architects Registration Council, and may not be fully covered by professional indemnity insurances. Their fees are invariably highly negotiable, and they will usually submit our plans for approval, find you builders, and supervise work if required. They will give you as much or as little help as you require. Make sure there is a clear understanding of your budget, and of the fees which they require.

USING A DESIGN FROM THIS BOOK

A full set of drawings for a design from this book will cost less than 1% of the cost of the building, and standard designs can be altered to meet your own requirements. The drawings come with very detailed advice on submitting your own planning and building regulation applications, or you can get a local surveyor or estate agent to do this for you, or P.S.S. Ltd who sell the drawings may arrange this.

The majority of P.S.S. clients choose to telephone the company to discuss their requirements before placing an order. The P.S.S. staff welcome this, and a chat of this sort is useful to both parties.

BUILDING WARRANTIES

Warranties or guarantees that a new house or bungalow is properly built are usually a condition of a mortgage on it. If you are building without using mortgage finance, such a warranty will probably be required by someone purchasing the property at a later date, particularly if they are getting a mortgage on it.

There are three alternatives in this — a warranty issued by the National Housebuilders Council (or N.H.B.C.), or a similar warranty issued by the Municipal Mutual Insurance Company which is called Foundation 15, or to get the architect who has appropriate professional indemnity insurance cover to certify the work. This matter is dealt with at length in this book's companion volume *Building Your Own Home*, and everyone having a new home built should make themselves familiar with every detail of these options. Both the N.H.B.C. and Foundation 15 have leaflets on their services which are essential reading. If you are using a builder who is registered with the N.H.B.C. or Foundation 15 he is obliged to offer you the appropriate warranty, and you must make sure that he does so. If you are a prospective selfbuilder it is usual to use a special Foundation 15 scheme for selfbuilders. If you want to rely on architects' certificates then you should discuss the insurance angle with the architect.

LOCAL BUILDING COMPANIES

By this we mean well established local firms who work in the area where you want to build. They are probably concerned with commercial or development work as well as with one-off houses, and may not welcome your enquiry unless the contract will be fairly large and the specification a high one. A phone call asking if they are interested in quoting for a job in your price bracket may save time and trouble. They are invariably N.H.B.C. or Foundation 15 registered. Check whether they will build for you using their own employees or whether they intend to sub-contract the job. This sort of firm should be able to help and advise you on every aspect of the project, but do make sure that you make your own decisions about the terms of your contract with them.

A LOCAL BUILDER

This is the fellow who puts up most one-off houses on the clients' own sites. He is usually a building tradesman who often works alongside his employees. He works from home where his wife takes the phone calls, and is probably N.H.B.C. or Foundation 15 registered. Do not be put off by his apparently meagre resources; he can do a first-class job and with the N.H.B.C. or Foundation 15 arrangements and the right contract you can be perfectly safe with him. His building work is usually better than his organising ability, and you may get involved in arranging for services and other matters.

THE NON REGISTERED BUILDER

If a builder who is not N.H.B.C. or Foundation 15 registered wants to take a contract for the whole job you must ask yourself why he is not registered. Take advice and be cautious. Perhaps you should treat him as a subcontractor and sign up for Foundation 15 yourself as a selfbuilder.

BUILDING CONTRACTS

If you employ an architect he will write a contract with a builder for you. Make sure it is a fixed price contract, with no escalation clauses to allow for inflation, and that any extras to be charged have to be approved by you as well as by the architect before the expenditure is incurred.

If you are using an established building firm they may present you with one of the various standard forms of contract used in the building industry.

A quotation from a small local builder may well be handwritten on one side of a piece of lined paper. This may seem to you to be casual in the extreme, but if the price if right and the builder is right it can be the basis of an excellent contract. What you do is to send him a letter accepting his offer and *referring to an attached specification and drawing*. The specification should be discussed with whoever designed the building. A good model specification will be found in *Building Your Own Home*.

In any arrangement to build a new home the essential is never to pay in advance for any work. Progress payment should always be for rather less than the actual value of the work done. Work that is extra to contract should also be costed and authorised in writing before it is put in hand. If these rules are followed, you will always be in the driving seat and will effectively control the contract. If you ever pay for anything in advance, or imply sanction for extra work for which you have not been quoted a firm price, you have lost control of the situation. 99% of disputes on contracts come from clients losing control of situations in this way.

QUOTATIONS AND PRIME COST SUMS

When you are seeking a price from a builder he will not want to quote for the particular kitchen that you require, and so will allow a prime cost sum for this. This is called a p.c. sum. If a p.c. sum is £900 he has allowed in his price for a kitchen with this value. If the kitchen that you want costs £500 more than this, then the contract price will be increased by £500; if less then there is saving on the contract price. Typical features covered by p.c. sums are kitchens, bathrooms, central heating, fitted furniture, fireplaces, feature staircases, wall tiling and floor tiling. It is a very useful arrangement, but make sure that you know the basis on which the extras or savings on p.c. sums will be charged — list price, trade price, special offer or what.

Another aspect of quotations is the obvious need to allow for unforeseen extra work in the foundations. This is dealt with by the builder quoting for the foundations as shown on the drawing. Any extra work in the foundation which is required by the Building Inspector or the N.H.B.C. or Foundation 15 Inspector is charged at standard trade rates; these are published monthly and are well known. Special features such as display shelving, parquet flooring, built-in hi-fi wiring or garden floodlights are best kept out of quotations and contracts altogether, and settled separately as extras to the contract. This has many advantages, one of which is that a request for elaborate sounding features in the basic quotation often gives the builder the idea that cost is not particularly important to you! Get your contract price fixed on a basic specification, with realistic p.c. sums, and obtain special quotations for extras later.

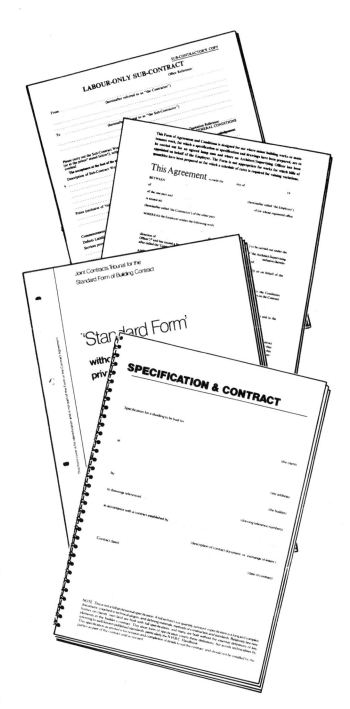

There are many forms of standard contract. If you use one, make sure that you read every word of it and understand all of it. Delete any paragraphs that do not suit you.

BUILDING USING SUB-CONTRACTORS OR YOUR OWN LABOUR

Any idea of building without having a contract with a builder who co-ordinates and controls the whole job takes you straight into the world of self-build. This is a practical proposition for those with organising ability and lots of confidence. Read *Building Your Own Home* — details are at the end of the book. It is the essential self-builder's handbook. Over ten thousand people build for themselves *every* year.

This owner-built house in Nottinghamshire was the original of our Woodchurch design.

Above: Colin Murray built his own home while serving in the RAF, using the D&M service. The house is the Blyth design.

Below: Tim Skelton of the Milton Keynes Land Office, Alan Lake of Barclays Bank who finances self build projects, and Tony Wilson, Secretary of the Self Build Managers Association, all of whom help people's dreams of a new home come true at Milton Keynes.

Timber frame building

If you are thinking of building a new home you are almost certainly reading all the magazine features on new houses that you can find, are sending for brochures, and you are collecting all the information that you can about your options. From this you will know of the choice between traditional construction and the newer timber frame systems, and you are probably a little uncertain about it all, particularly as both ways of building are promoted as being the *only* way of building. Let us look at this situation.

First of all, timber frame homes are neither better nor worse than traditionally built homes. They look exactly the same and are just as good an investment. The costs are generally comparable. The difference is in the way in which they are constructed.

Timber frame houses and bungalows have a wooden frame which supports the roof. This usually has a skin of brickwork or other masonry outside. There is lots of insulation and damp proofing material around the frame itself, and the walls inside are formed by an inner skin of plasterboard or 'dry lining'.

Traditional housing usually has walls with two skins of masonry, with insulating blockwork as the inner skin. The walls between rooms are usually built in solid blockwork, at any rate on the ground floor, and all interior surfaces are finished with traditional wet plastering that takes some time to dry out.

There are various half-way compromises between these two systems of construction: traditionally built houses can be dry lined, and first floor walls between bedrooms are often timber framed. However, the essential difference between traditional and timber frame construction is that a timber frame supports the roof of the building, and gives the whole dwelling its structural stability. In traditional construction this structural stability comes from the masonry.

All new housing in the UK has to comply with some of the strictest building regulations in the world, and all new homes, traditional or timber framed, are built to exceptionally high standards. Timber frame housing is particularly closely controlled, and because the components are factory made there is an assurance of a measure of 'built-in' quality. The timber frame home will last as long as a traditionally built home, will be no better and no worse a fire risk, and will be just as easy to insure, and just as easily mortgaged. Their advantages and disadvantages compared with traditional construction are very minor matters in the whole context of building yourself a new home. On the other hand, a decision to build one way or the other is a very fundamental one, and you have to make your mind up early in the whole scheme of things. To help you in this, here are the points you should keep in mind.

1. Timber frame housing is very effectively advertised by the frame manufacturers, and their trade associations do an excellent public relations job. As a result you can go to the Ideal Homes Exhibition and collect an armful of timber frame brochures. You will not find many stands promoting traditional construction. This is a pity. It gives a one sided view because there are no comparable organisations concerned with the older way of building.

2. The proportion of timber frame used for one-off housing varies enormously in different parts of the country. In Scotland it has almost taken over the market, in some parts of England it is no more popular than it was 10 years ago. Beware generalisations, and look out for other new homes being built locally to get an idea of the way the trend is going in your own county.

3. Timber frame houses can be built more quickly than traditional buildings. The speed of construction comes from the walls being reared and the roof put on in two or three working days compared with two or three weeks for bricks and mortar. More importantly, the plasterboard internal surfaces do not have to dry out like traditional plastering, and this can save another month. However, the foundations, drains, drive, services and fitting out all take just as long whichever way you build. Ignoring the publicity stunts (the writer once built a traditional house in 7 days!), if time is important you can hope to move into a timber frame house 2 months after a start is made on site, and into a traditionally built home in 4 months. This will be after an average of between 3 and 4 months considering design, getting planning and building regulation consents, and waiting for the builder to start. If speed is essential, timber frame will save you 2 months, and perhaps more in bad weather.

4. Timber frame houses have a high level of thermal insulation. All the frame manufacturers put more insulation into the structure than the building regulations require, and more than is provided in most traditionally built homes. Of course, whatever insulation you wish can be specified in any new home, however it is constructed, but timber frame companies offer exceptional insulation as standard. Rather more importantly timber frame walls do not soak up heat themselves the way that blockwork walls do, so the house will warm up quickly when the heat is turned on. It will also cool down quickly when you turn the heat off, but then you won't be in to notice! This low thermal capacity and quick thermal response of a timber frame house is a very real advantage if your home is going to be unoccupied for part of the day, or when both husband and wife are at work.

5. Costs are more or less comparable. The only meaningful comparisons are the final costs per square foot for the finished job, and timber frame houses are firmly in the middle of traditional costs. Certainly if you are wanting to build for yourself using sub-contractors you will probably find it cheaper to build traditionally, and at the very top end of the market you can pay more for a traditional home than average timber frame costs, but in most cases the prices that you will be quoted will be in the same general bracket.

6. Most timber frame companies will handle everything for you from planning application onwards, and because they are so concerned to advertise they are customer conscious, and will look after you. They usually have show houses for you to inspect before you

settle anything at all, and the nationally known companies have got where they are by giving a good service. Usually they have an area manager who will act as your liaison man in everything as the job progresses, and perhaps the real appeal of timber frame to those building on their own land is that it is all made so easy.

7. Finally, as with all major decisions to be made when building a new home, go to see timber framed homes from a frame manufacturer who quotes you for a service. Reputable companies will encourage it.

This traditional style house is by Prestoplan, and has a timber frame

A Prestoplan home on the Isle of Man, exterior and interior.

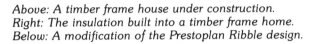

Above: A timber frame house under construction.
Right: The insulation built into a timber frame home.
Below: A modification of the Prestoplan Ribble design.

Virtually all single and two storey homes can be built in timber frame, but there are obvious advantages in using designs that were specifically drawn for this type of construction. In particular, a building regulation application to build using a frame requires the submission of special drawings with the structural design calculations, and usually can only be handled by the trade manufacturer.

Twenty of the designs in this book are by Prestoplan, Britain's leading timber frame manufacturer. Plans for these designs are available from Plan Sales Services like the plans for all the other designs in the book, and these are for making planning applications only. Prestoplan have the full frame drawings and structural calculations for building regulation applications for all these designs, and purchasers of drawings are put in touch with the company who will quote for their full service. If one of these designs is built using a Prestoplan frame, the company will refund the sum paid to Plan Sales Services for the basic plan.

Photographs for this feature were provided by Prestoplan Homes Limited, timber frame housing specialists, who may be contracted at Four Oaks Road, Walton Summit Centre, Preston, PR5 8AS. Their telephone number is 0772 627373. They have staff in all parts of the country who can advise on designs, costs etc.

The package companies

There are many ways of arranging to build a new home, and one very straightforward approach is to use one of the companies that offer a specialised service to those who have their own land. There are a number of them to choose from, and they can be very useful indeed to those who feel they want help in co-ordinating the whole job.

Many of the designs in this book are from Design & Materials Limited, who specialise in traditional construction. Whether you buy plans from this book, or other plans from the D & M range, or whether you want a design drawn specially for you, D & M will be happy to quote you for making a site survey, advising you in detail on costs and many other matters, handling your planning and building regulation applications, obtaining quotations from builders for you, and supplying all the structural shell materials for your home. They have experienced field staff who cover the whole of Britain except the Scottish Highlands and N. Ireland, and have an associated company in Eire.

A proportion of the plans are by Prestoplan Ltd, and were specially drawn for timber-frame construction. As with the D & M plans, buying these drawings does not involve you in any obligation to use a Prestoplan timber-frame, but obviously Prestoplan will be delighted to quote you. Again, they will handle everything for you, from discussing the potential of your site through to arranging the actual building work. Prestoplan will also quote for help with any of the other designs in the book which are suitable for this type of construction. It must be emphasised that if you are building with a timber-frame you will have to use the services of a specialist supplier to provide you with the design calculations that will be needed for your building regulation application. It is not practicable for the average home builder to handle this himself, and advice on this subject in many American publications is not relevant to British conditions.

Besides D & M and Prestoplan there are many other companies in this field, and most of them will help you to build using a set of plans purchased using the order form at the back of this book. They should all be able to give you firm quotations for everything they offer to do for you, and the best way of evaluating the service offered is to ask to see their completed homes and jobs under construction for ordinary clients — *not* show houses. If you are buying their experience, make sure how wide it is and ask how many houses they handle a year. This is particularly important when talking to agents for continental firms.

The D & M Avonmere design.

A question often asked is whether it is more economical to buy materials through a package company. The answer is that in direct terms there is probably no saving, and that given the bill of quantities, the time to spare, and the right contacts you can probably just beat the price that they quote. However, it is the convenience and efficiency of their total service that is the real attraction, together with the advice that they can give about local builders, sub-contractors, insurances and many other matters. People tend to get involved with a package company at project planning stage, and are more concerned at the ability of the company to help them realise their total objective within their budget than with the possibility of buying their double glazing units marginally cheaper elsewhere.

All the package companies aim at the middle and top end of the market, and their specifications are always very high, with above average standards of insulation. Materials supplied are invariably first class, especially the joinery, which they usually manufacture themselves. Walling materials and tiles which they supply come directly from the manufacturer's works against long term contracts, and this enables them to guarantee

deliveries — something which is very important when work starts on site.

Package companies will not usually enter into a contract to build for you themselves, instead they obtain competing quotations for you from local builders and help you to place a contract direct with the contractor whose tender you wish to accept. This procedure avoids legal complications, and the client has the direct benefit of the builders N.H.B.C. Certificate with its ten year warranty.

Those who are building on their own using sub-contractors find a package service even more useful, as it takes one whole area of organisation and uncertainty out of their hands. This enables them to concentrate on the job that only they can do, which is to see that the work on site is carried out properly, on programme, and at the right price. They also find that professionally prepared estimates of costs from the package companies are useful in putting up their proposals to building societies and banks who are providing loan finance, besides getting help from package companies in arranging for the architect's progress certificates which will be required as a condition of obtaining loan finance.

All the materials for a new home. The photograph was posed for The Sunday Times *by D & M Ltd., and shows their clients with the architect, the engineer, the materials manager, and*

everyone else involved in providing the D & M service. In the background are the materials supplied — a giant Lego set.

Above: A bungalow in Wales built in traditional materials using a package from RBS Limited.

Below: A D&M house drawn to the client's own requirements.

The legal side

PLANNING

Serious consideration cannot be given to building a new home without an understanding of the various consents and approvals necessary before you can even make a start. This subject is not nearly as simple or straight-forward as you may think it should be, and applications to build a home must be made with care, and with an understanding of the options. It is equally important to understand how the system works, and find out how you can best arrange to get the various permissions that you want. This involves all sorts of special procedures, and sometimes these do not seem to have much relevance to the commonsense fact that the plot of land that you are buying is obviously the best place for the bungalow of your dreams.

There are two basic rules to be observed in dealing with the planners and others concerned with all of this. One is to know what it is that you want, and the other is to ask for what you want in the way most likely to succeed. Often this is a job for a professional, but the general public have every right to handle these formal-ities themselves, and often do so. Whether employing an agent, or submitting applications yourself, you must know the way in which these things work, and how to use the system to have the best chance of obtaining the consents that are required with as little fuss as possible.

Planning consents are impersonal things, and it is always the land which obtains planning consent, not the person who made the application for it. When land with planning consent is sold, the consent is available to the new owner. One does not have to own a piece of land to apply for planning consent on it, and it is quite usual for a prospective purchaser to make an application before actually buying the land to which it relates, although he is legally obliged to advise the actual owner that he is doing this.

As a general rule the personal circumstances of the applicant play no part in consideration of a planning application. The criteria is that it should be seen to be a good thing for society at large that the proposed development should take place. A planning consent for a new home on a particular site is granted because new homes are required, and this is a good place for one, and not because the applicant is a good chap who deserves to be allowed to do what he wants. On a farm, consent will be given for a new farm bungalow because it is essential to the proper management of the farm, and not because a rise in milk prices enables the farmer to afford it. This is the theory behind the Planning Acts; the practice is sometimes different, but you have a better chance of arranging to get your own way if you understand the concept.

There are various types of planning consent, and the differences between them are important. They are as follows:

Outline Consent. This is simply permission for a dwelling of some sort to be built, and is normally granted subject to a large number of conditions or 'reserved matters'. These require that before any work starts it is necessary to submit details of the proposed design, materials, access, etc, and all these matters have to be approved. An application for Outline Consent can be made before any expense is incurred in buying plans.

Approval of Reserved Matters. This is given in respect of an application dealing with the reserved matters in the Outline Consent which has already been granted.

Full Planning Permission. This is granted when an application is made which covers everything regulated by the planning authority in one application. There may be reserved matters in such a consent, but they will deal with minor issues such as the bricks to be used, or the drainage arrangements.

Conditional Consent. This is a convenient term for a planning consent which has been issued on special conditions. This normally is that the dwelling should be occupied by a person whose job requires that he should live on the site. In these circumstances the actual wording used is most important. Typically it may read: 'Occupation shall be limited to a person solely employed in agriculture or forestry in the local area, or a person last so employed, or the widow of such a person'.

Such a consent makes it very difficult for the dwelling to be sold separately from the farm or other enterprise to which it relates, and this is the purpose of the condition. Sometimes this is reinforced by a condition requiring that the applicant enters into a legal agree-ment with the local authority promising not to sell the house or bungalow separately from the enterprise. This is called a Section 52 Agreement. As a general rule a dwelling covered by a conditional consent will not qualify for an ordinary building society mortgage.

Planning Applications. A planning application is a legal document in its own right, and has to be acted on by the planning authority within a set period. Once a decision has been given on a planning application it is a matter of record in the local authority planning register which is available for inspection by the general public.

A Planning Refusal. A refusal of a planning application is a matter of record but does not normally preclude a further application being made to do the same thing in a different way. However, a refusal of an application for approval of reserved matters may mean that any re-submission must be as a new full planning application, so that if problems arise in discussions with a planning officer it is usual to withdraw such an application before a decision is made.

Conservation Areas. These are areas of particular scenic importance where all proposals are subject to special scrutiny, and where any new building is expected to blend in perfectly with its surroundings. Conservation areas are usually found in the centre of old towns, in particularly attractive rural villages, in National Parks, and at beauty spots.

Green Belt, White Land, Residential Zoning, etc.

These are phrases which are often used in different ways and usually are not very specific. They relate to development plans for a town or village which have been adopted as a basis for dealing with planning applications. 'Green Belt' refers to land where no development is to be permitted, and 'White Land' is land not yet specifically zoned for residential development. This seems very simple, but only small areas of the country have development plans, and these are constantly being redrawn. In addition to this, they are regarded by different authorities in different ways, and may be considered as anything from a vague statement of principle to a firm policy. These terms are only really specific to a particular development plan, and the standing of that plan can vary.

Planning Appeals.

One can enter an appeal against a refusal of a planning application, or against the unreasonable imposition of reserved matters, or refusal to approve proposals covered by reservations in the consent. Just over a quarter of all planning appeals succeed and in certain areas where conservation groups and others put a lot of pressure on planning committees, there is a tendency to refuse any application in a sensitive situation knowing that the worthwhile applications will succeed at appeal. Planning appeals are dealt with by the Department of the Environment, and virtually all appeals relating to single houses are dealt with by exchange of letter. It is not at all unusual for private individuals to handle their own appeals, and the Dapartment of the Environment have a booklet giving help and advice in doing this. Anyone receiving a planning refusal is automatically sent full details of how to appeal against the decision.

The wording of any planning document has to be read very carefully. All the conditions mean exactly what they say, but there are some special things to look out for.

Any outline consent that reads: 'The area is of outstanding architectural importance, and a high standard of design and materials will be required' means that the local authority's requirements may be prohibitively expensive, and that this is certainly not a site on which anyone should consider building a low budget home without a lot of investigation into what will be permitted.

Any condition that requires that natural stone or natural slate shall be used, or which calls for the subsequent approval of materials in an area where stone, slates or small plain tiles may be required, may involve significant additional costs.

A planning consent for a building on a site where there are trees which are protected by a Tree Preservation Order will normally have a condition drawing attention to this. If it does not, the Planning Consent certainly does not cancel the Tree Preservation Order. You will have to seek separate approval to fell any trees that are in the way. If you have to do this it is always a good idea to offer to plant replacement trees elsewhere on the site.

Most planning refusals list half a dozen reasons why the application has failed. Some planning authorities set out as many reasons for their decision as possible. The only reason for this can be that it makes entering an appeal rather more difficult, as each reason for refusal has to be challenged separately. On the other hand, when a planning refusal contains only a single reason for refusal, particularly when this relates to access or to some other particular aspect of the proposal, it can be taken as an indication that a further application which meets the authority's requirements in this particular respect will be approved.

When one looks at the different sorts of consent it seems sensible to apply first for outline consent to

Outline consent to build on a site like this will be subject to very stringent and expensive conditions.

establish whether a house or bungalow can be built at all, and when this is granted to have detailed plans prepared and submit an application for approval of the reserved matters. However, this is a lengthy procedure, and frequently it is preferable to make a full planning application as a first approach to the authority. This saves time, and is often believed to demonstrate that an application is for a new home that someone really wants to build, and is not simply being made to establish an enhanced value for a piece of land. Another advantage of this approach is that it clears any uncertainty regarding the conditions in an outline consent. This can be very important as such conditions can often make a very significant difference in the total cost of a new home.

The general public have free access to planning officers, who invariably have set times at which they are available to discuss planning matters with members of the public. At most council offices they have an interview room set aside for this purpose where their treatment of visitors is invariably friendly and open compared with, for instance, the attitude at the rating office. However, in dealing with them, whether by letter or face to face, it is important to recognise two things. Firstly, no planning officer will discuss planning policy, but must restrict himself to advising how planning

policy will affect your proposals, without committing himself or the council in any way. Secondly, if you ask for advice you will get it — but you may wish you hadn't had it! To elaborate the first point, a planning officer will advise that an application 'could normally be expected to be approved' or that he 'would not anticipate being able to recommend approval'. He is not allowed to be more specific, and it is pointless, and rude, to try to tie him down.

What he will do is to explain policy in such a way that there are plenty of lines to read between. What he will not do is debate the policy itself, or give any sort of promise regarding an application. The only exception to this is when he is discussing reserved matters in a full consent, such as a requirement that a type of brick or design detail should be approved by him under powers delegated to him by the planning committee. In these matters he will be specific, and will often negotiate a compromise.

The second point concerns detailed advice given by a planning officer. This advice, although obviously the best advice as to how the planning authority view a situation, is a counsel of perfection, and it may not suit you to take it. For instance, suppose you are buying a particularly attractive site with outline consent. As a first stage in establishing a design you may decide to

TP 6P   NOTICE OF PLANNING PERMISSION   Planning Reference No. 326/C/172883

TOWN AND COUNTRY PLANNING ACT
THE SHERWOOD DISTRICT COUNCIL having considered an Application
by or on behalf of Mr & Mrs J.B. Smithson
to erect a detached two storey dwelling with garage
on part O.S. 371 at Clay Lane, Carlton
as shown on the plans submitted with the application, which application and plans and any relevant correspondence are hereinafter referred to as "the application" hereby in pursuance of their powers under the above mentioned Act.

GRANT PERMISSION

for the development in accordance with the application, subject to compliance with the conditions imposed and or the reasons set out below.

CONDITIONS

1   The development hereby permitted must be begun either before the expiration of 5 years from the date of this outline permission, or the expiration of 2 years from the final approval of the reserved matters.
2   Application for approval of reserved matters must be made no later than the expiration of 3 years from the date of this outline planning permission.
3   Details of the siting, design and external materials for the dwelling and the means of access thereto shall be the subject of a separate application for the approval of reserved matters.
4   The colour type and finish of all external material shall be approved by the planning authority before development commences.
5   Any gates provided shall be set back at a distance of 4.5 metres from the edge of the carriageway of the adjoining highway.
6   The access shall be splayed back at an angle of 45°.
7   Provision shall be made for the parking of a minimim of 2 cars within the boundary of the site.
8   An adequate turning space should be provided on the site to enable vehicles to enter and leave the highway in a forward gear.
9   A landscaping scheme shall be submitted and approved before any work starts on site.
10 The existing trees and hedges shall be protected to the satisfaction of the planning authority while all the work is in progress.
11 The occupation of the dwelling shall be restricted to a person solely employed in agriculture, or in forestry, or a pensioner last so employed or the widow of such a person.

REASONS
To comply with section 41 of the Town and Country Planning Act 1971.

Date..................

Authorised Officer

An Outline Planning Consent.

call at the planning office to ask for the free advice which is available there. If you do this you will be well received, and you will be impressed by the trouble which will be taken to explain how the site needs a house of sensitive and imaginative design to do justice to its key position. You may be shown drawings of the sort of thing that the planning officer has in mind, or a sketch may be drawn for you while you watch. All this is splendid, until you realise that the ideal house being described suits neither your life-style nor your pocket. You will then wonder what the reaction is going to be to your application for the quite different house that you want, and which is all you can afford. The simple answer is that your application will be dealt with on its merits and that the planning officer has an obligation to approve what is acceptable, and not what he thinks best. However, it is obviously preferable to discuss your own specific requirements which have been drawn up for you before the meeting.

Planning Applications are made by filling in forms which you obtain from your local planning office, and sending them in together with four or five copies of your plans — the number of plans required varies from council to council. The various details that have to be shown on the plans are explained in a leaflet which will accompany the application forms. Plans purchased for

designs in this book come with elaborate notes on making planning applications.

Fees are payable in respect of planning applications, and although there are various exceptions, the general rule is that every time you sign a planning application you will have to pay a fee. The fee is increased regularly in line with inflation. There is only one fee if you are making a full planning application, but if you make an outline application followed by an application for the approval of reserved matters, then you will be paying two fees. Everyone grumbles about these fees but they are negligible in the context of the total cost of the project.

If you have got planning consent and want to make an alteration to the design it is not usually necessary to make a fresh application. The alteration should be shown on an amended drawing and two copies be sent to the Planning Office with a letter asking that they are accepted as 'amendments to the approved drawing'. There is rarely any difficulty over this if the alteration does not significantly change the appearance of the building.

BUILDING REGULATION APPLICATIONS

Our building regulations grew out of early public health legislation. The original intention was to ensure that new buildings were healthy, with minimum standards of ventilation and damp proofing. Over the years this has gradually changed to concern that the building is structurally sound and built according to the best building practice from wholly durable materials. More recently still this has been extended to concern over safety features, such as the design of balustrades, and the latest regulations are now concerned with standards of insulation. There are no building regulations yet about fixing curtain rails, but at the present rate of progress we will have them before long!

It is usual to make a building regulation application at the same time that one submits a planning application, but it is not essential. If you are not in a hurry it may be a good idea to get planning consent first. Fees for building regulations are payable on a fixed scale and like planning fees are regularly increased in line with inflation. When the approval certificate is received it is accompanied by a sheaf of post cards which have to be sent back to the local authority at various stages as the building progresses, and the building inspector will then visit the site to ensure that the work is up to standard. Not surprisingly there are fees payable for these inspections as well — usually twice as much again as the original application fee. There is no escape from any of this, and if these procedures are disregarded you can be legally required to take parts of the building to pieces so that hidden workmanship can be inspected, and in the last resort a sub-standard dwelling may have to be demolished. Things rarely come to this, but, as with planning legislation, building regulations must be taken very seriously.

The application is made by filling in a simple form and sending it to the local authority with two copies of the plans. Here it will be examined and invariably you will get a letter asking for further information, usually requiring various details to be shown on the drawing with a note about how they conform with the building regulations. If this is dealt with within a statutory five

Building Regulation Inspection Notices.

week period (which *you* can extend by a further three weeks to enable you to deal with queries), then the approval will be issued. If not, a refusal notice will be sent as the council is legally obliged to make a decision within six weeks. Do not worry too much about a refusal notice of this sort because when you send the information required the file will be reopened without you paying any more fees.

A whole schedule of queries on a building regulation application is quite usual, and does not imply that whoever drew your plans is less than competent. Individual local authorities have a great deal of freedom in how they interpret the building regulations, and no two authorities ask for additional information on the same topics. Architects expect these queries, which can vary from a request for a soil stability investigation and full foundation design calculations to a request to show the actual headroom half way up the stairs.

Sometimes building regulation queries can only be dealt with by going to considerable expense in having a structural engineer provide the information required. This usually happens when the application is to build a house or bungalow in a mining area, or over a geological fault, or where the design proposed is unusual. Your architect or whoever drew your plans will usually arrange this for you, but the fees will have to be paid by you, and it is a good idea to arrange to pay them direct, with the bill made out to you as the client, so that you have the direct benefit of the engineer's professional indemnity insurance.

*Building Regulations — **what** you build*
*N.H.B.C. standards — **how** you build*

CONTRACTS, CONVEYANCES AND COVENANTS

This part of the book is about legal procedures, and so we include a brief look at the terms used when you build your new home. However, this is not a D.I.Y. guide for doing without a solicitor, and it is extremely unwise for most people to enter into any commitment to buy or sell land without legal help. A title to a house is sometimes conveyed without a solicitor, and there are savings to be made by doing this. Whether they are worthwhile is a matter of opinion. However, buying a piece of land on which to build a new home involves many more factors. A solicitor is essential. Some of the terms that he or she will use are as follows:

A Reservation Fee or **Reservation Deposit** may be paid to an estate agent or to the vendor simply to establish your interest in buying the land. Ensure that it is no more than this by writing on the back of your cheque 'returnable deposit — subject to contract'. This is as far as you should ever get without a solicitor.

Searches are investigations which are made by your solicitor into the title and all aspects of it. They take at least a month, during which time you will be looking very carefully at whether you can build the home you want within the terms of any existing planning consent, and within your budget.

A Contract is a firm undertaking to buy the land, and once you have signed it you cannot back out. It is usual to pay 10% of the purchase price when the contract is signed.

A Conveyance is the final transfer of the title to the land, and usually takes place a month after the contract is signed. This is when the balance of the money is paid over and the land becomes yours.

Covenants are specific obligations which you undertake when you sign the contract, and which you cannot escape without a great deal of difficulty, if at all. They are very important, and their long term implications must be considered with great care. Your solicitor will advise. Typical covenants might be: 'not to use the land conveyed other than for the erection of a *single* dwelling of one storey'. This is bad news if you want to build a two storey house and would like to build another in the garden if you could *ever* get planning permission in the future. 'To keep the east boundary wall in good repair at all times'. The east boundary wall may be O.K. now, but what would it cost to replace if it started to lean in twenty years' time? 'To obtain the written approval of the vendor to the design of all buildings erected on the land'. A very common one. You must get 'Such consent not to be unreasonably withheld' added to it.

Discuss each and every covenant with your solicitor, and remember that you will have to pass on these obligations to anyone who buys from you in the future. This is important; you may not object to a covenant which prohibits keeping pets, but this may make it difficult for you to sell to a dog lover in the future.

Easements are formal permissions given by another landowner to let you do something on his land. Many people who build on their own land in the eighties are building on in-fill plots, and share access and services with others. The arrangements for them to do this are called easements, and they are important to both parties.

Beware any arrangement to share an access or service without a formal easement, even if another member of your family is involved. When you sell your house — and remember than on average every house is sold every seven years — the purchaser will certainly not want to buy it without formal easements, and at that time you may find that you cannot arrange things easily. To fall out with any neighbour is unfortunate, but to fall out with one who controls your drains can be disastrous. In the same way, do not grant any easement other than on a formal basis. If an informal use of an easement goes on for long enough a presumptive right is established, and this may extend to far more than you would have permitted in a formal arrangement.

Easements for shared drains and shared drives usually involve shared responsibility for maintenance and repairs. Look at the wording of such arrangements carefully, and consider how they are likely to work in the future. Who is to say when a drive needs to be repaired, or when a drain needs maintenance? Your solicitor will advise on this, and his fees for arranging the right wording for an easement are well worth the money.

Easements for overhead power lines are a great source of heartbreak to those who build on in-fill plots. If there are electricity lines running over the site for your new home, then a previous owner of your land has given the electricity board an easement to have them there. Now, if the easement was granted under one of the original nineteenth century electricity supply acts, there may be a condition in it that any owner of the land can serve a notice on the board to move the power lines at the board's expense if he wants to build a house for himself. If the easement was granted under modern legislation it will probably say that the board has to do the same, but at the landowner's expense. The difference can be thousands of pounds. However, beware taking this for granted. In the 1950's the electricity

boards offered the other parties to their easements small sums of money to extinguish these rights, and a claim that the board has to move its power lines out of the way of your new home at its own expense may be met by evidence that your predecessor in title accepted £10 to extinguish this right in 1952!

There are similar situations when other main services are buried in a plot. There will be an easement somewhere that sets out the terms on which they are allowed to be there, and the exact wording of this can be very important.

RIGHTS OF WAY
Rights of way for others to cross your land are a common feature of rural in-fill building plots. Often the site was left undeveloped precisely because there was a right of way across it, which was then in use, but is not now used. The right of way as a legal right is invariably still there, and can cause problems. Again, this is a job for a solicitor.

If you have a public footpath across your building plot you can often get it diverted, but will have to tread very carefully in dealing with this. The procedures involved are lengthy, and any proposal of this sort has to be widely advertised and can easily become a conservationist's *cause celebre*. Remember that use of public footpaths or bridle paths are among the oldest of our civil rights, and politely ask all concerned for their support as a favour. Avoid calling the footpath 'disused' — there are those who dedicate their lives to re-establishing disused footpaths.

More usual rights of way concern access to neighbouring fields, or sometimes to properties which no longer exist. In these cases someone owns the right of way over your land in the way that you own the land itself. It is your land, but he can use it for access. This will have happened in one or two ways; either it will be written into his title to his own land (and should also be noted in your deeds), or else it is an acquired right which results from it having been used for a certain number of years. If it is not used it may be possible to buy it, so that only you have a right of way over your own land. If this is not possible then it is important to know exactly the extent of the right, and here your solicitor will advise.

Easements and rights of way can be very important indeed.

SERVICES

The standard services to be considered when thinking about a new house are water, electricity, gas and telephones. Compared with much else with which you will be involved these are comparatively simple matters as the authorities concerned are in business selling their services, and will want you as a customer. However, there are things to watch.

A water supply is provided by the local water authority who will want a formal application for a supply, and a connection fee. They may also want a separate application for a tap for water for the builder to use while he is building, and may make a special building water charge. Many people building on an in-fill site arrange a temporary water supply from another dwelling, and thus avoid the building water charge. This can be well worth doing.

The water authority will be concerned that all plumbing work meets their own standards, and will want to inspect it before they provide the permanent connection. Your plumber will know their requirements, and is probably on Christian name terms with the Inspector. A connection is made at the boundary of your property, and you have to provide the pipe from the boundary to the house.

The electricity supply is arranged in much the same way, and it is worth noting that a temporary supply can be made to a building site if a locked box is provided for the meter. This enables electric mixers and other power tools to be used, and is often a good idea. When filling in the application form for the permanent supply it is important to give consideration to the possible advantages of opting for the Economy 7 Tariff, with cheap electricity after midnight. If you are considering a heat pump it is also worth asking if a three phase supply is available without extra charge.

One matter, which is very important, is to settle exactly where the meter box is to be fixed. These boxes are supplied by the electricity boards for building into the outside wall of a house so that the meters can be read without entering the premises. The Boards expect them to be fixed in a prominent position, preferably by the front door. Now these boxes are singularly unattractive in appearance, and it is unlikely that you will want the meter box to be a key feature on the front of the building. If this is so, you will have to say very clearly to all concerned at an early stage and settle where it is to be. The board may ask for a few pounds extra to cover the additional length of cable: pay it, it is worthwhile.

If you are building in the country you may find that the electricity board will quote for an overhead supply. If you want a buried cable they will quote for this as well, and you may be able to get the price down if you offer to dig the trench for them. This must be a trench on its own, and may not be shared with other services.

If there is a gas main within reach to give you a gas supply, the procedures are exactly the same as those for an electricity supply, even down to the meter box. If there is a gas supply available but you doubt if you will want to use it, it may be worth considering putting in the supply simply to enhance the value of your house when you sell it.

Telephones are becoming more and more part of our lives, and arrangements to put them in a new house should be planned as carefully as the other services. You will probably want the wires underground, and once again you may be able to negotiate on the cost of this if you offer to dig the trench. When the time comes to put the wiring in the trench, try asking the foreman to drop in a two pair cable as you expect to have a second phone before long. He will usually oblige and you can give your teenagers their own phone in the future. (Whether or not this is a good idea is a matter of opinion, but you will have the option.) A spare line may also be useful for cable t.v. or a burglar alarm link.

ROADS AND DRAINS

The drive and the drains from your new home are yours where they are inside your boundary, but what is the legal position outside your boundary? For most people the answer is that their drive leads across the council's footpath to a council road, and that their drains connect into the water authority's sewers, and their planning consent implies that the Council permits them to use the road and sewers. These roads and sewers are maintained by the authorities as a charge on the rates, and in exchange for this they will require either that their own workmen make the necessary sewer connections or footpath crossings at your expense, or else that your workmen do the job to their own exacting and expensive requirements.

Another possibility is that the road and sewers have been recently constructed by whoever sold you the land, and that the authorities will not take them over until all the new properties have been built. In these circumstances you will almost certainly have bought your land with the benefit of Road and Drainage Bonds which are guarantees that the local authority will eventually take over the road at no expense to you. These are often called Section 40 or Section 18 agreements.

The alternative is that you are involved in a special situation where your access is off a private road, or an unadopted road. In these circumstances it is likely that your drains are either your responsibility although they run under someone else's land, or else you share them with others. In some parts of the Home Counties these arrangements are not uncommon, and if this is your case it is essential that you understand clearly what your rights are when you think the services need repair or improvement, and what your obligations are to help pay for it. Your solicitor will advise on this.

Road charges are payments which are sometimes demanded by local authorities for making up or improving sub-standard roads which give access to a property. Again, this is more common in some parts of the country than others, and any liability to road charges will be discovered by your solicitor when you purchase the land. If you already have the land—perhaps a paddock at the bottom of your garden, or a plot which has been inherited—then it is a very good idea to check whether by building a house on it you are incurring a liability for road charges. The answer will probably be 'No' but it is nice to be sure.

Drains. A new dwelling requires two sorts of drains, and while this presents no problems when buying a serviced plot in a built up area, the options for a rural site without main drains can be confusing. The difference in costs between different arrangements can be considerable, and it is important not just to find out what is practicable, but also which is the cheapest of any alternatives. Whatever is approved will be satisfactory from a technical viewpoint, as the building regulations standards are very high.

Surface water drains take rainwater from the roof and from any drains in a drive, and nothing else. Except in urban areas they usually lead to soakaways, which are simply large holes which have been filled with stones and covered over. Soakaways have to be a minimum distance from the house, and wholly on your own land. Make sure they are not constructed in a place where you might want to build an extension at some time in the future. If you are a farmer you can avoid soakaways by simply leading surface water drains into land drains, or into a ditch. Incidentally surface water is called top water in some parts of the country.

All the other drains are foul drains, and take bath water, and water from the kitchen sink besides connecting

Right: A cess pool being installed. It will need to be emptied every two weeks.

Below: A Conder septic tank, which is ready to connect up to the inlet and outlet pipes as soon as the hole is backfilled.

to W.C.s. They are normally connected to council sewers (alias main drains) and the details of how this is to be done have to be shown very precisely on the plans which accompany your building regulation application. It is not essential that they should connect directly to the sewer, and it is often acceptable that they connect into a neighbour's drain instead. This can save you a great deal of money and it is often well worthwhile paying a neighbour a couple of hundred pounds and meeting the legal costs of an easement to do this if it avoids an expensive drain connection in the road. Such an arrangement is called a shared system, although in East Anglia some local authorities insist on calling it a combined system. Everywhere else a combined system means an arrangement for surface water to be put into foul drains.

If you are building a new home where there is not a sewer available at a depth where your drains can run into it at an acceptable gradient, you are involved in a special situaiton, and require advice from someone who has a great deal of relevant recent experience. Recent experience is important as drain technology is changing quickly. There are many options.

First of all, if there is a sewer within your reach but it is uphill from the new house you can install your own sewage pump. These have improved tremendously in recent years, and the whole installation, including sophisticated automatic controls, is hidden in a manhole below ground and costs about £1000. This seems a large sum, but if it enables a house to be built where it would otherwise be impossible to build it, it may be worthwhile. Usually it is only a small fraction of the value of the finished property.

Next we move to septic tanks, mini sewage systems and cess pools, which are not a very glamorous subject, but as the difference in cost is enormous it is worthwhile reading on. Septic tanks are digesters, being tanks with a series of baffles inhabited by bacteria that break down the solids in the raw sewage and render it unobjectionable. When they have done the job the effluent runs out of the exit pipe from the septic tank, and is disposed of in some suitable way. It is clean and odourless, but not surprisingly the authorities will take a very keen interest in what happens to it. Their requirements vary in different areas and the differences are sometimes inexplicable. If the site is isolated and the sub-surface drainage is good, a simple soakaway may be acceptable. More usually a system of land drains is required. Often a sand filter chamber is required between the septic tank and the final discharge point. In some areas a special permit is required to discharge septic tank effluent anywhere near a watercourse, and the building regulation consent for the installation will be conditional on obtaining the permit.

Septic tanks have changed a great deal in recent years, and are now invariably prefabricated in either fibreglass or concrete. The 600 gallon size for a single household costs under £500. The solids which accumulate in the bottom of a septic tank have to be pumped out every year or two, and it should be situated where the tanker can reach it. There are also statutory requirements that it should be at least 16 yards from a dwelling.

Where there is a high water table, or in some water

supply catchment areas, it may not be possible to obtain approval for a septic tank or a mini sewage system, and a cess pool is required. This is simply a very large buried tank which is pumped out by a sewage tanker at intervals — at least monthly — and not only is the initial installation costly, but the cost of emptying it can be significant. Sometimes the council provides this service on the rates, sometimes charges are levied which vary from high to exorbitant. The general rule is to try to avoid having a cess pool if at all possible, and to get the best advice on sophisticated digester systems.

The septic tank and cess pool units illustrated on the previous page are manufactured by Conder Products Limited, Abbots Barton House, Worthy Road, Winchester, Hants. The phone number is 0962 841313, and Conder will advise on the best way of meeting your own special situation if you are unable to connect to the main drains.

A Clearwater Filtaclere mini sewage system installed in the garden of a house built in an area where a septic tank would not have been acceptable. Units like this are easily concealed by a small shrubbery.

Another alternative is to install a mini sewage system such as the Clearwater Filtaclere unit illustrated. This is a packaged unit incorporating electric pumps etc which enable the effluent to meet very stringent requirements in a very simple and cost effective way. It is manufactured by Clearwater, LMS House, Riverway Estate, Old Portsmouth Rd, Guildford GU3 1LZ, phone 0483 33831. They will advise on statutory requirements, and on the appropriate ways of meeting them. Effluent control is a fast changing scene, and the people who are best able to give you up to date advice are the specialist manufacturers.

Finance

If you buy a house from a developer or through an estate agent you will find that the person who you are dealing with will advise and help you with the various financial arrangements that have to be made. Usually they will be anxious to arrange a mortgage for you, and to sell you insurances. This help is not available if you are arranging to build on your own land, and you will have to handle all the financial planning yourself. This is not at all difficult providing that you have a clear view of your long term objectives.

Start by considering your position when the new home is completed, and you have moved in. Will you want a mortgage? If not, then you are very fortunate and your only problem is to work out whose name is to be on the title deeds in order to put your family in the best Capital Transfer Tax situation.

If you will be involved with a mortgage then there are various alternatives, from endowment insurance-linked mortgages at one end of the scale to Option Mortgages on the other. Your mortgage may be with either a bank or a building society. All of this may be something with which you are very familiar, or you may need specialist advice. If you need advice the best people to start with are your Bank Manager, or a reputable mortgage broker. The important thing is to consider these long term objectives quite separately from the actual business of financing the building work.

Paying for the land and the actual construction work is something which has to be carefully budgeted, and arranged with care, as all the people who will be working for you are working for money. They will expect to be paid on time, and you will find that their cooperation and help will evaporate very quickly if anything goes wrong with your arrangements to meet your bills. To maintain the enthusiasm of all concerned you must be a good payer, and must be seen to be a good buyer.

If you do not already have a site then the first thing that you have to pay for is the land, and the solicitor's fees and land registry charges involved in buying the land. The only exception is if you are buying a serviced plot from one of the local authorities who will give you a licence to build on the land, and only require you to pay for the plot itself when the house is finished. This sounds a good idea, but it can make it difficult for you to borrow the money for the building work as you will not have the deeds to the land to offer as security. In this case the authority selling the land will help with advice on how to get round this problem.

The next commitment is to pay your architect or designer, to pay planning and building regulation application fees, and perhaps to pay some special insurance premiums. None of these will be very large sums, but it is important to pay them promptly and to start the way you intend to go on.

At this stage you will be getting firm price quotations for the actual building work, and will be relieved to find these are in line with the guideline project costs which you have been using so far. If you are placing a contract with a builder then he will almost certainly want stage payments — typically 20% when the ground floor slab is cast, 25% when the roof is tiled 25% when the house is plastered out, and the balance when you move in. Your contract with him probably involves deducting a 5% retention from each payment, which you will pay at the end of a three month period after the builder has returned to deal with any minor snags.

Building using sub-contractors involves many more payments to be made, and you will have to draw up your own cash flow projection, probably using a book like *Building Your Own Home* as a guide.

If you are building using one of the package service companies they will help you to establish your budget, will give you a firm quotation for their own work which will explain exactly when their bills have to be paid, and will advise on budgeting for other expenditure.

At the end of the whole job you will move into your new home, and will probably get the mortgage which we have already discussed. When you know where you are going to get this, and what sort of a mortgage it is going to be, you can find out if you can get progress payments as the building goes up, or whether the mortgage money can only be paid when the building is completed. If you can get progress payments then you will need only a modest bank balance or overdraft to pay the bills that come along before the first progress payment arrives, and another advantage of a mortgage with progress payments is that you will also get the tax benefits of the mortgage right from the start.

If you cannot arrange progress payments on the particular mortgage that you want then you must get a bridging loan to cover the cost of the work until you receive the mortgage money on the finished job. This is an arrangement with the bank to lend you all the money that you require to build, sometimes as a lump sum loan, but preferably as an overdraft. As a security the bank will want your personal guarantee and also the title deeds to the land and whatever you build on it. When you finish the bank will transfer the deeds to your building society, and the building society will transfer its cash direct to the bank. The banks and building societies are well used to working together in this way.

A disadvantage of this arrangement is that the bank will want rather more interest than a building society, and may insist on a fixed loan instead of an overdraft, which is more expensive still. They will sometimes demand a commitment fee on top of everything else. Tax relief can be claimed on the interest, but not normally until you make your annual tax return.

If your mortgage is with a bank then all of this is arranged by your bank manager. If you are getting a building society mortgage your bank manager will want to see a letter from your building society confirming that a mortgage will be available in due course before he authorises a bridging loan.

As an alternative to using the title to the land on which you are building as security for all of this, it is sometimes preferable to take out a second or increased mortgage on your existing home. It is all very complicated, but the banks and building societies are in business to lend money, and they will help and advise on the various ways in which everything can be arranged. When you find that you are about to sign the relevant papers to commit yourself to all of this, you will be less than human if you do not start wondering exactly what you have let yourself in for, and what will happen if you become ill, or fall under a bus. This is where you start thinking about insurance.

INSURANCES

Having made arrangement to build a new house, probably using borrowed money, you will be very conscious that you have entered into some pretty formidable obligations and that you must try to cover any risks with appropriate insurance. This is relatively easy, and the premiums involved are quite small.

First of all, once you have bought the land you are liable to third party claims arising from anything to do with the land. The obvious hazard is that a tree may fall and injure someone. Third party claims of this sort may be covered by your existing householder's insurances, but once you start any building operations the risks are very real and you must make sure that they are covered.

If you have a formal contract with a builder then the wording of the contract itself should put the responsibility on him to insure against all risks, including the risk of the uncompleted building catching fire. However, if you are handling any part of the work yourself, either working yourself or using sub-contractors, you should certainly take out your own insurance cover, as well as insisting that your builder has the insurances required under his contract. You will need contractors 'All Risk' insurance, employers' liability insurance if you are employing any one at all, and standard third party insurance. The latter is essential; you must realise that if you have any responsibility for a building site a trespassing child who falls off your scaffold may have a valid claim for damages against you.

The Norwich Union insurance company have a special policy for selfbuilders which covers 'All Risk' insurance, Employers' Liability insurance and Third Party cover. Details and a proposal form will be found at the back of this book.

If you think that the success of the whole project depends on you, and that your own supervision is necessary for everything to be the huge success that it will be, then you must take out special insurance cover to enable someone to take over if you are killed or taken ill. This is even more important if you are building using sub-contractors, or relying on some of your own labour. Short term life insurance for one year only is very cheap, and a special policy for a sum adequate to enable your executors to employ the best builder in town to get the job finished is a very sensible investment. Short term health insurance may be equally appropriate. Everyone's personal situation is different in this, but whatever it is, suitable arrangements must be made.

VAT

The VAT situation for new homes is all good news. If you are building a completely new home, and are not altering, renovating or otherwise involved with an existing building, you will get back virtually all the VAT which you pay whether or not you are VAT registered. The VAT position for extensions, alterations, or repairs is different and complex, but for a completely new building it is quite simple.

If you are already VAT registered with a business of some sort, and the new house is financed as part of the business, as on a farm or at a garden centre, then you simply reclaim the VAT through your normal returns.

If a builder has a contract for the whole job he will 'zero rate' the VAT and you will not have to pay the VAT on anything that he buys for you. If you want to buy any fittings yourself — light fittings for example — give him the receipt and ask him to put it through his books as if he had brought it himself. All the normal fittings and fixtures can be zero rated except for a few unusual items. These are mainly items of kitchen equipment as opposed to kitchen units — cookers, washing machines, etc. Some fitted furniture is also outside the scope of the regulations, as are for some reason, extractor fans.

If you are building using sub-contractors then you reclaim the VAT using what are called 'Notice 719 procedures'. This is a bit involved; full details and the relevant Customs and Excise notice are given in *Building Your Own Home*. The essential is to keep all your bills, as you will need them to support your claim for a VAT refund when the house is finished.

New 'User-Friendly' version of VAT Notice 719 which is available from your local VAT office.

116

Design Page Index

All of these designs are for new homes that can be built at realistic unit costs. All of them have been built, and a large proportion have been built many times.

When choosing a design it is essential to consider the constraints of the site and the requirements of the planning authorities as detailed in earlier chapters. All the designs can be built using any materials acceptable under the Building Regulations, and there is considerable scope for making alterations to windows and roof styles. Other alterations are often practicable but may increase unit construction costs.

This index is in alphabetical order. The areas given are the areas enclosed by the internal faces of the external walls. They are expressed in square feet instead of using metric units as this is still common parlance.

Detailed working drawings for all the designs are available from Plan Sales Services Ltd., with the exception of the designs of pages 182 to 191 which are only available from Design and Material Limited as part of their standard service. The design on page 122 is available from Shire Country Homes Limited. Purchase of drawings from PSS Ltd. conveys authority for the construction of the property to which they relate.

INDEX

INDEX

Designs featuring a Sunken Lounge

Holiday Homes

Designs often built as Farmhouses

Designs with a large Study or Office for those who want to work at home

INDEX

Designs suitable for a Narrow Site
SEE PAGES:
237, 240, 242, 248, 254, 255, 264, 273, 340, 350, 352, 356.

Designs with a Granny Flat or other self-contained accommodation
SEE PAGES:
126, 136, 153, 228, 234, 266, 267, 312, 334, 344, 352, 356, 363, 367, 371.

Designs of interest to the Disabled
SEE PAGES:
267, 352, 356, 360, 371.

Small Family Houses of less than 1200 sq.ft.
SEE PAGES:
148, 149, 154, 155, 161, 298, 340, 341, 342, 343, 346, 347, 348, 349, 350, 351, 352, 353, 365, 371.

Designs suitable for a Sloping Site or with a Split Level Layout
SEE PAGES:
127, 150, 151, 152, 153, 164, 165, 166, 167, 177, 196, 223, 225, 226, 236, 238, 244, 250, 252, 274, 282, 284, 294, 295, 300, 303, 322, 343, 344, 345.

Small family bungalows of less than 1000 sq.ft.
SEE PAGES:
225, 240, 241, 242, 244, 246, 247, 248, 255, 257, 258, 261, 264, 273, 280, 334.

Small Retirement Bungalows
SEE PAGES:
225, 241, 247, 252, 257, 258, 261, 264, 273, 280.

SHIRE

This is a design from Shire Country Homes, who are a specialist company which manages the construction of individual homes for a limited number of clients, many of whom work abroad while their home is being built in the UK. This large and impressive house is under construction in Kent.

Design Number 92201

Floor Area	3681 sq. ft.	342 sq. m.
Dimensions overall	56' x 60'8"	17.05 x 19.50
Lounge	20' x 14'6"	6.10 x 4.42
Kitchen	13' x 14'6"	3.96 x 4.42
Dining	13' x 14'6"	3.96 x 4.42
Family	10' x 14'9"	3.05 x 4.49
Utility	9'6" x 7'9"	2.90 x 2.37
Bed 1	17'6" x 10'	5.33 x 3.05
Sitting Area	7' x 7'2"	2.13 x 2.18
En/suite	10'2" x 5'2"	3.10 x 1.57
Bed 2	13' x 10'10"	3.96 x 3.30
Bed 3	13' x 10'10"	3.96 x 3.30
Bed 4	11'10" x 9'4"	3.61 x 2.84
Bed 5	11'10" x 9'4"	3.61 x 2.84
Garage (max.)	19'8" x 22'4"	6.00 x 6.80

This design was drawn for a client of Shire Country Homes Ltd. who used their management service. For details see page 396.

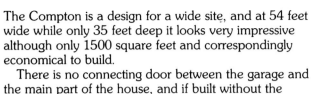

COMPTON

The Compton is a design for a wide site, and at 54 feet wide while only 35 feet deep it looks very impressive although only 1500 square feet and correspondingly economical to build.

There is no connecting door between the garage and the main part of the house, and if built without the detached garage this long thin house will suit a shallow infill plot in a village street very effectively.

Design Number 92156 Compton

Floor Area	1517 sq.ft.	141 sq.m.
Dimensions overall	53'8" x 35'	16.35 x 10.67
Lounge	17' x 13'6"	5.18 x 4.10
Kitchen	12'8" x 10'4"	3.86 x 3.14
Dining	10'6" x 11'	3.22 x 3.36
Utility	9'5" x 6'9"	2.86 x 2.05
Study	8'11" x 11'	2.10 x 3.36
Bed 1	13'5" x 10'	4.10 x 3.04
Bed 2	12'8" x 9'6"	3.86 x 2.90
Bed 3	9'5" x 7'6"	2.86 x 2.29
Sewing room	10'6" x 11'	3.22 x 3.36
Garage	17'10" x 16'3"	5.42 x 4.95

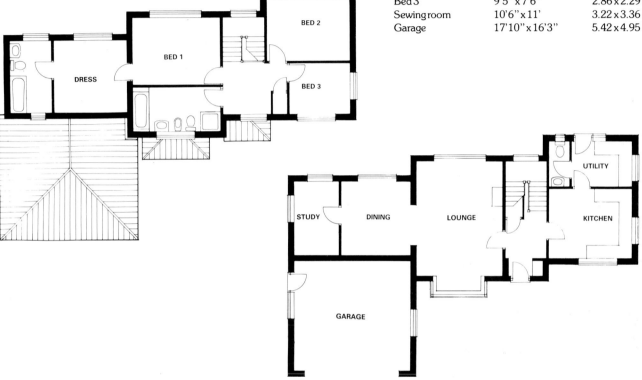

CROXTONBANK

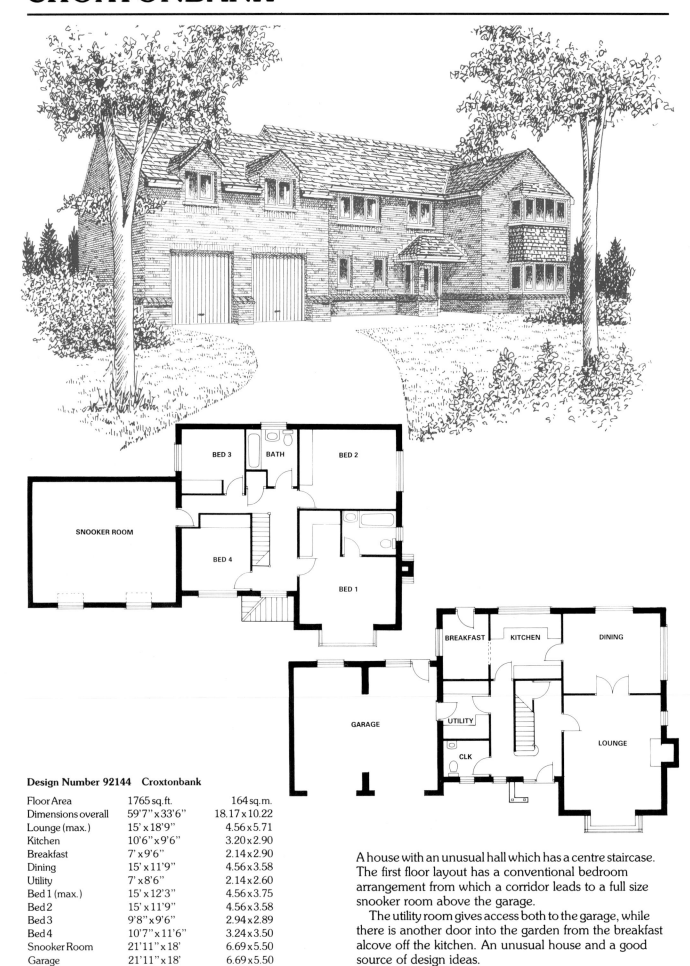

Design Number 92144   Croxtonbank

Floor Area	1765 sq. ft.	164 sq. m.
Dimensions overall	59'7" x 33'6"	18.17 x 10.22
Lounge (max.)	15' x 18'9"	4.56 x 5.71
Kitchen	10'6" x 9'6"	3.20 x 2.90
Breakfast	7' x 9'6"	2.14 x 2.90
Dining	15' x 11'9"	4.56 x 3.58
Utility	7' x 8'6"	2.14 x 2.60
Bed 1 (max.)	15' x 12'3"	4.56 x 3.75
Bed 2	15' x 11'9"	4.56 x 3.58
Bed 3	9'8" x 9'6"	2.94 x 2.89
Bed 4	10'7" x 11'6"	3.24 x 3.50
Snooker Room	21'11" x 18'	6.69 x 5.50
Garage	21'11" x 18'	6.69 x 5.50

A house with an unusual hall which has a centre staircase. The first floor layout has a conventional bedroom arrangement from which a corridor leads to a full size snooker room above the garage.

The utility room gives access both to the garage, while there is another door into the garden from the breakfast alcove off the kitchen. An unusual house and a good source of design ideas.

ADDINGTON

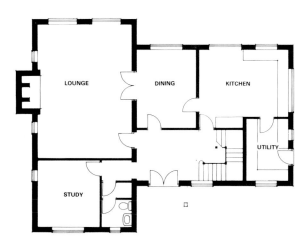

This five bedroom home has been built many times as a farmhouse, and looks equally well whether rendered as shown here, built in brick or stone, or half timbered. In the farmhouse role it usually has a back porch with a w.c. added, which extends the overall width to 58 feet and also adds to the complexity of the design which is important to the appearance of a big house in a rural area.

The en suite bathroom in the master bedroom suite is shown with a shower, but can be re-arranged for a bath if required.

Design Number 92102   Addington

Floor Area	2520 sq.ft.	234 sq.m.
Dimensions overall	50'9" x 38'	15.45 x 11.55
Lounge	17'2" x 24'	5.24 x 7.32
Kitchen	16'4" x 12'	4.98 x 3.65
Dining	11' x 14'	3.35 x 4.27
Study	11'4" x 12'	3.46 x 3.65
Utility	7'6" x 11"	2.29 x 3.35
Bed 1	16'4" x 12'	4.98 x 3.65
Bed 2	9' x 14'	2.75 x 4.27
Bed 3	15' x 10'6"	4.58 x 3.20
Bed 4	11'3" x 9'9"	3.43 x 2.98
Bed 5	10'6" x 13'3"	3.20 x 4.05

ABERCROMBIE

The Abercrombie is another design with a granny flat. This is becoming a very popular feature of the larger new homes being built in the 90s, one reason being that it provides a very tax effective way in which an elderly person can contribute to the cost of a new home. By arranging for the granny flat accommodation to be self-contained, with its own front door as well as a connecting door into the main house, an elderly person can enjoy a sense of still having their own home while having the security of being under the same roof as the

Design Number 92101   Abercrombie

Floor Area	2013 sq. ft.	187 sq. m.
Dimensions overall	55'3" x 33'10"	16.85 x 10.32
Lounge	12' x 23'5"	3.65 x 7.14
Kitchen/Dining	12' x 23'5"	3.65 x 7.14
Study	10' x 11'6"	3.05 x 3.50
Bed 1	12' x 14'6"	3.65 x 4.42
Bed 2	12' x 9'3"	3.65 x 2.80
Bed 3	12' x 9'6"	3.65 x 2.90
Bed 4	10'2" x 8'3"	3.10 x 2.50
Granny Annex		
Living Room (min)	13'9" x 9'6"	4.20 x 2.90
Bed 5	13'9" x 8'3"	4.20 x 2.50

BARROWFORD

Another three level house. The plans for this one are most easily understood if you start at the top, where the bedrooms are all at the same level. Below them the dining room, kitchen and hall are on the same level as the front entrance, and the lounge is down four steps. The prototypes of this design were built speculatively in Nottinghamshire in 1991, and proved very popular. Changes of level always make a house seem larger than it really is.

Design Number 92147 Barrowford

Floor Area	1464 sq. ft.	136 sq. m.
Dimensions overall	36'1" x 36'10"	11.00 x 11.23
Lounge	13'2" x 15'7"	4.00 x 4.75
Kitchen	11'2" x 9'3"	3.40 x 2.82
Dining	9' x 8'3"	2.75 x 2.50
Bed 1 (max.)	17' x 11'	5.18 x 3.35
Bed 2	11'2" x 10'9"	3.40 x 3.27
Bed 3	11'2" x 6'9"	3.40 x 2.05
Garage	16'5" x 17'10"	5.00 x 5.42

AVON

A deceptively simple four bedroom house which offers a great deal of accommodation in only 1668 square feet. This is largely due to the positioning of the stairs, which facilitate a very small first floor landing and yet are well lit by their own dormer window on the front elevation.

Half timbered homes like this are usually built on large sites in rural areas, but the Avon will also suit a tight plot in suburban surroundings, having no windows in side walls. The garage, shown set back but sharing a party wall with the house, can be constructed as a detached building if appropriate.

Design Number 92104   Avon

Floor Area		
(exc. garage)	1668 sq. ft.	155 sq. m.
Dimensions overall		
(inc. garage)	62'6" x 33'6"	19.05 x 10.22
Lounge	14'6" x 18'	4.42 x 5.49
Kitchen	13' x 10'2"	3.96 x 3.10
Dining	12'6" x 11'5"	3.80 x 3.49
Study	12' x 10'	3.65 x 3.05
Bed 1	14'6" x 11'4"	4.42 x 3.46
Bed 2	12'6" x 11'3"	3.80 x 3.43
Bed 3	10' x 10'2"	3.05 x 3.10
Bed 4 (max.)	8' x 10'2"	2.44 x 3.10

This is a large five bedroom home of 2422 square feet which, built with the right materials, will look well anywhere in Britain. Here it is shown constructed in rustic brick with some tile hanging under a plain tile roof, which is as it might be built in Kent. In the Cotswolds it would look every bit as much in place built in stone, or in wire cut bricks in the Midlands.

The choice of staircase is always important to a home like this, and so is the decision whether to have single or double doors between the hall and the lounge, and between the lounge and the drawing room, and whether they should be solid or glazed.

Design Number 92103   Akenham

Floor Area	2422 sq.ft.	225 sq.m.
Dimensions overall	57'6" x 34'	17.53 x 10.37
Lounge	22' x 13'	6.71 x 3.96
Kitchen/Breakfast	24' x 10'	7.32 x 3.05
Dining	12' x 14'	3.65 x 4.27
Study	9' x 10'	2.75 x 3.05
Utility	8' x 9'6"	2.44 x 2.90
Family Room	12' x 17'6"	3.65 x 5.34
Bed 1	12' x 14'	3.65 x 4.27
Bed 2	12' x 14'	3.65 x 4.27
Bed 3	12' x 13'	3.65 x 3.96
Bed 4	12' x 8'	3.65 x 2.44
Bed 5	9' x 9'	2.75 x 2.75

BAGSHOT

The Bagshot design house is only 1440 square feet, but its striking appearance makes it look far larger. Much of this effect comes from the high window which lights the stairs, and if it is appropriate this can be moved into the side wall so that sunlight streams down the length of the hall if the house faces in the right direction for this.

The small utility room need not be built if the budget will not stretch to it, but it does add complexity to the building, and with it a feeling of size.

The plan shows how a conservatory can be built in the angle between the lounge and the dining room.

Design Number 92106   Bagshot

Floor Area	1440 sq.ft.	135 sq.m.
Dimensions overall	50'5" x 28'1"	15.36 x 8.57
Lounge	20' x 14'	6.10 x 4.27
Kitchen/Breakfast	15'3" x 12'	4.65 x 3.65
Dining	13' x 12'	3.96 x 3.65
Utility	7' x 8'	2.13 x 2.45
Bed 1	11' x 12'	3.35 x 3.65
Bed 2	11'3" x 12'	3.43 x 3.65
Bed 3	11'6" x 10'8"	3.50 x 3.25

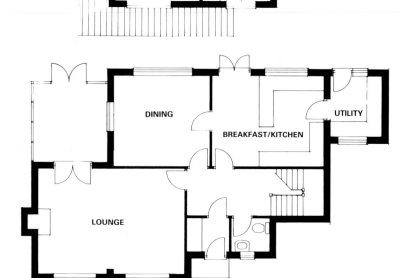

ARBORFIELD

This large house is for a site where it can be seen and admired from a distance, and there is a lot to admire. The four gabled dormers and the complexity of the front elevation give it a period appearance, which must be matched by the materials chosen for the walls, roof and the garage doors. In the sketch the artist has shown windows with shallow arches to the heads. This conveys a period effect when used with rustic bricks.

There are three bathrooms on the first floor but no cloakroom on the ground floor. If a cloakroom is required, it can be built at the expense of the size of the study.

Design Number 92105　Arborfield

Floor Area		
(inc. garage)	2650 sq. ft.	246 sq. m.
Dimensions overall	64'3" x 28'	19.59 x 8.54
Lounge	14' x 24'11"	4.27 x 7.60
Kitchen	13' x 11'1"	3.96 x 3.39
Dining	14' x 11'1"	4.27 x 3.39
Study	13' x 10'	3.96 x 3.05
Utility	9'3" x 7'2"	2.80 x 2.19
Workshop	8'4" x 7'2"	2.54 x 2.19
Garage	17'10" x 18'5"	5.44 x 5.60
Bed 1	17'10" x 13'6"	5.44 x 4.10
Bed 2	14' x 11'6"	4.27 x 3.49
Bed 3	14' x 10'10"	4.27 x 3.31
Bed 4	14' x 11'6"	4.27 x 3.49
Bed 5	13' x 11'8"	3.96 x 3.55

BESSACAR

A four bedroom house for a site with a narrow frontage: in fact it can be fitted onto a 40 foot plot.

It is illustrated here built in brick with diamond patterning and contrasting header courses. This was typical of houses built in many suburbs in the first half of the century, and this style is appropriate to infill plots in these areas, which now command very high prices.

The simple canopy porch which is shown is more appropriate to a rural than an urban setting: almost any style of porch for a front door in the angle between two wings of the house can be used. The choice is yours!

Design Number 92107   Bessacar

Floor Area	1378 sq.ft.	128 sq.m.
Dimensions overall	32'2" x 33'4"	9.82 x 10.16
Lounge	18'1" x 12'6"	5.52 x 3.80
Kitchen/Breakfast	18'1" x 10'	5.52 x 3.05
Dining	12' x 10'6"	3.65 x 3.20
Bed 1	12'10" x 12'6"	3.92 x 3.80
Bed 2	12' x 10'6"	3.65 x 3.20
Bed 3	9'7" x 10'	2.92 x 3.05
Bed 4	8'3" x 9'4"	2.50 x 2.85

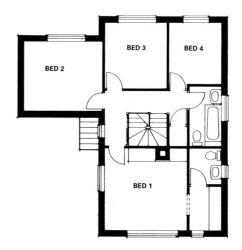

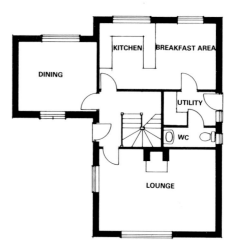

132

BARNSTABLE

The Barnstable design is just under 2000 square foot and is deeper than it is wide, suiting a narrow plot or a site where there are no side views.

The large and unusually shaped hall gives a lot of character to the attractive ground floor layout. The dining room with the large adjacent cloakroom can be used as a fifth bedroom or a granny flat if required.

On the first floor there is provision for more built in cupboards and wardrobes than are usual. The flat roof outside the master bedroom window can be used as a balcony if required.

Design Number 92109   Barnstable

Floor Area	1981 sq.ft.	184 sq.m.
Dimensions overall	32'3" x 51'2"	9.84 x 15.59
Lounge	16'1" x 19'	4.90 x 5.79
Kitchen	13' x 13'3"	3.96 x 4.05
Dining	14'1" x 14'11"	4.29 x 4.54
Study	10'2" x 9'6"	3.09 x 2.90
Utility	8'9" x 7'	2.66 x 2.13
Cloaks	8'9" x 5'11"	2.66 x 1.80
Bed 1	14'1" x 10'4"	4.29 x 3.14
Bed 2	10' x 11'11"	3.05 x 3.64
Bed 3	9' x 12'7"	2.75 x 3.85
Bed 4	7'9" x 12'7"	2.35 x 3.85

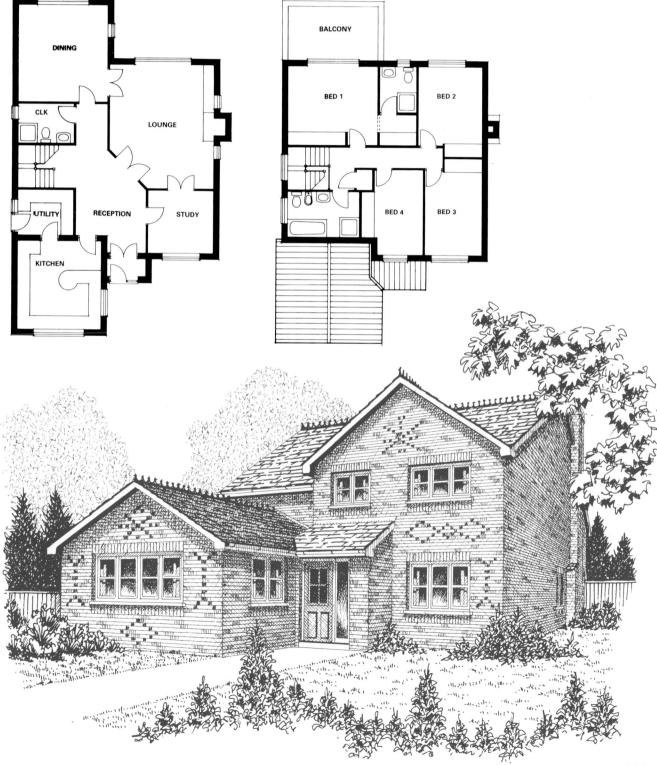

BROWNLOW

A very simple four bedroom house which is extremely cost-effective to build. One of its advantages for those on a tight budget is that it can be built in stages: the house first, and then the garage with the link block later.

Design Number 92110   Brownlow

Floor Area		
(exc. garage)	1680 sq.ft.	156 sq.m.
Dimensions overall		
(inc. garage)	61'10" x 25'7"	18.86 x 7.79
Lounge	13' x 20'	3.96 x 6.10
Kitchen	10' x 13'2"	3.05 x 4.00
Dining	10' x 13'2"	3.05 x 4.00
Utility	6'9" x 8'	2.05 x 2.44
Bed 1	10' x 12'9"	3.05 x 3.90
Bed 2	8' x 12'9"	2.44 x 3.90
Bed 3	11'8" x 12'	3.58 x 3.65
Bed 4	8'5" x 7'8"	2.58 x 2.35
Garage	18'2" x 18'	5.54 x 5.50

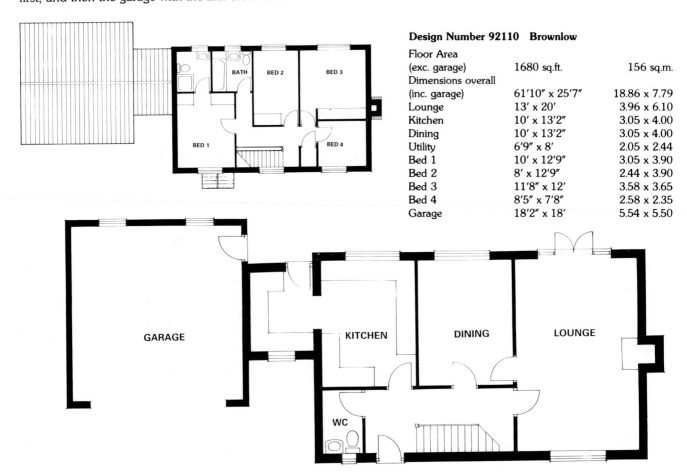

DEEPDALE

Design Number 92108   Deepdale

Floor Area	1464 sq. ft.	136 sq. m.
Dimensions overall	33'4" x 33'	10.16 x 10.08
Lounge	12'6" x 18'11"	3.80 x 5.78
Kitchen/Breakfast	10' x 15'	3.05 x 4.58
Dining	11'3" x 12'	3.43 x 3.65
Utility	8'5" x 8'7"	2.56 x 2.63
Bed 1	12'6" x 18'11"	3.80 x 5.78
Bed 2	10' x 11'9"	3.05 x 3.58
Bed 3	11'3" x 12'	3.43 x 3.65

An angled front porch leads to an unusual hall in this interesting house of under 1500 square feet, and determines that two of the doors from the hall open into the angled corners of the dining room and the kitchen. This always raises the questions of how they should be hung — to open to the left or to the right. Look at the one in the kitchen. Would you want it as shown, or opening to the other hand? Sorting out this sort of thing and getting exactly what you like is what building your own home is all about.

The two bathrooms which serve the three bedrooms are larger than usual in a house of this size, and have room for bath, basin, bidet and wc without being cramped. There is plenty of cupboard space as well.

BALCOME

A house that meets unusual design requirements. It was commissioned by a client who wanted a home to be built in the country, on a site with all round views, with three bedrooms which all required their own bathrooms, one of which had to be on the ground floor for an elderly person.

The outcome was the Balcome design which has an interesting shape with three separate roofs. It provides all the accommodation required in a little over 1600 square feet, and is a very cost effective structure to build.

Note the old fashioned ventilated larder and the three large walk-in cupboards which were also part of the original design brief.

Design Number 92136 Balcome

Floor Area	1636 sq. ft.	152 sq. m.
Dimensions overall	46'5" x 37'10"	14.16 x 11.54
Lounge	14'8" x 18'3"	4.47 x 5.56
Kitchen/Break/Fam	18'3" x 16'10"	5.56 x 5.15
Dining	10'6" x 9'10"	3.20 x 3.00
Bed 1	14'7" x 13'	4.46 x 3.96
Bed 2	12'2" x 11'8"	3.70 x 3.56
Bed 3	12'9" x 9'10"	3.90 x 3.00

CARCASTLE

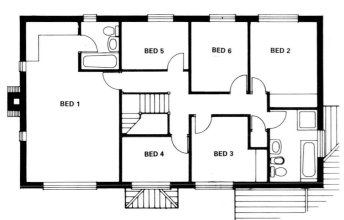

One of the few six bedroom houses in this book, the Carcastle is a straight forward design for a house with a lot of room to be built as cost effectively as possible.

The garage need not be constructed unless required, in which case the door into the utility room can be moved into the side wall, and its window moved to the front of the home.

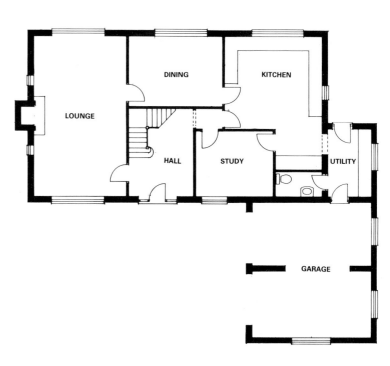

Design Number 92121 Carcastle

Floor Area		
(exc. garage)	2196 sq. ft.	204 sq. m.
Dimensions overall		
(inc. garage)	54'9" x 45'9"	16.70 x 13.94
Lounge	14' x 23'5"	4.27 x 7.14
Kitchen	14'8" x 19'6"	4.48 x 5.94
Dining	14'4" x 10'2"	4.37 x 3.10
Study	12'1" x 9'8"	3.70 x 2.94
Utility	6'7" x 9'11"	2.00 x 3.03
Bed 1	14' x 23'5"	4.27 x 7.14
Bed 2	10' x 12'5"	3.05 x 3.80
Bed 3	11'10" x 9'	3.60 x 2.94
Bed 4	10'2" x 6'7"	3.10 x 2.00
Bed 5	10'2" x 6'11"	3.10 x 2.10
Bed 6	8'6" x 10'2"	2.60 x 3.10
Garage	19'8" x 18'	6.00 x 5.50

AMESBURY

The Amesbury is an interesting house, taking a lot of its character from the four large bay windows and the tall window which lights the hall from the stairs. It is shown here with the two projecting wings of the house rendered above a brick plinth, which is a return to a feature of Edwardian homes that is now becoming very popular.

Note the long run of cupboards between the kitchen and the family room, enough for all the outdoor clothes for even the largest of families and their guests.

Design Number 92111   Amesbury

Floor Area	2552 sq. ft.	237 sq. m.
Dimensions overall	54'11" x 37'3"	16.75 x 11.36
Lounge	15'4" x 24'	4.69 x 7.32
Kitchen/Breakfast	15'4" x 12'	4.69 x 3.66
Dining	15'10" x 11'10"	4.82 x 3.62
Utility	14' x 8'	4.27 x 2.44
Family	15'4" x 13'	4.69 x 3.96
Bed 1	15'4" x 15'5"	4.69 x 4.70
Bed 2	15'10" x 11'10"	4.82 x 3.62
Bed 3	10' x 12'	3.05 x 3.66
Bed 4	15'4" x 9'3"	4.69 x 2.80
Bed 5	11'1" x 7'11"	3.39 x 2.40

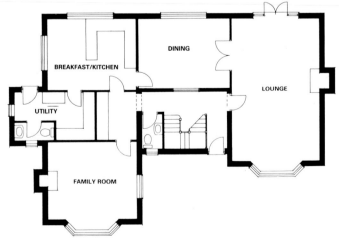

This four bedroomed house has a width of only 37 feet, and because it has no windows to rooms at the sides, it can be built close to the boundaries of a narrow plot. (Kitchens and bathrooms, etc. are not rooms for this purpose as far as the regulations are concerned). This makes it a very convenient design in a suburban setting, where its crisp appearance and unusual front elevation will help it to seem larger than it is.

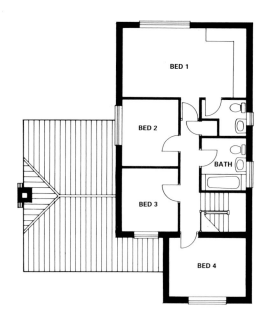

Design Number 92120   Aldergrove

Floor Area	1701 sq.ft.	158 sq.m.
Dimensions overall	36'8" x 42'7"	11.19 x 12.98
Lounge	13' x 19'6"	3.96 x 5.95
Kitchen	19'6" x 10'2"	5.95 x 3.10
Dining	13'2" x 10'6"	4.01 x 3.20
Utility	6' x 10'6"	1.84 x 3.20
Study	12' x 9'	3.65 x 2.75
Bed 1	19'6" x 10'6"	5.95 x 3.20
Bed 2	9' x 10'2"	2.73 x 3.10
Bed 3	9' x 9'6"	2.73 x 2.90
Bed 4	12' x 9'	3.65 x 2.75

BENINGTON

Design Number 92113   Benington

Floor Area	2304 sq.ft.	214 sq.m.
Dimensions overall	44'7" x 45'9"	13.60 x 13.95
Lounge	18'4" x 19'	5.60 x 5.79
Kitchen	11'8" x 15'	3.55 x 4.56
Dining	16'3" x 14'9"	4.94 x 4.50
Utility	7' x 10'10"	2.13 x 3.30
Family Room	23'5" x 13'	7.14 x 3.96
Bed 1	16'3" x 14'9"	4.94 x 4.50
Bed 2	11'8" x 15'	3.55 x 4.56
Bed 3	18'4" x 9'10"	5.60 x 3.00
Bed 4	14'9" x 8'10"	4.50 x 2.69

This large impressive home suits a site with all round views and is more likely to be built in the country than in an urban setting.

It is shown here constructed in stone, and the actual type of stone to be used will determine many of the features, such as the possible use of stone window surrounds, and even the style of a coping at the top of the chimney. This need to use stone in the traditional local way is discussed at length on pages 24-31.

EVENWOOD

Five bedrooms and three bathrooms in a house of just over 2000 square feet make this a popular design for those with a large family, and with the integral double garage it requires a minimum plot of only 60 feet, or even less if the utility room is not built.

One of the many alterations which can be made to this basic design is to build an extension to the first floor landing above the front porch, as shown in the inset sketch.

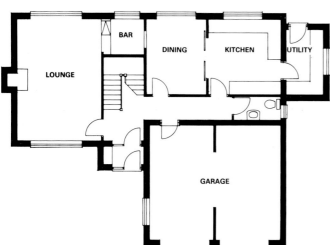

Design Number 92114   Evenwood

Floor Area	2045 sq. ft.	190 sq. m.
Dimensions overall	48'8" x 34'6"	14.83 x 10.53
Lounge	13' x 18'	3.96 x 5.48
Kitchen	11' x 11'2"	3.35 x 3.40
Dining	9' x 11'2"	2.74 x 3.40
Utility	5'9" x 9'8"	1.75 x 2.95
Bed 1	13' x 18'	3.96 x 5.48
Bed 2	11' x 11'1"	3.35 x 3.38
Bed 3	9' x 11'2"	2.74 x 3.40
Bed 4	11' x 8'3"	3.35 x 2.50
Bed 5	8'4" x 14'	2.55 x 4.28
Garage (each)	9'8" x 17'	2.95 x 5.18

ALCASTON

The Alcaston design has a lean-to roof over the front porch, which is wholly appropriate to the site in Wales on which it was built. In other parts of Britain it may be preferable to consider a pitched roof to the porch, moving the bathroom window to the other wall to allow for this. This style of porch would suit a solid door with narrow windows in the porch side walls. Like so much else, this sort of thing depends on the regional design features in the area where you want to build: those who buy drawings for designs in this book invariably have them altered to suit their own site.

The utility/breakfast room wing need not be built if it is not required, and of course the big Inglenook fireplace with its little side windows can be replaced with a fireplace in any other style if required.

Design Number 92116   Alcaston

Floor Area	2530 sq.ft.	235 sq.m.
Dimensions overall	59'8" x 42'9"	18.21 x 13.03
Lounge	13' x 23'9"	3.96 x 7.24
Kitchen	17'5" x 12'	5.33 x 3.65
Dining	12'4" x 12'	3.75 x 3.65
Breakfast/Utility	10'4" x 20'4"	3.15 x 6.20
Study	13' x 12'	3.96 x 3.65
Reception	16'9" x 18'1"	5.11 x 5.52
Bed 1	13' x 16'5"	3.96 x 5.00
Bed 2	15'4" x 12'	4.68 x 3.65
Bed 3	14'5" x 12'	4.40 x 3.65
Bed 4	10'8" x 11'5"	3.27 x 3.49
Bed 5	10'2" x 14'9"	3.10 x 4.50

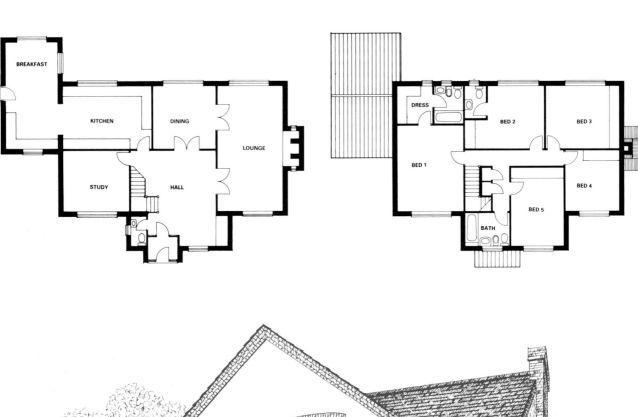

BIRCHGROVE

A four bedroom house with a self contained office over an integral double garage.

The office has its own entrance at the top of external steps and these are on the opposite side of the garage from the front door and quite separate from it. This helps to emphasize that the office is not simply a spare room in the house, which is often important to someone working from their home.

Although shown as an office, this part of the building can also be used as self contained living space, perhaps as a flat or bed and breakfast accommodation. Indeed, to meet some situations it may be appropriate to make a planning application for this building with the office accommodation shown as bedrooms, with a link through to the landing.

If the workshop on the ground floor is not required it can become a utility room, which will make a considerable cost saving.

Design Number 92115   Birchgrove

Floor Area	2368 sq. ft.	220 sq. m.
Dimensions overall	49'6" x 40'3"	15.09 x 12.28
Lounge	13' x 19'8"	3.96 x 6.00
Kitchen	11' x 13'6"	3.35 x 4.10
Dining	9' x 10'2"	2.75 x 3.10
Utility	5'9" x 9'8"	1.75 x 2.95
Study	7' x 10'2"	2.15 x 3.10
Bed 1	13' x 19'8"	3.96 x 6.00
Bed 2	11' x 9'	3.35 x 2.75
Bed 3	9' x 10'2"	3.35 x 2.75
Bed 4	7' x 10'2"	2.15 x 3.10
Office (overall)	19'8" x 17'1"	6.00 x 5.20
Garage (each)	9'8" x 17'1"	2.95 x 5.20
Workshop	7'8" x 5'11"	2.35 x 1.80

BURNSIDE

The Burnside was originally built in a suburban setting using Butterley bricks from the Kirton Works, with the eaves features, header courses and patterns in the brickwork shown in the artists drawing.

A design requirement was that the study should be as large as possible at the expense of the hall. Many would wish to have a wider hall and a smaller study, giving room for a solid front door with a window on each side. One of the advantages of building for yourself is that you have an opportunity to make your own decisions on matters like this.

Design Number 92117 Burnside

Floor Area	2605 sq. ft.	242 sq. m.
Dimensions overall	59'6" x 33'3"	18.13 x 10.15
Lounge	15'9" x 26'9"	4.81 x 8.15
Kitchen	14'10" x 11'	4.53 x 3.35
Dining	13' x 11'	3.96 x 3.35
Utility	8' x 11'	2.43 x 3.35
Study	12'9" x 8'2"	3.89 x 2.50
Bed 1	14'5" x 11'6"	4.40 x 3.50
Bed 2	13' x 14'3"	3.96 x 4.35
Bed 3	13' x 12'2"	3.96 x 3.70
Bed 4	10'4" x 12'	3.15 x 3.65
Bed 5	11'6" x 8'2"	3.50 x 2.50
Garage	18'7" x 19'8"	5.68 x 6.00

FRAMLINGTON

A four bedroom home which was first built in Kent, which is why it is shown here with the tile hanging that is so typical of the South East. A variation of this design is to combine the kitchen with its breakfast alcove with the utility room to give a very large farmhouse kitchen, perhaps adding a porch to the back door.

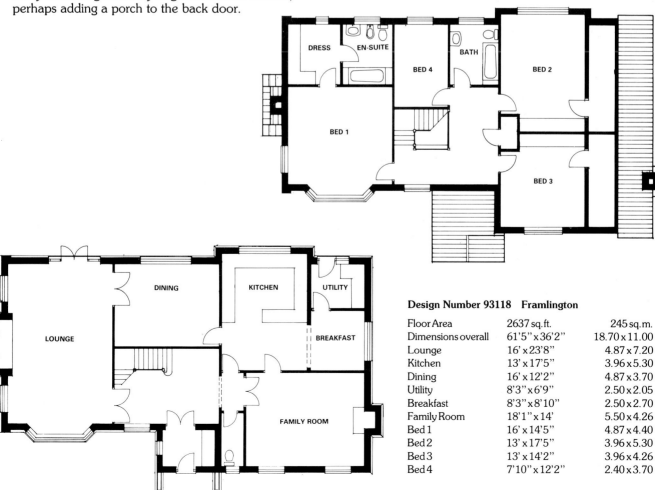

Design Number 93118   Framlington

Floor Area	2637 sq.ft.	245 sq.m.
Dimensions overall	61'5" x 36'2"	18.70 x 11.00
Lounge	16' x 23'8"	4.87 x 7.20
Kitchen	13' x 17'5"	3.96 x 5.30
Dining	16' x 12'2"	4.87 x 3.70
Utility	8'3" x 6'9"	2.50 x 2.05
Breakfast	8'3" x 8'10"	2.50 x 2.70
Family Room	18'1" x 14'	5.50 x 4.26
Bed 1	16' x 14'5"	4.87 x 4.40
Bed 2	13' x 17'5"	3.96 x 5.30
Bed 3	13' x 14'2"	3.96 x 4.26
Bed 4	7'10" x 12'2"	2.40 x 3.70

BRAMPTON

The Brampton design is drawn to suit a narrow urban or suburban site where an integral garage is required to the rear of the property. It is shown here with a large balcony over the garage with access onto it from the landing as well as through the patio doors from the master bedroom.

In order to keep the overall width of the house to under 40 feet there is no room for separate windows beside the front door, and a glazed door in a frame with glazed side screens is used to light the hall. This is appropriate to a suburban setting, but would have to be given further consideration if the house is to be built in the country.

The small false gable on the front elevation is a popular decorative feature in the 90s. If you like it, it can stay there, but it can be ignored if you wish.

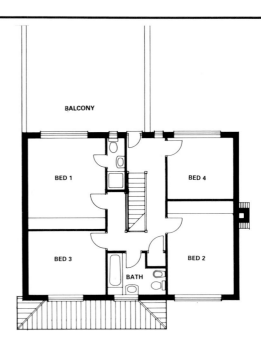

Design Number 92119   Brampton

Floor Area	2411 sq.ft.	224 sq.m.
Dimensions overall	38'4" x 59'6"	11.68 x 18.14
Lounge	14'5" x 25'7"	4.40 x 7.81
Kitchen/Breakfast	19'11" x 14'3"	6.08 x 4.35
Dining	12'4" x 14'9"	3.77 x 4.49
Utility	10' x 8'6"	3.05 x 2.60
Study	9'7" x 8'6"	2.93 x 2.60
Bed 1	13'3" x 14'9"	4.05 x 4.50
Bed 2	11'2" x 15'3"	3.40 x 4.66
Bed 3	13'3" x 10'6"	4.05 x 3.21
Bed 4	11'2" x 10'	3.40 x 3.05
Garage	20' x 18'2"	6.10 x 5.55

AYLEFORD

Design Number 92112   Ayleford

Floor Area
(exc. garage)	2077 sq. ft.	193 sq. m.
Dimensions overall		
(inc. garage)	64'4" x 40'3"	19.60 x 12.25
Lounge	19'5" x 18'	5.90 x 5.48
Kitchen	12'7" x 13'	3.85 x 3.96
Dining	13'6" x 12'	4.12 x 3.65
Utility	10'11" x 13'	3.54 x 3.96
Bed 1	12'8" x 13'	3.85 x 3.96
Bed 2	14'2" x 12'	4.32 x 3.65
Bed 3	19'5" x 9'8"	5.90 x 2.94
Bed 4	15'9" x 8'0"	4.80 x 2.44
Garage	20'1" x 18'2"	6.12 x 5.53

A front door set in the angle between two wings of a house is not only an interesting feature itself, but also leads to an unusual layout for the hall, enabling it to appear larger than it really is. This four bedroom family house demonstrates this very clearly.

It has other interesting features as well, including a corner fireplace in the lounge which mirrors the angled double doors, and another fireplace in the dining room. The utility room is very large, as appropriate if this new home is being built in the country. However, if required this room can be reduced in size and the house built without the projecting rear wing, resulting in a significant cost saving.

FOXDALE

This small three bedroom home in a Tudor style will suit either a rural setting or a narrow plot in a built up area. Depending on the character of adjacent buildings it may be appropriate to consider a gabled roof to the porch, and above it a false gable at the eaves of the main roof. If this is required then the window lighting the stairs can be moved above the half landing.

Design Number 92122   Foxdale

Floor Area	1173 sq.ft.	109 sq.m.
Dimensions overall	31'6" x 28'8"	9.60 x 8.75
Lounge	12' x 18'3"	3.65 x 5.56
Kitchen	10' x 10'2"	3.15 x 3.11
Dining	12' x 8'4"	3.65 x 2.54
Utility	5'3" x 10'2"	1.60 x 3.11
Bed 1	12' x 10'9"	3.65 x 3.60
Bed 2	12' x 11'6"	3.65 x 3.50
Bed 3	9'2" x 10'2"	2.80 x 3.11

BARRHILL

The Barrhill design is a modification of the Foxdale house opposite wih a granny bed-sit or a bedroom for an invalid on the ground floor. This is a common design requirement, and the house is usually built with provision for the downstairs WC to be opened into the hall at a later date to become a cloakroom. The bedsit then becomes the lounge with a dining room at the front of the house. The first floor is identical with that of the Foxdale.

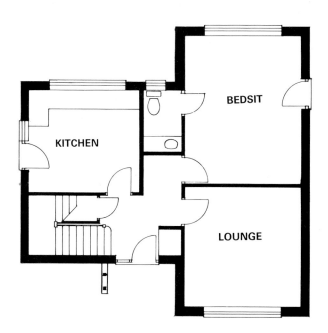

Design Number 92123   Barrhill

Floor Area	1173 sq.ft.	109 sq.m.
Overall Dimension	31'6" x 28'8"	9600 x 8750
Lounge	12' x 11'10"	3650 x 3600
Kitchen	11'8" x 10'2"	3550 x 3110
Bed Sit	12' x 14'9"	3650 x 4500
Bed 1	12' x 16'1"	3650 x 4900
Bed 2	12' x 10'6"	3650 x 3200
Bed 3	9'2" x 10'2"	2800 x 3110

CANNONBURY

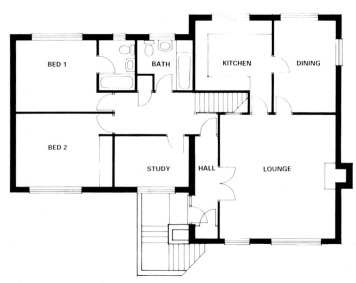

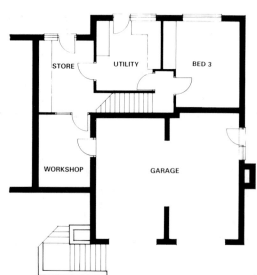

Design Number 92126   Cannonbury

Floor Area	2196 sq. ft.	204 sq. m.
Dimensions overall	51'5" x 34'4"	15.69 x 10.48
Lounge	18' x 18'7"	5.48 x 5.68
Kitchen	12' x 13'7"	3.65 x 4.15
Dining	9'7" x 13'7"	2.93 x 4.15
Study	11'6" x 7'7"	3.50 x 2.31
Utility	9'11" x 10'4"	3.03 x 3.15
Bed 1	12'6" x 10'8"	3.81 x 3.27
Bed 2	15' x 10'10"	4.56 x 3.31
Bed 3	11'7" x 12'10"	3.55 x 3.90
Workshop	7'11" x 10'10"	2.40 x 3.30
Garden Store	8'5" x 7'4"	2.58 x 2.25
Garage (overall)	21'11" x 18'10"	6.68 x 5.75

This is another example of a single level bungalow built on a sloping site with a garage below, with internal access to the garage level and some accommodation at the lower level.

The rooms adjacent to the garage are shown as a study and workshop, but this area could easily be laid out as a self contained flat.

Design Number 92125   Crawford

Floor Area	2497 sq. ft.	232 sq. m.
Dimensions overall	54'5" x 39'0"	16.58 x 10.88
Lounge/Dining	28'3" x 23'4"	8.63 x 7.13
Kitchen/Breakfast	23'4" x 12'	7.13 x 3.65
Utility	10'10" x 8'8"	3.30 x 2.65
Bed 1	16'4" x 12'	4.98 x 3.65
Bed 2	11'6" x 14'11"	3.50 x 4.55
Bed 3	11'7" x 9'	3.53 x 2.75
Bed 4	8'5" x 7'11"	2.58 x 2.40
Workshop	10'10" x 9'9"	3.30 x 2.98
Garage (overall)	23'4" x 19'8"	7.13 x 6.00

A stone bungalow with a low pitch roof built on a sloping site over a double garage like this is typical of homes offering B & B accommodation in Wales and the West Country. The layout of the Crawford design was drawn with this in mind.

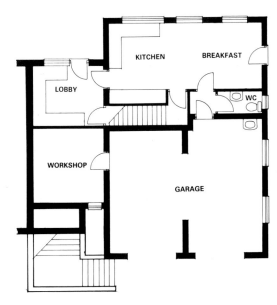

CARSTAIRS

Design Number 92127   Carstairs

Floor Area	1991 sq.ft.	185 sq.m.
Dimensions overall	50'11" x 31'9"	15.51 x 9.68
Lounge	20' x 15'2"	6.10 x 4.62
Kitchen	9' x 10'	2.75 x 3.05
Dining	10'8" x 10'	3.25 x 3.05
Utility	12' x 9'4"	3.65 x 2.85
Study	7' x 8'9"	2.13 x 2.67
Bed 1	12'6" x 12'11"	3.81 x 3.95
Bed 2	12'6" x 12'2"	3.81 x 3.72
Bed 3	12' x 9'8"	3.65 x 2.95
Garage	11'11" x 25'6"	3.64 x 7.77

A popular approach to a sloping site is this three level house — garage below, up six steps to living accommodation, and then up another seven steps to the bedrooms. In the Carstairs design this concept has been developed further by providing a utility room and a study or workshop at the garage level, so that the appearance of this part of the house matches the bedroom area above, giving a more balanced appearance than many split level homes.

False gables are shown above four windows on the front elevation. These are ornamental features and whether or not the roof is built in this way will depend on your preference, and whether the planners think it appropriate in the local area.

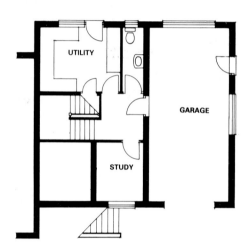

CORNWALL

Design Number 92128   Cornwall

Floor Area	1926 sq. ft.	179 sq. m.
Dimensions overall	51'3" x 32'5"	15.63 x 9.90
Lounge	20' x 15'6"	6.10 x 4.72
Kitchen	13'3" x 9'8"	4.05 x 2.95
Dining	14'9" x 9'8"	4.50 x 2.95
Utility	10'6" x 6'7"	3.20 x 2.02
Study	8'8" x 8'9"	2.65 x 2.67
Bed 1	18'8" x 12'3"	5.70 x 3.75
Bed 2	10'6" x 13'10"	3.20 x 3.92
Bed 3	13'9" x 9'8"	4.20 x 2.95
Garage	10'6" x 18'1"	3.20 x 5.50

This is a design for a sloping site which takes a little time to understand. The front entrance has the same intermediate floor level as the bedroom wing, but the same ceiling level as the upper floor living accommodation, giving an unusually lofty hall. The lounge is reached by seven steps, and three glazed screens in the lounge wall ensure plenty of light for the staircase and the entrance hall generally.

Another six steps lead down to the ground floor accommodation, with three rooms and a cloakroom or bathroom. The arrangement of rooms here can be varied to meet any requirement: family accommodation, a self-contained flat, or simply storage space.

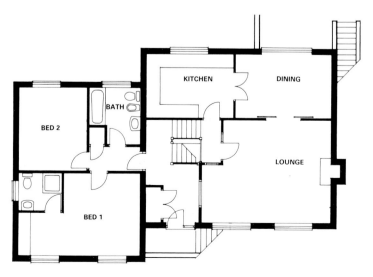

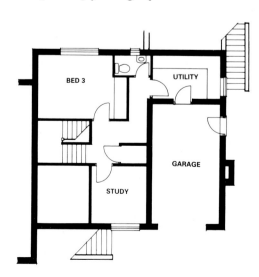

BLANDFORD

Design Number 92130   Blandford

Floor Area	1098 sq. ft.	102 sq. m.
Dimensions overall	26'5" x 33'	8.05 x 10.06
Lounge	12'2" x 17'8"	3.70 x 5.40
Kitchen	12'2" x 12'3"	3.70 x 3.97
Dining	12'2" x 8'4"	3.70 x 2.54
Utility	7' x 5'9"	2.10 x 1.77
Bed 1	12'2" x 8'8"	3.70 x 2.65
Bed 2	12'2" x 8'8"	3.70 x 2.65
Bed 3	12'2" x 8'8"	3.70 x 2.65

A small three bedroom cottage of less than 1100 square feet which is shown with a half hip roof. It is an ideal 'village street' cottage, although there are parts of the country where it would be more appropriate to build it with a gable roof.

A cost saving option if the sides of the house are at least four metres from the boundary is to replace the dormers in the two rear bedrooms with windows in the gable walls.

Note that the fireplace is shown centrally on the lounge wall on the plan, but in the sketch it is positioned as it needs to be if the fireplace is to be in the corner of the room, which is how the prototype was built.

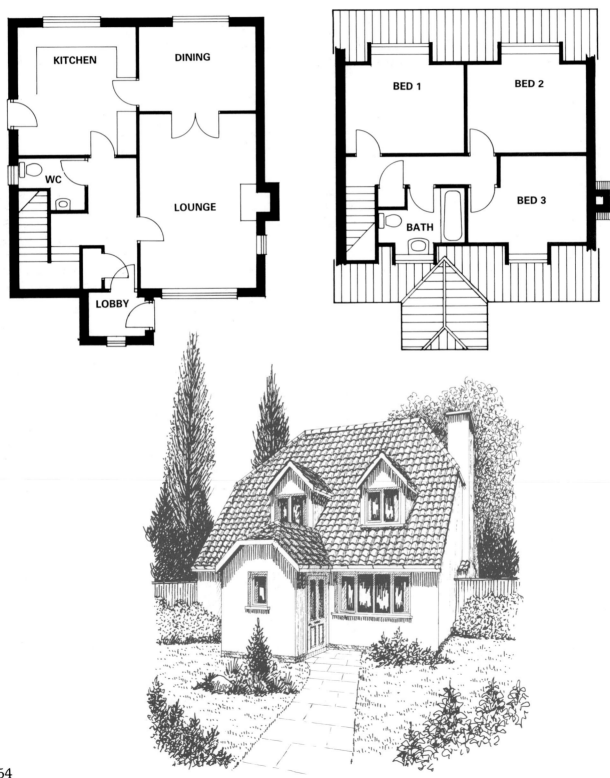

Design Number 92129   Clifton

Floor Area	1076 sq.ft.	100 sq.m.
Dimensions overall	26'5" x 28'2"	8.05 x 8.59
Lounge	12'2" x 17'8"	3.70 x 5.40
Kitchen	12'2" x 13'	3.70 x 3.92
Dining	12'2" x 8'4"	3.70 x 2.54
Bed 1	12'2" x 11'10"	3.70 x 3.60
Bed 2	12'2" x 8'8"	3.70 x 2.65

A compact two bedroom cottage with luxury features for a home of this size, including two bathrooms and a ground floor cloakroom.

It is illustrated here with rendered walls above a brick plinth, but can also be built with Victorian features or in a more austere style for the Midlands or North, and would fit happily on a vacant plot in a village street anywhere.

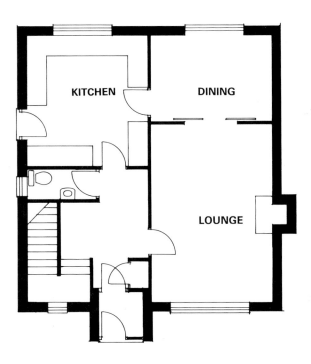

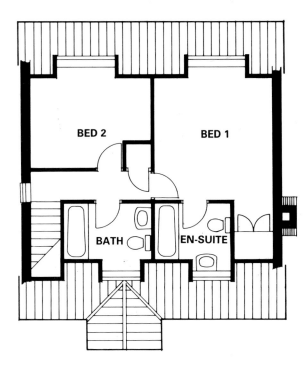

FINCHFIELD

Another four bedroom home that can be built on a plot only 40 feet wide, in this case with an integral garage.

This is the most popular room layout in speculative housing in Britain, although the roof arrangement often varies. In choosing between designs based on this room arrangement it is important to compare room sizes. There are a number of designs which are derivatives of this concept in this book.

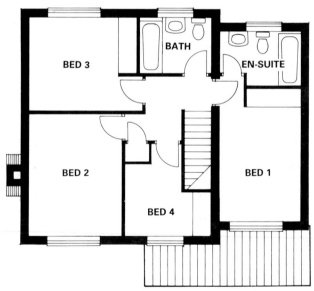

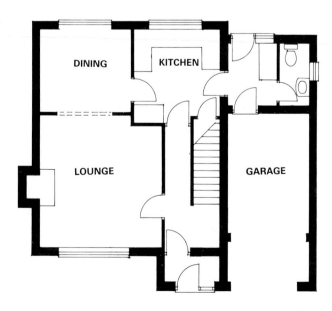

Design Number 92131　Finchfield

Floor Area	1345 sq. ft.	125 sq. m.
Dimensions overall	33'2" x 28'9"	10.12 x 8.78
Lounge	13'6" x 14'1"	4.10 x 4.30
Kitchen	9'8" x 10'	2.94 x 3.05
Dining	10' x 8'11"	3.06 x 2.70
Bed 1	9' x 14'3"	2.75 x 4.35
Bed 2	11'9" x 12'11"	3.10 x 3.95
Bed 3	11'9" x 10'	3.60 x 3.05
Bed 4	9'6" x 9'10"	2.90 x 3.00
Garage	9' x 18'	2.75 x 5.50

CORNHILL

The Cornhill house is a variant of the Finchfield design opposite with the same four bedroom first floor layout but a different ground floor arrangement. The hall is much smaller, with access to the kitchen through the lounge instead of alongside the stairs. This gives a significantly larger lounge and more storage space in the kitchen.

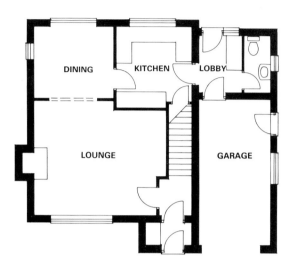

Design Number 92132   Cornhill

Floor Area	1292 sq. ft.	120 sq. m.
Dimensions overall	33'2" x 28'9"	10.12 x 8.78
Lounge	16'9" x 14'1"	5.10 x 4.30
Kitchen	9'8" x 10'	2.94 x 3.05
Dining	10' x 8'11"	3.06 x 2.70
Bed 1	9' x 15'5"	2.75 x 4.70
Bed 2	11'9" x 12'11"	3.10 x 3.95
Bed 3	11'9" x 10'	3.60 x 3.05
Bed 4	9'6" x 9'10"	2.90 x 3.00
Garage	9' x 18'	2.75 x 5.50

BRIDESWELL

The Brideswell house was designed as a vicarage, and will also suit others who work from their homes and have visitors at all hours. This requires that there should be a large porch — visitors tend to arrive when it is raining — and a spacious office or study which is sufficiently far from the living accommodation for the television not to be heard by those discussing matters of importance. A cloakroom adjacent to the study is another requirement.

This design meets all these criteria in a well laid out family home of under 2000 square feet. At this size it meets the cost guide lines of most church authorities, and has proved very popular.

Design Number 92133   Brideswell

Floor Area	1980 sq. ft.	184 sq. m.
Dimensions overall	56'3" x 28'5"	17.15 x 8.68
Lounge	13'11" x 21'7"	4.24 x 6.59
Kitchen	9'4" x 13'5"	2.86 x 4.09
Breakfast	7'10" x 8'10"	2.40 x 2.70
Dining	11'3" x 9'10"	3.43 x 3.00
Utility	8'8" x 8'10"	2.65 x 2.70
Vicarage	9'4" x 13'	2.86 x 3.94
Bed 1	13'11" x 11'5"	4.24 x 3.49
Bed 2	9'4" x 11'5"	2.86 x 3.49
Bed 3	13'11" x 9'10"	4.24 x 3.00
Bed 4	9'10" x 9'4"	3.00 x 2.86
Garage	16'11" x 18'10"	5.15 x 5.76

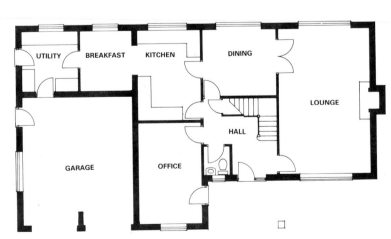

DOWNSEND

Design Number 92134   Downsend

Floor Area	1750 sq. ft.	163 sq.m.
Dimensions overall	39'3" x 32'2"	11.97 x 9.79
Lounge	14' x 17'	4.26 x 5.18
Kitchen/Breakfast	10'11" x 13'7"	3.33 x 4.15
Dining	14' x 13'	4.26 x 3.96
Utility	7'4" x 6'10"	2.24 x 2.10
Bed 1	14' x 12'	4.26 x 3.65
Bed 2	14' x 13'	4.26 x 3.96
Bed 3	10'9" x 15'9"	3.29 x 4.80
Garage	10'9" x 17'	3.29 x 5.18

The Downsend design is a small house of 1250 square feet with a lot of character and an interesting three bedroom layout.

It is shown here with an island fireplace between the lounge and the dining room. This was a very popular feature in the 70s but is rarely seen today: the wall concerned can be built solid if required and will suit any sort of fireplace. Alternatively the hearth and chimney can be moved to the outside wall on the right hand side of the house.

The stairs will be a key feature in this small home, and should be chosen with care to give an appropriate 'cottage' feel.

ARDROSSAN

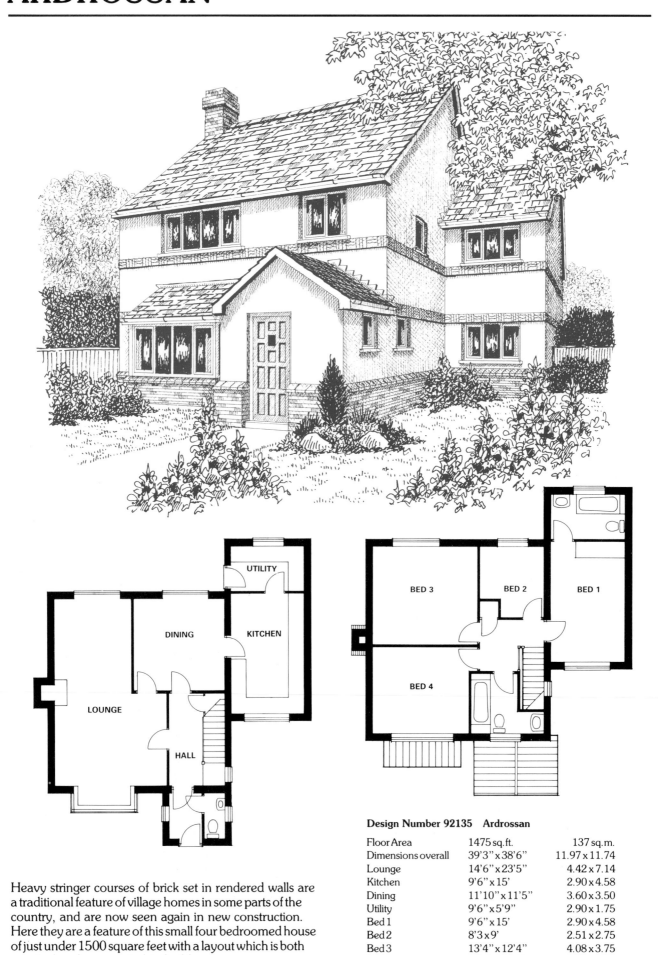

Design Number 92135   Ardrossan

Floor Area	1475 sq.ft.	137 sq.m.
Dimensions overall	39'3" x 38'6"	11.97 x 11.74
Lounge	14'6" x 23'5"	4.42 x 7.14
Kitchen	9'6" x 15'	2.90 x 4.58
Dining	11'10" x 11'5"	3.60 x 3.50
Utility	9'6" x 5'9"	2.90 x 1.75
Bed 1	9'6" x 15'	2.90 x 4.58
Bed 2	8'3 x 9'	2.51 x 2.75
Bed 3	13'4" x 12'4"	4.08 x 3.75
Bed 4	12'4" x 10'9"	3.75 x 3.29

Heavy stringer courses of brick set in rendered walls are a traditional feature of village homes in some parts of the country, and are now seen again in new construction. Here they are a feature of this small four bedroomed house of just under 1500 square feet with a layout which is both practical and economical to build.

BRIGHTSTONE

This economical three bedroom cottage of under 1200 square feet has an unusual roof arrangement which is not seen on the artists sketch, but which can be understood by reference to the first floor plan and the elevation drawing.

The third bedroom and the very large bathroom are lit by Velux roof lights, but if required these can be augmented with small windows in the end gables. Alternatively, if the budget will stretch to it, these rooms can have small tiled dormers like the two bedrooms at the front.

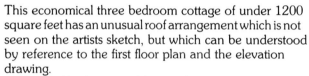

Design Number 92139   Brightstone

Floor Area	1196 sq. ft.	112 sq. m.
Dimensions overall	32'3" x 30'8"	9.84 x 9.37
Lounge	12' x 17'3"	3.65 x 5.26
Kitchen	9'9" x 13'9"	2.99 x 4.20
Dining	8'8" x 11'4"	2.65 x 3.46
Utility	6'10" x 8'1"	2.09 x 2.48
Bed 1	12'6" x 10'2"	3.83 x 3.10
Bed 2	13'4" x 6'9"	4.06 x 2.07
Bed 3	12' x 8'8"	3.65 x 2.65

AVIEMORE

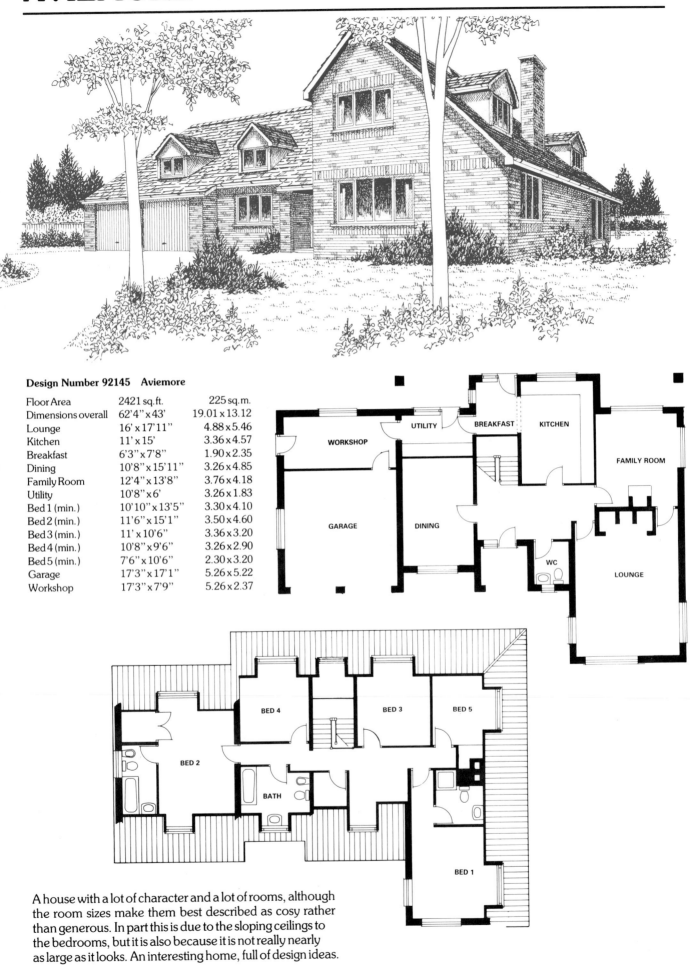

Design Number 92145 Aviemore

Floor Area	2421 sq.ft.	225 sq.m.
Dimensions overall	62'4" x 43'	19.01 x 13.12
Lounge	16' x 17'11"	4.88 x 5.46
Kitchen	11' x 15'	3.36 x 4.57
Breakfast	6'3" x 7'8"	1.90 x 2.35
Dining	10'8" x 15'11"	3.26 x 4.85
Family Room	12'4" x 13'8"	3.76 x 4.18
Utility	10'8" x 6'	3.26 x 1.83
Bed 1 (min.)	10'10" x 13'5"	3.30 x 4.10
Bed 2 (min.)	11'6" x 15'1"	3.50 x 4.60
Bed 3 (min.)	11' x 10'6"	3.36 x 3.20
Bed 4 (min.)	10'8" x 9'6"	3.26 x 2.90
Bed 5 (min.)	7'6" x 10'6"	2.30 x 3.20
Garage	17'3" x 17'1"	5.26 x 5.22
Workshop	17'3" x 7'9"	5.26 x 2.37

A house with a lot of character and a lot of rooms, although the room sizes make them best described as cosy rather than generous. In part this is due to the sloping ceilings to the bedrooms, but it is also because it is not really nearly as large as it looks. An interesting home, full of design ideas.

ALCONBURY

Design Number 92146   Alconbury

Floor Area	2841 sq.ft.	264 sq.m.
Dimensions overall	47'6" x 39'5"	14.47 x 12.03
Lounge	15'11" x 23'10"	4.84 x 7.28
Kitchen/Breakfast	15'2" x 14'9"	4.62 x 4.50
Dining	12'2" x 12'	3.71 x 3.65
Study	15'2" x 9'8"	4.62 x 2.95
Utility	11'4" x 7'9"	3.45 x 2.38
Music Room	15'11" x 8'8"	4.84 x 2.65
Bed 1	15'11" x 15'	4.84 x 4.58
Bed 2 (min.)	15'2" x 10'9"	4.62 x 3.28
Bed 3	14'5" x 9'2"	4.39 x 2.80
Bed 4	9' x 12'	2.75 x 3.65
Bed 5	10'8" x 8'	3.25 x 2.45

This large family home of nearly 3000 square feet is nearly square, making it very easy to arrange for alterations to the internal layout to suit your own lifestyle. The arrangements for the little courtyard between the two wings of the house at the rear will determine the character of the music room and dining room, and should be carefully planned at an early stage. A fountain, a piece of sculpture or just paving with a raised bed and a stone bench — there are many options.

On the first floor, a door has been shown between the master suite dressing room and the small bedroom at the front of the house. This was a feature of the prototype for this design, and was arranged to suit a family with a small baby. A special door like this can be built so that it is easily removed and replaced with a solid wall at a later date.

BREDEN HILL

If you have a site which is so steep that the house will be at least 10 feet above the driveway, one approach is to build with a garage directly in front of the property, so that the flat roof forms a terrace. This requires a minimum of excavation, which can be important where the subsoil is rock.

The Breden Hill design demonstrates this with a conventional four bedroom house which has a patio window to the drawing room leading onto the terrace.

The terrace is the key element in the appearance of the home and it is imporant that it is finished to a high standard with carefully chosen ballustrading.

Design Number 92149   Breden Hill

Floor Area		
(exc. garage)	1755 sq. ft.	163 sq. m.
Dimensions overall		
(inc. garage)	47'8" x 34'7"	14.53 x 10.54
Lounge	17'9" x 14'	5.40 x 4.26
Kitchen	10'6" x 11'	3.20 x 3.35
Dining	10'6" x 14'	3.20 x 4.26
Utility	10'6" x 5'4"	3.20 x 1.63
Study	12'6" x 9'9"	3.80 x 2.98
Bed 1 (min.)	14' x 14'	4.26 x 4.26
Bed 2	12'6" x 9'9"	3.80 x 2.98
Bed 3	11'2" x 8'9"	3.40 x 2.68
Bed 4	10' x 7'6"	3.05 x 2.30
Garage	16'5" x 17'9"	5.00 x 5.42

CARRICKMORE

The Carrickmore design is a smaller version of the Breden Hill house, designed to be built on a sloping site behind a garage which has a flat roof forming a terrace. The terrace ballustrading can be compared with that of the Breden Hill : it is a very important element in the appearance of a house built in this way and should be chosen with care.

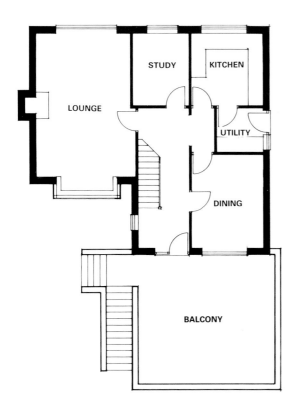

Design Number 92150   Carrickmore

Floor Area	1356 sq. ft.	126 sq. m.
Dimensions overall	46'4" x 34'8"	14.13 x 10.57
Lounge	18' x 13'	5.50 x 3.96
Kitchen	9'2" x 9'4"	2.80 x 2.85
Dining	11'10" x 9'4"	3.60 x 2.85
Utility	5'7" x 6'1"	1.70 x 1.85
Study	9' x 7'3"	2.75 x 2.20
Bed 1	14'11" x 10'6"	4.55 x 3.20
Bed 2	10' x 9'8"	3.05 x 2.95
Bed 3	7'10" x 12'4"	2.40 x 3.76
Bed 4	7'10" x 13'	2.40 x 3.96
Garage	16'5" x 17'9"	5.00 x 5.42

CLEVELAND

A four level house, with only a single stair well. Enter at the front door and you can turn left into the lounge or alternatively you can go down four steps to the dining room and kitchen level. If instead you had gone up the stairs you would have passed two bedrooms after nine steps, and found the master bedroom suite after four more. This can be a very useful way of tackling a sloping site where rock under the surface makes excavation difficult.

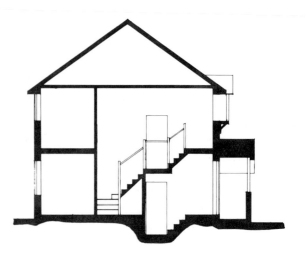

Design Number 92151   Cleveland

Floor Area	1572 sq.ft.	146 sq.m.
Dimensions overall	36'10" x 24'4"	11.21 x 7.40
Lounge	13'6" x 22'6"	4.12 x 6.85
Kitchen	12'4" x 10'	3.75 x 3.05
Dining	12'4" x 12'2"	3.76 x 3.70
Bed 1	13'6" x 14'9"	4.12 x 4.50
Bed 2	12'4" x 10'	3.76 x 3.05
Bed 3	12'4" x 10'2"	3.76 x 3.10

Another house which adjusts to a sloping site by having rooms at four different levels. In this case this is arranged easily and economically by having a landing for the intermediate level on a single flight of stairs.

Design Number 92152   Denby Dale

Floor Area	1604 sq. ft.	149 sq. m.
Dimensions overall	37'5" x 24'4"	11.41 x 7.40
Lounge (min)	13'6" x 22'6"	4.12 x 6.85
Kitchen	12'4" x 10'	3.76 x 3.05
Dining	12'4" x 12'2"	3.76 x 3.70
Bed 1	12'4" x 14'9"	3.76 x 4.50
Bed 2 (min.)	13'6" x 8'	4.12 x 2.45
Bed 3	11'11" x 7'1"	3.62 x 2.15
Bed 4 (max.)	8'3" x 7'1"	2.50 x 2.15

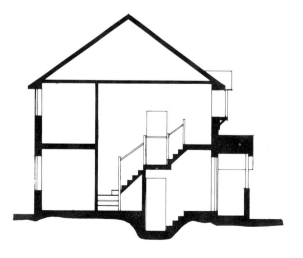

CLUMBER

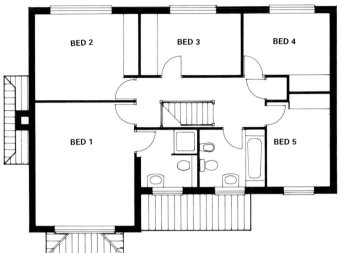

This five bedroom home was designed in the style of a Victorian cottage, but has a lot more space than you would expect from the outside. There are five bedrooms and two bathrooms, with generous cupboard space.

The scalloped barge boards, crested ridge tiles and other Victorian features demand a careful choice of setting for this design. If it does not match its surroundings, the roof pitch can be dropped and the house can be built in either brick or stone, possibly deleting the lounge bay window if this would not be in keeping with a regional style.

The Inglenook fireplace is not strictly in character with the front elevation, but the family commissioning the prototype of this design loved it, and it is a very attractive part in their living room.

Design Number 92157 Clumber

Floor Area	1830 sq.ft.	170 sq.m.
Dimensions overall	42'7" x 30'7"	13.30 x 9.33
Lounge (min.)	13'6" x 26'6"	4.12 x 8.08
Kitchen	11'3" x 15'6"	3.42 x 4.72
Dining	12'10" x 10'9"	3.91 x 3.28
Utility	8'1" x 5'11"	2.47 x 1.80
Bed 1	11'11" x 15'5"	3.94 x 4.70
Bed 2	13'6" x 10'9"	4.12 x 3.28
Bed 3	12'10" x 7'6"	3.91 x 2.28
Bed 4 (min.)	11'3" x 7'6"	3.42 x 2.28
Bed 5 (min.)	8'1" x 9'11"	2.47 x 3.04

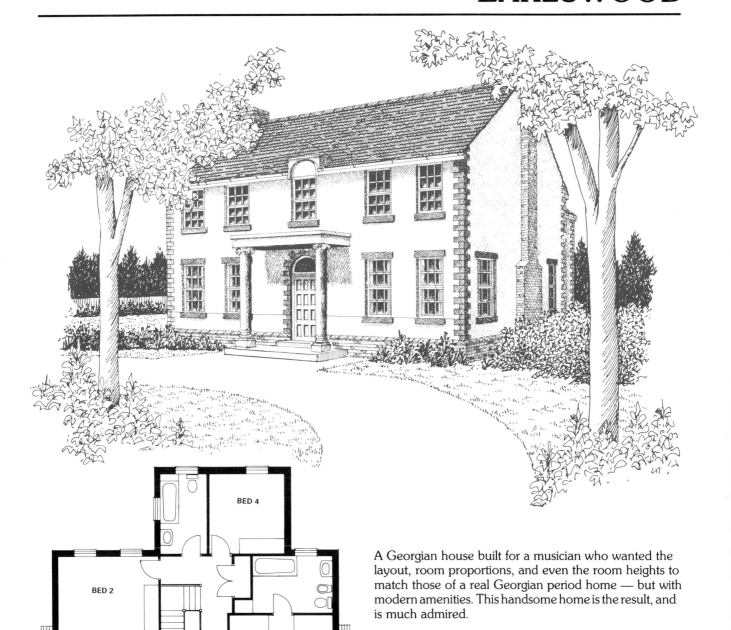

A Georgian house built for a musician who wanted the layout, room proportions, and even the room heights to match those of a real Georgian period home — but with modern amenities. This handsome home is the result, and is much admired.

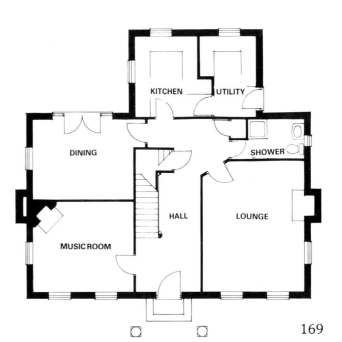

Design Number 92155   Earlswood

Floor Area	2034 sq. ft.	189 sq. m.
Dimensions overall	42'6" x 35'5"	12.96 x 10.80
Lounge	13'10" x 17'1"	4.21 x 5.21
Kitchen	8'7" x 7'5"	2.63 x 2.26
Dining	13'10" x 10'6"	4.21 x 3.21
Utility	7'9" x 7'5"	2.36 x 2.26
Study/Music Room	13'10" x 12'	4.21 x 3.61
Bed 1	13'10" x 14'9"	4.21 x 4.51
Bed 2	13'10" x 10'6"	4.21 x 3.21
Bed 3	13'10" x 12'	4.21 x 3.61
Bed 4	10'1" x 10'8"	3.08 x 3.26

169

APPERKNOWLE

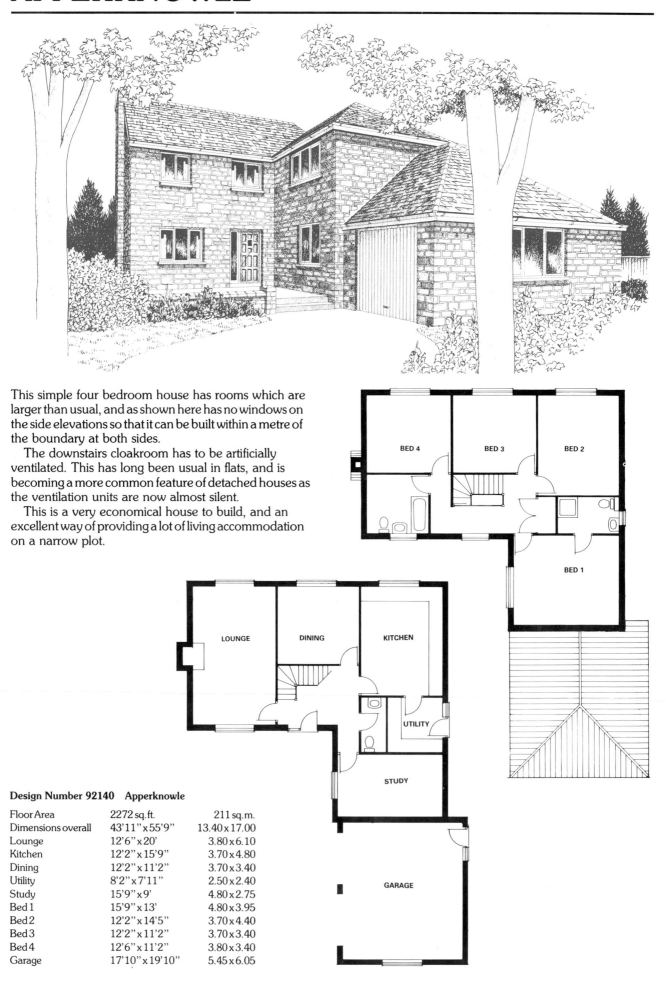

This simple four bedroom house has rooms which are larger than usual, and as shown here has no windows on the side elevations so that it can be built within a metre of the boundary at both sides.

The downstairs cloakroom has to be artificially ventilated. This has long been usual in flats, and is becoming a more common feature of detached houses as the ventilation units are now almost silent.

This is a very economical house to build, and an excellent way of providing a lot of living accommodation on a narrow plot.

Design Number 92140   Apperknowle

Floor Area	2272 sq. ft.	211 sq.m.
Dimensions overall	43'11" x 55'9"	13.40 x 17.00
Lounge	12'6" x 20'	3.80 x 6.10
Kitchen	12'2" x 15'9"	3.70 x 4.80
Dining	12'2" x 11'2"	3.70 x 3.40
Utility	8'2" x 7'11"	2.50 x 2.40
Study	15'9" x 9'	4.80 x 2.75
Bed 1	15'9" x 13'	4.80 x 3.95
Bed 2	12'2" x 14'5"	3.70 x 4.40
Bed 3	12'2" x 11'2"	3.70 x 3.40
Bed 4	12'6" x 11'2"	3.80 x 3.40
Garage	17'10" x 19'10"	5.45 x 6.05

FLAMBOROUGH

Design Number 92138   Flamborough

Floor Area	3197 sq. ft.	297 sq. m.
Dimensions overall	65'11" x 60'10"	20.09 x 18.54
Lounge (Vaulted)	16' x 23'9"	4.88 x 7.25
Kitchen	12'11" x 12'	3.94 x 3.65
Dining	12'5" x 11'2"	3.80 x 3.40
Family	21' x 26'1"	6.69 x 7.94
Bed 1	21' x 14'	6.69 x 4.26
Dress	10' x 11'2"	3.05 x 3.40
En/suite	11'7" x 11'2"	3.54 x 3.40
Bed 2	14'5" x 10'	4.40 x 3.05
Bed 3	11' x 10'	3.35 x 3.05
Bed 4	11' x 10'	3.35 x 3.05

This is an interesting home. The master bedroom suite is all that there is on the first floor, and the hall and lounge have high vaulted ceilings to the full height of the roof. The other three bedrooms are at the other end of the building, which has a staggered front elevation which adds to the impressive appearance of this large and unusual home.

171

DUFFUS

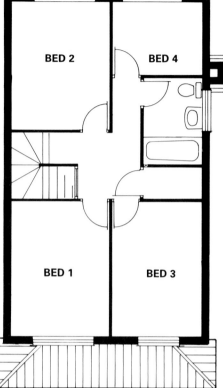

The small Duffus house with four bedrooms is just over 20 feet wide, and having no side windows it will fit on a plot that is only 30 feet from side to side.

It has a dining/hall, with a front door opening directly into it, which is more usually found in very grand houses three times the size. If the family prefer to eat in the lounge it can easily become a study/hall!

This design concept is just about the only way of providing four bedrooms plus a garage on a very narrow plot, and it is very useful for infill sites in towns.

Design Number 92143   Duffus

Floor Area	1303 sq.ft.	121 sq.m.
Dimensions overall	22'4" x 37'5"	6.81 x 11.40
Lounge	9'2" x 15'5"	2.79 x 4.70
Kitchen/Dining	9'3" x 15'5"	2.82 x 4.70
Study (min.)	9'2" x 12'11"	2.79 x 3.94
Bed 1	9'3" x 12'11"	2.82 x 3.94
Bed 2	9'4" x 12'2"	2.85 x 3.70
Bed 3	9'2" x 12'11"	2.79 x 3.94
Bed 4	9' x 6'11"	2.76 x 2.10
Garage	8'8" x 16'5"	2.66 x 5.00

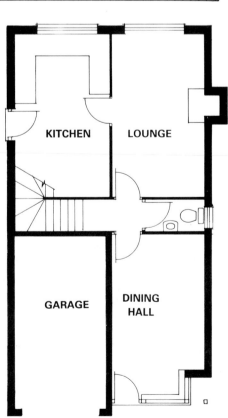

BOREHAM

A four bedroom suburban home of just under fifteen hundred square feet which will suit a plot of thirty six feet width, although it will look rather better with more space around it.

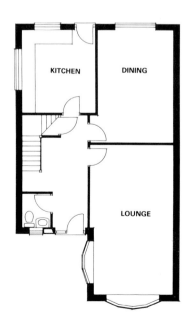

Design Number 92154   Boreham

Floor Area	1496 sq.ft.	139 sq.m.
Dimensions overall	24'3" x 40'	7.40 x 12.20
Lounge	12'3" x 21'7"	3.73 x 6.58
Kitchen	11' x 12'	3.35 x 3.64
Dining	11'2" x 16'3"	3.40 x 4.97
Bed 1	11' x 16'1"	3.35 x 4.90
Bed 2	10'2" x 9'9"	3.10 x 2.97
Bed 3	10' x 12'	3.05 x 3.65
Bed 4	9'11" x 12'	3.03 x 3.66

173

FOSDYKE

A three bedroom house of only 1400 sq. ft. for a wide frontage plot, which makes it appropriate to rural areas where land prices are lower than in towns. The hall is only lit by the window on the half landing, but as it is 1200mm wide this is perfectly adequate, especially as there is a similar window on the first floor landing.

The en-suite bathroom is of a size usually found in very large houses, and there is scope for the rearrangement of the whole of the first floor to meet individual requirements.

Design Number 92158   Fosdyke

Floor Area	1410 sq. ft.	131 sq.m.
Dimensions overall	48'2" x 24'	14.69 x 7.33
Lounge	17' x 13'6"	5.18 x 4.10
Kitchen	12'8" x 17'4"	3.86 x 5.29
Dining	12' x 12'	3.64 x 3.64
Bed 1	13'5" x 10'	4.10 x 3.04
Bed 2	12'8" x 9'6"	3.86 x 2.90
Bed 3	13'5" x 7'	4.10 x 2.04

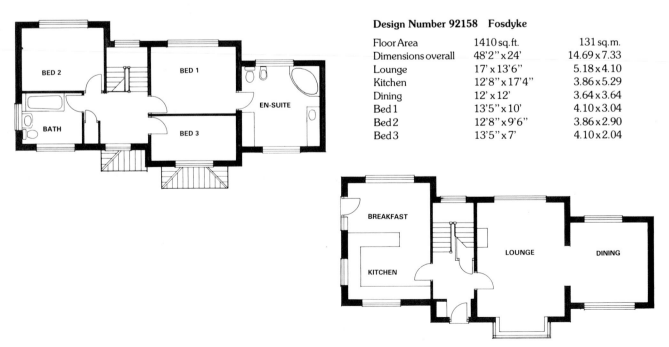

CHURCH NORTON

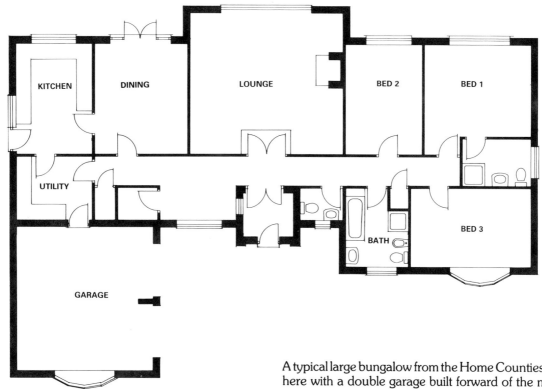

Design Number 92153   Church Norton

Floor Area

(inc. garage)	2013 sq.ft.	187 sq.m.
Dimensions overall	69'1" x 49'6"	21.06 x 15.08
Lounge	20' x 18'	6.10 x 5.49
Kitchen	10' x 14'	3.05 x 4.27
Dining	12' x 14'	3.65 x 4.27
Utility	10' x 8'	3.05 x 2.45
Bed 1	14' x 11'9"	4.27 x 3.58
Bed 2	10' x 14'	3.05 x 4.27
Bed 3	16' x 10'	4.87 x 3.04
Garage	18' x 20'5"	5.49 x 6.21

A typical large bungalow from the Home Counties, shown here with a double garage built forward of the main building. The elm boarding below the 'Hampshire hip' gables is typical of the area, but requires a very careful choice of rustic bricks and tiles if it is not to appear contrived.

Large bungalows with design features that emphasize a low roof line such as this need to be set in large gardens. If space is at a premium it is usually preferable to opt for a steeper roof pitch and a more vertical emphasis in the design detailing.

BILBOROUGH

A design for a site with important views to the front, a slope running from one side to the other so that the garage of the house is lower than the front door.

The way that this is dealt with in this design is with a straight flight of stairs with a landing half way up, and from the landing a door giving access into the lounge above the garage. On the upper floor there are two bedrooms and a bathroom, and a small third bedroom or study is on the ground floor.

Very much a house for a site with a sea view, and the style in which it is shown would be wholly appropriate to this.

Design Number 92148   Bilborough

Floor Area	1646 sq. ft.	153 sq. m.
Dimensions overall	43'7" x 28'2"	13.28 x 8.58
Lounge	18'9" x 16'	5.67 x 4.85
Kitchen	14' x 7'	4.27 x 2.75
Dining (max.)	14' x 11'7"	4.27 x 3.55
Utility	8'8" x 5'	2.63 x 1.53
Bed 1	11'4" x 16'2"	4.27 x 4.93
Bed 2	14' x 9'10"	4.27 x 3.00
Bed 3	16'9" x 10'6"	2.05 x 3.20
Garage	18'9" x 16'	5.67 x 4.85

BALTIMORE

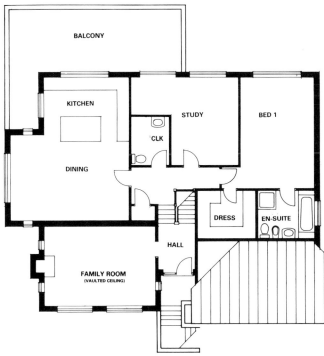

This complex design with many unusual features is based on a home in the USA which was built diagonally across a sloping site.

The mid level entrance shares a vaulted ceiling with the family room, and beyond there are two flights of stairs. One goes up to the kitchen, dining room and study, and the other down to the lounge which has access to the garden. The master bedroom suite is at the upper level and the other two bedrooms are at the other end of the house on the lower level. Having the largest bedroom isolated from the others is very common in new homes across the Atlantic, enabling one partner to murder the other without disturbing the rest of the household.

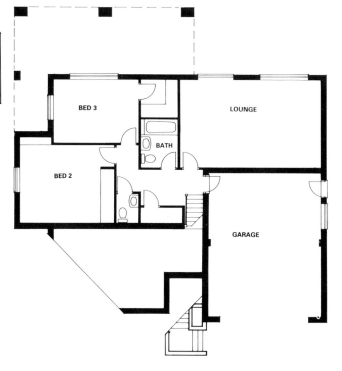

Design Number 92137 Baltimore

Floor Area	2691 sq.ft.	250 sq.m.
Dimensions overall	51'4" x 39'7"	15.64 x 12.08
Lounge	23'1" x 14'1"	7.05 x 4.30
Kitchen	14' x 10'2"	4.26 x 3.10
Dining	19'5" x 12'7"	5.94 x 3.85
Study	17'4" x 14'1"	5.30 x 4.30
Family (Vaulted)	18'2" x 12'7"	5.55 x 3.85
Bed 1	12' x 17'8"	3.65 x 5.40
Dress	9'8" x 7'6"	2.85 x 2.30
Bed 2	15'6" x 12'7"	4.74 x 3.85
Bed 3	14' x 10'2"	4.26 x 3.10
Garage	18'6" x 22'9"	5.65 x 6.95

BECKINGHAM

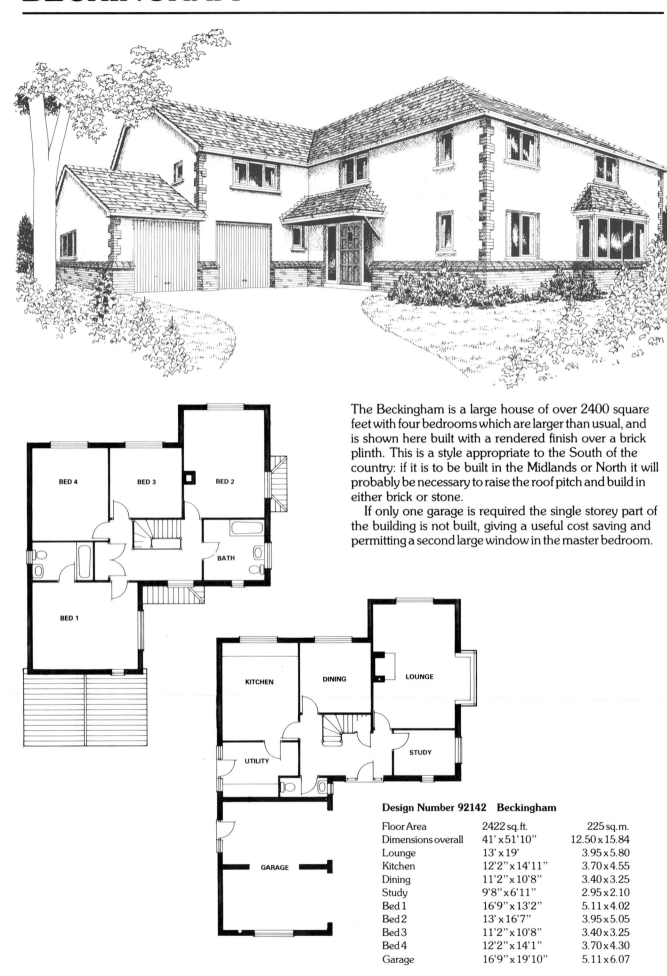

The Beckingham is a large house of over 2400 square feet with four bedrooms which are larger than usual, and is shown here built with a rendered finish over a brick plinth. This is a style appropriate to the South of the country: if it is to be built in the Midlands or North it will probably be necessary to raise the roof pitch and build in either brick or stone.

If only one garage is required the single storey part of the building is not built, giving a useful cost saving and permitting a second large window in the master bedroom.

Design Number 92142   Beckingham

Floor Area	2422 sq. ft.	225 sq. m.
Dimensions overall	41' x 51'10"	12.50 x 15.84
Lounge	13' x 19'	3.95 x 5.80
Kitchen	12'2" x 14'11"	3.70 x 4.55
Dining	11'2" x 10'8"	3.40 x 3.25
Study	9'8" x 6'11"	2.95 x 2.10
Bed 1	16'9" x 13'2"	5.11 x 4.02
Bed 2	13' x 16'7"	3.95 x 5.05
Bed 3	11'2" x 10'8"	3.40 x 3.25
Bed 4	12'2" x 14'1"	3.70 x 4.30
Garage	16'9" x 19'10"	5.11 x 6.07

BAMFORD

A four bedroom home that can be built with or without the double garage shown. This is a very popular design concept for a site with the main views to the rear, and gives the feeling of a far larger property than its 1800 square feet. Without the garge it can be built on a plot with a 50 foot frontage.

Note the winding stairs without quarter landings. This means that they take up less of the hall than they otherwise would. If quarter landings are preferred, possibly to suit an elderly person, then the whole hall area will have to be redesigned.

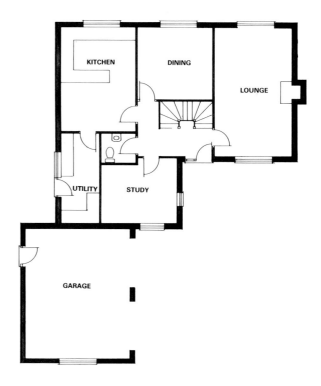

Design Number 92141 Bamford

Floor Area	1841 sq.ft.	171 sq.m.
Dimensions overall	46'1" x 52'8"	14.06 x 16.05
Lounge	12'6" x 19'8"	3.80 x 6.00
Kitchen/Breakfast	11'10" x 16'1"	3.63 x 4.90
Dining	12' x 11'	3.65 x 3.35
Utility	6' x 13'7"	1.83 x 4.15
Study	12'2" x 10'	3.70 x 3.05
Bed 1	11'10" x 16'1"	3.63 x 4.90
Bed 2	12' x 11'	3.65 x 3.35
Bed 3	12'6" x 10'6"	3.80 x 3.20
Bed 4	9'2" x 8'10"	2.80 x 2.70
Garage	16'11" x 20'	5.16 x 6.10

FRESHFORD

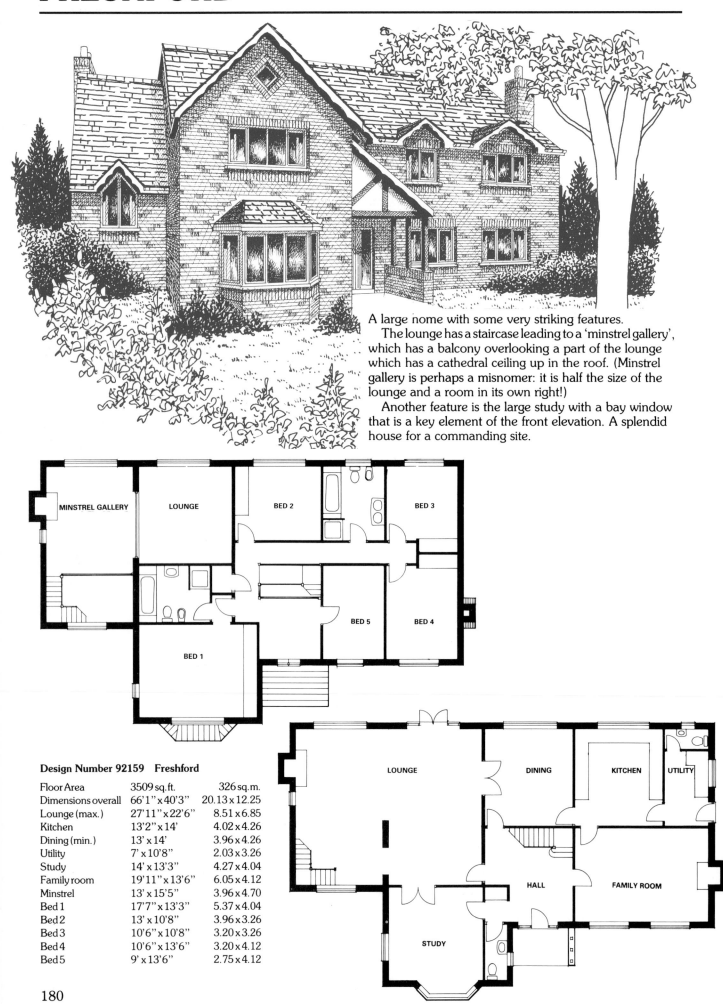

A large nome with some very striking features.

The lounge has a staircase leading to a 'minstrel gallery', which has a balcony overlooking a part of the lounge which has a cathedral ceiling up in the roof. (Minstrel gallery is perhaps a misnomer: it is half the size of the lounge and a room in its own right!)

Another feature is the large study with a bay window that is a key element of the front elevation. A splendid house for a commanding site.

Design Number 92159   Freshford

Floor Area	3509 sq.ft.	326 sq.m.
Dimensions overall	66'1" x 40'3"	20.13 x 12.25
Lounge (max.)	27'11" x 22'6"	8.51 x 6.85
Kitchen	13'2" x 14'	4.02 x 4.26
Dining (min.)	13' x 14'	3.96 x 4.26
Utility	7' x 10'8"	2.03 x 3.26
Study	14' x 13'3"	4.27 x 4.04
Family room	19'11" x 13'6"	6.05 x 4.12
Minstrel	13' x 15'5"	3.96 x 4.70
Bed 1	17'7" x 13'3"	5.37 x 4.04
Bed 2	13' x 10'8"	3.96 x 3.26
Bed 3	10'6" x 10'8"	3.20 x 3.26
Bed 4	10'6" x 13'6"	3.20 x 4.12
Bed 5	9' x 13'6"	2.75 x 4.12

180

BILLINGHURST

The Billinghurst is a compact four bedroom house of 1670 square feet with the feel of a much larger property. In particular, the large open front porch and the stairs with a gallery around three sides are impressive features. Like all half timbered buildings, the detailing has to be in accordance with the local regional style, and in many areas this house would be built with a knee high plinth to the brickwork as on the inset sketch.

Design Number 92124   Billinghurst

Floor Area	1670 sq.ft.	155 sq.m.
Dimensions overall	36'10" x 32'7"	11.24 x 9.93
Lounge	12' x 22'1"	3.65 x 6.74
Kitchen	12'1" x 12'	3.69 x 3.65
Dining	10'4" x 12'	3.15 x 3.65
Bed 1	12' x 12'	3.65 x 3.65
Bed 2	12' x 9'9"	3.65 x 2.99
Bed 3	10'4" x 12'	3.15 x 3.65
Bed 4	12'1" x 13'5"	3.69 x 4.10
Garage	11'6" x 18'	3.51 x 5.48

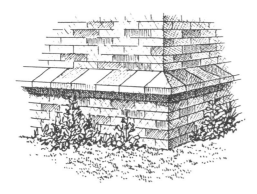

D & M INDIVIDUAL DESIGN 92310

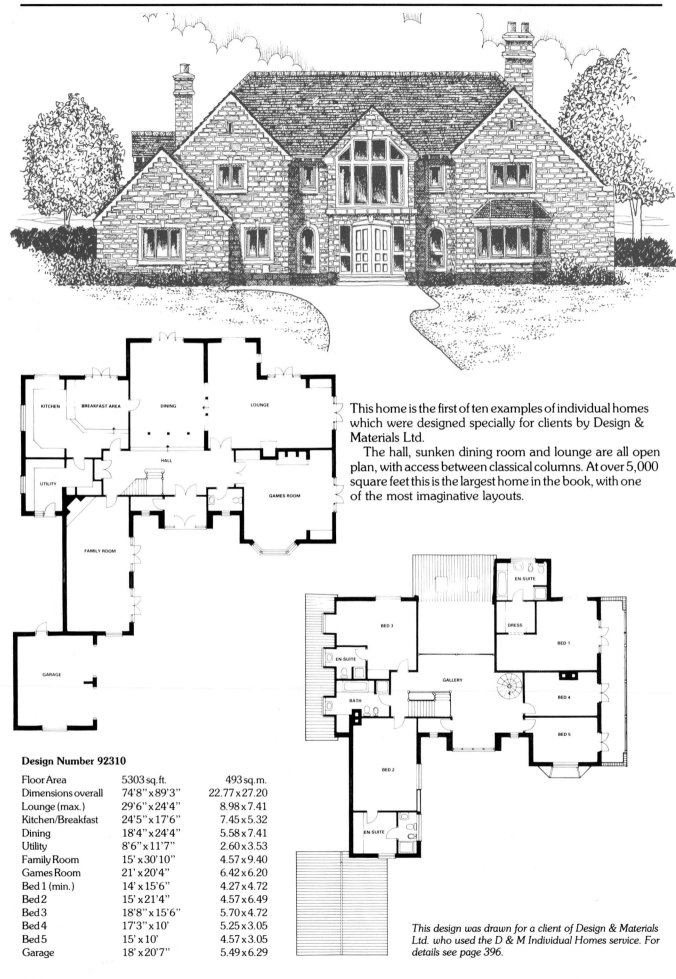

This home is the first of ten examples of individual homes which were designed specially for clients by Design & Materials Ltd.

The hall, sunken dining room and lounge are all open plan, with access between classical columns. At over 5,000 square feet this is the largest home in the book, with one of the most imaginative layouts.

Design Number 92310

Floor Area	5303 sq. ft.	493 sq. m.
Dimensions overall	74'8" x 89'3"	22.77 x 27.20
Lounge (max.)	29'6" x 24'4"	8.98 x 7.41
Kitchen/Breakfast	24'5" x 17'6"	7.45 x 5.32
Dining	18'4" x 24'4"	5.58 x 7.41
Utility	8'6" x 11'7"	2.60 x 3.53
Family Room	15' x 30'10"	4.57 x 9.40
Games Room	21' x 20'4"	6.42 x 6.20
Bed 1 (min.)	14' x 15'6"	4.27 x 4.72
Bed 2	15' x 21'4"	4.57 x 6.49
Bed 3	18'8" x 15'6"	5.70 x 4.72
Bed 4	17'3" x 10'	5.25 x 3.05
Bed 5	15' x 10'	4.57 x 3.05
Garage	18' x 20'7"	5.49 x 6.29

This design was drawn for a client of Design & Materials Ltd. who used the D & M Individual Homes service. For details see page 396.

D & M INDIVIDUAL DESIGN 92308

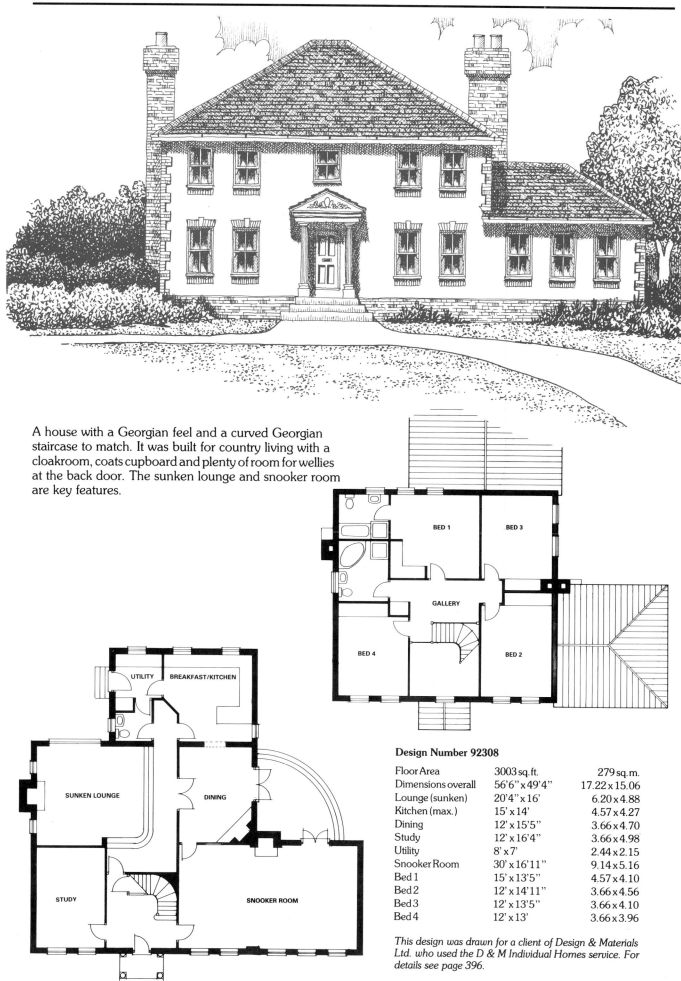

A house with a Georgian feel and a curved Georgian staircase to match. It was built for country living with a cloakroom, coats cupboard and plenty of room for wellies at the back door. The sunken lounge and snooker room are key features.

Design Number 92308

Floor Area	3003 sq.ft.	279 sq.m.
Dimensions overall	56'6" x 49'4"	17.22 x 15.06
Lounge (sunken)	20'4" x 16'	6.20 x 4.88
Kitchen (max.)	15' x 14'	4.57 x 4.27
Dining	12' x 15'5"	3.66 x 4.70
Study	12' x 16'4"	3.66 x 4.98
Utility	8' x 7'	2.44 x 2.15
Snooker Room	30' x 16'11"	9.14 x 5.16
Bed 1	15' x 13'5"	4.57 x 4.10
Bed 2	12' x 14'11"	3.66 x 4.56
Bed 3	12' x 13'5"	3.66 x 4.10
Bed 4	12' x 13'	3.66 x 3.96

This design was drawn for a client of Design & Materials Ltd. who used the D & M Individual Homes service. For details see page 396.

D & M INDIVIDUAL DESIGN 92305

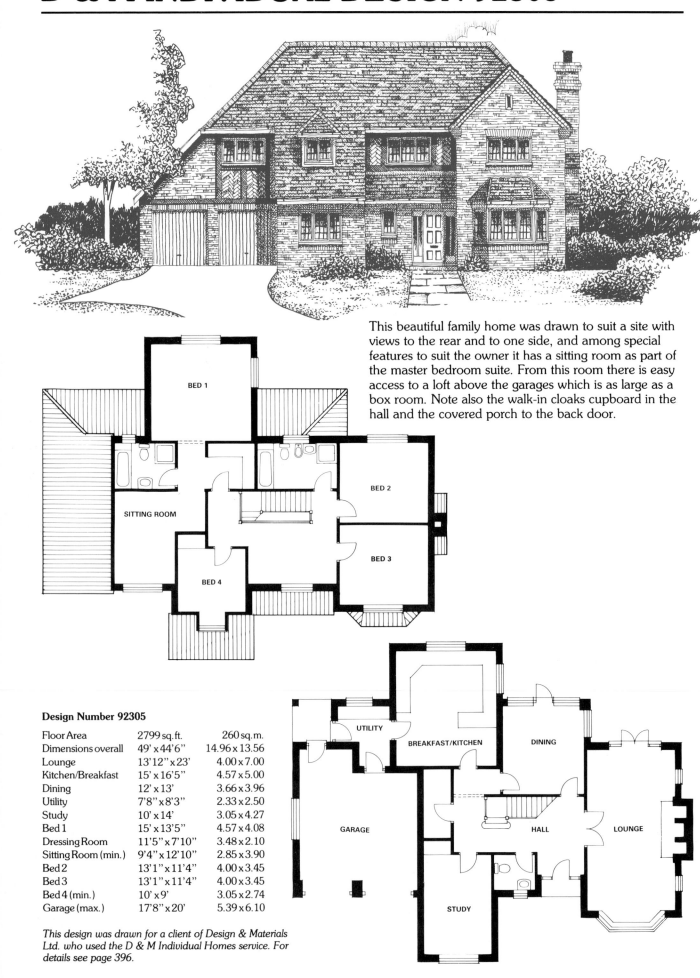

This beautiful family home was drawn to suit a site with views to the rear and to one side, and among special features to suit the owner it has a sitting room as part of the master bedroom suite. From this room there is easy access to a loft above the garages which is as large as a box room. Note also the walk-in cloaks cupboard in the hall and the covered porch to the back door.

Design Number 92305

Floor Area	2799 sq. ft.	260 sq. m.
Dimensions overall	49' x 44'6"	14.96 x 13.56
Lounge	13'12" x 23'	4.00 x 7.00
Kitchen/Breakfast	15' x 16'5"	4.57 x 5.00
Dining	12' x 13'	3.66 x 3.96
Utility	7'8" x 8'3"	2.33 x 2.50
Study	10' x 14'	3.05 x 4.27
Bed 1	15' x 13'5"	4.57 x 4.08
Dressing Room	11'5" x 7'10"	3.48 x 2.10
Sitting Room (min.)	9'4" x 12'10"	2.85 x 3.90
Bed 2	13'1" x 11'4"	4.00 x 3.45
Bed 3	13'1" x 11'4"	4.00 x 3.45
Bed 4 (min.)	10' x 9'	3.05 x 2.74
Garage (max.)	17'8" x 20'	5.39 x 6.10

This design was drawn for a client of Design & Materials Ltd. who used the D & M Individual Homes service. For details see page 396.

D & M INDIVIDUAL DESIGN 92307

This is the only bungalow among the individual designs from Design & Materials in this book, and has a distinctive copper roof to the lounge which is a bold and unusual feature on the front elevation. The lounge ceiling is raised to suit it, giving the room the feel of a conservatory while being an integral part of the structure.

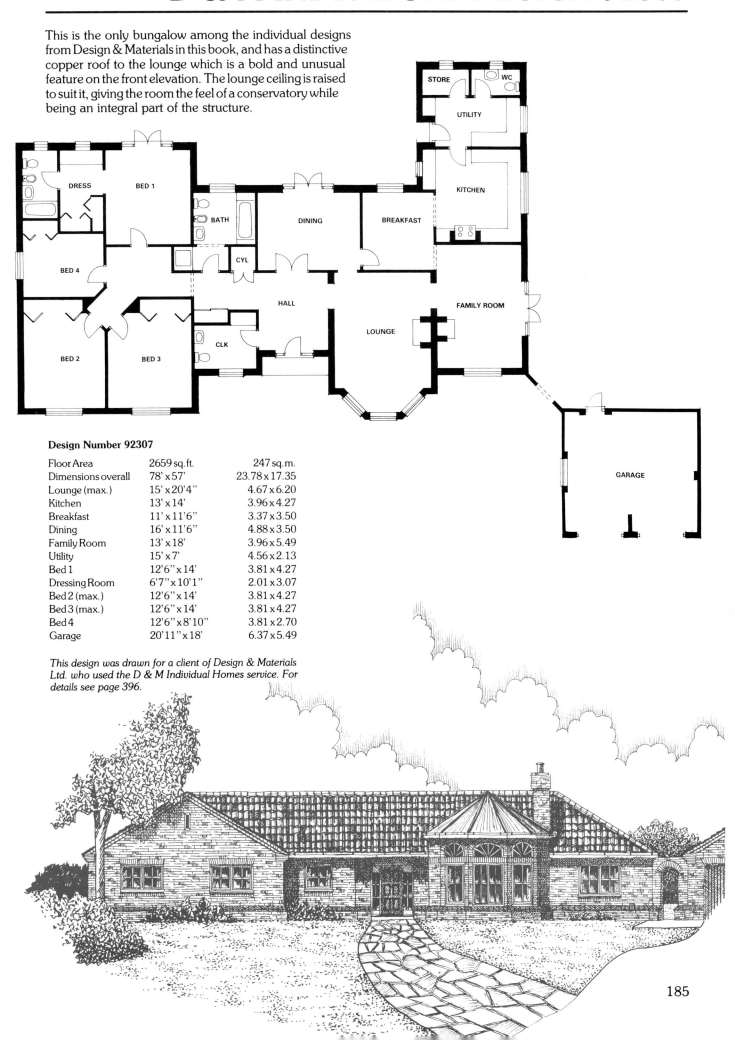

Design Number 92307

Floor Area	2659 sq.ft.	247 sq.m.
Dimensions overall	78' x 57'	23.78 x 17.35
Lounge (max.)	15' x 20'4"	4.67 x 6.20
Kitchen	13' x 14'	3.96 x 4.27
Breakfast	11' x 11'6"	3.37 x 3.50
Dining	16' x 11'6"	4.88 x 3.50
Family Room	13' x 18'	3.96 x 5.49
Utility	15' x 7'	4.56 x 2.13
Bed 1	12'6" x 14'	3.81 x 4.27
Dressing Room	6'7" x 10'1"	2.01 x 3.07
Bed 2 (max.)	12'6" x 14'	3.81 x 4.27
Bed 3 (max.)	12'6" x 14'	3.81 x 4.27
Bed 4	12'6" x 8'10"	3.81 x 2.70
Garage	20'11" x 18'	6.37 x 5.49

This design was drawn for a client of Design & Materials Ltd. who used the D & M Individual Homes service. For details see page 396.

D & M INDIVIDUAL DESIGN 92303

An interesting five bedroomed house with a hip roof that gives a striking front elevation.

Considerable care has to be taken in selecting the tiles for a roof as large as this, with a choice to be made between cost effective interlocking tiles and very expensive small plain tiles.

Design Number 92303

Floor Area	2900 sq.ft.	269 sq.m.
Dimensions overall	66'8" x 31'3"	20.33 x 9.52
Lounge	22'10" x 17'1"	6.94 x 5.20
Kitchen/Breakfast	17'6" x 17'1"	5.33 x 5.20
Dining	14' x 12'	4.27 x 3.66
Utility	7'10" x 10'	2.40 x 3.05
Study	12'8" x 8'	3.86 x 2.44
Play Den	16'6" x 12'	5.03 x 3.66
Bed 1	15' x 17'1"	4.57 x 5.20
Bed 2	14'3" x 10'7"	4.33 x 3.23
Bed 3	14' x 10'	4.27 x 3.05
Bed 4	10'1" x 9'	3.07 x 2.74
Bed 5	12'8" x 8'	3.86 x 2.44

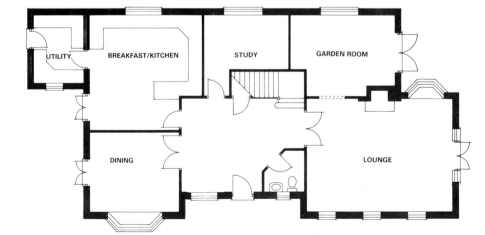

This design was drawn for a client of Design & Materials Ltd. who used the D & M Individual Homes service. For details see page 396.

D & M INDIVIDUAL DESIGN 92306

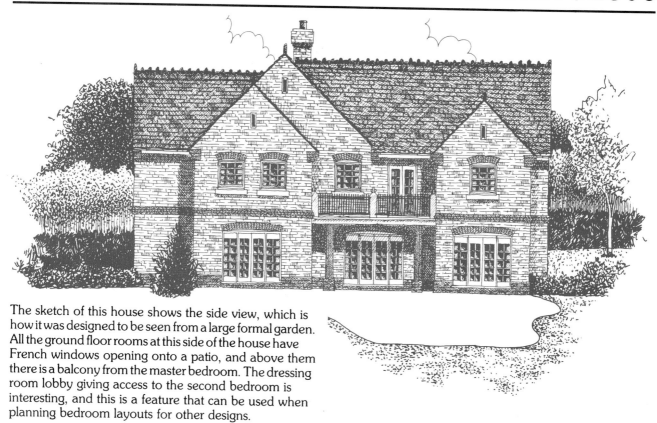

The sketch of this house shows the side view, which is how it was designed to be seen from a large formal garden. All the ground floor rooms at this side of the house have French windows opening onto a patio, and above them there is a balcony from the master bedroom. The dressing room lobby giving access to the second bedroom is interesting, and this is a feature that can be used when planning bedroom layouts for other designs.

Design Number 92306

Floor Area	3353 sq. ft.	312 sq. m.
Dimensions overall	51' x 55'6"	15.53 x 16.91
Lounge (max.)	18'4" x 17'6"	5.59 x 5.33
Kitchen/Breakfast	23'7" x 13"	7.19 x 3.96
Dining	18' x 14'	5.49 x 4.27
Study	10' x 12'	3.05 x 3.66
Family Room	14' x 16'	4.27 x 4.89
Bed 1	14' x 18'	4.27 x 5.49
Bed 2 (max.)	16' x 11'7"	4.88 x 3.53
Bed 3	18' x 14'	5.49 x 4.27
Bed 4	15' x 13'	4.57 x 3.96
Bed 5	10' x 12'	3.05 x 3.66
Bed 6	12'2" x 8'	3.70 x 2.44

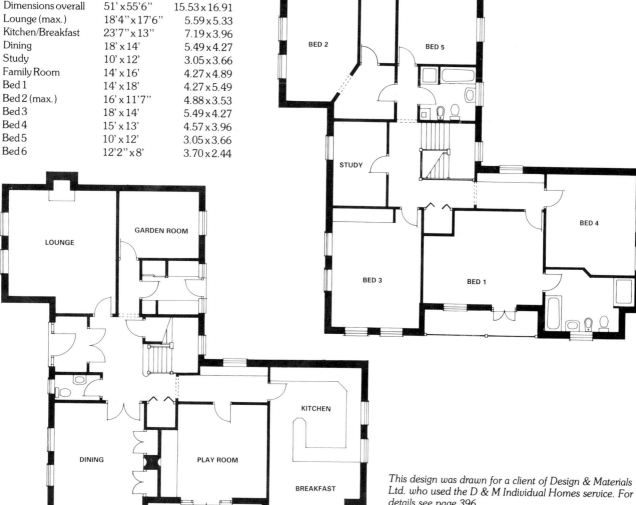

This design was drawn for a client of Design & Materials Ltd. who used the D & M Individual Homes service. For details see page 396.

D & M INDIVIDUAL DESIGN 92302

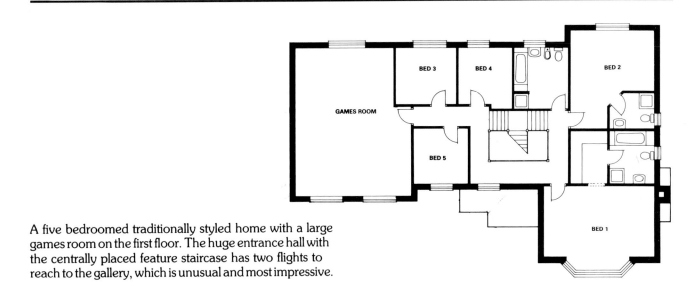

A five bedroomed traditionally styled home with a large games room on the first floor. The huge entrance hall with the centrally placed feature staircase has two flights to reach to the gallery, which is unusual and most impressive.

Design Number 92302

Floor Area	3660 sq.ft.	340 sq.m.
Dimensions overall	68'5" x 43'2"	20.87 x 13.16
Lounge (max.)	20' x 22'	6.10 x 6.70
Kitchen/Breakfast	20'1" x 10'6"	6.13 x 3.20
Dining	15' x 17'1"	4.57 x 5.20
Utility	10'2" x 9'10"	3.10 x 3.00
Study	9' x 13'4"	2.75 x 4.06
Games Room (max.)	21'2" x 25'8"	6.46 x 7.83
Bed 1	20' x 12'7"	6.10 x 3.84
Bed 2	15' x 17'1"	4.57 x 5.20
Bed 3	10'9" x 9'10"	3.28 x 3.00
Bed 4	9'9" x 10'6"	2.98 x 3.20
Bed 5	9'7" x 9'8"	2.93 x 2.96
Garage (max.)	21'2" x 25'8"	6.46 x 7.83

188

This design was drawn for a client of Design & Materials Ltd. who used the D & M Individual Homes service. For details see page 396.

D & M INDIVIDUAL DESIGN 92304

Design Number 92304

Floor Area	3190 sq. ft.	296 sq. m.
Dimensions overall	68'11" x 58'3"	21.00 x 17.60
Lounge	18' x 24'	5.49 x 7.32
Kitchen/Breakfast	19'9" x 12'8"	6.03 x 3.87
Dining	15' x 13'	4.57 x 3.96
Utility	20' x 8'	6.00 x 2.40
Family Room	16' x 11'	4.88 x 3.35
Office	12' x 10'	3.66 x 3.05
Bed 1	18' x 15'	5.49 x 4.57
Bed 2	10' x 13'	3.05 x 3.96
Bed 3	12'5" x 10'	3.79 x 3.05
Snooker Room	16' x 24'4"	4.88 x 7.42
Garage	18' x 20'8"	5.49 x 6.30

Another house with a snooker room from which there is access to the balcony over the utility room. Note the self-contained office suite adjacent to the front door and the sauna in the master bedroom suite.

This design was drawn for a client of Design & Materials Ltd. who used the D & M Individual Homes service. For details see page 396.

D & M INDIVIDUAL DESIGN 92309

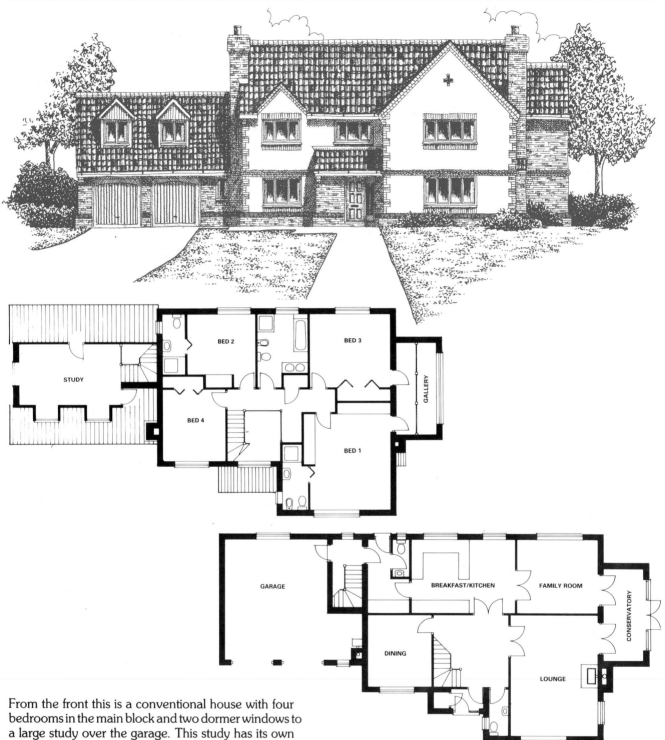

From the front this is a conventional house with four bedrooms in the main block and two dormer windows to a large study over the garage. This study has its own staircase from the back porch.

On the south side of the house there are some very original features. The projecting sun room on the ground floor has a window which is virtually a glass wall reaching up the full height of the building, and there is a first floor gallery projecting into it from two of the bedrooms. Access from the bedrooms to the gallery are shown through standard single doors, but a gallery like this can be arranged in many ways, and sliding glass doors from at least one of the bedrooms is an interesting alternative.

This design was drawn for a client of Design & Materials Ltd. who used the D & M Individual Homes service. For details see page 396.

Design Number 92309

Floor Area	2918 sq.ft.	272 sq.m.
Dimensions overall	75'2" x 34'2"	22.90 x 10.42
Lounge	15' x 20'	4.57 x 6.10
Kitchen/Breakfast	18' x 12'	5.49 x 3.66
Dining	11' x 12'	3.35 x 3.66
Family Room	14' x 12'	4.27 x 3.66
Sun Room	7' x 15'3"	2.13 x 4.69
Bed 1 (max.)	15' x 16'1"	4.57 x 4.90
Bed 2	11'11" x 12'	2.64 x 3.66
Bed 3	14' x 12'	4.27 x 3.66
Bed 4	11' x 12'	3.35 x 3.66
Study	18'2" x 10'	5.53 x 3.05
Garage (max.)	24'4" x 20'	7.41 x 6.10

190

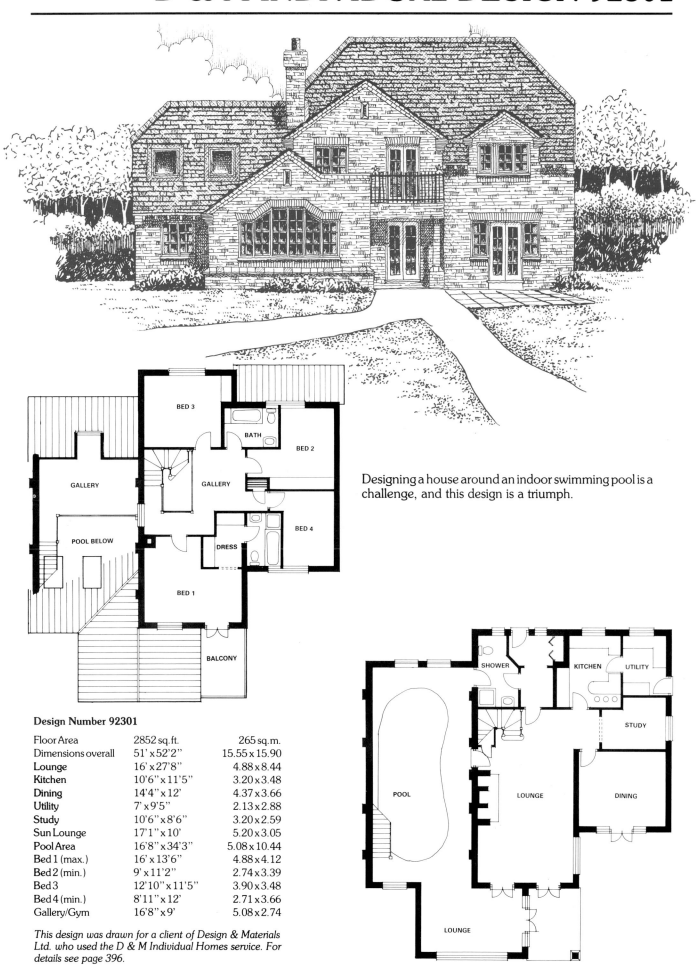

Designing a house around an indoor swimming pool is a challenge, and this design is a triumph.

Design Number 92301

Floor Area	2852 sq. ft.	265 sq. m.
Dimensions overall	51' x 52'2"	15.55 x 15.90
Lounge	16' x 27'8"	4.88 x 8.44
Kitchen	10'6" x 11'5"	3.20 x 3.48
Dining	14'4" x 12'	4.37 x 3.66
Utility	7' x 9'5"	2.13 x 2.88
Study	10'6" x 8'6"	3.20 x 2.59
Sun Lounge	17'1" x 10'	5.20 x 3.05
Pool Area	16'8" x 34'3"	5.08 x 10.44
Bed 1 (max.)	16' x 13'6"	4.88 x 4.12
Bed 2 (min.)	9' x 11'2"	2.74 x 3.39
Bed 3	12'10" x 11'5"	3.90 x 3.48
Bed 4 (min.)	8'11" x 12'	2.71 x 3.66
Gallery/Gym	16'8" x 9'	5.08 x 2.74

This design was drawn for a client of Design & Materials Ltd. who used the D & M Individual Homes service. For details see page 396.

191

HARBURY

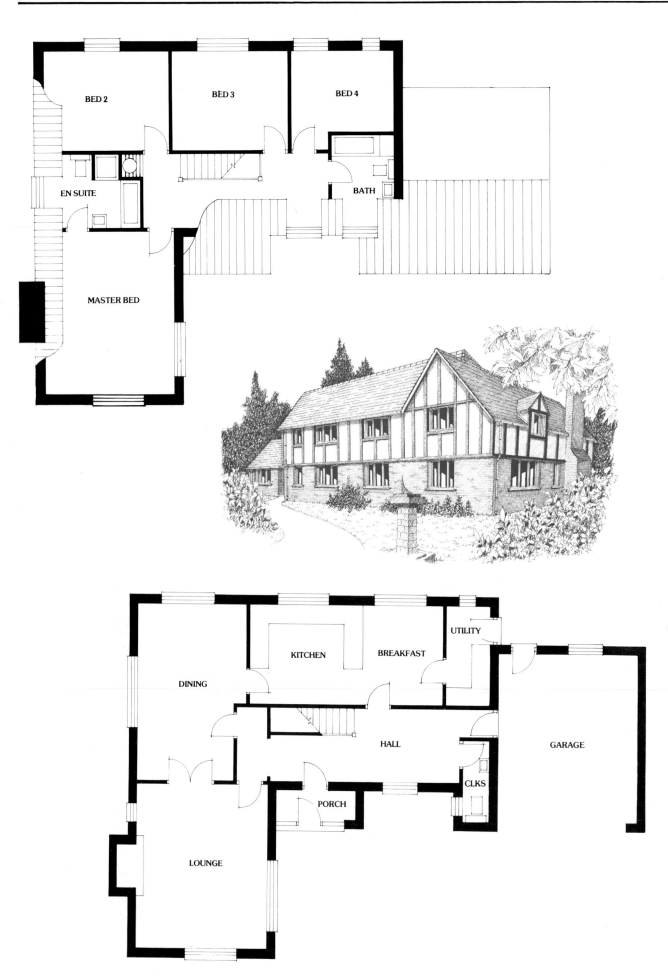

BED 2

BED 3

BED 4

EN SUITE

BATH

MASTER BED

KITCHEN

BREAKFAST

UTILITY

DINING

HALL

GARAGE

CLKS

PORCH

LOUNGE

The new Harbury design has a very large hall and a large landing, reflecting todays concern that the front door of a substantial house should lead into an imposing hall, with appropriate furnishings. A window in the hall which is well separated from the door helps to give just this effect, and the stairs are intended to be a key feature, perhaps made in oak or other hardwood.

A home for a generous plot of land, in an area to suit either the half timbering which is shown, or with tile hanging to the first floor.

Design Number 84501

Floor Area		
(exc. garage)	2088 sq.ft.	194 sq.m.
Dimensions overall		
(inc. garage)	58'8'' x 39'6''	17.88 x 12.04
Lounge	18'0'' x 15'0''	5486 x 4572
Dining	19'4'' x 12'6''	5891 x 3810
Kitchen	11'0'' x 13'0''	3353 x 3962
Breakfast	9'0'' x 11'0''	2743 x 3353
Utility	5'0'' x 11'0''	1524 x 3353
Garage	18'0'' x 15'9''	5486 x 4805
Master Bed	18'0'' x 15'0''	5486 x 4572
Bed 2	11'0'' x 15'0''	3353 x 4572
Bed 3	13'0'' x 11'0''	3962 x 3353
Bed 4	11'6'' x 11'0''	3505 x 3353

NETHERBURY

There is another version of this design known as the Netherbury, reference 84502, which has a study between the lounge and dining room.

RUFFORD

This new 1984 farmhouse design is very adaptable and sure to become a favourite. It has the huge farmhouse kitchen and family room which is wanted by so many who build in the country, and this can be fitted out in many ways to suit the family concerned. There are four generous bedrooms and a single large family bathroom: if required a second bathroom can be provided at the end of the corridor, and another small gable window put in the front elevation to light the landing.

Design Number 84503

Floor Area	1787 sq. ft.	166 sq. m.
Dimensions overall	43'8'' x 36'5½''	13.30 x 11.11
Lounge	18'6'' x 13'0''	5638 x 3962
Family Room	17'3½'' x 13'0''	5267 x 3962
Dining	12'0'' x 9'8''	3650 x 2951
Kitchen	17'0'' x 13'0''	5182 x 3962
Bed 1	17'0'' x 13'0''	5182 x 3962
Bed 2	13'0'' x 10'8½''	3962 x 3267
Bed 3	11'2'' x 13'0''	3404 x 3962
Bed 4	10'0'' x 9'8''	3050 x 2951

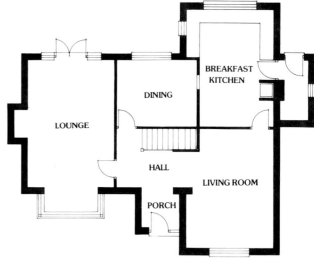

The Heathfields design is shown illustrated with a porch roof extending across the front of the building, supported on feature gallows brackets on either side of the dining room windows. This is a house for those who like big rooms, and has a particularly large en-suite bathroom with a separate shower and bath. This is something which is becoming increasingly popular, and there is a growing tendancy to require that the bathroom in the master suite should be at least as large and well equipped as the family bathroom. After all — who pays for the house!

Design Number 84504

Floor Area		
(exc. porch)	2109 sq. ft.	196 sq. m.
Dimensions overall	48'2" x 28'0"	14.68 x 8.54
Lounge	26'2" x 15'0"	7975 x 4572
Dining	11'6" x 13'0"	3500 x 3962
Kitchen	13'0" x 9'2"	3962 x 2800
Utility	10'0" x 6'0"	3050 x 1830
Master Bed	14'0" x 13'0"	4267 x 3962
Bed 2	14'0" x 15'0"	4267 x 4572
Bed 3	15'0" x 11'10"	4572 x 3598
Bed 4	13'9" x 9'4½"	4184 x 2862

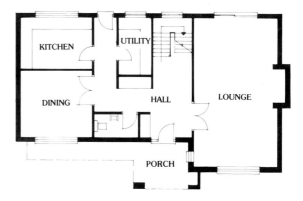

BROOKFIELD

Another version of the Heathfields features a farmhouse kitchen with a generous dining area, and a separate study replacing part of the former dining room. This is known as the Brookfield, reference 84505, and is particularly suited to those living in the country.

DOVEDALE

The Dovedale is a "four level" design for a sloping site — the garage is below, up six steps to the front door, up a half landing to the master bedroom suite, and then up again to the other four bedrooms and main bathroom

Although originally designed for a site in Somerset, where it was built in 1983, this house was named Dovedale by the architect because it is so typical of many new houses which we design for the Peak District, where most sites are sloping! It has a very practical layout for a large home, and is sure to be built in many different parts of the country.

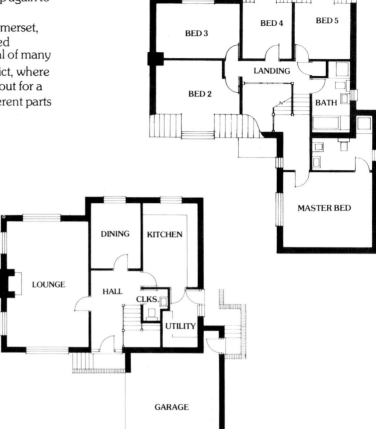

Design Number 84505

Floor Area

(inc. garage)	2291 sq.ft.	212 sq.m.
Dimensions overall	40'3" x 47'6½"	12.26 x 14.49
Lounge	22'4" x 15'1"	6800 x 4600
Dining	8'10" x 11'10"	2700 x 3598
Kitchen	9'10" x 14'11"	3000 x 4548
Utility	10'4" x 6'7"	3152 x 2000
Garage	19'2" x 15'9"	5850 x 4800
Master Bed	15'9" x 13'1½"	4800 x 4000
Bed 2	15'1" x 12'5½"	4600 x 3800
Bed 3	15'1" x 9'6"	4600 x 2900
Bed 4	12'9½" x 8'10"	3900 x 2700
Bed 5	12'9½" x 9'10"	3900 x 3000

The Norton house provides a lot of accommodation in less than 1700 sq. ft., and can be built either with or without the garage as required. This gives scope for the garage to be added at a later date.

The dormer windows to the bedrooms give an attractive period appearance to the rear elevation, or if required the drawings for this design can be altered to raise the roof to the main building by 3 ft., with the soffit at the head of the windows and small dormer roofs above. This allows trussed rafters to be used, and saves on construction costs.

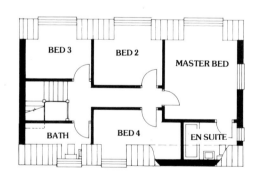

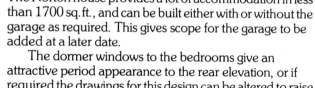

Design Number 84507

Floor Area (exc.garage)	1680 sq.ft.	156 sq.m.
Dimensions overall	48'3½'' x 47'5''	14.72 x 14.45
Lounge	20'0'' x 12'0''	6096 x 3658
Study	10'0'' x 8'0''	3048 x 2438
Dining	12'0'' x 10'0''	3658 x 3048
Living Room	10'0'' x 13'3''	3048 x 4048
Kitchen	17'0'' x 13'0''	5182 x 3962
Garage	17'0'' x 18'5''	5182 x 5620
Master Bed	11'0'' x 14'1''	3348 x 4296
Bed 2	11'0'' x 9'0''	3358 x 2743
Bed 3	10'0'' x 8'0''	3048 x 2438
Bed 4	13'6'' x 7'4''	4100 x 2253

ASHBOURNE

This house was designed in 1983 for a site in the Peak National Park; hence the name. The use of stone, with traditional stone window surrounds and stone tabling to the gables gives it a very expensive look, but it is a straight-forward property to build, and the construction costs should reflect this. As usual with our 1983 designs, the hall is large, with a feature staircase facing the front door. The generous ground floor accommodation, with a lounge, living room, dining room and study makes this an ideal family home.

ELDERSTONE

The Elderstone is a sister design which has a large garage and workshop replacing the lounge shown here, and within the same 'shell' features a drawing room in place of the living and dining rooms of the Ashbourne. The study illustrated here becomes the dining room. The reference number of the Elderstone is 84509.

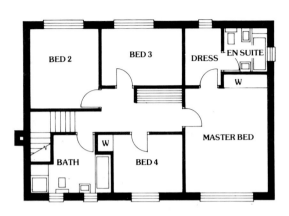

Design Number 84508

Floor Area	1937 sq. ft.	180 sq. m.
Dimensions overall	49'4½" x 29'0"	15.05 x 8.8
Lounge	23'5" x 12'0"	7140 x 3658
Living Room	10'0" x 11'6"	3048 x 3500
Dining	12'0" x 14'7"	3648 x 4450
Kitchen	12'0" x 12'0"	3658 x 3658
Study	12'0" x 8'6"	3648 x 2590
Master Bed	14'9" x 12'0"	4490 x 3658
Bed 2	10'0" x 11'6"	3048 x 3500
Bed 3	12'0" x 8'4"	3648 x 2550
Bed 4	10'4" x 8'4"	3096 x 2540

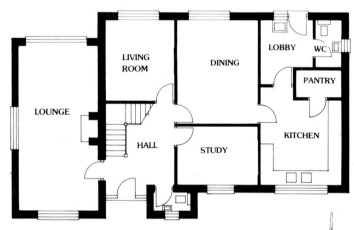

MARLBOROUGH

The Marlborough design is a house with a period appearance, and the period feel goes with a layout where the hall is a room in its own right. The lounge, dining room, kitchen and all four bedrooms look out to the rear, and this is definitely a home where the main garden and the principal view are on the opposite side of the building from the access.

This is a simple and straightforward building to construct, and is one of a number of new designs introduced in 1984 with seemingly complex roofs based on the use of trussed rafters to give very cost effective construction.

Design Number 84510

Floor Area

(exc. garage)	1959 sq. ft.	182 sq.m.
Dimensions overall	45'0'' x 48'2''	13.72 x 14.67
Lounge	20'0'' x 14'0''	6100 x 4266
Dining	12'0'' x 10'8½''	3658 x 3266
Kitchen	10'6'' x 14'0''	3200 x 4266
Utility	10'6'' x 7'0''	3200 x 2134
Study	10'0'' x 9'0''	3050 x 2743
Garages (each)	18'0'' x 10'3½''	5486 x 3132
Master Bed	12'0'' x 15'0''	3658 x 4570
Bed 2	10'0'' x 14'0''	3050 x 4266
Bed 3	9'8'' x 14'0''	2950 x 4266
Bed 4	10'6'' x 11'6''	3200 x 3500

LOXLEY

Design Number 84512

Floor Area	2615 sq.ft.	243 sq.m.
Dimensions overall	47'7'' x 38'6''	14.50 x 11.73
Lounge	17'2'' x 24'0''	5240 x 7315
Dining	10'7'' x 14'0''	3234 x 4267
Kitchen/Breakfast	16'4'' x 12'0''	4986 x 3667
Study	12'0'' x 11'4''	3658 x 3464
Utility	7'3'' x 11'1''	2216 x 3373
Master Bed	16'4'' x 14'0''	4986 x 4267
Bed 2	10'7'' x 12'0''	3234 x 3667
Bed 3	10'7'' x 13'4''	3240 x 4056
Games Room	17'2'' x 23'0''	5240 x 7017

This large half timbered home is in the Manor House style which is once again popular for large sites and country settings. It is shown here as drawn for a site in Derbyshire where a large games room big enough for a billiards table was required on the first floor, with a window to take advantage of the spectacular view. A more conventional use of this space would be to provide two more bedrooms, and this can be easily arranged as in our Maplehurst design, reference 84531

The large inglenook fireplace is very much in character, as is the staircase with two quarter landings that winds around one end of the hall. A prestige house for a prestige site.

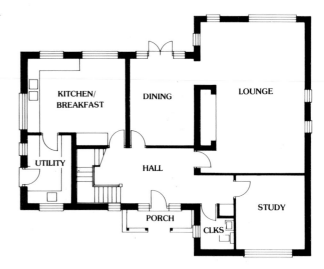

BURFORD

This is a condensed version of our very popular Cotswold design, and should prove to be just as popular. Although it is only 1560 sq. ft. it has all the essential features of the larger design — a big hall with a feature staircase at one end, a through lounge with views to both front and rear, and a large farmhouse kitchen.

The kitchen area can be altered in many different ways provided that the feature pillar is retained, as this provides support for a wall above, and there is room for a small study if required. Our architects have been concerned with many variants of the basic design, and their advice is readily available.

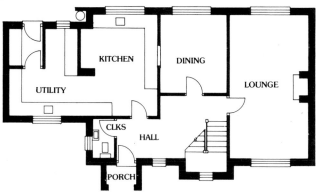

Design Number 84513

Floor Area	1560 sq. ft.	145 sq. m.
Dimensions overall	47'0" x 26'6½"	14.32 x 8.09
Lounge	12'0" x 21'0"	3658 x 6405
Dining	10'0" x 11'6"	3048 x 3505
Kitchen	12'0" x 15'1"	3658 x 4605
Utility	10'6" x 6'11"	3200 x 2100
Breakfast Area	4'11" x 7'0"	1500 x 2134
Master Bed	10'6" x 12'8"	3196 x 3867
Bed 2	12'0" x 11'0"	3658 x 3353
Bed 3	12'0" x 9'8"	3658 x 2952
Bed 4	10'6" x 8'0"	3196 x 2438

HENLEY

BED 5

BED 4

BED 3

BED 4

BED 2

STUDY

DINING

KITCHEN

UTILITY

LOUNGE

HALL

PLAYROOM

CLKS

Another new design for 1984 with four reception rooms and five bedrooms in only 2200 sq.ft. It was specifically drawn to be built with tudor half timbering to the first floor, but it can be constructed in other materials to suit a local style provided that care is taken over the details. We will be pleased to advise on this.

The illustration shows a front door frame with narrow vertical lights on either side of the door: it is interesting how this style of frame suits both traditional and ultra-modern homes. However, it does mean that the letter box is set either in the door or in a wall adjacent to the frame rather than in the frame itself. The latter is more popular.

Design Number 84514

Floor Area	2195 sq. ft.	204 sq. m.
Dimensions overall	45'3'' x 34'3½''	14.09 x 10.45
Lounge	13'0'' x 20'4''	3962 x 6196
Dining	14'0'' x 12'0''	4267 x 3658
Study	10'0'' x 8'0''	3050 x 2438
Playroom	11'0'' x 11'4''	3353 x 3450
Kitchen	14'0'' x 10'0''	4267 x 3050
Utility	9'5'' x 10'0''	2870 x 3050
Bed 1	14'0'' x 12'0''	4267 x 3658
Bed 2	11'0'' x 11'4''	3353 x 3450
Bed 3	14'0'' x 10'0''	4267 x 3050
Bed 4	11'0'' x 9'8½''	3353 x 2962
Bed 5	10'0'' x 8'0''	3050 x 2438

RAINFORD

The Rainford was specially designed as a large house to be
built on a relatively narrow plot. It was originally
drawn for a situation where there was no access to any
kitchen door down the right hand side of the building, and
this determined the position of the back door as shewn.
The drawings are easily altered to shew a door directly into
the kitchen, and the kitchen itself is quite big enough for a
washing machine and deep freezer so that the utility room
can become a cloakroom if required.

The morning room is an 'optional extra' which can be
built at a later stage or together with the rest of the building.

Design Number 84515

Floor Area	2012 sq.ft.	187 sq.m.
Dimensions overall	49'10'' x 34'5''	15.19 x 10.50
Lounge	11'6'' x 21'0''	3500 x 6400
Kitchen	10'0'' x 15'9''	3050 x 4800
Morning Room	14'0'' x 9'3''	4267 x 2800
Garage	10'6'' x 17'6½''	3200 x 5350
Master Bed	11'0'' x 17'8''	3350 x 5400
Bed 2	11'6'' x 18'8''	3500 x 5700
Bed 3	11'0'' x 11'6''	3353 x 3500
Bed 4	14'0'' x 9'0''	4267 x 2750

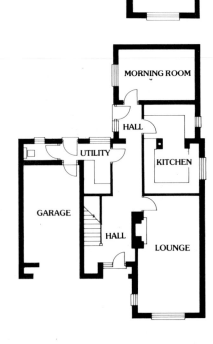

ESKDALE

The Eskdale is one of our designs that always manages to look larger than it really is, and it has an interesting and unusual layout. The lounge is at the end of a passage, which always helps a house to seem generously proportioned, and the window and fireplace in the lounge can be moved around to suit the views and the site on which the house is to be built.

The two dormer windows are frankly an extravagence, as the main bedroom and the stair well could be lit from gable windows, but they add enormously to the character and the period feel of the building.

This house can easily be built without the garage if desired.

Design Number 84516

Floor Area		
(exc. garage)	1614 sq. ft.	150 sq. m.
Dimensions overall		
(inc. garage)	59'9½" x 25'8½"	18.22 x 7.84
Lounge (max.)	18'0" x 13'6"	5486 x 4116
Dining	11'5" x 12'5½"	3486 x 3800
Kitchen	13'0" x 10'1½"	3962 x 3086
Study	12'0" x 8'6"	3658 x 2590
Garage	18'0" x 18'0"	5486 x 5486
Bed 1 (max.)	18'0" x 13'4½"	5486 x 4078
Bed 2	12'0" x 10'1½"	3658 x 3090
Bed 3	10'1½" x 9'10"	3086 x 3000
Bed 4	8'0" x 10'1½"	2438 x 3086

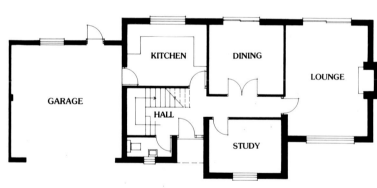

HOLMWOOD

The Holmwood is a country house in the traditional Kent or Sussex style, with rendered walls below a tile hung first floor and a huge inglenook fireplace with its own roof. The rooms are all generous in size, and the hall and landing are particularly large, with windows giving plenty of light and a spacious feel to the whole house.

Design Number 84517

Floor Area	2066 sq. ft.	192 sq.m.
Dimensions overall	48'10'' x 28'11''	14.89 x 8.81
Lounge	23'5'' x 14'0''	7140 x 4267
Dining	14'0'' x 11'1½''	4267 x 3390
Kitchen	13'0'' x 13'1''	3962 x 3990
Study	13'0'' x 10'0''	3962 x 3050
Bed 1	14'0'' x 11'11''	4267 x 3635
Bed 2	14'0'' x 11'6½''	4267 x 3520
Bed 3	14'0'' x 11'6½''	4267 x 3520
Bed 4	13'0'' x 13'1''	3962 x 3990

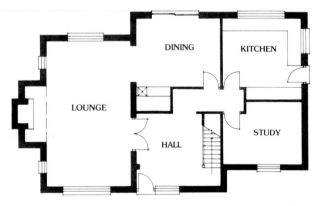

VERWOOD

This striking bungalow with its distinctive arched windows and Hampshire hips to the roof deserves a large site which can be landscaped to suit it, and where the principal views are to the front. It is illustrated with the walls in random stonework, but it would look equally well with a rendered finish and contrasting hardwood joinery, with hardwood barge boards on the gables to match.

This is a design for an outstanding site but in spite of all its character it is relatively inexpensive to build.

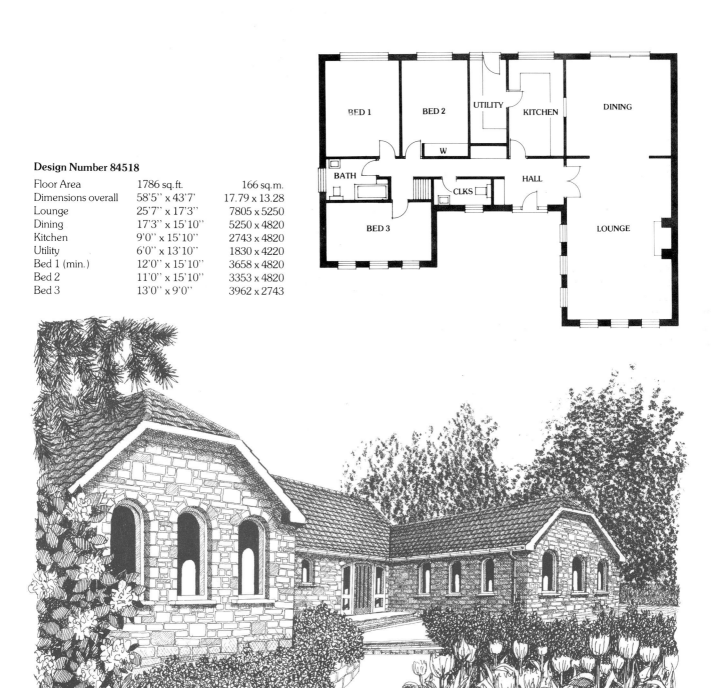

Design Number 84518

Floor Area	1786 sq.ft.	166 sq.m.
Dimensions overall	58'5'' x 43'7'	17.79 x 13.28
Lounge	25'7'' x 17'3''	7805 x 5250
Dining	17'3'' x 15'10''	5250 x 4820
Kitchen	9'0'' x 15'10''	2743 x 4820
Utility	6'0'' x 13'10''	1830 x 4220
Bed 1 (min.)	12'0'' x 15'10''	3658 x 4820
Bed 2	11'0'' x 15'10''	3353 x 4820
Bed 3	13'0'' x 9'0''	3962 x 2743

CASTLETON

This interesting house has a lounge with two deep window nooks that give a lot of character and are well suited to period furnishings. The first floor walls above the lounge are carried by two steel joists, and these can be either concealed between the ceiling and the upper floor, or else they can be cased in wood as 'period' oak beams.

This is another design where the windows can be altered to suit the outlook, and the patio windows in the dining room can be moved into the lounge, or put in the back wall of the dining room, or dispensed with altogether.

Design Number 84519

Floor Area	1235 sq. ft.	115 sq. m.
Dimensions overall	40'10½" x 25'9½"	12.46 x 7.86
Lounge	20'0" x 13'7½"	6100 x 4150
Dining	13'0" x 10'0"	3962 x 3050
Kitchen	15'3" x 10'0"	4648 x 3050
Bed 1	17'0" x 10'0"	5182 x 3050
Bed 2	11'3" x 10'0"	3428 x 3050
Bed 3	11'6" x 10'8"	3500 x 3250

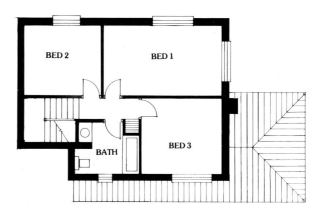

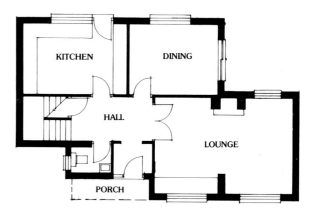

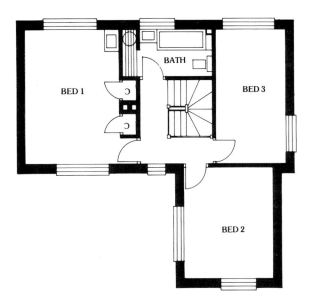

The Brierley is a very economical three bedroom house with a winder staircase and a landing that has its own window, both features that are very unusual in houses of less than 1100 sq. ft.

The spans of the two wings of the house are dissimilar, so that there is the option of having roofs of the same height but of different pitches, or of having roofs of the same pitch with one ridge lower than the other. Your choice can depend on the style of adjacent properties, or on your own preference. Most people will not notice which you have chosen, but it is the opportunity of having a choice of this sort that makes building your own home so worthwhile.

Design Number 84520

Floor Area	1087 sq. ft.	101 sq. m.
Dimensions overall	31'0'' x 28'3''	9.46 x 8.61
Lounge	12'6'' x 14'7''	3800 x 4450
Dining	11'6'' x 10'2''	3500 x 3100
Kitchen	14'7'' x 7'10''	4450 x 2400
Bed 1	10'6'' x 14'7''	3200 x 4450
Bed 2	11'6'' x 10'2''	3500 x 3100
Bed 3	14'7'' x 7'10''	4450 x 2400

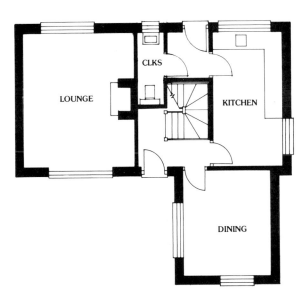

RUNCORN

This large house is better suited to a peri-urban site than to the depths of the country, and was originally designed for a prestige site in the North West. It is shown here with six bedrooms and three bathrooms, but as originally drawn, the two bedrooms and bathroom above the garage formed a self contained flat, with a bedroom, sitting room and services for an elderly member of the family. We have also prepared plans for this house with this area as a billiards room, complete with bar!

Design Number 84521

Floor Area		
(inc. garage)	2938 sq. ft.	273 sq.m.
Dimensions overall	49'0'' x 47'4''	14.93 x 14.42
Lounge	17'0'' x 15'0''	5182 x 4572
Dining	10'0'' x 14'5''	3050 x 4400
Study	10'0'' x 13'1''	3050 x 3983
Kitchen	12'0'' x 13'0''	3658 x 3962
Master Bed	15'0'' x 14'0''	4572 x 4267
Bed 2	15'0'' x 13'6''	4572 x 4115
Bed 3	11'0'' x 10'0''	3353 x 3050
Bed 4	10'0'' x 9'0''	3050 x 2900
Bed 5	19'0'' x 9'0''	5800 x 2900
Guest Bed	10'10'' x 8'8''	3300 x 2650

ELSTEAD

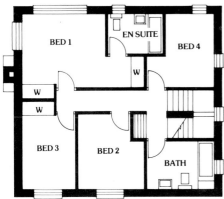

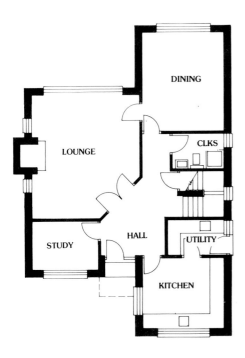

The Elstead is a new design for 1984 with a lot of unusual features. The hall and lounge have off-set double doors, giving character to both rooms, and the position of the kitchen, with a kitchen window looking at the front door, is as practical as it is unusual. The house is illustrated with Hampshire hip roofs, but can be built with gables or full hips to suit the local style.

With all the main rooms looking out to the back, this is a design for a north facing site with plenty of room all round the building.

Design Number 84522

Floor Area	1600 sq.ft.	149 sq.m.
Dimensions overall	30'3'' x 44'3''	9.22 x 13.49
Lounge	15'11'' x 17'9''	4900 x 5400
Dining	14'0'' x 12'0''	4250 x 3660
Kitchen	10'0'' x 12'0''	3050 x 3660
Study	10'1½'' x 6'11''	3090 x 2100
Utility	8'9'' x 5'3''	2660 x 1600
Bed 1	12'4'' x 9'9''	3760 x 2973
Bed 2	11'3'' x 8'3''	3427 x 2510
Bed 3	10'11'' x 7'10½''	3327 x 2400
Bed 4	10'1'' x 7'0''	3073 x 2134

RIVERDALE

The Riverdale design, with large rooms and a simple straightforward shape is one of the most economical homes to build in this book in terms of cost per sq.ft. It is a particularly well proportioned home which looks well in a wide range of settings and materials.

The proto-type was built in Nottinghamshire with a step down into the lounge as shown on the drawing, and details are available of this and of the feature fireplace that was linked with the steps. However, this is not an essential part of the design.

When built as a farmhouse the single garage can be turned into a farm office, with a window to the front and its own side or rear entrance. If required this entrance can link with the back porch, which has its own cloakroom. This is an arrangement which many farmers find useful.

Design Number 84523

Floor Area		
(inc. garage)	2242 sq.ft.	207 sq.m.
Dimensions overall	45'5" x 35'4"	13.84 x 10.76
Lounge	22'0" x 19'0"	6700 x 5800
Dining	11'10" x 14'9"	3600 x 4500
Kitchen	9'10" x 14'9"	3000 x 4500
Garage	9'10" x 18'2½"	3000 x 5550
Master Bed	22'0" x 19'0"	6700 x 5800
Bed 2	18'2½" x 9'10"	5550 x 3000
Bed 3	11'10" x 14'9"	3600 x 4500
Bed 4	11'6" x 9'10"	3500 x 3000

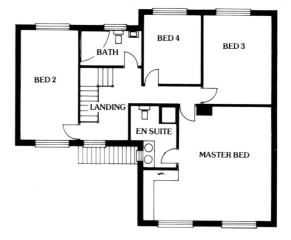

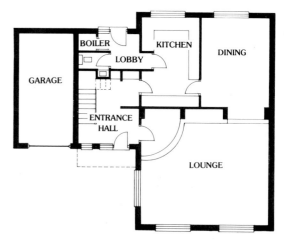

ROSMORE

Tile hanging above brickwork, with dormers and wooden supports to a porch, always seems to go with a woodlands setting as shown here, although this unusual design can be built in a variety of materials and styles. The large hall provides all sorts of interesting furnishing opportunities. The fourth bedroom is small but with an angled door and a deep dormer it has a great deal of character, and would make a splendid childs room with a desk for homework in the window.

The side door can be moved from the back to the front of the utility room if this is better suited to the access.

Design Number 84524

Floor Area	1880 sq.ft.	175 sq.m.
Dimensions overall	47'11'' x 35'5''	14.59 x 10.79
Lounge	21'7½'' x 13'0''	6587 x 3962
Dining	16'7'' x 11'0''	5050 x 3353
Study	9'0'' x 7'0''	2743 x 2134
Kitchen	18'0'' x 10'0''	5486 x 3050
Utility	10'0'' x 6'7½''	3050 x 2020
Master Bed	16'7'' x 11'0''	5050 x 3353
Bed 2 (max.)	11'6'' x 20'8''	3505 x 6300
Bed 3 (max.)	8'8½'' x 11'6''	2650 x 3505
Study (max.)	10'0'' x 9'10''	3050 x 3000

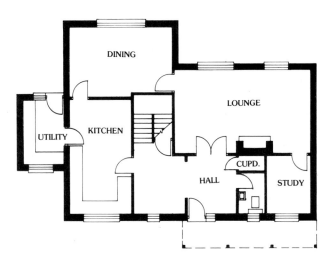

EVERDALE

If you want a new home in a country setting that looks like a small manor house, this is it. With an area of only 1720 sq.ft. and designed for ease of construction, this D & M design by Tim Woods is a winner in every way.

It is shown here built in random coursed stone, with stone window heads and cills, and this is the material for which it was originally designed for a site in Derbyshire. However, it would look equally well in brick, with careful attention paid to the brick detailing. A splendid home for a prestige site.

RIDGEHAVEN

An equally attractive home is the four bedroom version of this design, known as the Ridgehaven, reference number 84526, which features upper floor accommodation over the study/lounge projection, giving a total floor area of approximately 1900 sq.ft.

Design Number 84525

Floor Area	1720 sq.ft.	160 sq.m.
Dimensions overall	50'7" x 30'2"	15.42 x 9.20
Lounge (overall)	18'0" x 24'9"	5486 x 7552
Dining	15'0" x 10'0"	4572 x 3050
Study/Playroom	9'3" x 8'10"	2825 x 2700
Kitchen	17'0" x 8'5"	5182 x 2572
Laundry	5'9" x 9'10"	1750 x 3000
Bed 1	15'0" x 15'10½"	4572 x 4850
Bed 2	15'0" x 10'1½"	4572 x 3086
Bed 3	10'5" x 8'5"	3182 x 2572

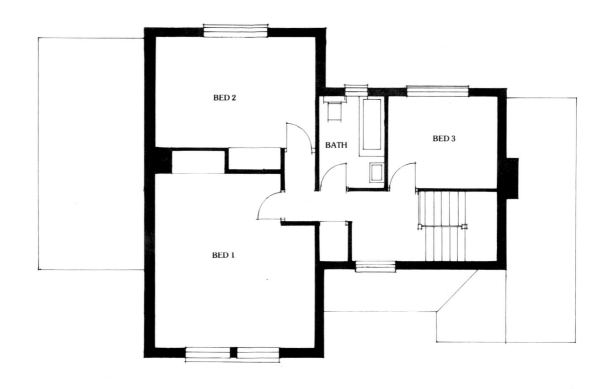

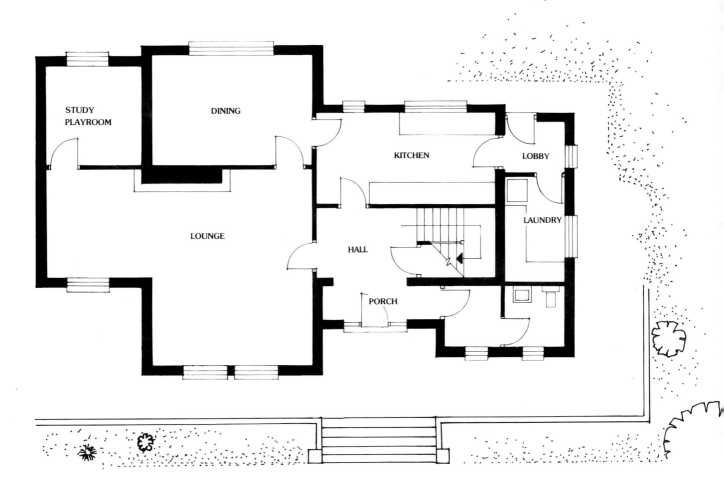

PRINCETON

This attractive cottage style home has more accommodation than one expects, and can be built either with or without the garage that is shown. Similarly the utility room can be omitted if required. The heads of the dormer windows are below the roof soffits, so that trussed rafters can be used with consequent cost savings. Indeed, this is in every way a very economical home to build, and a very attractive property.

Design Number 84527

Floor Area		
(exc. garage)	1130 sq.ft.	105 sq.m.
Dimensions overall		
(inc. garage)	55'6'' x 19'10''	16.91 x 6.05
Lounge	18'0'' x 11'6''	5486 x 3505
Dining	8'10'' x 10'10''	2700 x 3300
Kitchen	9'4'' x 10'10''	2845 x 3300
Utility	6'6'' x 7'1''	1828 x 2151
Garage	16'1'' x 18'0½''	4894 x 5496
Master Bed	13'0'' x 9'5''	3964 x 2870
Bed 2	9'10'' x 9'10''	3000 x 3000
Bed 3	7'6½'' x 9'10''	2300 x 3000
Bed 4	7'10'' x 8'6''	2386 x 2590

THAMESMEAD

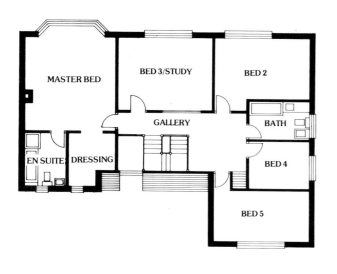

This large house with five bedrooms suits a site with views to both the front and the rear, and will suit a large family who want a living room at one end of the house that is well away from the lounge and dining room at the other. The drawings show a rear bay window feature to both the lounge and the master bedroom above it, but this can be omitted if not required.

A feature of the Thamesmead is the high window with its own gabled roof which lights both the hall and the landing. This can be arranged in a number of different ways, and gives a great deal of character to the property, both inside, and to the front elevation.

Design Number 84528

Floor Area	2430 sq. ft.	226 sq. m.
Dimensions overall	67'11'' x 59'1''	20.7 x 18.01
Lounge (max.)	15'3'' x 24'0''	4658 x 7315
Dining	15'10'' x 12'0''	4820 x 3658
Kitchen/Breakfast	16'0'' x 12'0''	4877 x 3658
Utility o/all	14'0'' x 8'0''	4267 x 2438
Family Room	16'0'' x 12'0''	4877 x 3658
Garage	18'1'' x 18'0''	5500 x 5486
Master Bed	15'3'' x 15'5''	4658 x 4695
Bed 2	16'0'' x 10'0''	4877 x 3048
Bed 3/Study	15'10'' x 12'0''	4820 x 3658
Bed 4	10'0'' x 8'6''	3048 x 2438
Bed 5	16'0'' x 8'0''	4877 x 2448

KIMBERLEY

The Kimberley design has a nice "cottage" feel to it, and is one of the designs that seems to suit sites in all parts of the country. It can be built with the garage changed to a bedroom and shower room for an elderly person living with the family, and as the drains are all at the left hand side of the building this is an economical way of arranging for granny flat accommodation.

The dormer style windows set below an economical trussed rafter roof give a traditional cottage appearance with the advantages of flat bedroom ceilings and modern cost effective construction.

Design Number 84529

Floor Area (inc. garage)	1290 sq. ft.	120 sq. m.
Dimensions overall	31'2" x 31'8½"	9.50 x 9.66
Lounge	20'0" x 12'6"	6096 x 3810
Kitchen	14'2" x 11'11"	4315 x 3634
Garage	10'0" x 17'0"	3055 x 5182
Bed 1 (max.)	12'6" x 20'0"	3810 x 6096
Bed 2	10'4½" x 10'0"	3166 x 3050
Bed 3	13'8" x 8'7"	4166 x 2622

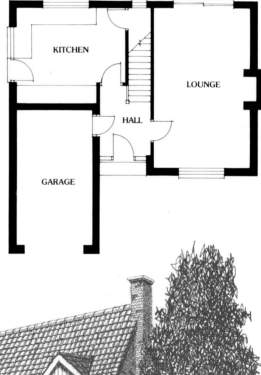

ROTHWELL

The Rothwell is one of a group of designs with the front door set in the angle between two wings of the building. This always gives an interesting shape to the hall, and in this case this feature follows through to the lounge.

On the first floor this is another design with the master bedroom suite quite separate from the other bedrooms — a feature which seems to be growing in popularity.

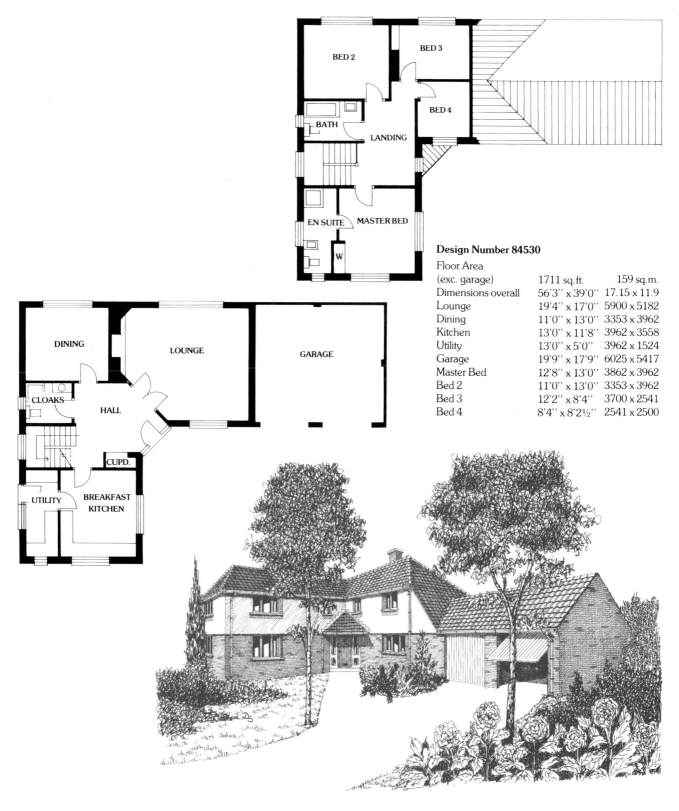

Design Number 84530

Floor Area

(exc. garage)	1711 sq.ft.	159 sq.m.
Dimensions overall	56'3'' x 39'0''	17.15 x 11.9
Lounge	19'4'' x 17'0''	5900 x 5182
Dining	11'0'' x 13'0''	3353 x 3962
Kitchen	13'0'' x 11'8''	3962 x 3558
Utility	13'0'' x 5'0''	3962 x 1524
Garage	19'9'' x 17'9''	6025 x 5417
Master Bed	12'8'' x 13'0''	3862 x 3962
Bed 2	11'0'' x 13'0''	3353 x 3962
Bed 3	12'2'' x 8'4''	3700 x 2541
Bed 4	8'4'' x 8'2½''	2541 x 2500

CARLTON

This large and imposing bungalow has been built on more than 100 sites in one form or another, and at one time was the design used by D & M Limited as its trademark. Designed by Jean Dunkley, R.I.B.A., in 1973, it seems to be nearly everyone's idea of a dream home for a dream site. In the real world it requires a site with at least a 100ft. frontage, preferably with some trees about to give a broken skyline behind the simple roof.

The Carlton is a very economical structure, with no load bearing internal walls and a simple trussed rafter roof. It is illustrated with landscape style windows, with top opening lights, which suit it better than casement windows although it can be built with either. In both sketches it is shown in a garden which slopes away from the front door. When building on a site like this it is most important to establish the floor level at just the right height for the building to look at its best. So often clients who are most concerned about the exact position of the corner pegs for a new home seem content to leave the actual floor level to others. It is much too important for that.

The recess off the back porch of this bungalow is for the central heating boiler with short pipe runs to the large airing cupboard, but sometimes the boiler is put in the back of the porch itself, giving more cupboard space in the utility room.

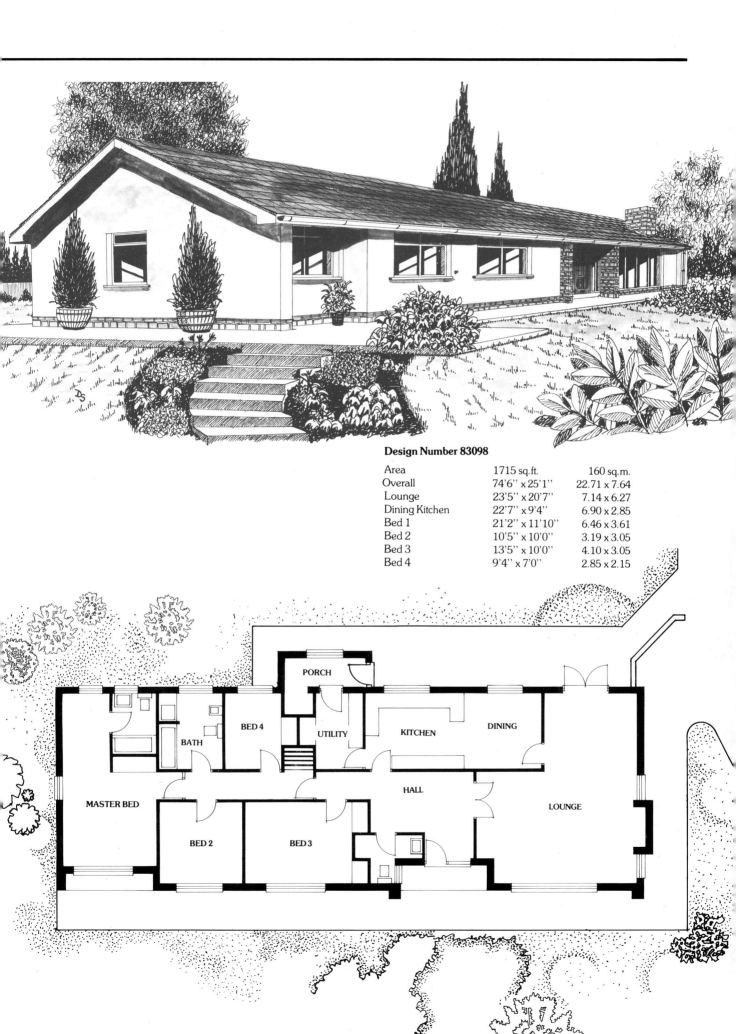

Design Number 83098

Area	1715 sq.ft.	160 sq.m.
Overall	74'6'' x 25'1''	22.71 x 7.64
Lounge	23'5'' x 20'7''	7.14 x 6.27
Dining Kitchen	22'7'' x 9'4''	6.90 x 2.85
Bed 1	21'2'' x 11'10''	6.46 x 3.61
Bed 2	10'5'' x 10'0''	3.19 x 3.05
Bed 3	13'5'' x 10'0''	4.10 x 3.05
Bed 4	9'4'' x 7'0''	2.85 x 2.15

HUCKNALL

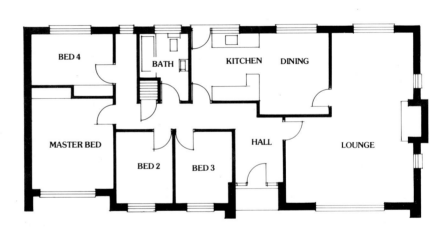

Design Number 83100

Floor Area	1270 sq.ft.	118 sq.m.
Overall dimensions	56'1'' x 26'4½''	17.0 x 8.0
Lounge (overall)	23'5'' x 18'6''	7.14 x 5.64
Kitchen/Dining (overall)	19'7'' x 11'4''	5.96 x 3.45
Master Bed	12'2'' x 11'11''	3.70 x 3.63
Bed 2	10'0'' x 8'0''	3.05 x 2.43
Bed 3	10'0'' x 8'0''	3.05 x 2.43
Bed 4	11'11'' x 6'10''	3.63 x 2.08

This is a variant of our popular ''Carlton'' bungalow, with the overall length reduced from 74ft to 56ft. There are two arrangements shown, one with an en suite bathroom to the master bedroom, and one with a single family bathroom. In the latter layout we show a window in a recess at the head of the passage, but this can easily be omitted and the window recess used for a separate W.C. or a walk-in airing cupboard.

NEWARK

How do you arrange a patio window in a living room that is the full width of a gable? Just the single opening rarely looks right from outside, but it is invariably what is needed when considered from inside. One answer is to have a narrow slit window on each side of the main opening as in this successful design.

Another feature is the sunken lounge, with two steps down to the new level. This gives a remarkable feeling of space to the whole bungalow, and is the one feature of the house that guests always remember. An incidental result of this arrangement is that a whole flight of steps is required up to the front door, which gives the emphasis to the entrance that is so necessary when it is in the angle between the two wings of the building.

This is a big bungalow, with four bedrooms and study that can become a fifth bedroom if required, but it is a very cost effective design. The only problem area is the chimney, which comes through the roof far too near the valley for simple construction — but where else can the fireplace go? Never mind — our drawings include a special detail to show how the chimney, the roof and the valley all relate to each other!

Design Number 83095

Floor Area	1700 sq.ft.	158 sq.m.
Dimensions Overall	68'10'' x 34'1½''	20.97 x 10.40
Lounge	15'3½'' x 20'4''	4.66 x 6.20
Dining	9'6'' x 11'11½''	2.90 x 3.64
Kitchen	15'2½'' x 10'0''	4.64 x 3.05
Study	9'6'' x 7'10½''	2.89 x 2.40
Utility	10'0'' x 7'10½''	3.05 x 2.40
Cloaks	6'0'' x 7'10½''	1.80 x 2.40
Master Bed	15'1'' x 11'7½''	4.60 x 3.54
Bed 2	10'7½'' x 11'7½''	3.24 x 3.54
Bed 3	12'6'' x 7'10½''	3.82 x 2.40
Bed 4	12'6'' x 7'4½''	3.82 x 2.25

This bungalow can be built in two stages if required, without bedrooms 3 and 4, and extended later if desired. The smaller version is called the Collingham and the reference is 82095.

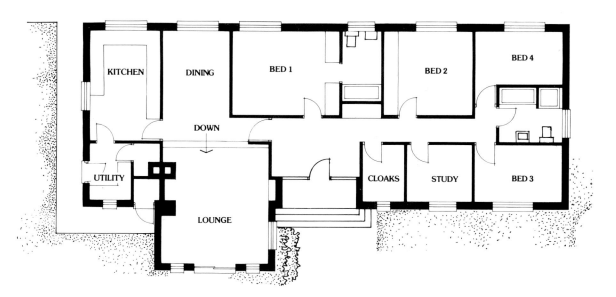

LAMBOURNE

A dream design in a dream setting, though not a figment of our architect's imagination, but a home that has been built and looks every bit as attractive as the drawing.

This is a big bungalow, and it must be emphasised that in many parts of the country the planners will suggest that our architectural tradition is that a home of this size is built as a two storey house. However, if it is built as part of a complex of single storey farm buildings, or integrated well into the landscape, the planning application should not be too much real trouble.

One of the advantages of a 'U' shaped design is that different parts of the house can be kept quite separate. The lounge/family room/dining room are grouped around the main entrance, the bedroom wing is quite separate, and the garage/farm office/farm kitchen form the third unit. Perhaps this is the ultimate modern farm bungalow.

The Plumpton design is a four bedroom version of this bungalow. The reference no. is 82164.

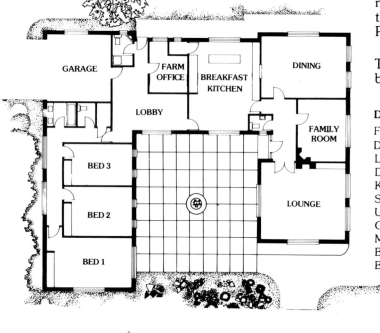

Design Number 83164

Floor area (inc. garage)	3203 sq.ft.	297 sq.m.
Dimensions overall	62'2" x 76'4"	18.9 x 23.2
Lounge	21'3" x 18'3"	6.46 x 5.56
Dining	21'3" x 14'9"	6.46 x 4.50
Kitchen	21'3" x 17'8"	6.46 x 5.39
Study	12'0" x 14'10"	3.65 x 4.52
Utility (overall)	9'6" x 12'2"	2.88 x 3.70
Garage	15'9" x 16'1"	4.80 x 4.90
Master Bed	21'3" x 12'0"	6.46 x 3.65
Bed 2	16'11" x 12'0"	5.16 x 3.65
Bed 3	16'11" x 9'10"	5.16 x 3.00

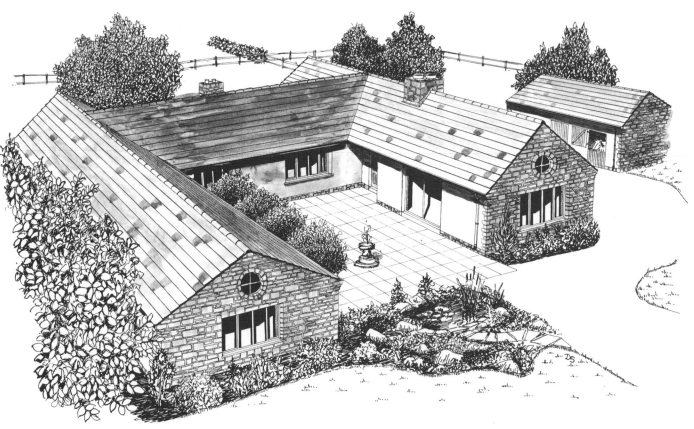

WHEATLEY

The planners loved this design when it was first drawn for a very sensitive site in 1980. It takes a moments thought to appreciate the internal arrangement. The front door leads into a very high hall, lit by windows above the entrance screen. From this hall there are two separate flights of stairs, one leading discretely up left to the bedrooms, while the other goes to a gallery leading to the living area. This is one of the most impressive entrances in any of our designs, and provides a marvellous setting for period furniture.

Although it is particularly well suited to a sloping site, this design can be built on level ground if care is given to landscaping, and soil can be obtained to build up the garden level around the single storey wing.

Note that there are three doors from the garage — into the hall, into the utility room, and into a large work room or store. The utility room is a long way from the kitchen, but the latter is large enough to avoid this being a problem.

Design Number 83163

Floor Area (exc. garage)	1640 sq.ft.	152 sq.m.
Dimensions Overall	59'7'' x 29'8''	18.16 x 9.05
Lounge	19'11'' x 13'1''	6.06 x 3.99
Dining/		
Kitchen (overall)	10'0'' x 23'6''	3.04 x 7.16
Workroom	12'0'' x 9'2''	3.65 x 2.79
Utility	11'1'' x 9'2''	3.39 x 2.79
Garage	23'5'' x 18'4''	7.14 x 5.59
Master Bed (overall)	11'9'' x 13'10''	3.59 x 4.22
Bed 2	11'9'' x 9'3''	3.59 x 2.81
Bed 3	11'1'' x 9'2''	3.39 x 2.79
Bed 4	12'0'' x 7'3''	3.65 x 2.19

WOODCHURCH

GLYNDEBOURNE

226

This attractive bungalow has a conservatory next to the kitchen, which is an ideal arrangement for a family with young children, and a big garden. It suits a site where the view is to the front, and is another design that is popular with those housewives who think the kitchen window is the most important window in the house.

Design Number 83106

Floor Area	1452 sq. ft.	135 sq. m.
Overall dimensions	60'6" x 36'1"	18.43 x 11.0
Lounge (overall)	14'0" x 20'0"	4.26 x 6.10
Dining	9'8" x 13'4"	2.96 x 4.08
Kitchen	10'6" x 13'0"	3.20 x 3.96
Utility	7'0" x 7'8"	2.13 x 2.35
Sunroom	11'0" x 10'0"	3.43 x 3.05
Bed 1	12'6" x 14'0"	3.81 x 4.26
Bed 2	11'9" x 10'8"	3.58 x 3.25
Bed 3	12'6" x 10'0"	3.81 x 3.05

Originally built for a distinguished musician, the Glyndebourne design provides the maximum of gracious living in a sensible overall size for a two bedroomed home. It is a derivative of our very popular "Carlton" bungalow, and has the same front elevation but with a small projecting gable to the rear.

It is shown here with a rendered finish on a stone plinth, with stone window sills. The junction of the rendered wall and the plinth is always very important, and the specification for the plasterer should require a bell shaped aluminium render stop to give a clean edge that is at least an inch clear of the stone work. The stone sills are a regional feature; until recent times they would have been installed in the full thickness of the wall; however, modern legislation discourages such "cold bridges" in today's thermally efficient cavity walls. We are aware of this and our drawings embody suitable methods of solving the problem.

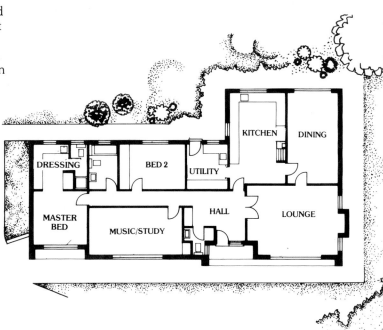

Design Number 83107

Floor Area	1800 sq. ft.	167 sq. m.
Overall	67'11" x 36'0"	20.69 x 10.97
Lounge	19'8" x 14'10"	5.99 x 4.52
Dining	11'0" x 19'4"	3.35 x 5.89
Kitchen	12'1" x 19'4"	3.69 x 5.89
Music/Study/		
Guest Room	20'6" x 10'0"	6.25 x 3.05
Utility	9'2" x 9'6"	2.80 x 2.89
Master Bed	11'6" x 11'5"	3.49 x 3.47
Bed 2	14'8" x 9'6"	4.46 x 2.89

EXETER

HAWKHURST

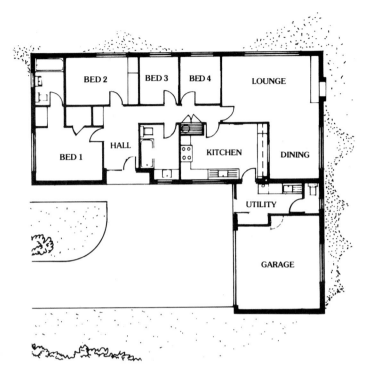

The Exeter design is an old favourite, particularly in rural areas. It is a bungalow that needs plenty of space around it. The main block of the design does not often change, but the variations to the garage wing have been endless. One of the most common is to reduce the size of the utility room to little more than a porch and to build a farm office behind it. Another interesting possibility is to arrange for the garage foundations to be built to suit its conversion into a granny flat at a later date.

The huge walk-in wardrobe with hanging rails on either side is an unusual feature, and one that has proved very popular. We now often incorporate it in new designs.

Design Number 83112

Area (exc. garage)	1650 sq. ft.	153 sq.m.
Overall	57'6'' x 40'3''	17.54 x 15.29
Lounge	19'2'' x 12'7''	5.84 x 3.84
Dining	10'10'' x 9'10''	3.30 x 3.00
Kitchen	17'3'' x 10'6''	5.25 x 3.20
Bed 1	14'1'' x 13'1''	4.30 x 3.99
Bed 2	14'5'' x 9'0''	4.40 x 2.74
Bed 3	9'0'' x 7'9''	2.74 x 2.35
Bed 4	9'0'' x 7'9''	2.74 x 2.35

A five bedroom version of this design is the Honiton, reference 82112 with a gable extension to the rear.

This design has some unusual and attractive features. The large living area has a big island fireplace which splits it into two halves — an informal living room, and a more formal lounge. The fireplace itself is the first thing that is seen when one enters through the front door. This is real "open plan" living — attractive to some, and less so to others. The decision as to whether this is for you may depend on whether all the family like the same television programme. At any rate, the layout can be built with solid dividing walls if required.

Two bathrooms and exceptionally large wardrobes give luxury bedroom accommodation, and if required the main bathroom can be reduced in size to permit a cloakroom at the front door.

As drawn the garage roof arrangement depends on differential floor levels; if the site requires that the garage floor is at the same level as the bungalow floor, then a gable roof will be required over the garage door.

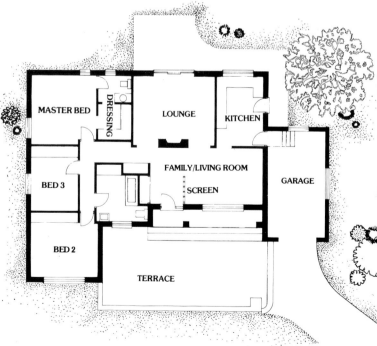

Design Number 83113

Floor Area (exc. garage)	1230 sq. ft.	114 sq.m.
Dimensions Overall	59'0'' x 39'6''	18.00 x 12.04
Lounge	15'9'' x 13'0''	4.80 x 3.96
Family/Living Room	10'6'' x 15'0''	3.20 x 4.57
Kitchen	9'0'' x 13'0''	2.74 x 3.96
Garage	11'3'' x 20'0''	3.43 x 6.10
Master Bed	12'6'' x 13'0''	3.81 x 3.96
Bed 2	13'0'' x 12'0''	3.96 x 3.65
Bed 3	12'0'' x 9'0''	3.65 x 2.74

CRANBROOK

Design Number 83118

Floor Area
(exc. garage etc.)	1120 sq.ft.	104 sq.m.

Dimensions overall
inc. out buildings as

in this layout	84'6" x 42'0"	25.7 x 12.8
Lounge	18'2" x 13'0"	5.53 x 3.96
Dining	10'0" x 8'0"	3.05 x 2.43
Kitchen	13'6" x 8'7½"	4.12 x 2.63
Bed 1	11'0" x 12'6"	3.35 x 3.81
Bed 2	11'0" x 13'0"	3.35 x 3.96
Garden Store	11'2" x 7'6"	3.40 x 2.29
Garage	9'0" x 16'8"	2.74 x 5.07
Workshop	7'0" x 12'0"	2.13 x 3.66

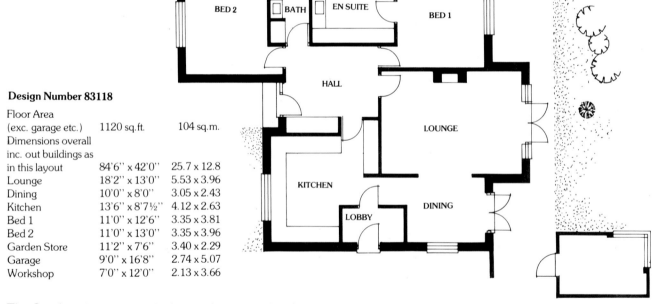

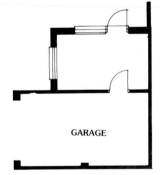

The Cranbrook was originally designed for a woodland site in Lincolnshire and was built in stone under a pantile roof instead of the flat tiles shewn in our sketch. Unpainted softwood joinery was specified and this was stained to a dark oak colour. The result was one of the most attractive bungalows ever built to our drawings.

Note that the biggest bathroom is en suite with the main bedroom: this is a growing trend, with more and more of those who pay the mortgages deciding that they deserve the best washing facilities!

The little building by the dining room window is an amateur radio station, and was built at the same time as the bungalow to match it in materials and style. If you have a hobby, then make provision for it in your plans and do not let it be an afterthought.

PENHURST

The Penhurst bungalow was drawn by John Gwilliam RIBA for a large and valuable site on the W. coast, where only a 58' strip could be used for the building. The open plan layout was designed in conjunction with the clients, who wanted a clear view from the kitchen across the dining area and through the glazed screen into the lounge. It all worked very well indeed, and became a striking and much admired home.

The car port has wrought ironwork in the arched openings. This is a very effective way of giving character to a screen wall, and looks particularly well when associated with generous areas of paving.

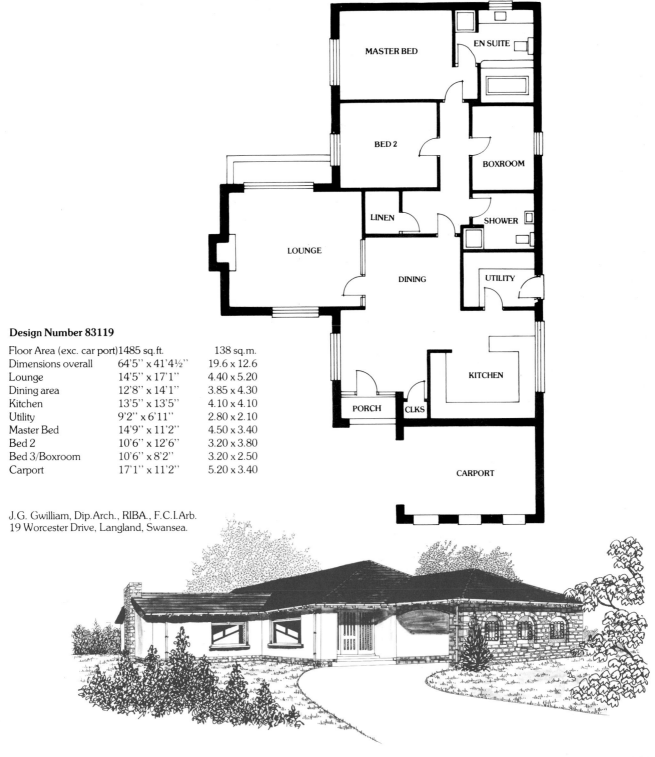

Design Number 83119

Floor Area (exc. car port)	1485 sq.ft.	138 sq.m.
Dimensions overall	64'5'' x 41'4½''	19.6 x 12.6
Lounge	14'5'' x 17'1''	4.40 x 5.20
Dining area	12'8'' x 14'1''	3.85 x 4.30
Kitchen	13'5'' x 13'5''	4.10 x 4.10
Utility	9'2'' x 6'11''	2.80 x 2.10
Master Bed	14'9'' x 11'2''	4.50 x 3.40
Bed 2	10'6'' x 12'6''	3.20 x 3.80
Bed 3/Boxroom	10'6'' x 8'2''	3.20 x 2.50
Carport	17'1'' x 11'2''	5.20 x 3.40

J.G. Gwilliam, Dip.Arch., RIBA., F.C.I.Arb.
19 Worcester Drive, Langland, Swansea.

FARNBOROUGH

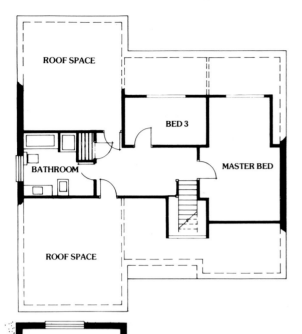

A common design requirement is for a home with one bedroom and its bathroom downstairs, and the other bedrooms and another bathroom above. The Farnborough demonstrates one way of providing this accommodation with two big roof space areas that will not be counted for rating purposes when the house is built, but which can be turned into additional bedrooms if ever required.

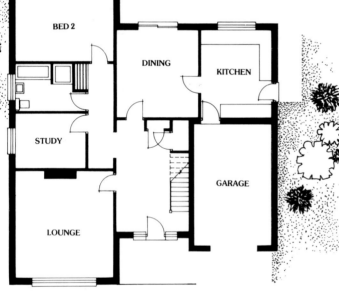

Design Number 83120

Floor area (inc. garage)	1808 sq. ft.	168 sq.m.
Dimensions overall	41'3'' x 43'7''	12.5 x 13.2
Lounge	14'9'' x 15'11''	4.50 x 4.85
Dining	13'0'' x 13'0''	3.96 x 3.96
Kitchen	13'0'' x 11'0''	3.96 x 3.35
Study	8'0'' x 10'6''	2.43 x 3.20
Garage	12'0'' x 18'0''	3.65 x 5.48
Master Bed	12'7'' x 18'4''	3.83 x 5.60
Bed 2	14'9'' x 9'10''	4.50 x 3.00
Bed 3	13'0'' x 7'0''	3.96 x 2.13

SHERWOOD

The Sherwood bungalow is a very popular D & M design, and particularly appeals to housewives who want the kitchen windows to look out over the drive to give a good view of everything that is going on. This is well illustrated in the sketch, but what the artist was not able to show is the projecting gable on the rear elevation, with wide patio doors. The lounge is big enough to have two sets of double doors leading into it, and these are very important features. The pattern of door should be chosen with great care, as it will give a lot of character to the room.

This design can also be drawn with a sunken lounge, and the lounge gable can be extended if required. For one client we provided plans for the lounge increased in depth by 10ft, with room for a grand piano on the right of the door from the hall, and two steps down from this level to a conservatory area with doors out to a very special garden.

A four bedroom version of this design is called the Thoresby, reference 82121

Design Number 83121

Area	1485 sq. ft.	138 sq. m.
Overall	61'3'' x 31'8''	18.66 x 9.66
Lounge	20'6'' x 16'1''	6.25 x 4.91
Dining	12'0'' x 11'5½''	3.65 x 3.49
Kitchen	13'6'' x 11'8''	4.11 x 3.55
Bed 1	15'2'' x 13'1''	4.61 x 3.66
Bed 2	14'7'' x 10'0''	4.45 x 3.05
Bed 3	12'0'' x 10'0''	3.65 x 3.05

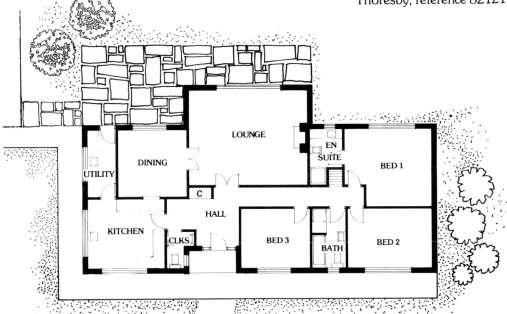

PARKLANDS

The Parklands bungalow is another design which suits a site with all round views. The angled fireplace is the principal feature in the large living room, and is often built of stone or handmade bricks and these may be used for the adjacent walls. This layout is particularly popular with those who like plenty of space around them, especially if they do a lot of entertaining. However, if this is not your scene the Parklands can be built with a dividing wall between the dining and the lounge areas. In this case the double doors are replaced with two ordinary doors into the hall, one from each room.

If the garage is not required it is usual to build a small porch at the back door, and this can have either a flat or a pitched roof depending on the area, and the probable requirements of the Planning Officer. The decision whether to build an integral garage or a detached one is not easy: the convenience of an integral garage has to be set against a detached garage being cheaper to build. Another factor is that a separate garage can be built at a later date, and those who are building on their own using sub-contractors often like to arrange to delay starting their garage until they know that the main building is going to be within their budget costs.

Design Number 83130

Area (exc. garage)	1060 sq.ft.	99 sq.m.
Overall	47'11" x 25'1"	14.61 x 7.64
Lounge	19'9" x 11'0"	6.01 x 3.36
Dining	12'4" x 8'11"	3.78 x 2.72
Kitchen	12'0" x 10'6"	3.68 x 3.19
Bed 1	14'4" x 10'11"	4.37 x 3.33
Bed 2	12'1" x 10'1"	3.71 x 3.07
Bed 3	8'10" x 8'1"	2.71 x 2.47

This bungalow is sometimes built with the garage turned into a small flat to give separate accommodation for an elderly relative. The design for this is called the Newhall, and has the reference number 82130

MOORCROFT

The Moorcroft bungalow was originally drawn for a north country site, where it was built in stone with the stone tabling to the gables that is illustrated. In a softer landscape in the south it would probably be built in brick or have a rendered finish and so look far less austere.

The room sizes are very generous, and this is definitely a luxury home. The layout can be re-arranged to provide a two bedroom — two bathroom home if required. A very attractive bungalow for a retired couple looking for larger-than-average rooms.

Design Number 83123

Floor Area	1240 sq.ft.	115 sq.m.
Dimensions overall	48'5'' x 38'6½''	14.7 x 11.7
Lounge/Dining (overall)	26'4½'' x 20'7''	8.04 x 6.27
Kitchen	10'0'' x 11'5''	3.05 x 3.48
Utility	6'6'' x 10'0''	1.98 x 3.05
Master Bed	15'1'' x 12'0''	4.60 x 3.65
Bed 2	10'0'' x 11'1''	3.05 x 3.38
Bed 3	8'0'' x 8'0''	2.43 x 2.43

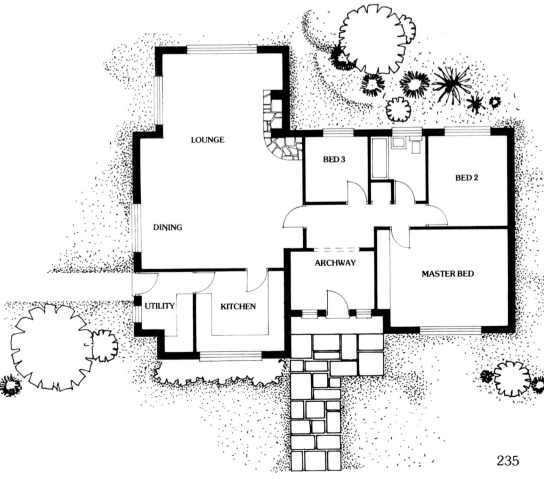

BIDDENDEN

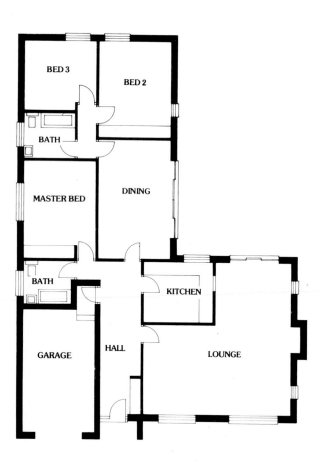

This large bungalow uses a family room as a passage to give access to the second and third bedrooms, and as these are usually childrens bedrooms this is a logical and sensible arrangement. (Incidentally it is as common in American designs as it is unusual here.)

The dining table can either be in the family room or in the lounge as required: if the latter then a door can be opened from the lounge into the kitchen.

The Biddenden is illustrated here with a barbeque built against the outside of the chimney breast, using a special fire built into the chimney when the house was built. If you like out-of-doors entertaining this is an excellent way of ensuring that the smoke keeps out of your guests eyes!

Design Number 83124

Floor area (inc. garage)	1722 sq.ft.	160 sq.m.
Dimensions Overall	62'2'' x 44'7''	18.95 x 13.59
Lounge (overall)	23'7'' x 23'5''	7.20 x 7.14
Kitchen	11'0'' x 9'0''	3.35 x 2.74
Garage	11'6'' x 19'0''	3.50 x 5.80
Family Room	11'6'' x 18'2''	3.50 x 5.55
Master Bed	15'0'' x 11'6''	4.57 x 3.50
Bed 2	14'9'' x 11'6''	4.50 x 3.50
Bed 3	11'6'' x 11'0''	3.50 x 3.35

ELMHURST

This interesting design demonstrates a way of getting a large luxury bungalow on a site with a width of only 45ft, while enjoying most of the advantages of a home on a far larger frontage. The lounge and dining room have patio doors which open to an enclosed Courtyard and the bedroom wing has views to the rear. If your problem is how to build a large single storey home on a narrow plot then the Elmhurst or modification of the Elmhurst may provide the answer.

A four bedroom version of this bungalow is the Ashgrove, reference 82125

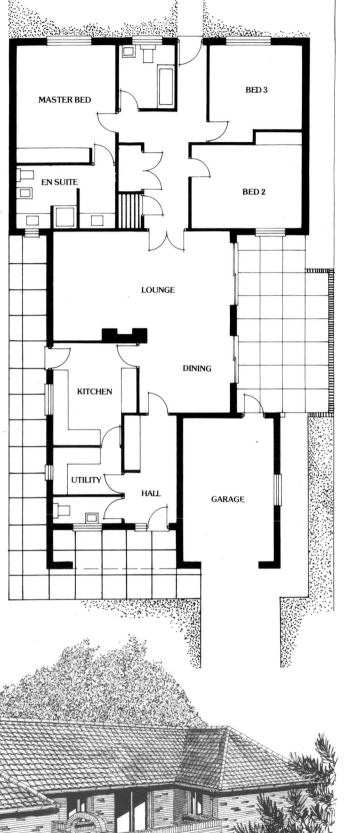

Design Number 83125

Floor Area (inc. garage)	1851 sq.ft.	172 sq.m.
Dimensions overall	39'6" x 67'4"	12.0 x 20.5
Lounge/Dining (overall)	23'5" x 23'0"	7.14 x 7.01
Kitchen	13'0" x 11'1"	3.96 x 3.38
Utility	7'3" x 6'0"	2.20 x 1.83
Garage	18'0" x 12'0"	5.48 x 3.65
Master Bed	13'1½" x 13'0"	4.00 x 3.96
Bed 2	14'5" x 10'6"	4.40 x 3.20
Bed 3	12'7" x 12'2½"	3.84 x 3.72

LICHFIELD

The Lichfield design bungalow has a very large living area combined with three double bedrooms, a utility room that can have the external door omitted so that it can be used as a small fourth bedroom or study, and two bathrooms. The lounge/dining/kitchen layout can be varied to suit the clients requirements and the opportunities offered by the site.

In the plan we show the lounge floor dropped to give feature steps up to double doors that lead into the hall, with extra ceiling height. The roof carries on at the same level, so the cost of this is minimal while the effect can be most impressive and gives enormous character to the home. The only snag with this arrangement is that changes of levels in bungalows are not always popular with prospective purchasers when the property is sold. The choice is yours.

The Tamworth design is a 4 bedroom version of this bungalow. The design reference number is 82126

Design Number 83126

Area	1431 sq.ft.	136 sq.m.
Overall	62'0'' x 29'6''	18.89 x 8.99
Lounge	23'4'' x 13'2''	7.11 x 4.02
Dining	12'5'' x 10'6''	3.80 x 3.20
Kitchen	12'5'' x 12'6''	3.80 x 3.81
Bed 1	13'5'' x 11'8''	4.10 x 3.56
Bed 2	16'5'' x 9'10''	5.00 x 3.00
Bed 3	10'6'' x 9'10''	3.21 x 3.00
Utility	9'2'' x 8'1''	2.78 x 2.46

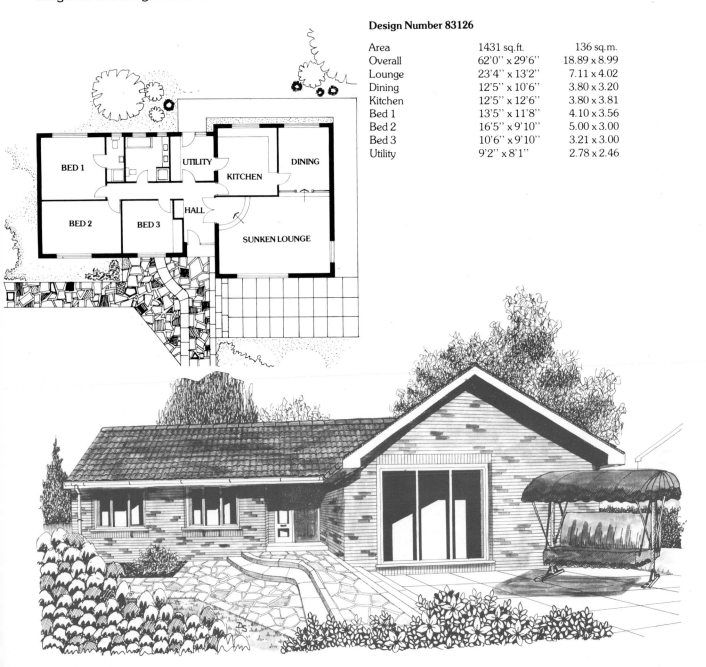

COLWYN

The Colwyn bungalow was originally designed for a splendid coastal site at Colwyn in North Wales. With a study isolated from the rest of the accommodation, it has proved particularly popular with those who work from their own homes, as well as for clergymen and others who wish to talk to callers away from family hubbub.

The two gables give it an interesting appearance from all angles, and the "window seat" window in the lounge adds a lot of character. The dining room usually has a patio window, but this can be changed if required.

Note the walk-in airing cupboard with the cylinder on one side of the door and linen racks to the ceiling on the other.

Design Number 83127

Area (inc. garage)	1880 sq. ft.	176 sq.m.
Overall	62'0'' x 46'6''	18.89 x 14.16
Lounge	23'5'' x 12'4''	7.14 x 3.76
Dining	12'3'' x 11'6''	3.74 x 3.50
Kitchen	14'9'' x 11'10''	4.50 x 3.60
Bed 1	13'0'' x 12'3''	3.97 x 3.72
Bed 2	16'2'' x 10'10''	4.92 x 3.31
Bed 3	10'10'' x 10'6''	3.31 x 3.20

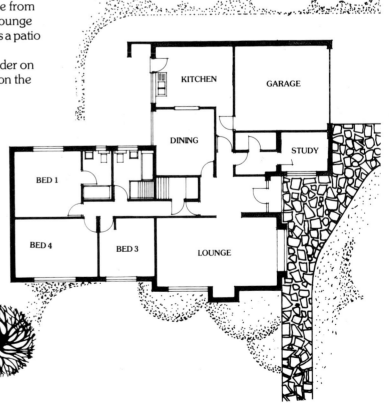

GAINSBOROUGH

The Gainsborough bungalow is another design for sites where the view and outlook are to the rear, and the entrances have to be to the front. It is shown here with the big kitchen/family room arrangement which suits those who work in the country, and has a chimney breast which is central to the internal walls of both the lounge and the kitchen. This can take flues from both the fire in the lounge and from an Aga type cooker up the same stack — it is surprising how many of our farming clients list "room for an Aga" at the top of their list of design requirements. The three large bedrooms have built-in cupboards and there are two more and a large airing cupboard in the hall. If the shower is not required in the bathroom it can be replaced by the airing cupboard, giving an extra cupboard in the hall.

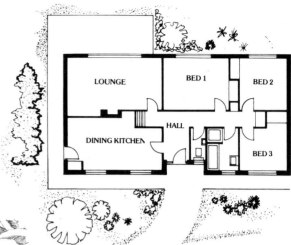

Design Number 83111

Area	1060 sq. ft.	99 sq.m.
Overall	47'11" x 25'1"	14.61 x 7.64
Lounge	19'9" x 12'1"	6.01 x 3.69
Dining Kitchen	19'9" x 11'0"	6.01 x 3.35
Bed 1	13'10" x 10'7"	4.23 x 3.24
Bed 2	10'7" x 10'1"	3.24 x 3.07
Bed 3	10'1" x 10'0"	3.07 x 3.05

CONWAY

In architects jargon this is a "north frontage" design for a house where the view is to the rear. The large living room and main bedroom face the view, bringing the kitchen and bathroom windows into the front elevation. The area is only 840 sq. ft., yet the living room is 24ft long, giving a wide choice of ways of dividing off the dining end of the room. The windows in the lounge can be moved about to suit a client's particular requirements, although if unit cost is to be kept to a minimum no windows should be closer to a corner of the building than 2ft. 3".

The roof is entirely supported by the external walls, and although the walls between the rooms are built in solid block work to give good sound insulation, they can be moved around to change the room sizes. A common change is to combine the bathroom and W.C. to give a larger hall.

The bungalow is shown here with a chimney for a coal fire, although this need not be constructed if it is not required. The heating requirement of this compact home when built with modern standards of insulation is so low that all the radiators required for full central heating can be run from the back boiler of a coal or gas fire in the living room.

Design Number 83142

Area	840 sq. ft.	79 sq.m.
Overall	38'4" x 25'1"	11.69 x 7.64
Living Room	24'2" x 11'0"	7.36 x 3.36
Kitchen	12'0" x 10'6"	3.68 x 3.19
Bed 1	12'2" x 11'0"	3.72 x 3.36
Bed 2	10'11" x 10'1"	3.32 x 3.08

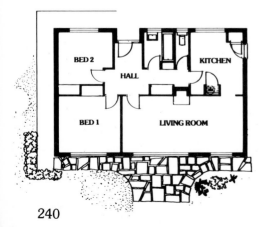

BERKLEY & FOLKESTONE

BERKLEY

The Berkley bungalow is only 700 square feet, and is usually built as a weekend cottage, although it has all the features of a home to be permanently occupied and makes an economical retirement home.

It is this versatility which makes it a good investment as a second home, as the re-sale potential is much better. Small chalets and wooden holiday homes are often depreciating assets, while a miniature full size home in permanent material will appreciate with the housing market.

The illustration shows the rear elevation with a 12ft. patio window. Patio windows of this size in a small lounge have to be double glazed if the house is to be used all year round, and triple glazing can be appropriate in these circumstances. Of course, the patio window can be replaced with an ordinary window if required, or a smaller french window into the end wall. Provided that the end of the window is 2ft. 3 inches from the corner of the building this is easily done, but a true corner window requires special consideration as it may have to be a structural part of the building. We are well used to dealing with this.

Design Number 83134

Area	700 sq.ft.	65 sq.m.
Overall	31'8'' x 25'1''	9.66 x 7.64
Living Room	16'8'' x 12'1''	5.09 x 3.69
Kitchen	11'0'' x 8'2''	3.35 x 2.50
Bed 1	13'0'' x 10'2''	3.97 x 3.09
Bed 2	11'0'' x 9'10''	3.35 x 3.01

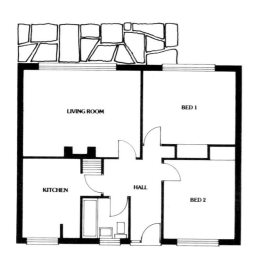

FOLKESTONE

This holiday bungalow has the living accommodation in the centre of the building, with two bedrooms at each end. This arrangement is very convenient for two families going on holiday together, and the open plan layout certainly suits holiday living.

A vacation home like this in permanent materials is a much better investment than a timber chalet, particularly as far as maintenance is concerned.

Design Number 83135

Floor Area	882 sq.ft.	82 sq.m.
Dimensions overall	39'6½'' x 25'3''	12.0 x 7.7
Lounge/Dining (overall)	18'8'' x 13'6''	5.70 x 4.11
Kitchen	7'0'' x 6'0''	2.13 x 1.83
Bed 1	11'6'' x 10'4''	3.51 x 3.15
Bed 2	12'10'' x 9'7''	3.91 x 2.92
Bed 3	9'7'' x 7'3½''	2.92 x 2.22
Bed 4	8'0'' x13'6''	2.43 x 4.11

KESWICK

YARMOUTH

242

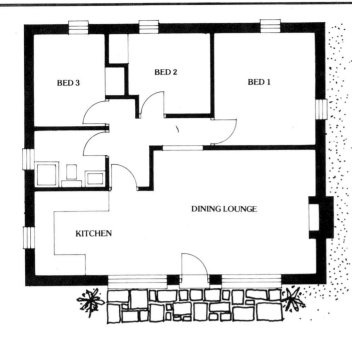

This holiday bungalow of only 650 sq.ft. was designed for holiday living in an area where a simple traditional design is a basic planning requirement. The accommodation is arranged on the basis that a family on holiday in these surroundings will want one double bedroom and two separate sets of bunk beds for children. The kitchen is open plan with the living room, and the windows are as big as one can realistically hope to get the approval of the planners.

A holiday home built in permanent materials like this is a much better investment than the wooden chalet that is often the alternative. The simple design, with the roof wholly supported on the external walls, lends itself to being built as a part time project, perhaps using local sub-contractors for the shell and finishing off the building oneself.

Remember the chimney and fireplace have to be massive to get the right effect with this design.

Design Number 83136

Area	648 sq.ft.	60 sq.m.
Dimensions overall	29'10'' x 25'0''	9.0 x 7.6
Lounge	16'0'' x 12'0''	4.87 x 3.65
Dining/Kitchen	12'0'' x 8'0''	3.65 x 2.43
Bed 1	10'0'' x 10'10''	3.05 x 3.30
Bed 2	8'2'' x 7'10''	2.50 x 2.38
Bed 3	7'0'' x 8'10''	2.13 x 2.70

A holiday bungalow has to be quite different from an ordinary home, and should be designed to suit holiday living — the realities of holiday living, not the image. One reality is that you will not spend all of the holiday sunbathing or fishing, and that the holiday home must have a character and a feel to it that will reflect and enhance a holiday mood.

The huge fireplace which is the key feature of this design gives interest and an outdoor living feel, as well as separating the living area from the galley and dining area. There are two double bedrooms and lots of storage. Storage is important in holiday homes, particularly these days when they are often shared by two or more families, and a large ceiling hatch so that one set of holiday clothes can be up in the roof space in suitcases when someone else is using the bungalow is an important design feature.

With two sliding glass doors on the key elevation, this design is suited to a situation where vacation homes are an established part of the landscape.

The Cromer bungalow, reference 82137 is a 3 bedroom version of the Yarmouth.

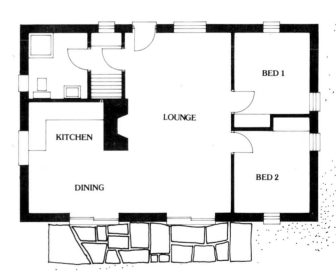

Design Number 83137

Area	713 sq.ft.	66 sq.m.
Dimensions overall	36'2'' x 22'1''	11.0 x 6.7
Lounge	13'0'' x 21'0''	3.96 x 6.40
Dining/Kitchen		
(overall)	12'0'' x 13'0''	3.65 x 3.96
Bed 1	9'0'' x 9'6''	2.74 x 2.90
Bed 2	9'0'' x 9'6''	2.74 x 2.90

NEWQUAY

TRURO

244

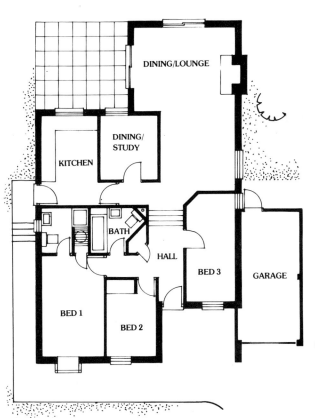

This interesting bungalow is from the drawing board of Robert J. Wood, a well known Architectural practice that moved to Torquay from London some years ago, and which has two bungalow designs in this book. Both are in the rather special style which is typical of the Devon coast.

The Newquay is designed for a sloping site, with four steps down from the hall into the lounge, dining room and kitchen. The shallow span permits an economical purlin roof of unequal span, as shown in the small scale section.

Design Number 83138

Floor Area	990 sq. ft.	92 sq.m.
Overall dimensions	46'6" x 36'8½"	14.1 x 11.4
Lounge/Dining (overall)	21'11¾" x 14'1"	6.70 x 4.30
Kitchen	11'10" x 8'0½"	3.60 x 2.45
Dining/Study	8'3" x 8'6"	2.50 x 2.60
Bed 1	14'0" x 8'10"	4.25 x 2.70
Bed 2	8'8½" x 7'3"	2.65 x 2.20
Bed 3	14'9" x 6'9"	4.50 x 2.05
Garage	17'0" x 8'3"	5.18 x 2.50

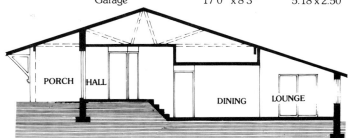

The second bungalow by Robert J. Wood is designed for a narrow site where the view from the principal rooms is to be to the rear.

The massive stone supports for the porch roof, and the sideways facing entrance, help the Truro to look larger than it really is. If necessary the garage can be dispensed with altogether, and the gable roof falling below the main roof will ensure that the bungalow is as distinctive as it is practical.

Design Number 83139

Floor Area	742 sq. ft.	69 sq.m.
Overall dimensions	30'8" x 40'8"	9.35 x12.41
Lounge/Dining (overall)	20'4" x 17'10½"	6.20 x 5.45
Kitchen	8'6" x 8'2½"	2.60 x 2.50
Garage	8'0½" x 17'7"	2.45 x 5.35
Bed 1	8'10" x 11'2"	2.70 x 3.40
Bed 2	7'10" x 11'2"	2.40 x 3.40
Garage	8'2" x 17'9"	2.49 x 5.4

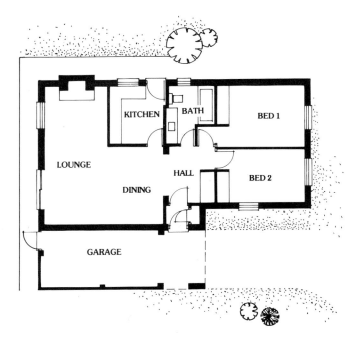

Robert J. Wood, Chartered Architect
70 — 71 Fleet St, Torquay, Devon.

LANGDALE

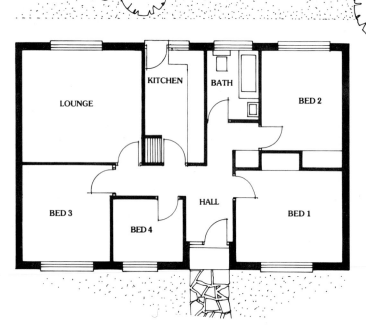

Design Number 83140

Floor Area	840 sq. ft.	79 sq. m.
Overall dimensions	25'3'' x 38'6½''	7.7 x 11.7
Lounge	13'3½'' x 13'6½''	4.05 x 4.12
Kitchen	7'0'' x 13'3½''	2.13 x 4.05
Bed 1	12'4'' x 10'1''	3.76 x 3.08
Bed 2	9'2'' x 11'0''	2.80 x 3.36
Bed 3	9'11'' x 10'1''	3.02 x 3.08
Bed 4	8'0'' x 6'10''	2.43 x 2.08

The Langdale bungalow provides four bedrooms in only 840 sq. feet, and to give this accommodation the lounge has to be fairly small. It is shown here in a rural setting with the windows to the front and rear, but if it has to be fitted on a narrower plot they can be moved into the gable walls.

This design is also useful as a holiday home or fishing cottage, providing the maximum of sleeping accommodation for those who expect to spend the whole day out of doors.

CRESSWELL & WELBECK

CRESSWELL

Clients who are building a home for their retirement often ask for a design of modest overall size, easily run, but with big rooms that suit furniture bought for a larger home. This is a design that meets all the requirements where the site has its principal views to the rear. An alternative version with views to the front is the Welbeck below.

Although the Cresswell will fit on a 45ft plot, both the lounge and the master bedroom are over 20ft. long. The unusually deep wall between the hall and the bedroom accommodates display shelves with concealed lighting, and many other features of this sort can be built into this attractive, but cost effective design.

Design Number 83108

Floor Area		
(exc. garage)	1020 sq.ft.	95 sq.m.
Dimensions Overall	36'10½'' x 34'2''	11.2 x 10.4
Lounge/Dining	13'0'' x 23'0''	3.96 x 7.00
Kitchen (overall)	12'6'' x 13'6''	3.81 x 4.11
Master Bed	20'4'' x 11'6''	6.20 x 3.50
Bed 2	12'6'' x 10'4''	3.81 x 3.15

WELBECK

This is the ''views to the front'' version of our popular Cresswell design which is illustrated above.

When it was designed by Tim Woods the specification was for a retirement bungalow about 1,000 sq.ft. with two bedrooms, one of which was to be at least 20ft. long. The size of the rooms, and the well balanced proportions give this bungalow the feel of a far larger property, and it is in many ways the ideal retirement bungalow.

Design Number 83109

Floor Area	1020 sq.ft.	95 sq.m.
Dimensions Overall	30'10½'' x 34'2''	11.2 x 10.4
Lounge	18'1'' x 12'6''	5.50 x 3.81
Kitchen	12'6'' x 13'6''	3.81 x 4.11
Bed 1 (overall)	20'0'' x 11'6''	6.10 x 3.50
Bed 2	13'0'' x 10'4''	3.96 x 3.15

WINDERMERE & ULLSWATER

The Windermere and Ullswater designs meet a specific requirement in the most practicable way, and are good examples of a design concept that evolved to meet building regulation requirements for narrow sites.

Both designs provide 3 bedroom accommodation with all the bedrooms grouped at one end of the home, and to achieve this one bedroom window has to be in a side wall. A bedroom is classified by the authorities as a "habitable room", unlike a bathroom or kitchen, and the principal window of a habitable room must be at least 12 feet from a boundary.

On the other side of these designs there are nearly 40 square feet of window and door openings, and another building regulation requirement is that they should be at least 3 feet from any boundary.

The third critical dimension is that the most cost effective span for a simple rectangular structure with a trussed rafter roof is about 25 feet.

Add these dimensions together and we arrive at a minimum 40 foot plot width for the standard solution to the problem. If three bedrooms are required on a plot which is less than 40 feet wide, then either two bedrooms have to be at one end and one at the other, or else a structure with a more complex shape is involved.

The Ullswater has the kitchen door on the same side as the bedroom window, and the 12 foot distance to the boundary is wide enough for the drive and a garage adjacent to the back door. The Windermere is obliged to have the garage and drive on the opposite side to the back door. The two bungalows are otherwise the same.

Both designs have an optional cloakroom at the front door, which, if it is not required is just the right size for a cloaks cupboard and somewhere to leave a pram — a requirement that is often overlooked in a compact house, but which is a very important matter.

The 12 foot width for a garage enables it to be built right up to the boundary, with a 3 foot gap between the garage and the main building. This space is often advantageously filled with a wrought iron gate or similar feature.

WINDERMERE

Design Number 83128

Area	850 sq.ft.	79 sq.m.
Overall	38'4'' x 25'1''	11.69 x 7.64
Living Room	16'8'' x 13'1''	5.08 x 3.99
Kitchen	10'6'' x 10'0''	3.19 x 3.05
Bed 1	12'1'' x 10'6''	3.68 x 3.20
Bed 2	11'0'' x 10'6''	3.36 x 3.20
Bed 3	8'10'' x 6'11''	2.70 x 2.10

ULLSWATER

Design Number 83129

Area	850 sq.ft.	79 sq.m.
Overall	38'4'' x 25'1''	11.69 x 7.64
Living Room	16'8'' x 13'1''	5.08 x 3.99
Kitchen	10'6'' x 10'0''	3.19 x 3.05
Bed 1	12'1'' x 10'6''	3.68 x 3.20
Bed 2	11'0'' x 10'6''	3.36 x 3.20
Bed 3	8'10'' x 6'11''	2.70 x 2.10

DENHAM

This bungalow design with its twin staggered car ports comes from France, and is essentially for a site with the view to the rear. The windows on the rear elevation can be positioned to suit the view, the design of the back garden, or simply the decor of the room. This must be arranged with care, as the windows will determine the whole of the character of the lounge, which is very large for a home of this size.

From the road the appearance is dominated by the arrangement of the car ports. If appropriate the right hand one can be paved as a covered approach to the front door, leaving the car or cars on the left. Whatever the arrangement, the supporting pillar should be massive, with deep timbers at the eaves and masonry flower boxes or other features below to balance things up.

A very distinctive home with a lot of character within a very simple basic structure.

Design Number 83110

Area (exc. garage)	1304 sq.ft.	121 sq.m.
Dimensions overall	42'5'' x 53'10''	12.9 x 16.4
Lounge/Dining	31'4'' x 14'0''	9.55 x 4.26
Kitchen	12'0'' x 12'0''	3.65 x 3.65
Master Bed	12'0'' x 18'0''	3.65 x 5.50
Bed 2	11'0'' x 10'0''	3.35 x 3.05
Bed 3	9'0'' x 7'8''	2.74 x 2.35

A slightly larger 4 bedroom version of the Denham is the Harrow bungalow reference 82110

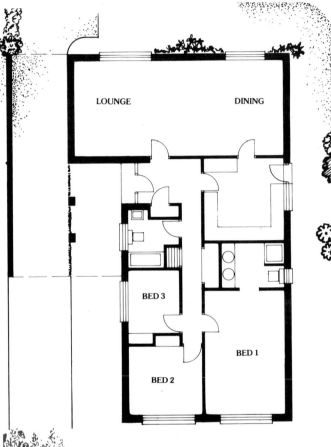

PEMBERTON

A three level house: the garage at ground level, up half a flight of stairs to the hall, lounge and kitchen, and then up another half flight to the bedrooms. This arrangement always seems to suit the use of contrasting materials for the walls to bedroom part of the house, shown here panelled in shiplap timber boarding. A rendered finish with a "bell" bottom edge over the stonework to the garage gives the same effect.

This design is often set back into a bank, and it is possible to save on excavations costs by omitting the store at the back of the garage if the levels permit this.

DINING

KITCHEN

MASTER BED

LOUNGE

D

D

BED 2

BED 3

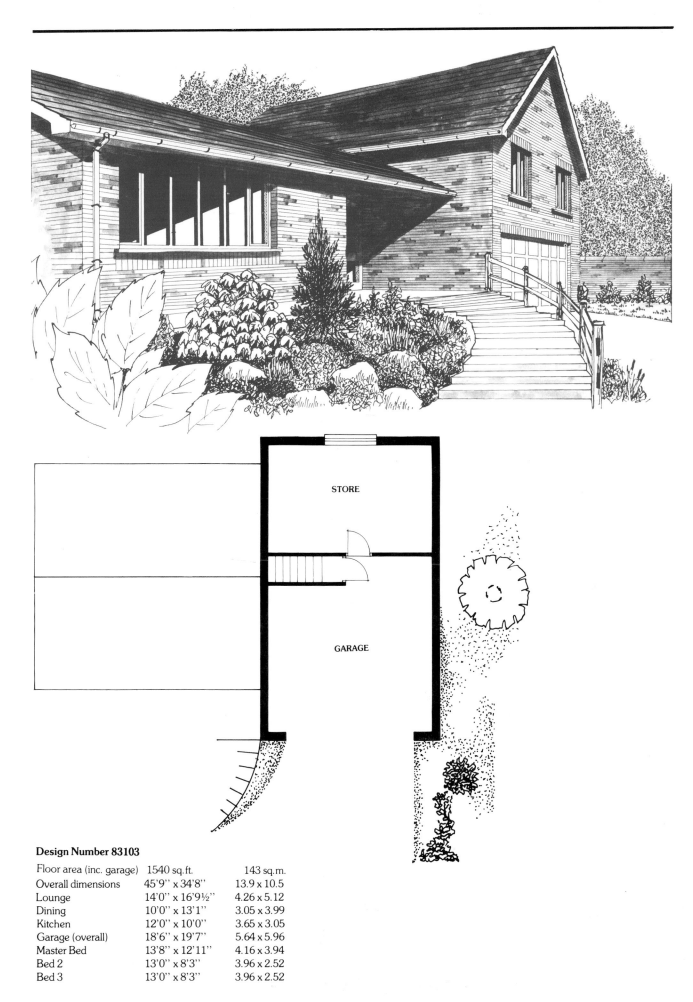

Design Number 83103

Floor area (inc. garage)	1540 sq. ft.	143 sq. m.
Overall dimensions	45'9'' x 34'8''	13.9 x 10.5
Lounge	14'0'' x 16'9½''	4.26 x 5.12
Dining	10'0'' x 13'1''	3.05 x 3.99
Kitchen	12'0'' x 10'0''	3.65 x 3.05
Garage (overall)	18'6'' x 19'7''	5.64 x 5.96
Master Bed	13'8'' x 12'11''	4.16 x 3.94
Bed 2	13'0'' x 8'3''	3.96 x 2.52
Bed 3	13'0'' x 8'3''	3.96 x 2.52

ALMONDBANK

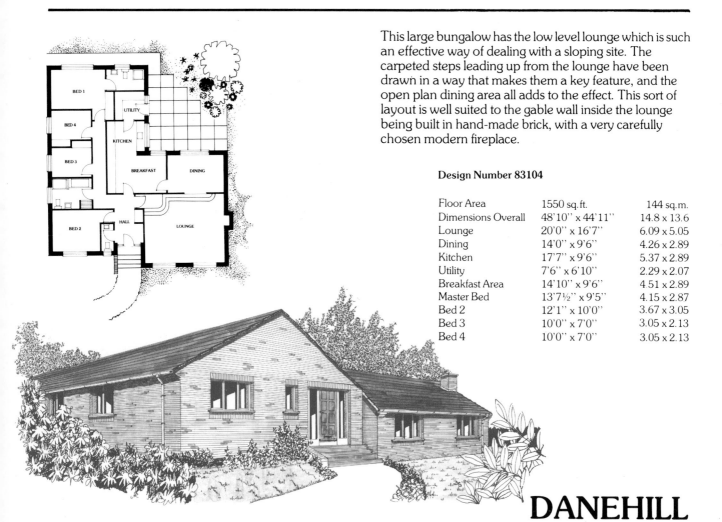

This large bungalow has the low level lounge which is such an effective way of dealing with a sloping site. The carpeted steps leading up from the lounge have been drawn in a way that makes them a key feature, and the open plan dining area all adds to the effect. This sort of layout is well suited to the gable wall inside the lounge being built in hand-made brick, with a very carefully chosen modern fireplace.

Design Number 83104

Floor Area	1550 sq. ft.	144 sq. m.
Dimensions Overall	48'10'' x 44'11''	14.8 x 13.6
Lounge	20'0'' x 16'7''	6.09 x 5.05
Dining	14'0'' x 9'6''	4.26 x 2.89
Kitchen	17'7'' x 9'6''	5.37 x 2.89
Utility	7'6'' x 6'10''	2.29 x 2.07
Breakfast Area	14'10'' x 9'6''	4.51 x 2.89
Master Bed	13'7½'' x 9'5''	4.15 x 2.87
Bed 2	12'1'' x 10'0''	3.67 x 3.05
Bed 3	10'0'' x 7'0''	3.05 x 2.13
Bed 4	10'0'' x 7'0''	3.05 x 2.13

DANEHILL

This is another design with the lounge at a lower level than the rest of the bungalow, with steps down from both the hall and back up again from the lounge into the dining room. This is a very effective way of showing off your dining room suite.

There are two large bedrooms and two bathrooms: the arrangement of these will be altered to suit individual clients requirements. Normally at least one bathroom will be en suite with a bedroom.

Design Number 83105

Floor Area	1360 sq. ft.	126 sq. m.
Dimensions Overall	46'1½'' x 38'10''	14.0 x 11.3
Lounge	21'8'' x 15'0''	6.60 x 4.57
Dining	13'3'' x 9'0''	4.03 x 2.74
Kitchen	16'11'' x 9'6''	5.15 x 2.89
Utility	9'6'' x 5'0''	2.89 x 1.54
Master Bed	12'1½'' x 11'7½''	3.69 x 3.55
Bed 2	15'4'' x 14'4½''	4.67 x 4.38

WASHINGTON

This interesting bungalow is unusual in having a hall that gives access to both the front and the back doors, and can be built with a screen door across the front of the porch to give a lobby at the front door if you are concerned about draughts!

There is a lot of cupboard space, and in many ways this is a very compact design, with a lot of accommodation in a small area. The garages need not be built if they are inappropriate.

Design Number 83101

Floor Area (exc. garage)	1076 sq.ft.	100 sq.m.
Dimensions Overall	51'6'' x 43'8''	15.7 x 13.3
Lounge/Dining	13'0'' x 21'8''	3.96 x 6.60
Kitchen	13'0'' x 10'0''	3.96 x 3.05
Bed 1	13'0'' x 11'0''	3.96 x 3.35
Bed 2	10'1'' x 11'0''	3.07 x 3.35
Study Bed	8'0'' x 8'9''	2.43 x 2.66
Garages (each)	9'0'' x 18'4''	2.74 x 5.60

MISTERTON

The Misterton design bungalow provides a large living area and an interesting and complex shaped structure that can be accommodated on a relatively narrow site. The frontage depends on the width of the garage required: with a single garage it can be built on a 40 foot side plot, and it only requires 54 feet for a double garage as shown.

The internal hall giving access to the bedrooms lacks a window and requires that at least 2 of the doors leading from it have glazed lights above. This is not an unusual arrangement. The wall between the utility room and the kitchen is not structural, and can be omitted if required.

Flat roofs are not as fashionable now as they were ten years ago, but in areas where they are an established feature of local architecture this design is deservedly popular.

Design Number 83122

Area (exc. garage)	1070 sq.ft.	102 sq.m.
Overall	46'7'' x 55'9''	14.20 x 17.00
Lounge	14'6'' x 15'9''	4.42 x 4.80
Dining	14'6'' x 9'10''	4.42 x 2.99
Kitchen	10'2'' x 8'10''	3.09 x 2.69
Bed 1	10'2'' x 10'6''	3.09 x 3.20
Bed 2	10'11'' x 10'6''	3.32 x 3.20
Bed 3	9'10'' x 8'6''	2.99 x 2.59
Garage	18'5'' x 15'6''	5.61 x 4.72

SHREWSBURY

Like many of our designs, the Shrewsbury bungalow was first drawn to meet a clients requirements, proved popular with others, and then became a standard. It is shown with an open-plan lounge/dining/kitchen arrangement, with these 3 rooms linked by wide arched openings that relate to each other in a particularly effective way. Open-plan living is a personal choice, and if desired these arches can be replaced by either single or double doors.

Building Regulations require that the window to bedroom 3 shall be 12 foot from any boundary, so the bungalow as drawn requires a minimum 53 feet width of plot. However, it has been built with the master bedroom increased in size and with bedroom 3 as an en suite bathroom. This arrangement will fit on a plot only 44 feet wide. It has also been modified for another client with a cloak room in the hall turned round to make a shower room to bedroom 2. The permutations are endless!

A two bedroom/two bathroom luxury version of this bungalow is the Parkhead, reference 82097.

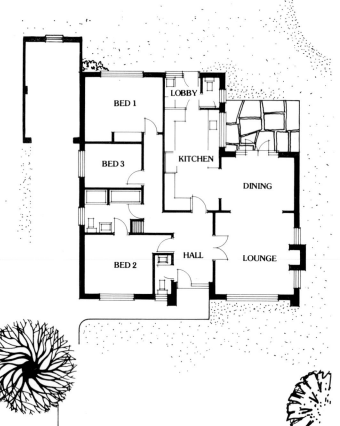

Design Number 83097

Area	1194 sq.ft.	211 sq.m.
Overall	38'4'' x 38'4''	11.69 x 11.69
Lounge	14'1'' x 13'10''	4.29 x 4.21
Dining	12'11'' x 9'0''	3.95 x 2.74
Kitchen	16'11'' x 9'6''	5.15 x 2.89
Bed 1	13'7'' x 11'5''	4.15 x 3.47
Bed 2	12'1'' x 10'0''	3.67 x 3.05
Bed 3	10'0'' x 7'0''	3.05 x 2.13
Garage	11'6'' x 18'0''	3.5 x 5.4

GRASMERE

This straight-forward bungalow for a 40ft. wide site has proved very successful over many years. The building is 25ft. wide, the garage can easily fit in a 12ft wide garden area, and there is a 3ft passage on the other side. This is the most practicable arrangement for a simple and cost effective rectangular structure on a plot of this size, and if it is possible to site the garage forward, as shown, the total effect is very attractive.

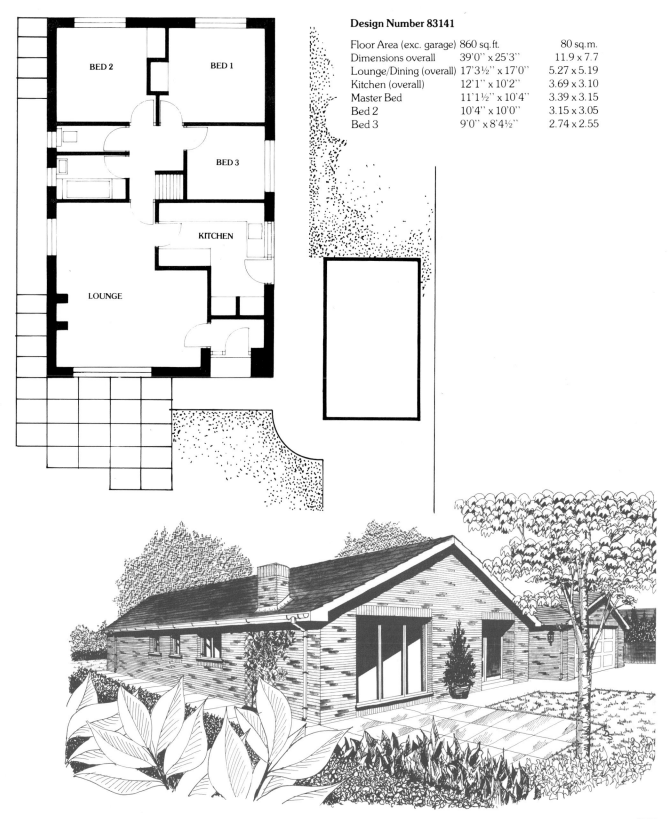

Design Number 83141

Floor Area (exc. garage)	860 sq. ft.	80 sq. m.
Dimensions overall	39'0'' x 25'3''	11.9 x 7.7
Lounge/Dining (overall)	17'3½'' x 17'0''	5.27 x 5.19
Kitchen (overall)	12'1'' x 10'2''	3.69 x 3.10
Master Bed	11'1½'' x 10'4''	3.39 x 3.15
Bed 2	10'4'' x 10'0''	3.15 x 3.05
Bed 3	9'0'' x 8'4½''	2.74 x 2.55

HAVERHILL

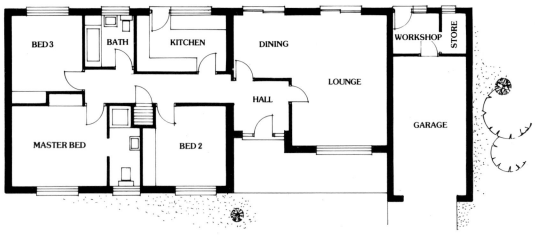

The Haverhill bungalow suits a site where a natural slope permits the garage floor to be significantly lower than the level of the living accommodation, giving an interesting and very cost effective roof arrangement. Although it is illustrated with flat tiles, this emphasis on the roof is very well suited to parts of the country where traditional pantiles are appropriate.

Design Number 83094

Floor Area	1150 sq.ft.	107 sq.m.
Dimensions overall	64'8'' x 26'6''	19.7 x 8.1
Lounge/Dining (overall)	21'6'' x 18'0''	6.55 x 5.48
Kitchen	11'6'' x 7'8½''	3.50 x 2.35
Garage	19'0'' x 10'2½''	5.79 x 3.11
Master Bed	13'6'' x 11'0''	4.11 x 3.35
Bed 2	12'0'' x 11'0''	3.65 x 3.35
Bed 3	10'0'' x 10'6''	3.05 x 3.20

FOREST GATE

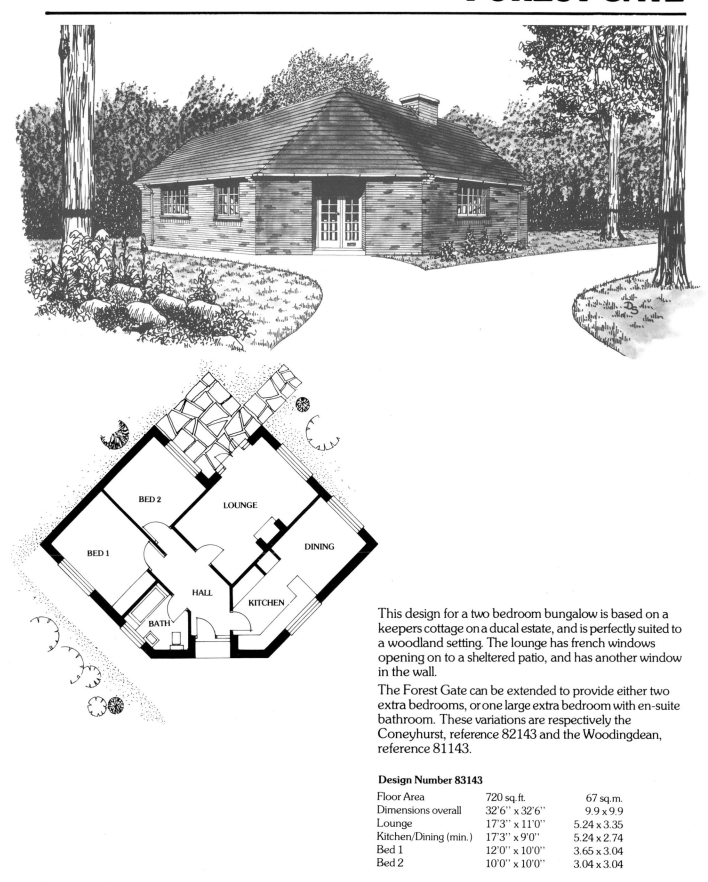

This design for a two bedroom bungalow is based on a keepers cottage on a ducal estate, and is perfectly suited to a woodland setting. The lounge has french windows opening on to a sheltered patio, and has another window in the wall.

The Forest Gate can be extended to provide either two extra bedrooms, or one large extra bedroom with en-suite bathroom. These variations are respectively the Coneyhurst, reference 82143 and the Woodingdean, reference 81143.

Design Number 83143

Floor Area	720 sq. ft.	67 sq.m.
Dimensions overall	32'6'' x 32'6''	9.9 x 9.9
Lounge	17'3'' x 11'0''	5.24 x 3.35
Kitchen/Dining (min.)	17'3'' x 9'0''	5.24 x 2.74
Bed 1	12'0'' x 10'0''	3.65 x 3.04
Bed 2	10'0'' x 10'0''	3.04 x 3.04

CARDIGAN

The Cardigan is an ideal retirement bungalow with a large living room which appeals to those who have been used to a larger house. The angled fireplace gives interest to the room, which has windows looking both front and rear. It is illustrated with a garage at the bedroom end of the house, which sometimes is unavoidable to suit an existing access. It is more usual to build it with a garage that gives access to the kitchen door, and this is shown in the inset plan. This arrangement, with the utility room at the back door, helps to keep draughts out of the kitchen.

The Cardigan is illustrated without a chimney, but we find that our clients who do not want an open fire invariably build a false chimney breast with an electric fire to give a focal point to the room.

In thinking how this bungalow would suit a site, remember that windows can be moved into the gable end wall to take advantage of a special view.

Design Number 83144

Area	840 sq. ft.	79 sq. m.
Overall	38'4'' x 25'1''	11.69 x 7.64
Lounge	19'0'' x 11'0''	5.79 x 3.36
Dining	12'5'' x 8'2''	3.78 x 2.50
Kitchen	12'1'' x 10'6''	3.68 x 2.19
Bed 1	11'7'' x 10'6''	3.54 x 3.21
Bed 2	10'7'' x 9'0''	3.23 x 2.75

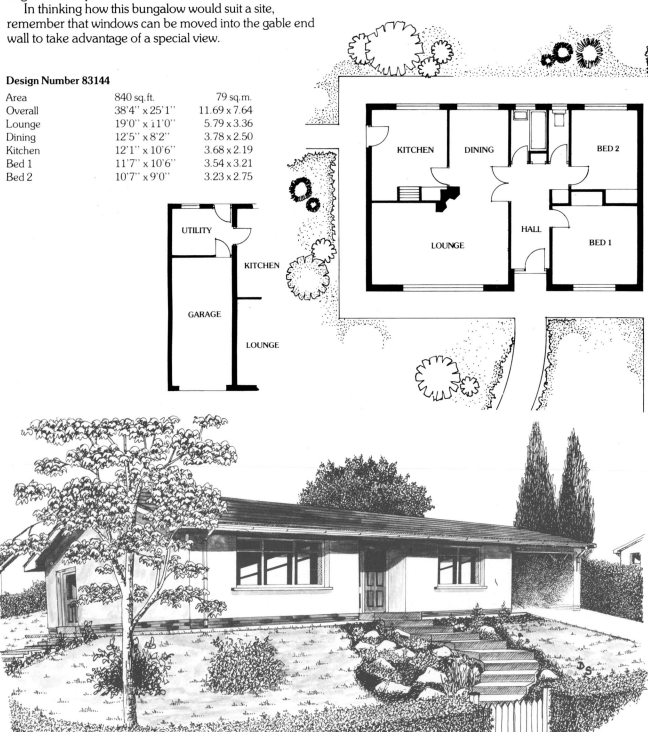

MARLOW

The Marlow is a 4 bedroomed version of the Parklands design opposite, and is very popular with those who like a really large living area in a bungalow of only 1060 square feet. There are two alternative bathroom arrangements, as we find that this house is often built by those with a large family who prefer one bathroom for the parents and a shower room for everyone else.

As with the Parklands, the garage need not be built, in which case it is usual to provide a porch of some sort or another at the back door.

Design Number 83131

Area (exc. garage)	1060 sq.ft.	99 sq.m.
Overall	47'11" x 25'1"	14.61 x 7.64
Lounge	19'9" x 11'0"	6.01 x 3.36
Dining	12'4" x 8'11"	3.78 x 2.72
Kitchen	12'0" x 10'6"	3.68 x 3.19
Bed 1	10'4" x 10'1"	3.14 x 3.07
Bed 2	10'4" x 10'1"	3.14 x 3.07
Bed 3	9'2" x 7'5"	2.80 x 2.27
Bed 4	9'2" x 6'7"	2.80 x 2.00

THORNHILL

The Thornhill bungalow suits either a site of generous size, where the lounge window can be in the side wall as illustrated, or a narrow plot where the lounge window changes place with the fireplace. There are other options as well, and one is to turn the en-suite bathroom to the guest room into a cloakroom with a door from the hall. Altogether it is a very versatile and popular design.

A five bedroom version of this bungalow is the Broadwell, reference 82096.

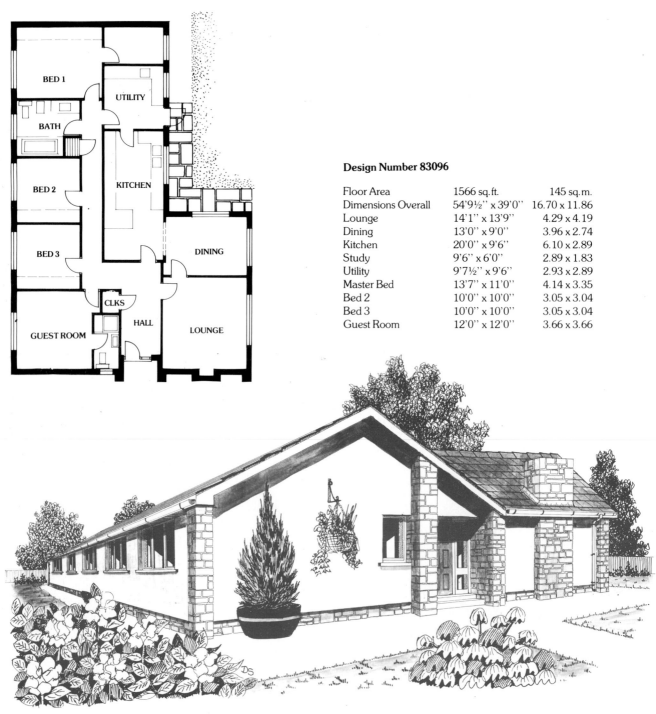

Design Number 83096

Floor Area	1566 sq.ft.	145 sq.m.
Dimensions Overall	54'9½'' x 39'0''	16.70 x 11.86
Lounge	14'1'' x 13'9''	4.29 x 4.19
Dining	13'0'' x 9'0''	3.96 x 2.74
Kitchen	20'0'' x 9'6''	6.10 x 2.89
Study	9'6'' x 6'0''	2.89 x 1.83
Utility	9'7½'' x 9'6''	2.93 x 2.89
Master Bed	13'7'' x 11'0''	4.14 x 3.35
Bed 2	10'0'' x 10'0''	3.05 x 3.04
Bed 3	10'0'' x 10'0''	3.05 x 3.04
Guest Room	12'0'' x 12'0''	3.66 x 3.66

EVESHAM

This is a D & M design, and has been built more often than any of the other D & M bungalows. The garage and utility room are often left off, sometimes with the intention of building them later, and when this is done the bungalow is still pleasantly proportioned and seems much larger than its modest 840 sq. ft.. The living room is a full twenty feet long, and if the fireplace is not required then the space which it occupies can be used to provide another cupboard in the hall. The kitchen is small: a decision has to be made whether to have a door from the kitchen to the living room, or whether to gain more space for kitchen units by having only a serving hatch.

We show this bungalow with a separate WC, but if required this can be moved into the bathroom, which will then have room for a shower, bidet, or airing cupboard. Once again, it is up to the householders to make their own decisions. There is room for another WC in the place of the utility room as shown on the inset drawing.

When built to todays high insulation standards this bungalow can have full central heating with the radiators run from the back boiler of either a coal fire or a gas fire in the lounge.

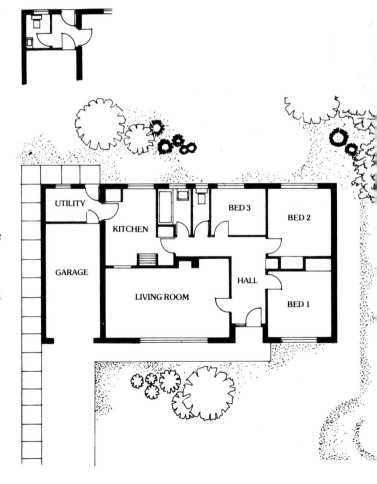

Design Number 83145

Area (exc. garage)	840 sq. ft.	79 sq. m.
Overall	38'4'' x 25'1''	11.69 x 7.64
Living Room	20'6'' x 11'0''	6.24 x 3.36
Kitchen	12'0'' x 8'4''	3.68 x 2.55
Bed 1	10'6'' x 10'2''	3.21 x 3.08
Bed 2	10'7'' x 10'2''	3.23 x 3.08
Bed 3	8'9'' x 7'2''	2.68 x 2.18

MIDHURST

TAUNTON

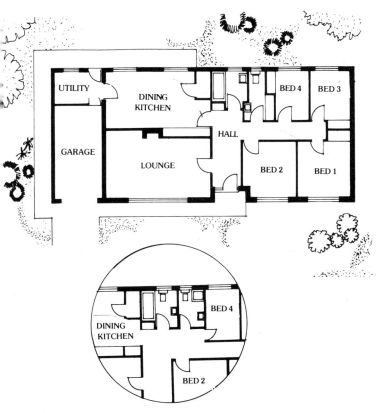

The Midhurst design is the 4 bedroomed version of our Ascot design, and is one of our series of rural designs with very large "living in" kitchens.

The garage and utility room shown can be omitted from the design altogether if required, and a small porch built at the back door for muddy boots and somewhere for the dogs to sleep!

The WC has its own wash basin, or room for a vanity unit, and is a very popular feature in a home with 4 bedrooms for a young family. Taking this concept further, the Midhurst has been built a number of times with a WC extended to become a shower room, although this cuts down the size of the 4th bedroom and involves moving the bedroom door. The inset drawing shows how this is arranged.

Design Number 83114

Area (exc. garage)	1060 sq.ft.	99 sq.m.
Overall	47'11'' x 25'1''	14.61 x 7.64
Lounge	19'9'' x 12'6''	6.01 x 3.81
Dining Kitchen	19'9'' x 10'7''	6.01 x 3.23
Bed 1	10'4'' x 10'1''	3.14 x 3.07
Bed 2	10'4'' x 10'1''	3.14 x 3.07
Bed 3	9'2'' x 7'5''	2.80 x 2.27
Bed 4	9'2'' x 6'7''	2.80 x 2.00

When you look at L shaped bungalow plans note carefully if a wall that supports the main roof continues straight through at the point where it joins the subsidiary roof. If it does, as with the Taunton, the roof design is simple, easy to build and cost-effective. Of course, there are many ways of building when this cannot be a design feature, but all of them involve special structural components which not only have to be designed, purchased and built in, but which also have to be approved by the local authority after the submission of structural engineers design calculations.

But enough of this — if you buy the plans from us we provide the design calculations anyway. The Taunton bungalow is a popular design with the single drawback that visitors to the front door have to walk down a passage to get to the lounge. Whether or not you think this a disadvantage is a personal choice. The windows in the lounge, and in the two end bedrooms, can be moved around to suit the view, and the back door can be moved from the back of the utility room to the front of it if this is desired.

Design Number 83115

Area including single garage	1616 sq.ft.	149 sq.m.
Overall	57'6'' x 45'9''	17.54 x 13.94
Lounge	23'4'' x 13'7''	7.11 x 4.15
Dining	11'10'' x 8'11''	3.60 x 2.72
Kitchen	13'5'' x 10'5''	4.10 x 3.18
Bed 1	13'0'' x 12'10''	3.96 x 3.92
Bed 2	13'0'' x 10'2''	3.96 x 3.08
Bed 3	10'6'' x 8'11''	3.21 x 2.72
Utility	15'11'' x 7'11''	4.89 x 2.42
Garage	15'11'' x 11'7''	4.89 x 3.51

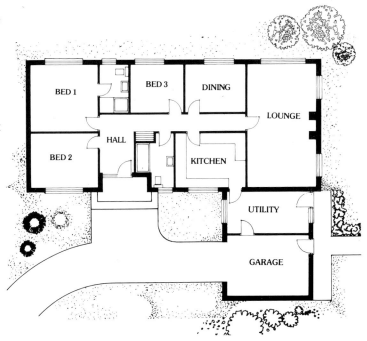

WINSLOW

This is another example of a small bungalow without a back door — a matter of personal choice that is a heresy to some, and commonsense to others. It suits a narrow plot, and without a second entrance one saves the cost of a path, gains room in the kitchen, and avoids having the milkman walking around the house in his heavy boots early in the morning!

The front porch feature is a relatively inexpensive way of giving character and prestige to what is basically a very economical rectangular structure. In the same way the angled fireplace and chimney breast can be built as a feature to house an electric fire without the expense of a chimney. This is how the bungalow is illustrated, although the chimney for an open fire can be built if required.

Design Number 83146

Area (exc. garage)	896 sq. ft.	83 sq. m.
Dimensions overall	33'11" x 41'6½"	10.34 x 13.88
Lounge	12'0" x 17'0"	3.65 x 5.20
Dining	10'6" x 10'0"	3.20 x 3.05
Kitchen	8'6" x 10'0"	2.59 x 3.05
Carport	9'0" x 17'9"	2.74 x 5.40
Master Bedroom	12'0" x 12'0"	3.65 x 3.65
Bed 2	10'0" x 12'0"	3.05 x 3.65
Bed 3	10'0" x 8'6"	3.05 x 2.59

BEECHWOOD

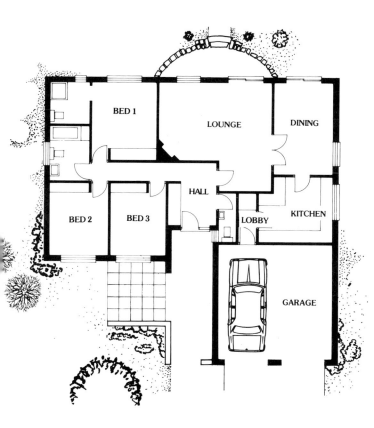

A narrow plot can make it necessary to build a garage projecting forward from a house or bungalow. If this is necessary it has to become an integral part of the whole design concept, and not "stuck on" as an after thought. This very attractive design achieves its effect by the clever balance between the different elements in the front elevation, and the unusually wide soffits to the roof. It is a striking and impressive building, and yet fits on a frontage of less than 60 feet.

Access from the garage into the kitchen is shown via a lobby with a useful store, or room for a deep freeze. As an alternative this lobby can be combined with the cloakroom, giving useful storage space. To comply with Building Regulations the door from the garage has to have a special fire-resistance rating and to be set in a frame with 25mm rebates. This is easily arranged.

If the width of the plot at the building line is very tight it is possible to reduce the width of this design slightly by substituting a double garage door for the two single garage doors shown. However, we feel that this unbalances the appearance slightly.

Design Number 83147

Area (inc. garage)	1690 sq.ft.	157 sq.m.
Dimensions overall	49'10"x 47'7"	15.1 x 14.5
Lounge (overall)	19'0" x 17'9"	5.79 x 5.41
Dining	10'0" x 15'0"	3.05 x 4.57
Kitchen (overall)	12'6" x 10'9"	3.81 x 3.28
Garage	19'4" x 19'0"	5.90 x 5.79
Master Bed	11'0" x 12'9"	3.35 x 3.90
Bed 2	10'0" x 12'0"	3.05 x 3.65
Bed 3	10'0" x 12'0"	3.05 x 3.65

YEOVIL

This is a version of the popular Exeter design bungalow with an integral Granny Flat. The flat has its own front door, an arrangement that is always very popular with Grannies who like to feel that they have retained their independence.

This design is suitable for a site with all round views, and the windows can be changed round to suit the clients' requirements.

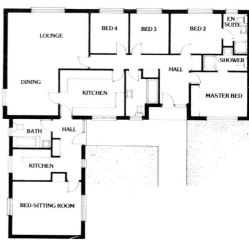

Design Number 83117

Floor Area (inclusive)	1765 sq.ft.	164 sq.m.
Dimensions Overall	57'9" x 52'4"	17.6 x 15.9
Lounge/Dining (overall)	23'5" x 19'2½"	7.14 x 5.85
Kitchen	10'5½" x 15'1"	3.18 x 4.60
Bed 1	13'1" x 10'2"	3.99 x 3.08
Bed 2	11'10" x 9'0½"	3.61 x 2.75
Bed 3	9'0" x 9'0½"	2.74 x 2.75
Bed 4	9'0" x 9'0½"	2.74 x 2.75
Annexe:		
Bed-Sitting Room	15'11" x 12'0"	4.89 x 3.65
Kitchen	7'0" x 9'0"	2.13 x 2.74

BRIDGWATER

This is a variant of the popular Taunton bungalow, with the double garage replaced by a Granny Flat. The overall dimensions are identical, and it is practicable to build the Bridgwater design with minimum additional foundations and lintels so that it can be turned into a Taunton if ever required. In the same way a Taunton can be built with everything ready for it to be turned into this design. Some clients have found this very convenient.

The windows in the Granny Flat can be moved about to suit the view.

Design Number 83116

Total Floor Area	1592 sq.ft.	148 sq.m.
Overall Dimensions	52'2" x 52'4"	15.8 x 15.9
Main Dwelling:		
Lounge	23'5" x 13'7"	7.14 x 4.15
Dining	11'10" x 9'0"	3.60 x 2.74
Kitchen	10'6" x 13'5"	3.19 x 4.10
Bed 1	13'0" x 13'0"	3.95 x 3.96
Bed 2	13'0" x 10'1½"	3.96 x 3.08
Bed 3	9'0" x 10'6"	2.74 x 3.21
Bedsitting	12'0" x 16'0"	3.65 x 4.87

This is a design with a self-contained flat for someone using a wheelchair who lives with the family — and it will all fit on a 51 ft. plot. There is a front porch with double doors which are easily managed, and then there are sliding doors into the flat, and all the doors inside the flat are opened in this way. When this design was originally built the three windows in the flat were constructed as narrow bays with very deep sills. The sills were fitted with lead trays as permanent window-boxes and the room had house plants in flower all the year round.

Design Number 83168

Floor Area (total)	1582 sq. ft.	147 sq. m.
Overall dimensions	44'4½'' x 56'3''	13.5 x 17.1
Main Dwelling:		
Lounge/Dining (overall)	23'5'' x 19'9''	7.14 x 6.01
Kitchen	10'6'' x 10'7''	3.20 x 3.24
Bed 1	10'7'' x 10'0''	3.24 x 3.05
Bed 2	12'5½'' x 10'0''	3.80 x 3.05
Bed 3	8'11'' x 12'1''	2.71 x 3.68
Annexe:		
Bedsitting Room		
(overall)	18'2½'' x 14'0''	5.55 x 4.26
Kitchen	10'0'' x 7'0''	3.05 x 2.13
Bath	9'5'' x 7'0''	2.87 x 2.13

ALLINGTON

Design Number 83169

This is an alternative version of the Clevedon design with a special flat for someone living in a wheelchair, but has the main accommodation with the lounge at the rear instead of the front. The overall size and floor area are the same, although some of the room sizes vary.

MARYLAND

The Maryland design bungalow features a large open plan dining hall with a full depth Georgian bay window. This is a most effective way of giving a prestige feel to a house of modest overall size, and it is an idea which is gaining in popularity. By pushing the garage forward the front elevation has a courtyard look, and flower boxes or other features can enhance this and make it a most striking home.

   The three bedroom layout includes a master suite that is shown with both a dressing room and a shower room, but of course the opportunities for arranging your own layout here are limitless.

   The massive chimney breast is designed to be a feature in both the lounge and the hall, to be built in either brick or stone as required. It can easily contain a gas fired central heating unit, with the controls hidden behind a specially designed door. This saves space in the kitchen and reduces pipe runs — and cost.

A five bedroom version of this bungalow with a gable extension to the rear is the Carolina design, reference 82150.

Design Number 83150

Area (exc. garage)	1188 sq.ft.	110 sq.m.
Dimensions overall	49'7'' x 47'2''	15.10 x 14.37
Lounge (overall)	13'0'' x 16'9''	3.96 x 5.10
Dining	11'0'' x 11'4''	3.35 x 3.45
Kitchen	13'1'' x 10'9''	4.00 x 3.28
Garage	21'0'' x 20'0''	6.40 x 6.10
Master Bed	11'0'' x 14'9''	3.35 x 4.50
Bed 2	11'0'' x 11'0''	3.35 x 3.35
Bed 3	12'0'' x 9'6''	3.65 x 2.90
Garage	18'3'' x 19'10''	5.64 x 6.06

Home Planners, Inc
23761 Reseach Drive
Farmington Hills, Michigan 48024, USA.

ALBANY

This large bungalow to an American design has many features which have been absent from our own domestic architecture for many years, but which are now coming back into fashion. The deep windows to the bedrooms are unusual, but give enormous character to the whole building. They can, of course, be replaced with windows of a standard sill height if required.

The deeply recessed porch with double doors gives a most prestigeous entrance. Our sketch shows classical pillars to the front of the porch. These are a key feature and must be absolutely right; in some situations it will be preferable to replace them with massive brick or stone piers. The choice will also depend on how it is intended to handle the landscaping of the garden in front of the porch.

A five bedroom version of this design is called the Maine, reference 82151.

Design Number 83151

Floor area (inc. garage)	1873 sq.ft.	174 sq.m.
Dimensions overall	61'3'' x 41'9''	18.6 x 12.7
Lounge	18'0'' x 18'6''	5.48 x 5.64
Dining	11'0'' x 19'2''	3.35 x 5.84
Kitchen	11'10'' x 10'0''	3.60 x 3.05
Utility	7'0'' x 10'0''	2.14 x 3.05
Garage	20'0'' x 21'4''	6.10 x 6.50
Master Bed	14'0'' x 12'2''	4.26 x 3.70
Bed 2	11'0'' x 11'0''	3.35 x 3.35
Bed 3	11'0'' x 9'0''	3.35 x 2.74

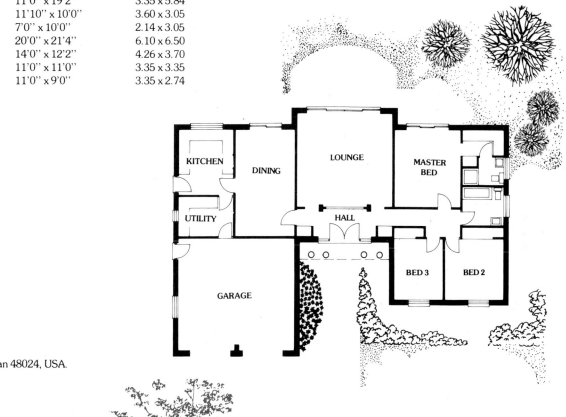

Home Planners, Inc
23761 Reseach Drive
Farmington Hills, Michigan 48024, USA.

269

CONNECTICUT

This is another typical American design, and is one that gets a great deal of character and interest in a layout that can suit a fairly modest plot — although it must be said that it will look its best with a lot more room around it. It looks complex and expensive; in fact it is not. All the three main roofs are at the same span, and the valley arrangements are simple and straight-forward. Shuttered windows to the garage match those in the living accommodation, and help to make the bungalow seem even larger than it is. The full depth bow window in the dining room rounds it off.

The dovecote above the garage doors is a fanciful feature — or is it? In the last century this sort of thing was commonplace, adding interest and character to a building. Then, for some reason, it was considered an architectural extravagance. Now the human values are reasserting themselves, and a good thing too.

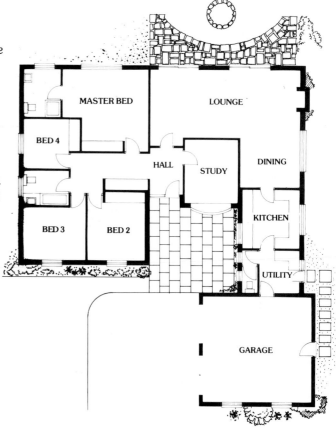

Design Number 83152

Area (exc. garage)	1767 sq.ft.	164 sq.m.
Dimensions overall	55'1'' x 63'7''	16.8 x 19.3
Lounge	13'0'' x 29'0''	3.96 x 8.83
Dining Area	11'6'' x 9'4''	3.50 x 2.85
Kitchen	11'0'' x 11'0''	3.35 x 3.35
Study	10'4'' x 12'0''	3.15 x 3.65
Utility	7'0'' x 6'6''	2.13 x 1.98
Garage	20'0'' x 21'0''	6.10 x 6.40
Master Bed (overall)	16'6'' x 15'6''	5.03 x 4.75
Bed 2	11'1'' x 13'0''	3.38 x 3.96
Bed 3	10'6'' x 12'0''	3.20 x 3.65
Bed 4	10'10'' x 9'4''	3.30 x 2.85

Home Planners, Inc
23761 Reseach Drive
Farmington Hills, Michigan 48024, USA.

DEANSGATE

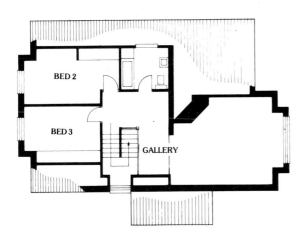

This is another American design by Home Plans Inc of Michigan which cleverly combines a traditional exterior with excitingly different floor plans. The idea of the internal arrangement takes some getting used to; the lounge has a sloping ceiling the full height of the house, overlooked by a minstrel gallery which is also the first floor landing. At the other end of the room is a massive floor to ceiling window which projects forward in a window wall, and which is shown here with a traditional stone surround. The master bedroom suite is on the ground floor and two other bedrooms and a bathroom above.

All this is in a floor area of under 1700 sq.ft., and can be accommodated on a fairly narrow plot if required. Unit building costs for this design are high, but this is a home that is an investment that will always keep well ahead of the market.

Incidentally this design can also be built with a gable porch to the front entrance, and in a suburban situation this would probably be preferable.

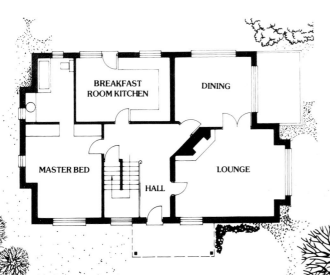

Design Number 83153

Floor Area	1661 sq.ft.	154 sq.m.
Dimensions overall	45'1'' x 33'0''	13.7 x 10.0
Lounge (overall)	17'6'' x 15'0''	5.32 x 4.55
Dining	13'6'' x 12'0''	4.13 x 3.65
Breakfast Kitchen	16'10'' x 11'6''	5.15 x 3.35
Master Bed (overall)	13'6'' x 16'0''	4.13 x 4.87
Bed 2	17'0'' x 9'4''	5.20 x 2.85
Bed 3	13'6'' x 9'6''	4.13 x 2.90

Home Planners, Inc
23761 Reseach Drive
Farmington Hills, Michigan 48024, USA.

OLLERTON

This bungalow was designed by Scattergood and Woodhams of Worksop, and has a distinctive appearance with an attractive balance between the wide glazed screen to the hall and the run of smaller windows on each side. To be seen at its best it needs a setting where the whole bungalow is in view, set well back in a large garden. A very interesting design.

Design Number 83154

Floor Area		
(exc. garage)	1270 sq.ft.	118 sq.m.
Overall dimensions	64'8'' x 32'7½''	19.7 x 9.46
Lounge	16'1'' x 20'0''	4.90 x 6.10
Dining	15'5'' x 9'0''	4.70 x 2.75
Kitchen	11'10'' x 11'10''	3.60 x 3.60
Utility	5'11'' x 9'6''	1.80 x 2.90
Bed 1	13'6'' x 10'10''	4.10 x 3.30
Bed 2	11'10'' x 9'10''	3.60 x 3.00
Bed 3 (overall)	8'10'' x 13'6''	2.70 x 4.10

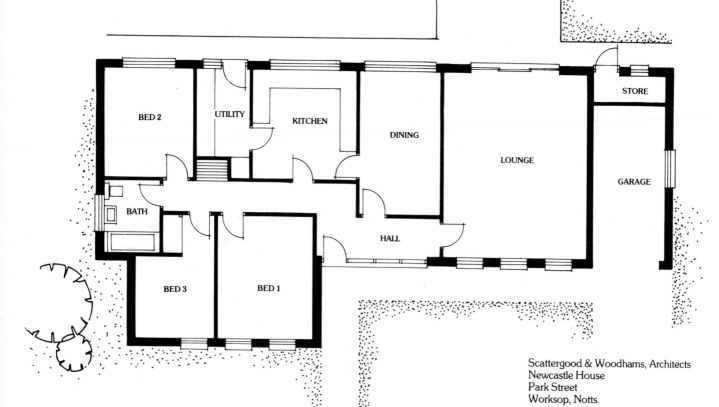

Scattergood & Woodhams, Architects
Newcastle House
Park Street
Worksop, Notts.

CAMBERLEY

This 840 sq. ft. 2 bedroom bungalow will sit on narrow sites, as all the windows which the Building Regulation requires to be at least 12ft from a boundary are in the gable end walls. However, it can also be used on a more spacious site like the one illustrated, and is useful in situations where as few windows as possible are wanted on the front elevation.

The Camberley has a very simple layout, and always feels larger than it really is. As with all small rectangular bungalows, the lower the roof pitch, the larger the building will seem.

If a storm porch is required there is room for a glazed screen and door inside the front door which is shown on the plan, and this is a popular feature with those who build the Camberley as a bungalow for their retirement.

Design Number 83148

Area	840 sq. ft.	79 sq. m.
Overall	38'4'' x 25'1''	11.69 x 7.64
Lounge	19'0'' x 11'0''	5.79 x 3.36
Dining	12'5'' x 8'2''	3.78 x 2.50
Kitchen	12'1'' x 10'6''	3.68 x 3.19
Bed 1	11'7'' x 10'6''	3.54 x 3.21
Bed 2	10'7'' x 9'0''	3.23 x 2.75

MENDIP

This design is for use on sites with very narrow frontages, and enables a three bedroom layout to be accommodated on a plot thirty five feet wide if a drive to a garage at the rear is required down the side of the bungalow, or only thirty one feet wide if access to a garage can be provided in some other way.

The Mendip design is fully reversible, and can be built with the lounge facing either the road or the back garden.

There is space for built-in wardrobes in all the bedrooms. If desired the bathroom and washbasin can be combined, giving room for a bidet or shower as well as the fittings shown, or else enabling the airing cupboard to be moved into the bathroom.

Design Number 83149

Area	840 sq. ft.	79 sq. m.
Overall	38'4'' x 25'1''	11.69 x 7.64
Living Room	17'5'' x 13'6''	5.30 x 4.11
Kitchen	13'6'' x 8'4''	4.11 x 2.54
Bed 1	11'6'' x 10'4''	3.51 x 3.15
Bed 2	11'10'' x 9'7''	3.61 x 2.92
Bed 3	9'7'' x 7'4''	2.92 x 2.22

PETWORTH

This is a D & M design, and D & M will never forget the client for whom this design was drawn as they took a vintage Bentley in part exchange for their service!

The low level lounge is entered down a feature staircase that leads from the dining room, which is completely open plan with the lounge except for the changes of levels and an attractive room divider.

The fireplace wall is in handmade brick. The whole effect is quite stunning and it is difficult to realise that the whole bungalow is only 1360 sq.ft. Note the small shower room off the main bedroom with a sliding door to save space.

Design Number 83132

Floor Area	1360 sq.ft.	126 sq.m.
Dimensions overall	51'0'' x 30'0''	15.5 x 9.1
Lounge	22'2'' x 16'7½''	6.75 x 5.07
Dining	12'6'' x 11'3''	3.81 x 3.42
Kitchen (overall)	17'8½'' x 11'3''	5.40 x 3.42
Master Bed	12'8'' x 10'9''	3.86 x 3.27
Bed 2	10'9'' x 10'3''	3.27 x 3.12
Bed 3	9'3'' x 9'0''	2.82 x 2.74

There is a four bedroom version of this bungalow called the Chesterton. The reference number is 82132.

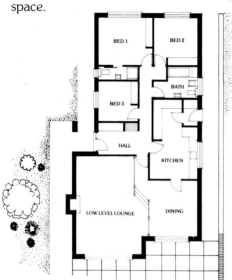

AMBERLEY

This is another design with a dropped lounge to take advantage of a sloping site, although it can be built on the level if required. The carpeted steps by the side of the fireplace lead up to the dining area. Your dining suite at this high level with windows behind it will look very striking, and add tremendous character. If required the bedroom wing can be at a higher level than the hall, as there is plenty of room in the passage between bedrooms 2 and 4 for the steps that would be required.

Design Number 83133

Floor Area	1920 sq.ft.	178 sq.m.
Dimensions overall	65'10½'' x 44'5''	20.0 x 13.5
Lounge	19'9'' x 20'0''	6.00 x 6.10
Dining	11'10'' x 10'10½''	3.60 x 3.30
Kitchen	16'5½'' x 10'10½''	5.01 x 3.30
Study	12'6'' x 8'7½''	3.82 x 2.63
Utility	10'10½'' x 7'6''	3.30 x 2.28
Master Bed	14'1'' x 11'7½''	4.30 x 3.54
Bed 2	15'1'' x 11'6''	4.59 x 3.50
Bed 3	17'1'' x 11'7½''	5.20 x 3.54
Bed 4	15'1'' x 9'6''	4.61 x 2.90

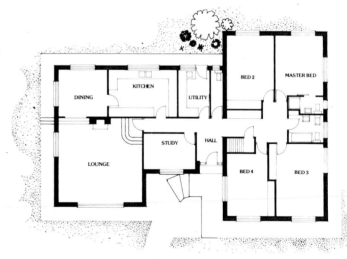

CHILTERN

This large 3 bedroomed bungalow has a layout to suit sites with a view to the rear. The large window in the lounge looks out to the back of the property, and another window or pair of french windows can be put in the gable end wall if required. As shown it has the lounge and dining room open-plan, but the internal walls can be re-arranged to divide them into separate rooms if required.

The cylinder cupboard is shown in the kitchen: This is a modern approach, based on the idea that the ironing will probably be done in the kitchen anyway, and that this is the most convenient place for the airing cupboard. This is a very individual sort of choice, and there are lots of alternative arrangements which can be made.

We are often asked for plans for this bungalow to be built with a patio window or french doors in the gable end wall of the lounge. There are no problems at all with this, but to meet building regulation requirements the size of the main window may have to be reduced slightly: we will advise on this when we know exactly what is required.

Design Number 83155

Area	1060 sq.ft.	99 sq.m.
Overall	47'11'' x 25'1''	14.61 x 7.64
Lounge	19'9'' x 11'0''	6.01 x 3.36
Dining	12'1'' x 8'11''	3.68 x 2.72
Kitchen	12'1 x 10'6''	3.68 x 3.19
Bed 1	13'10'' x 10'7''	4.23 x 3.24
Bed 2	10'7'' x 10'1''	3.24 x 3.07
Bed 3	10'1'' x 10'0''	3.07 x 3.05

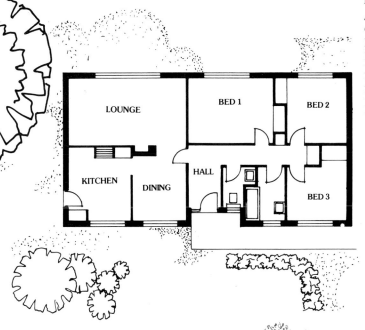

LOUNGE

BED 1

BED 2

KITCHEN

DINING

HALL

BED 3

BATTLEBRIDGE

This is another Irish design of the maximum size which qualifies for the Irish Government grant. Unfortunately the Dublin Government does not pay this to those who build this bungalow in Britain, but it is a very good design anyway, well suited to life in a rural area

Note that there are two doors into the bathroom, one from the hall, and a sliding door leading from the master bedroom. There is lots of storage space in this design, and one particularly attractive feature is the small window set in a run of wardrobes in the main bedroom.

As with so many of our designs which were first drawn for a site in Eire, there is a fireplace in the dining room. This need not be built if it is not required, in which case there is space for a pair of double doors between the lounge and the dining room.

Design Number 83156

Floor Area	1296 sq.ft.	120 sq.m.
Overall	52'10½'' x 32'2½''	16.11 x 9.81
Lounge	18'2'' x 12'0''	5.35 x 3.66
Dining	16'0'' x 12'3''	4.88 x 3.74
Kitchen	19'1'' x 12'3''	5.80 x 3.74
Utility (overall)	7'6'' x 9'2''	2.29 x 2.80
Master Bedroom	14'3'' x 10'0''	4.35 x 3.05
Bed 2	12'2'' x 10'0''	3.71 x 3.05
Bed 3	10'3½'' x 7'9''	3.14 x 2.35

A four bedroom version of the Battlebridge is called the Donegal, reference 82156.

Fergus Murray, Architect
Moatlands, Navan, Eire.

276

CROSSHAVEN

This large and impressive bungalow was originally designed for a rural site in Southern Ireland, where round arches are a common theme in new homes. As originally built the lounge was sunk two steps below the floor level everywhere else, so that the windowsills were at shoulder level. This was deliberately contrived to distract from an unsatisfactory view to the front, and to make the fireplace the focal point in the room, with the eye led up to the dining room and its patio door through to the garden beyond. An interesting approach, and one that worked very well. The architect was Fergus Murray, who works in Co. Meath.

Design Number 83157

Area	2030 sq. ft.	188 sq.m.
Dimensions overall	73'3'' x 32'2''	22.3 x 9.8
Lounge	23'9'' x 18'0''	7.25 x 5.48
Dining	14'0'' x 12'0''	4.26 x 3.65
Kitchen	12'0'' x 13'0''	3.65 x 3.96
Study	12'4'' x 8'0''	3.75 x 2.43
Utility	6'0'' x 12'0''	1.82 x 3.65
Breakfast Room	12'0'' x 9'6''	3.65 x 2.89
Master Bed	14'0'' x 10'2''	4.25 x 3.10
Bed 2	12'0'' x 12'0''	3.65 x 3.65
Bed 3	12'0'' x 11'6''	3.65 x 3.50
Bed 4	9'6'' x 14'3''	2.89 x 4.35

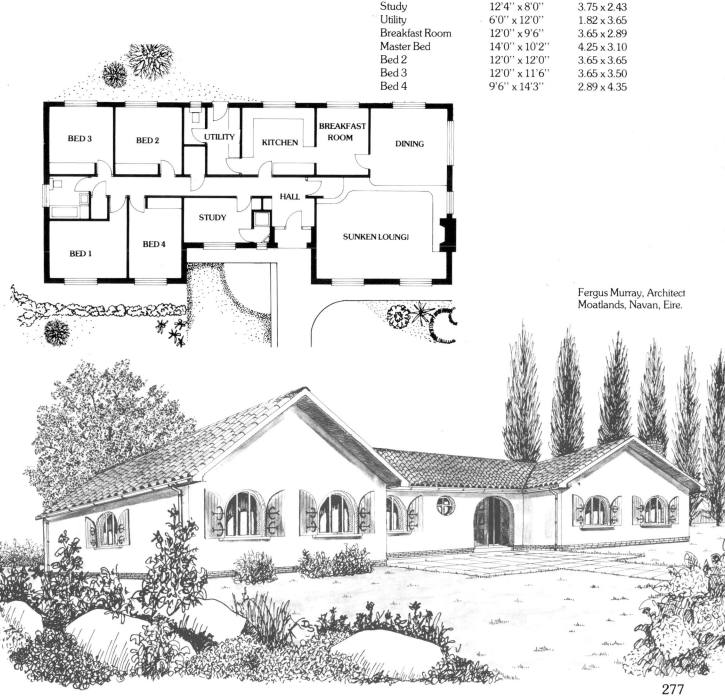

Fergus Murray, Architect
Moatlands, Navan, Eire.

HASLEMERE

ASCOT

Design Number 83158

Floor Area		
(exc. garage)	2948 sq. ft.	273 sq. m.
Dimensions overall	89'1'' x 75'5½''	27.1 x 23.0
Lounge	15'11'' x 23'7''	4.86 x 7.20
Dining	14'10'' x 15'6''	4.52 x 4.74
Kitchen	16'1'' x 14'1''	4.90 x 4.30
Study	14'10½'' x 15'6''	4.53 x 4.74
Utility	9'10'' x 11'10''	3.00 x 3.60
Garage	19'0'' x 28'7''	5.79 x 8.71
Master Bed	16'0'' x 15'6''	4.86 x 4.74
Bed 2	14'9'' x 15'6''	4.50 x 4.74
Bed 3	12'3'' x 14'9''	3.73 x 4.47
Bed 4	12'3'' x 14'9''	3.73 x 4.47

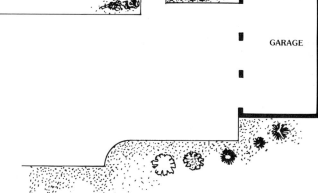

This is a design for sites where a large ranch style bungalow is wanted by the client, and where lots of gables are demanded by the planners!

Two bedrooms have en suite bathrooms, and as drawn the other two each have a door to the third bathroom. If this arrangement is not wanted it can easily be changed. The large store by the back door has been variously fitted out as a gun room, as a shower room on a stud farm, and as an office and drug store on a large dairy farm.

The window at the end of the long bedroom corridor deserves to be a feature, and can be either glazed to a low level sill or built as a little bay with a window seat.

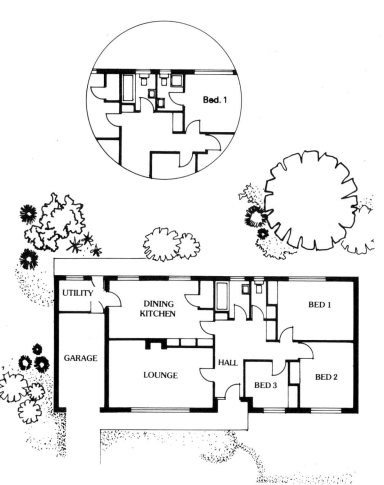

This big 3 bedroomed bungalow of 1060 square feet features the large kitchen/family room which is particularly popular with those who live and work in the country. There are built-in wardrobes to every bedroom, a cloaks cupboard and a broom cupboard in the hall, with an airing cupboard and a big walk-in larder in the kitchen. To match this generous storage with a feeling of size this bungalow is sometimes built with a glazed screen between the lounge and the hall, making both rooms feel even larger.

The Ascot is often built with the WC turned into a second bathroom serving the main bedroom, and the inset sketch shows how this is usually arranged.

The kitchen and utility room can be omitted, and this is often done when the bungalow is built on a farm where the car and landrover are parked elsewhere. In this case a porch is often built at the back door.

The 4 bedroomed version of this design is the Midhurst on page 114

Design Number 83159

Area	1060 sq. ft.	99 sq. m.
Overall	47'11'' x 25'1''	14.61 x 7.64
Lounge	19'9'' x 12'6''	6.01 x 3.81
Dining Kitchen	19'9'' x 10'7''	6.01 x 3.23
Bed 1	14'4'' x 10'11''	4.37 x 3.33
Bed 2	12'2'' x 10'1''	3.71 x 3.07
Bed 3	8'10'' x 8'1''	2.70 x 2.47

BANBURY

HYTHE

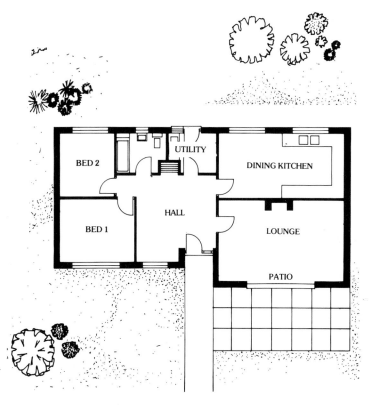

This attractive bungalow was originally designed for a Cotswold farmer as a bungalow for his retirement, and the design brief was that there should be a 20ft by 13ft lounge, a "decent sized hall", a kitchen big enough to take meals in, with everything else as compact as possible. The Banbury design resulted and has become very popular.

There is no provision for built-in furniture, but this can easily be arranged. Remember that most proprietary cupboard fronts are made to a 600mm module and as the dimensions on drawings are masonry dimensions before plastering, care has to be taken in working out exactly where cupboards can be fitted in. It is generally better to allow for a makeup piece on a run of cupboards than to plan to fill up a space exactly with doors.

The sketch shows this bungalow built in stone — as the original was — but it also looks very well with a rendered finish.

A three bedroom version of this bungalow is the Abingdon, reference number 82160.

Design Number 83160

Area	994 sq.ft.	92 sq.m.
Lounge	20'6" x 13'1"	6.24 x 3.99
Dining/Kitchen	20'6" x 10'0"	3.19 x 3.05
Utility	7'8" x 6'3"	2.38 x 1.90
Master Bed	10'2" x 12'1"	3.09 x 3.69
Bed 2	10'0" x 9'0"	3.04 x 2.74

This is another design to take advantage of a site where the outlook is to the rear, and it is illustrated here built in rendered insulating blocks with stone features. This style is very popular in some areas, and particulary in West Wales. It is important to ensure that the stone stands well proud of the rendered walling, and when discussing this with the bricklayer remember to allow for the thickness of the render.

In the inset plan we show an arrangement for an integral garage for this design, giving a porch at the back door, with the garage door recessed. This arrangement looks well, is very practical, — and we are at a loss to know why it is not more popular!

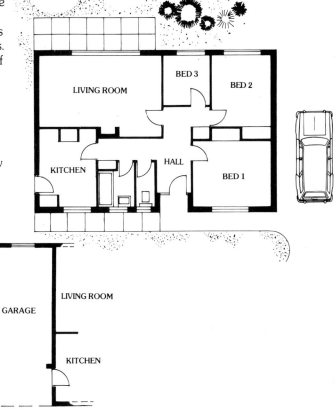

Design Number 83161

Area	840 sq.ft.	79 sq.m.
Overall	38'4" x 25'1"	11.69 x 7.64
Living Room	19'4" x 11'0"	5.90 x 3.36
Kitchen	12'0" x 9'0"	3.68 x 2.75
Bed 1	12'4" x 10'1"	3.76 x 3.08
Bed 2	11'0" x 9'2"	3.36 x 2.80
Bed 3	7'9" x 7'6"	2.36 x 2.29

RINGWOOD

We are often asked for drawings for a bungalow with a garage below the living accommodation and without any stairway to give access to it from inside the building. This saves space and minimizes costs. The Ringwood design meets these requirements, and is based on a bungalow built in Lincolnshire where the site had an old clay pit in the middle of it. This pit just fitted the garage, and everything else went on top. If you want this arrangement remember that there has to be a minimum of 8ft of difference in height between the garage floor level and the floor above it.

Design Number 83162

Floor Area

(exc. garage)	1470 sq. ft.	136 sq.m.
Dimensions overall	59'2'' x 27'5''	18.0 x 8.3
Lounge	18'0½'' x 13'5''	5.50 x 4.09
Dining	11'10'' x 11'10''	3.60 x 3.60
Kitchen	11'11½'' x 11'10''	3.64 x 3.60
Utility	9'9½'' x 5'8½''	2.99 x 1.74
Garage	25'6½'' x 17'8½''	7.79 x 5.40
Master Bed	13'5½'' x 11'10''	4.10 x 3.60
Bed 2	11'10'' x 11'10''	3.60 x 3.60
Bed 3	11'10'' x 9'9½''	3.60 x 2.99
Bed 4 (overall)	12'2½'' x 9'9½''	3.72 x 2.99

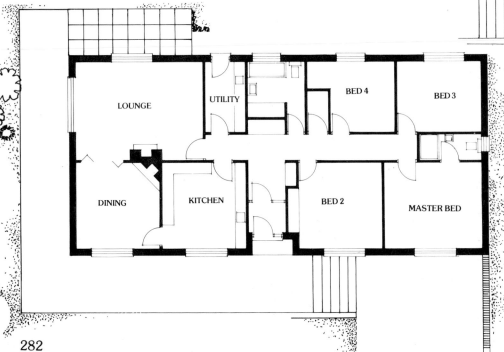

NORMANBY

This traditionally styled bungalow was originally drawn for a site in Shropshire and has many unusual features. The deep verandah outside the principal rooms, the traditional purlin roof, and the style of the porch at the front door are all reminiscent of the 20's and of the leisurely living that went with them. Not a budget home, but a very interesting one.

Design Number 83165

Floor Area (exc. garage)	2000 sq.ft.	185 sq.m.
Dimensions overall	51'5'' x 62'9''	15.6 x 19.1
Lounge	20'4'' x 14'0''	6.19 x 4.26
Dining	14'0'' x 14'0''	4.26 x 4.26
Kitchen	15'0'' x 11'0''	4.57 x 3.35
Utility	13'0'' x 8'0''	3.97 x 2.43
Garage	20'0'' x 16'0''	6.09 x 4.87
Sun Lounge	14'0'' x 11'6''	4.26 x 3.50
Master Bed	15'7'' x 12'0''	4.74 x 3.65
Bed 2	14'0'' x 9'8''	4.26 x 2.94
Bed 3	10'9'' x 9'0''	3.26 x 2.74

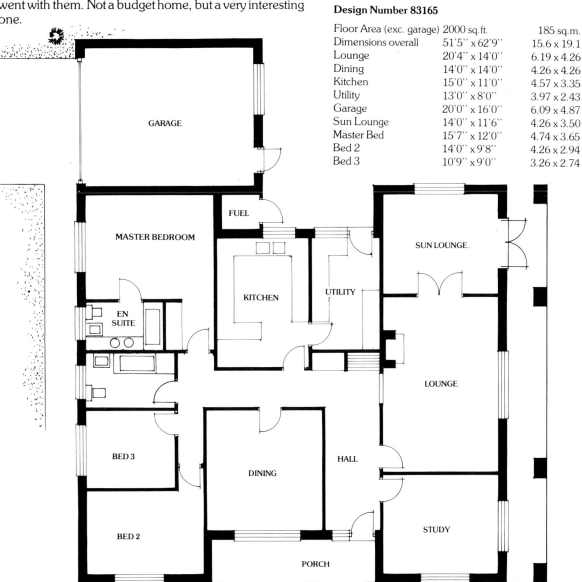

SHANNON

WATERBEACH

This large bungalow is another Irish design by Fergus Murray, and suits a site with a gentle slope. There is no direct access from the garage to the house, and this simplifies the structural design and reduces cost. However, there is plenty of room to re-arrange the layout to allow for stairs down to the garage if required, and we can provide drawings that show this. The actual arrangement depends on the position of the garage doors, which have to suit the access and the slope of the site.

This bungalow has been built on a level site in flat country with distant views, with the expense of the under-building to the bedrooms being justified by the commanding appearance of the structure. It all suited the site very well. Soil was brought in to build up the garden as appropriate, and this approach sometimes merits consideration on other sites.

Here the garage is approached from the side, and is sited under the forward projection of the lounge and family room, as shown on the inset plan.

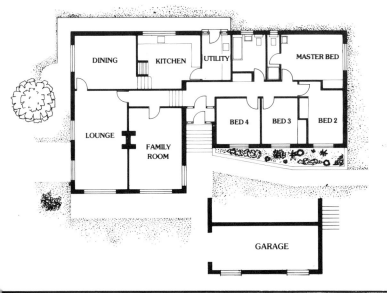

Design Number 83166

Floor Area (exc. garage)	1674 sq.ft.	155 sq.m.
Dimensions Overall	62'6'' x 36'1½''	19.06 x 11.01
Lounge	21'8'' x 12'0''	6.59 x 3.65
Dining	14'0'' x 12'4''	4.27 x 3.76
Kitchen	13'7'' x 12'4''	4.15 x 3.76
Utility	10'0'' x 6'6''	3.05 x 1.98
Garage	24'4'' x 9'2''	7.41 x 2.80
Family Room	17'11'' x 12'0'	5.47 x 3.65
Master Bed	14'0'' x 10'0''	4.27 x 3.05
Bed 2	12'0'' x 8'0''	3.66 x 2.44
Bed 3	8'0'' x 10'3½''	2.44 x 3.14
Bed 4	10'2'' x 10'3½''	3.09 x 3.14

Fergus Murray, Architect
Moatlands, Navan, Eire.

Arches to the front of the veranda which runs the whole length of the building are very popular with clients, but less so with the planners. Still, this design has been built on a number of occasions in Britain, and is very popular in Ireland. If the arches are in either brick or stone then the detailing of the masonry is most important, particularly at the point where the arch springs from the pillars. We always provide a drawing showing this particular feature, but there are many ways of doing it and often local practice is best. Discuss this with your builder or bricklayer.

Inside the bungalow the layout is orthodox, with a very large lounge. To suit the veranda outside the height of the rooms is nine feet, which gives a feeling of space and quality to the home.

Design Number 83167

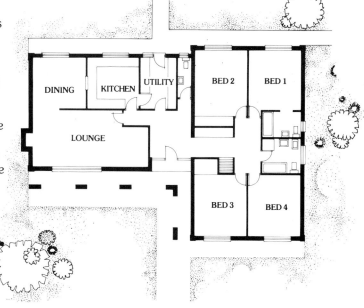

Floor Area	1750 sq.ft.	162 sq.m.
Dimensions Overall	61'5'' x 41'6''	18.71 x 12.65
Lounge	25'7½'' x 12'1½''	7.81 x 3.70
Dining	11'10'' x 10'11½''	3.60 x 3.34
Kitchen	11'6'' x 10'11½''	3.50 x 3.34
Utility	8'1'' x 10'11½''	2.46 x 3.34
Master Bed	12'7½'' x 11'7½''	3.85 x 3.54
Bed 2	14'1½'' x 11'6''	4.30 x 3.50
Bed 3	13'1½'' x 11'6''	4.00 x 3.50
Bed 4	13'1½'' x 11'7''	4.00 x 3.54

Fergus Murray, Architect
Moatlands, Navan, Eire.

FOXTON

Many of those building a new home on their own land are building it as part of a business venture. In these cases sometimes they want integral office or shop accommodation as in this canal side bungalow with a boat chandlery. This same design has been built on two different occasions as the owners home on caravan sites, and the layout proved to be very practical.

Design Number 83170

Floor Area	1720 sq.ft.	160 sq.m.
Overall dimensions	59'2½'' x 50'5½''	18.0 x 15.3
Shop	16'0½'' x 15'1''	4.89 x 4.60
Store	16'0½'' x 8'10½''	4.89 x 2.70
Lounge	19'0'' x 12'7''	5.79 x 3.84
Dining	11'4'' x 10'10''	3.45 x 3.30
Kitchen	17'4'' x 10'6''	5.29 x 3.20
Master Bed	14'1'' x 12'11½''	4.30 x 3.95
Bed 2	12'9½'' x 9'0''	3.90 x 2.74
Bed 3	10'9'' x 9'0''	3.29 x 2.74

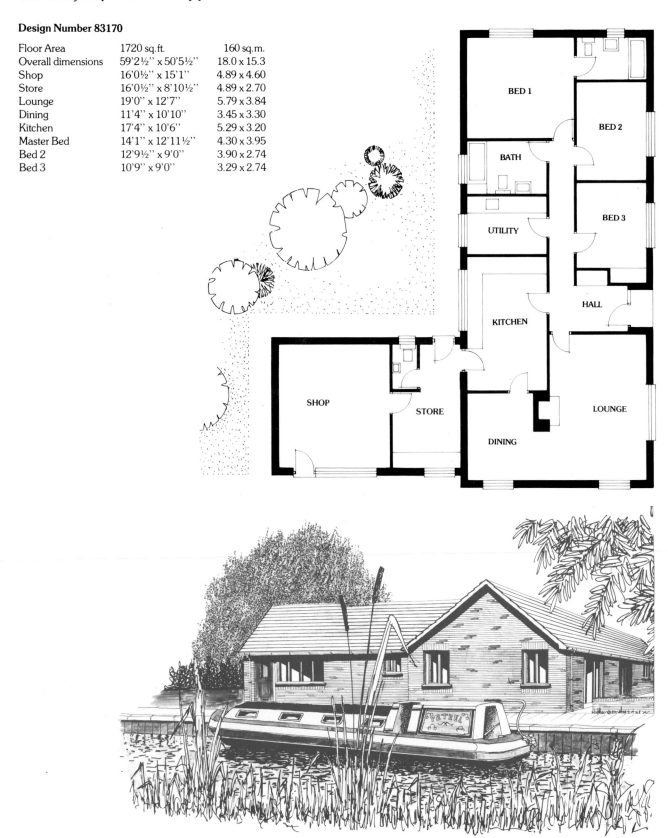

GLEN DUN

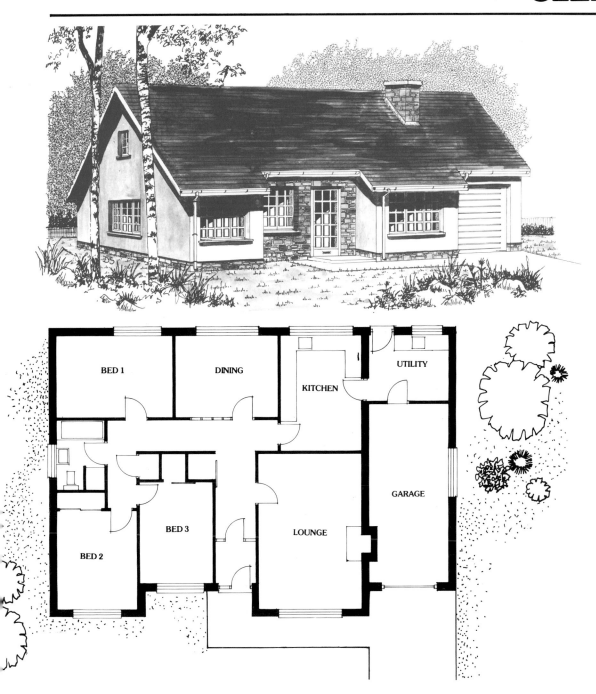

Design Number 83171

Floor Area		
(exc. garage)	1555 sq.ft.	144 sq.m.
Dimensions overall	50'7½" x 35'1½"	15.4 x 10.7
Lounge	13'0" x 19'0"	3.96 x 5.79
Dining	13'0" x 10'0"	3.96 x 3.04
Kitchen	10'0" x 14'0"	3.04 x 4.26
Utility	10'0" x 8'0"	3.05 x 2.44
Garage	10'0" x 21'9½"	3.05 x 6.64
Master Bed	14'4½" x 10'0"	4.38 x 3.04
Bed 2	12'0" x 10'0"	3.65 x 3.04
Bed 3	12'6" x 9'1"	3.80 x 2.76

The Glen Dun bungalow by Prestoplan was specially designed for timber frame construction, and the timber frame structure is available from Prestoplan Ltd.

This bungalow and the nineteen other designs which follow were all specially designed for timber frame construction by Prestoplan Ltd., and the construction kits are available from that company as detailed earlier in the book.

The Glen Dun bungalow is available in two versions. We illustrate the Mk.I. The Mk.II has further accommodation in the roof, and details are available on request. As its name suggests, this bungalow is popular in Scotland where it is usually built with the rendered finish shown in the illustration.

DOUGLAS

The Douglas is the largest of the Prestoplan timber frame bungalows in this book, and includes just about every feature of luxury living anyone could ask for. The lounge/dining area has an island fireplace which can be built in almost any style to suit one of the super new fires for a central hearth. There is a family room which can be just that, or else used as a Granny Flat or a Nursery. There are four bedrooms, one with a dressing room and en suite bathoom — the Douglas has it all.

This is essentially a home for a site with all round views, If the ground falls away in the front then this bungalow can be built with the floor to the lounge and dining room dropped by a couple of feet, with feature stairs into the room. Another alternative is to build it with the boarded sloping ceiling and cathedral windows illustrated: the options are endless, and Prestoplan will certainly incorporate your own design ideas in their drawings if you wish.

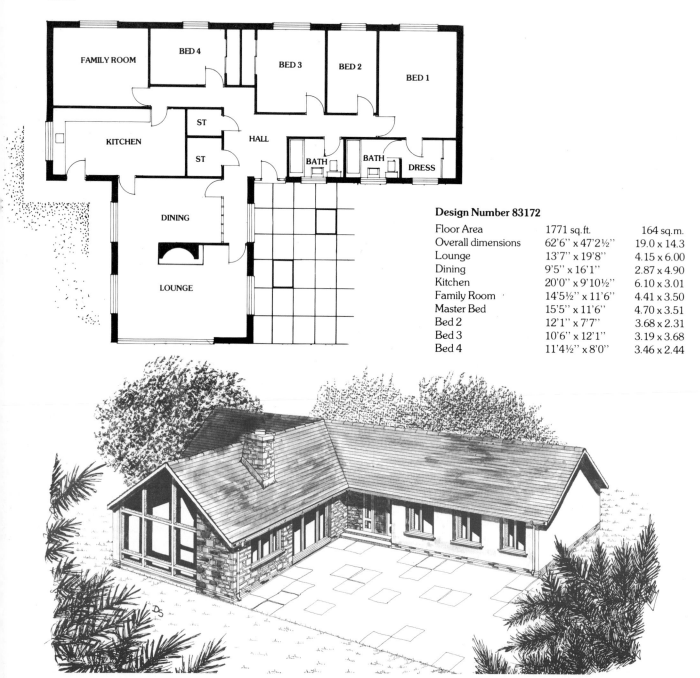

Design Number 83172

Floor Area	1771 sq.ft.	164 sq.m.
Overall dimensions	62'6" x 47'2½"	19.0 x 14.3
Lounge	13'7" x 19'8"	4.15 x 6.00
Dining	9'5" x 16'1"	2.87 x 4.90
Kitchen	20'0" x 9'10½"	6.10 x 3.01
Family Room	14'5½" x 11'6"	4.41 x 3.50
Master Bed	15'5" x 11'6"	4.70 x 3.51
Bed 2	12'1" x 7'7"	3.68 x 2.31
Bed 3	10'6" x 12'1"	3.19 x 3.68
Bed 4	11'4½" x 8'0"	3.46 x 2.44

ILKLEY

This is another Prestoplan design with a boarded sloping ceiling to the lounge and a matching cathedral window in the gable end. Although it is illustrated with a casement window in the side wall of the lounge, it is often built with a patio window in this position, making the lounge a splendid sun room.

Like all our Prestoplan designs, drawings and components for timber frame construction are available off the peg for this bungalow, and it is possible to re-position windows and make other alterations with the minimum of delay.

Design Number 83173

Floor Area (exc. garage)	1868 sq.ft.	173 sq.m.
Dimensions overall	41'0'' x 47'0''	12.5 x 14.3
Lounge	25'0'' x 12'9½''	7.60 x 3.90
Dining	13'5½'' x 12'6''	4.10 x 3.81
Kitchen	12'6'' x 11'2''	3.81 x 3.41
Master Bed	13'7'' x 10'6''	4.15 x 3.19
Bed 2	15'5½'' x 9'6½''	4.71 x 2.91
Bed 3	13'6'' x 9'10''	4.12 x 3.00
Bed 4	12'10'' x 9'5½''	3.92 x 2.88

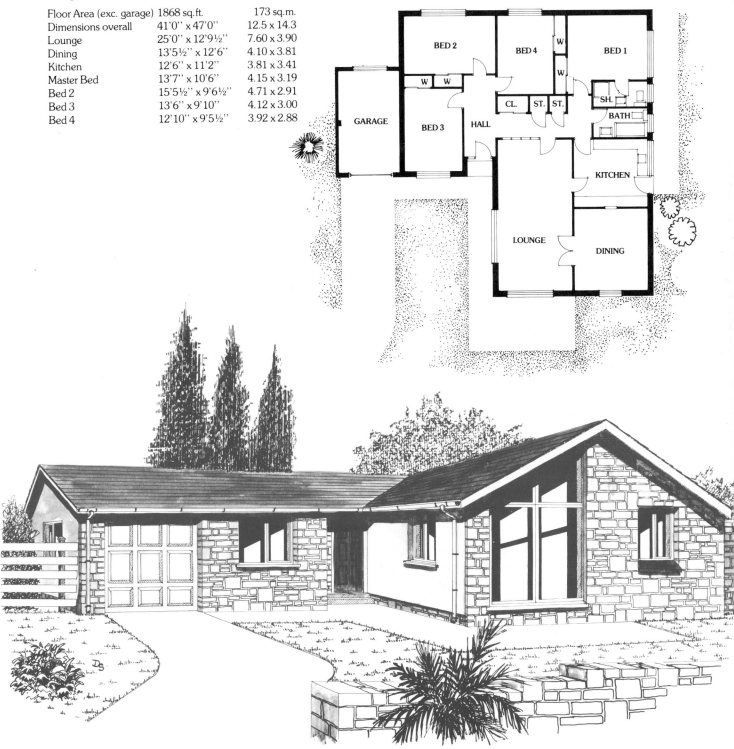

RICHMOND

This timber frame bungalow from Prestoplan has an interesting L shape layout with a hip roof that gives it a fashionable period appearance. The garage has a large recess for a workbench and connects with the utility room and kitchen via a useful lobby. The layout of all the rest of the accommodation shows a typical Prestoplan attention to detail — look at the angle corner of the lounge which gives space in the hall and adds interest to the lounge itself.

As with all our Prestoplan designs, a timber frame kit for this bungalow is available, together with the design calculations which will be required to support the building regulations application when you build in this way.

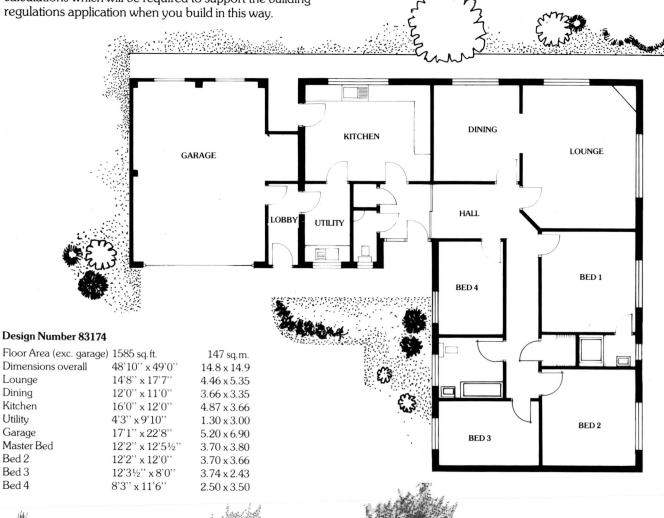

Design Number 83174

Floor Area (exc. garage)	1585 sq.ft.	147 sq.m.
Dimensions overall	48'10'' x 49'0''	14.8 x 14.9
Lounge	14'8'' x 17'7''	4.46 x 5.35
Dining	12'0'' x 11'0''	3.66 x 3.35
Kitchen	16'0'' x 12'0''	4.87 x 3.66
Utility	4'3'' x 9'10''	1.30 x 3.00
Garage	17'1'' x 22'8''	5.20 x 6.90
Master Bed	12'2'' x 12'5½''	3.70 x 3.80
Bed 2	12'2'' x 12'0''	3.70 x 3.66
Bed 3	12'3½'' x 8'0''	3.74 x 2.43
Bed 4	8'3'' x 11'6''	2.50 x 3.50

CHARNOCK

The Charnock is a very popular Prestoplan bungalow with a large study which makes it of particular interest to those who work from their homes. This room can also be used as a fourth bedroom, and as it is well separated from the other bedrooms this is popular with people who are building a home which they intend to share with an elderly relative.

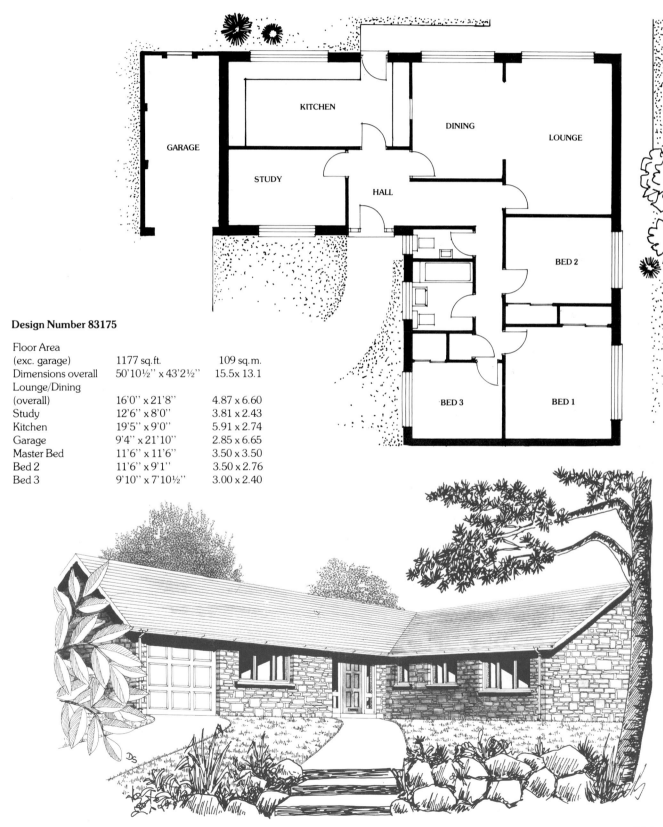

Design Number 83175

Floor Area
(exc. garage)	1177 sq.ft.	109 sq.m.
Dimensions overall	50'10½'' x 43'2½''	15.5x 13.1
Lounge/Dining		
(overall)	16'0'' x 21'8''	4.87 x 6.60
Study	12'6'' x 8'0''	3.81 x 2.43
Kitchen	19'5'' x 9'0''	5.91 x 2.74
Garage	9'4'' x 21'10''	2.85 x 6.65
Master Bed	11'6'' x 11'6''	3.50 x 3.50
Bed 2	11'6'' x 9'1''	3.50 x 2.76
Bed 3	9'10'' x 7'10½''	3.00 x 2.40

GLEN SHEE

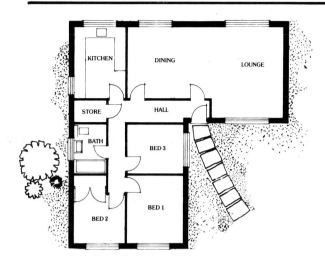

The Glen Shee bungalow was designed in Scotland at Prestoplan's Strathaven office to give the maximum accommodation in just over a thousand square feet. With both wings at the same span of 21 ft 4'', the building is well proportioned and the massive stone window-sills shown in the sketch are typical Scottish features that always help a home to look impressive.

The store in the hall is very popular, and every time this bungalow is built it seems to be used in a different way — larder, cloakroom, gun room or simply a glory-hole!

Design Number 83176

Floor Area	1026 sq. ft.	95 sq. m.
Dimensions overall	39'3'' x 39'7''	11.9 x 12.0
Lounge/Dining (overall)	15'9'' x 28'3''	4.80 x 8.60
Kitchen	9'2'' x 12'5''	2.80 x 3.80
Master Bed	10'4'' x 12'0''	3.15 x 3.65
Bed 2	9'0'' x 12'0''	2.75 x 3.65
Bed 3	8'8'' x 10'4''	2.65 x 3.15

GLEN FARG

This is another of a series of designs which were specifically drawn for Scotland in Prestoplan's office in Strathaven, but it has proved popular elsewhere, and espcially in N. Ireland. It is a very good example of a simple straight forward bungalow with an uncomplicated layout that is so well proportioned that it always looks bigger than it really is. The lounge is almost square; in an era when architects seem determined that all living rooms shall be rectangular it is a pleasant change, and is a deservedly popular feature.

Design Number 83177

Floor Area	1026 sq. ft.	95 sq. m.
Dimensions overall	45'2'' x 25'5½''	13.7 x 7.7
Lounge	14'1'' x 14'11''	4.30 x 4.55
Dining	10'2'' x 8'6½''	3.10 x 2.60
Kitchen	13'2'' x 8'6½''	4.00 x 2.60
Master Bed	13'9½'' x 11'8''	4.20 x 3.55
Bed 2	11'8'' x 9'10''	3.55 x 3.00
Bed 3	10'2'' x 9'8''	3.10 x 2.95

GLEN URQUHART

The Glen Urquhart is one of a series of homes which Prestoplan had specially designed to meet the demand in Scotland for simple bungalows with good proportions, good weather protection and sensible straight-forward layouts. This is one of the larger dwellings in this particular range and is deservedly popular.

The projection of the roof over the front door gives character to this design, and the treatment of the front porch is very important. Whether it is given a simple stanchion to support the roof with a dwarf wall below as shown, or whether it is a more elaborate feature, it must be designed to suit the building as a whole and to compliment the well balanced proportions

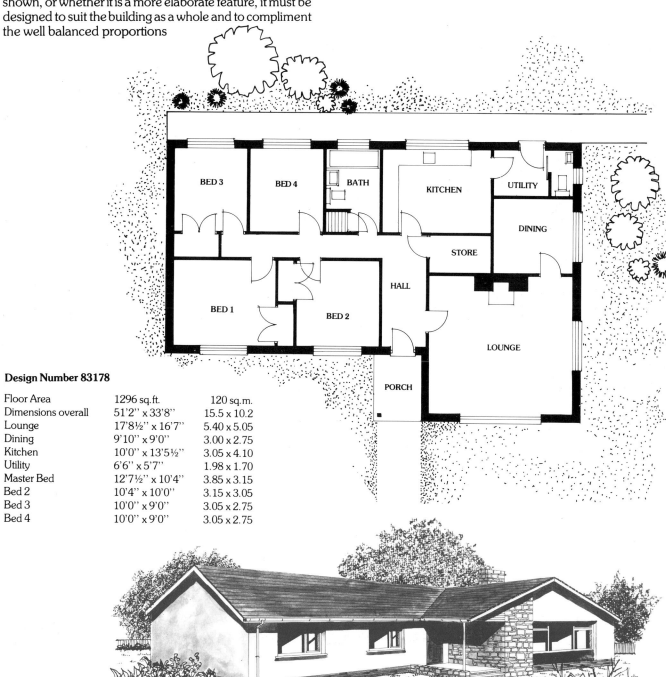

Design Number 83178

Floor Area	1296 sq.ft.	120 sq.m.
Dimensions overall	51'2" x 33'8"	15.5 x 10.2
Lounge	17'8½" x 16'7"	5.40 x 5.05
Dining	9'10" x 9'0"	3.00 x 2.75
Kitchen	10'0" x 13'5½"	3.05 x 4.10
Utility	6'6" x 5'7"	1.98 x 1.70
Master Bed	12'7½" x 10'4"	3.85 x 3.15
Bed 2	10'4" x 10'0"	3.15 x 3.05
Bed 3	10'0" x 9'0"	3.05 x 2.75
Bed 4	10'0" x 9'0"	3.05 x 2.75

BALMORAL

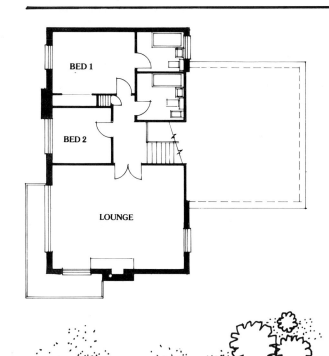

This is another house with the living accommodation on the upper floor to suit a site with panoramic distant views. Two bedrooms are on the same level as the garage, with three steps up to the hall, dining room and kitchen. The very large lounge with all round views and the two principal bedrooms are up a further flight of stairs which have a sloping ceiling above them. This unusual feature gives a lot of character to the hall.

The Balmoral is a timber framed design by Prestoplan.

Design Number 83180

Floor Area (inc. garage)	2690 sq.ft.	250 sq.m.
Dimensions overall	43'6'' x 45'5½''	13.2 x 13.8
Lounge	23'7½'' x 18'0½''	7.20 x 5.50
Dining	12'4'' x 10'8''	3.75 x 3.25
Kitchen	12'4'' x 10'8''	3.75 x 3.25
Utility	5'3'' x 7'0''	1.60 x 2.15
Garage	23'7½'' x 17'7''	7.20 x 5.35
Family Room	12'9'' x 11'2''	3.90 x 3.40
Master Bed	14'9'' x 10'6''	4.50 x 3.20
Bed 2	10'6'' x 9'10''	3.20 x 3.00
Bed 3	11'2'' x 10'2''	3.40 x 3.10
Bed 4	8'6'' x 10'2''	2.60 x 3.10

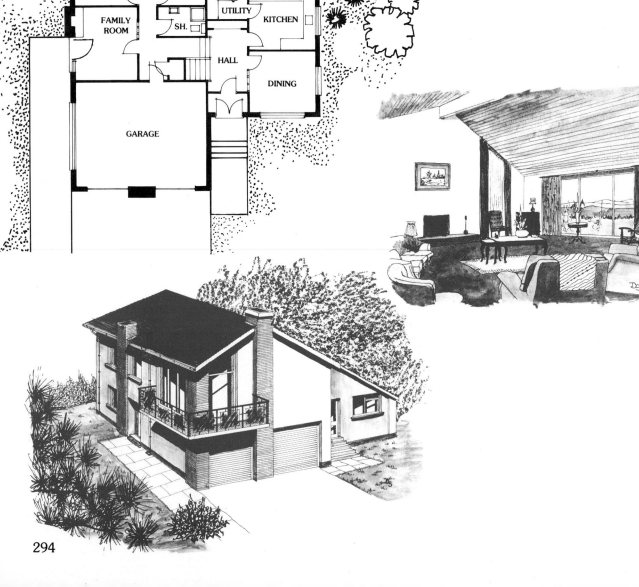

DUNVEGAN

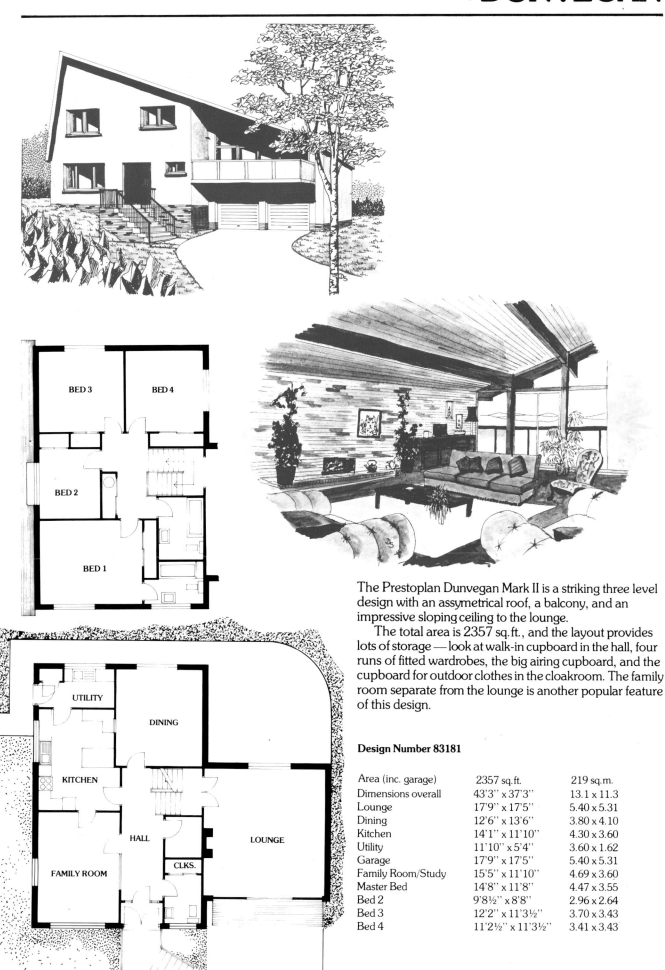

The Prestoplan Dunvegan Mark II is a striking three level design with an assymetrical roof, a balcony, and an impressive sloping ceiling to the lounge.

The total area is 2357 sq.ft., and the layout provides lots of storage — look at walk-in cupboard in the hall, four runs of fitted wardrobes, the big airing cupboard, and the cupboard for outdoor clothes in the cloakroom. The family room separate from the lounge is another popular feature of this design.

Design Number 83181

Area (inc. garage)	2357 sq.ft.	219 sq.m.
Dimensions overall	43'3" x 37'3"	13.1 x 11.3
Lounge	17'9" x 17'5"	5.40 x 5.31
Dining	12'6" x 13'6"	3.80 x 4.10
Kitchen	14'1" x 11'10"	4.30 x 3.60
Utility	11'10" x 5'4"	3.60 x 1.62
Garage	17'9" x 17'5"	5.40 x 5.31
Family Room/Study	15'5" x 11'10"	4.69 x 3.60
Master Bed	14'8" x 11'8"	4.47 x 3.55
Bed 2	9'8½" x 8'8"	2.96 x 2.64
Bed 3	12'2" x 11'3½"	3.70 x 3.43
Bed 4	11'2½" x 11'3½"	3.41 x 3.43

HAMBLETON

The Hambleton design by Prestoplan makes it clear that modern timber frame construction can look as "traditional" as you can wish. Although it is shown here with a cladding of natural stone, it looks equally effective in brick.

Two interesting features to this design — a very large dining room, which can easily be divided up to give a study, and the grouping of all the drainage to the front of the house which is very useful when the ground falls away to the rear.

Design Number 83182

Floor Area (exc. garage)	1675 sq.ft.	155 sq.m.
Dimensions overall	45'10" x 48'2"	13.9 x 14.6
Lounge	24'4" x 12'4"	7.41 x 3.76
Dining	18'4" x 11'0"	5.58 x 3.35
Kitchen	13'0" x 9'0"	3.96 x 2.74
Utility	14'0" x 6'6"	4.26 x 1.98
Garage	16'0" x 17'0"	4.87 x 5.18
Master Bed	13'0" x 12'4"	3.96 x 3.76
Bed 2	12'4" x 11'0"	3.76 x 3.35
Bed 3	11'0" x 10'0"	3.35 x 3.05
Bed 4	10'0" x 9'0"	3.05 x 2.74
Boxroom/Bed 5	8'6" x 8'0"	2.59 x 2.43

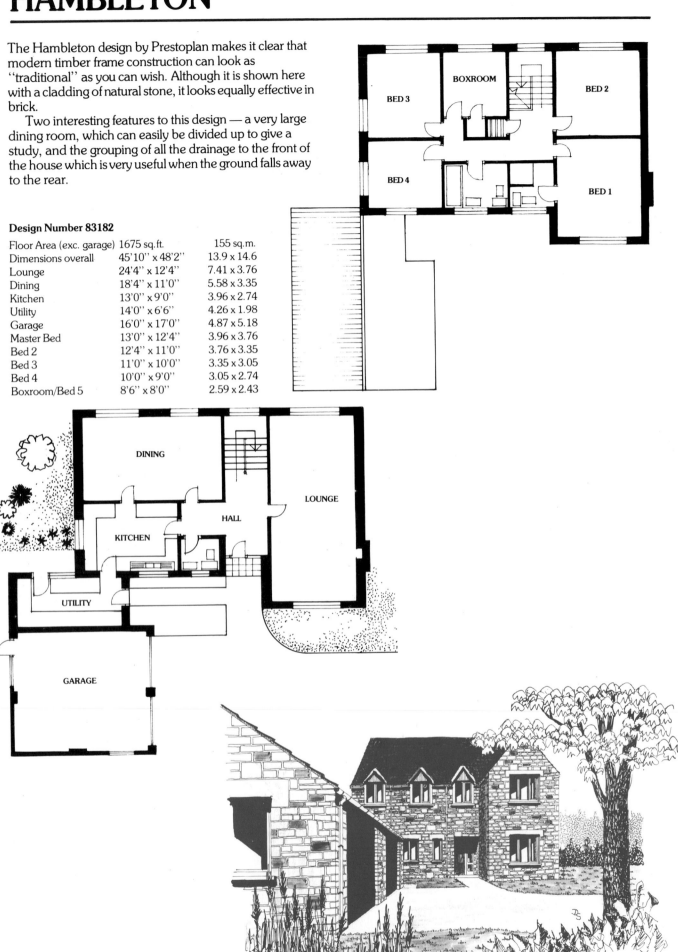

ROUNDHAY

The Roundhay house by Prestoplan is a conventional executive home with an attractive Georgian style bow window to the lounge, and with matching french windows at the rear. The layout follows a well proven pattern and it shows clearly how well timber frame construction can adapt to traditional house styles.

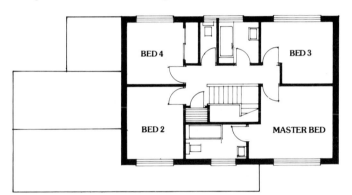

Design Number 83183

Floor Area (exc. garage)	1512 sq.ft.	140 sq.m.
Dimensions overall	52'3" x 27'3"	15.9 x 8.3
Lounge/Dining		
(overall)	23'4" x 21'8"	7.10 x 6.60
Kitchen	13'7" x 9'10"	4.13 x 3.00
Study	7'9½" x 9'10"	2.37 x 3.00
Utility	8'2" x 7'5½"	2.50 x 2.27
Garage	16'8" x 17'4½"	5.08 x 5.29
Master Bed	13'5½" x 11'7"	4.10 x 3.54
Bed 2	11'7" x 9'10"	3.54 x 3.00
Bed 3	11'6" x 9'9"	3.50 x 2.97
Bed 4	9'10" x 9'9"	3.00 x 2.97

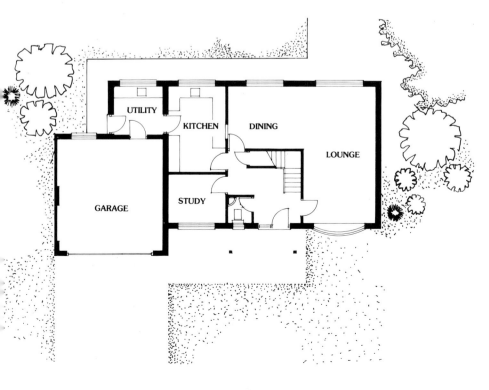

BEAUMONT

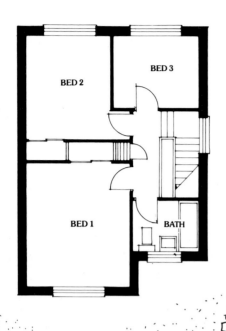

The Beaumont design by Prestoplan illustrates clearly how successfully a timber frame design can look completely traditional in every respect. This conventional house has a three bedroom layout that uses every last inch of floor area to the very best advantage, and still has room for a traditional larder — one reason why it is so often built as a farmhouse.

Note how the continuous run of cupboards between the master bedroom and the larger of the other two bedrooms is arranged to give the maximum of sound insulation.

Design Number 83184

Floor Area (inc. garage)	1248 sq. ft.	116 sq. m.
Dimensions overall	35'5'' x 29'5''	10.8 x 8.9
Lounge	11'10'' x 17'5''	3.60 x 5.31
Dining	9'10'' x 9'6½''	3.00 x 2.91
Kitchen (overall)	9'10'' x 9'10''	3.00 x 3.00
Garage (overall)	12'11½'' x 17'8½''	3.95 x 5.40
Master Bed	13'8'' x 11'10''	4.17 x 3.60
Bed 2	11'4'' x 9'6½''	3.45 x 2.91
Bed 3	9'10'' x 7'11''	3.00 x 2.40

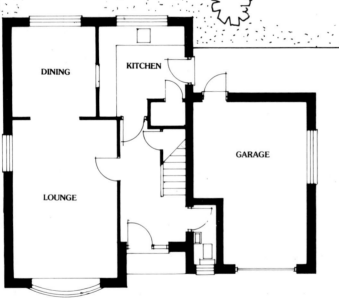

RIVINGTON & HAREWOOD

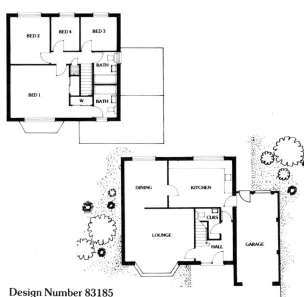

Design Number 83185

RIVINGTON

The Rivington Mk II house has a feature which many buying a new home feel they deserve but rarely find — a really big master bedroom with a dressing alcove and en suite bathroom in a house of only thirteen hundred square feet. If this is one of your priorities then this may be the design for you.

This is a Prestoplan design, and a timber frame kit is available for it. As with all timber frame homes it has a very high level of built in insulation.

Floor Area		
(exc. garage)	1328 sq.ft.	123 sq.m.
Dimensions overall	39'10" x 26'6"	12.1 x 8.0
Lounge	17'7½" x 12'9½"	5.37 x 3.90
Dining	10'8" x 11'6"	3.25 x 3.51
Kitchen	15'11" x 11'6"	4.86 x 3.51
Garage	21'8" x 10'8½"	6.60 x 3.25
Master Bed	15'0" x 12'9½"	4.58 x 3.90
Bed 2	11'6" x 10'1"	3.51 x 3.08
Bed 3	9'0" x 8'3"	2.74 x 2.52
Bed 4	8'3" x 7'2½"	2.52 x 2.20

HAREWOOD

The Harewood is one of Prestoplan's larger houses, and follows a traditional design concept that is always popular. The large hall with its imposing staircase, the 25ft lounge, and the study placed well away from family distraction make it an ideal executive home, and it is a firm favourite as such. The first floor has plenty of cupboard space and generously sized bathrooms. It all adds up to the sort of home that is a top-of-the-market investment, always has been, and always will be.

Design Number 83186

Floor Area (exc. garage)	1620 sq.ft.	150 sq.m.
Dimensions overall	55'0" x 27'5"	16.7 x 8.3
Lounge	13'9" x 25'7"	4.20 x 7.80
Dining	11'6" x 9'10"	3.50 x 3.00
Kitchen	9'4" x 13'5½"	2.85 x 4.10
Study	9'4" x 7'10½"	2.85 x 2.40
Utility	7'4½" x 8'0"	2.25 x 2.43
Garage	18'0" x 17'4½"	5.48 x 5.30
Master Bed	13'9" x 13'5½"	4.20 x 4.10
Bed 2	9'4" x 11'6"	2.85 x 3.50
Bed 3	13'9" x 11'10"	4.20 x 3.60
Bed 4	9'4" x 9'10"	2.85 x 3.00

GLEN MORE

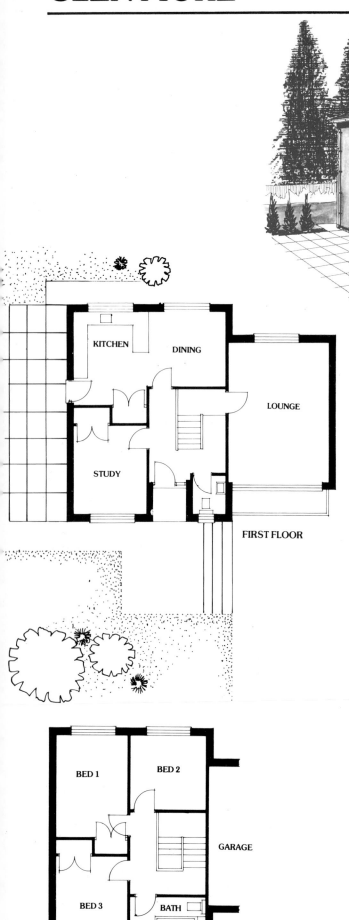

FIRST FLOOR

GROUND FLOOR

Another of the successful series of "Glen" designs from Prestoplan, with the split level accommodation and sloping ceiling to the lounge which are a feature of many Prestoplan designs. The highest point of the ceiling is over 12ft high, and slopes down to normal ceiling height. The rafters span the whole of the lounge and no beams are required to support them: however, if you are having a pine-boarded ceiling then you can incorporate a false beam to add to the character — the choice is yours. Whether the ceiling is boarded or plastered, it all gives enormous scope for imaginative decor and stunning lighting arrangements.

Design Number 83179

Floor Area (exc. garage)	1242 sq.ft.	115 sq.m.
Dimensions overall	27'4½'' x 35'9''	8.3 x 10.9
Lounge	13'5½'' x 17'9''	4.11 x 5.40
Kitchen/Dining (overall)	19'8'' x 12'0½''	6.00 x 3.67
Study	11'2'' x 9'6''	3.40 x 2.90
Garage	12'11½'' x 17'9''	3.95 x 5.40
Master Bed	12'0½'' x 9'6''	3.67 x 2.90
Bed 2	9'10'' x 9'9''	3.00 x 2.97
Bed 3	9'10'' x 9'6''	3.00 x 2.90

GRANTLEY

This Prestoplan design follows a popular and successful formula for getting a four bedroomed house with an integral garage on a site with an overall width of only 50ft. The two gable windows of the larger bedrooms help to give the Earlswood the appearance of being larger than it really is, as do the twin windows in the lounge.

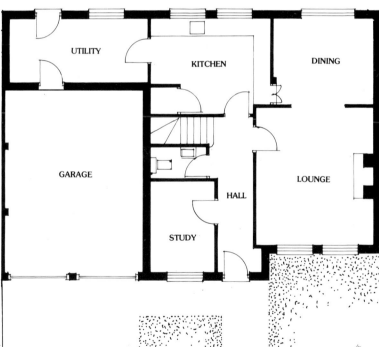

Design Number 83187

Floor Area (exc. garage)	1400 sq.ft.	130 sq.m.
Dimensions overall	43'0'' x 29'8½''	13.1 x 9.0
Lounge	15'1'' x 13'0''	4.60 x 3.96
Dining	9'6'' x 11'4''	2.90 x 3.45
Kitchen	13'6'' x 10'6''	4.10 x 3.20
Study	10'0'' x 7'0''	3.05 x 2.13
Utility	7'0'' x 15'9''	2.13 x 4.80
Garage	20'0'' x 15'9''	6.10 x 4.80
Master Bed	11'0'' x 13'0''	3.35 x 3.96
Bed 2	11'6'' x 11'0''	3.50 x 3.35
Bed 3	10'4'' x 9'10''	3.15 x 3.00
Bed 4	8'6'' x 7'3''	2.60 x 2.20

MILFORD

The Milford house is a Prestoplan design that incorporates projecting first floor bay windows that are now so much in fashion. The ground floor layout is straight-forward, with a larger study than usual which will appeal to those who work at home. On the first floor the room over the study has a large "walk-in" wardrobe which can be fitted out as a second en-suite bathroom if required. This arrangement is popular when a Grandparent shares a home with a family.

Design Number 83188

Floor Area (**exc.** garage)	1836 sq.ft.	170 sq.m.
Dimensions overall	62'8'' x 33'5''	19.1 x 10.1
Lounge	22'0'' x 13'0''	6.70 x 3.96
Dining	14'0'' x 12'0''	4.26 x 3.65
Kitchen	12'6'' x 10'6''	3.81 x 3.20
Study	11'0'' x 10'6''	3.35 x 3.20
Utility	10'0'' x 6'6''	3.05 x 1.98
Garage	17'0'' x 18'6''	5.18 x 5.64
Master Bed	14'0'' x 12'0''	4.26 x 3.65
Bed 2	13'0'' x 11'0''	3.96 x 3.35
Bed 3	12'9'' x 9'6''	3.88 x 2.89
Bed 4	12'9'' x 10'6''	3.88 x 3.20

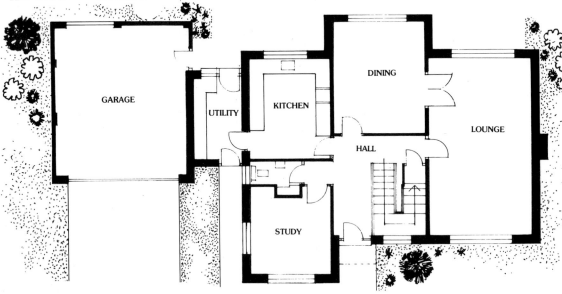

INVERNESS

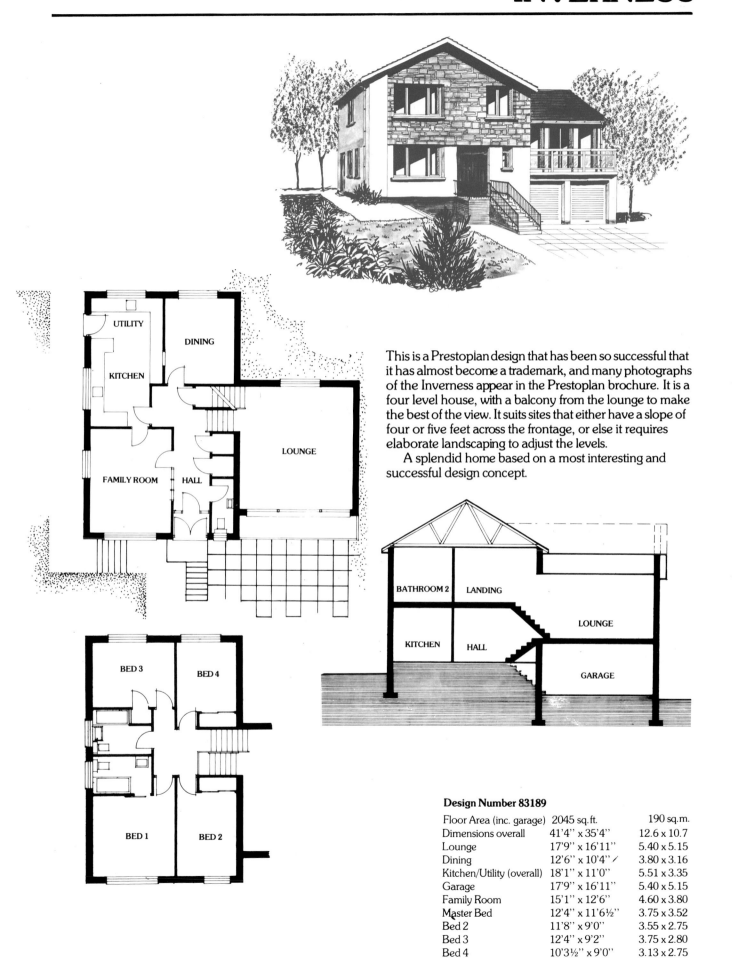

This is a Prestoplan design that has been so successful that it has almost become a trademark, and many photographs of the Inverness appear in the Prestoplan brochure. It is a four level house, with a balcony from the lounge to make the best of the view. It suits sites that either have a slope of four or five feet across the frontage, or else it requires elaborate landscaping to adjust the levels.

A splendid home based on a most interesting and successful design concept.

Design Number 83189

Floor Area (inc. garage)	2045 sq.ft.	190 sq.m.
Dimensions overall	41'4'' x 35'4''	12.6 x 10.7
Lounge	17'9'' x 16'11''	5.40 x 5.15
Dining	12'6'' x 10'4'' ✓	3.80 x 3.16
Kitchen/Utility (overall)	18'1'' x 11'0''	5.51 x 3.35
Garage	17'9'' x 16'11''	5.40 x 5.15
Family Room	15'1'' x 12'6''	4.60 x 3.80
Master Bed	12'4'' x 11'6½''	3.75 x 3.52
Bed 2	11'8'' x 9'0''	3.55 x 2.75
Bed 3	12'4'' x 9'2''	3.75 x 2.80
Bed 4	10'3½'' x 9'0''	3.13 x 2.75

303

BARDSEY

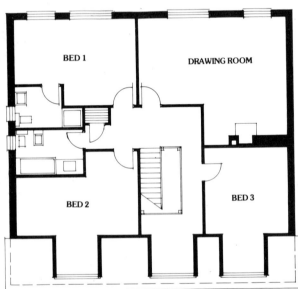

Another Prestoplan design with a thoroughly traditional appearance. This is a house for a site where the views are to the back of the home, and has the lounge/dining room, the kitchen, the first floor drawing room and the master bedroom all looking out to the rear. On the front elevation the three walk-in gables on the first floor are a most attractive feature, and the one on the landing is almost a little room in itself.

Note that there are fireplaces in both the lounge and the drawing room: this is our only design with a first floor fireplace!

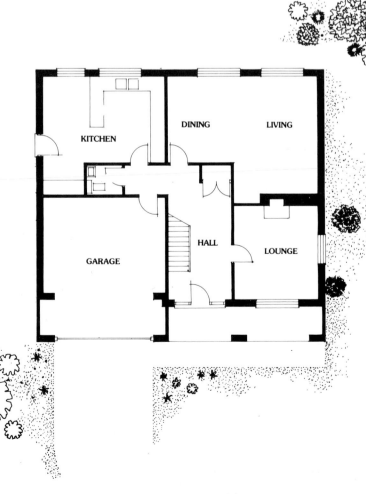

Design Number 83190

Floor Area	2106 sq. ft.	195 sq. m.
Dimensions overall	40'2½'' x 37'3''	12.2 x 11.3
Lounge/Dining (overall)	21'1'' x 17'5''	6.41 x 5.30
Kitchen	17'1'' x 11'10''	5.20 x 3.60
Study	11'8'' x 12'7½''	3.55 x 3.85
Garage	17'1'' x 18'9''	5.20 x 5.70
Master Bed (overall)	17'1'' x 11'10''	5.20 x 3.60
Bed 2 (overall)	17'1'' x 11'4''	5.20 x 3.45
Bed 3	11'10'' x 11'4''	3.60 x 3.45
Drawing Room (overall)	21'1'' x 17'5''	6.41 x 5.30

AVONMERE

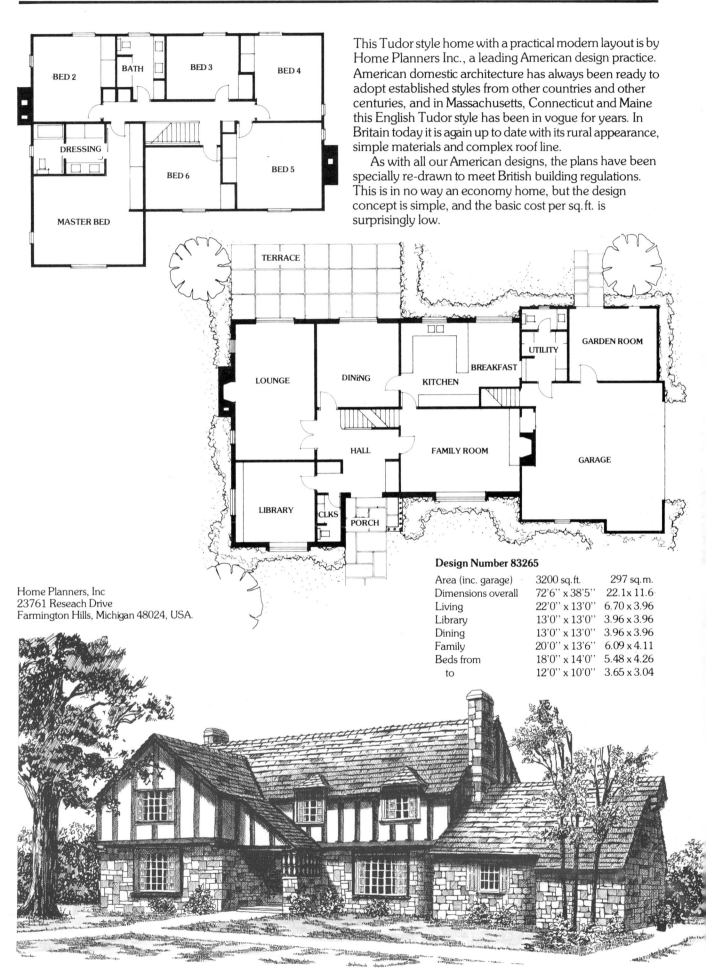

This Tudor style home with a practical modern layout is by Home Planners Inc., a leading American design practice. American domestic architecture has always been ready to adopt established styles from other countries and other centuries, and in Massachusetts, Connecticut and Maine this English Tudor style has been in vogue for years. In Britain today it is again up to date with its rural appearance, simple materials and complex roof line.

As with all our American designs, the plans have been specially re-drawn to meet British building regulations. This is in no way an economy home, but the design concept is simple, and the basic cost per sq. ft. is surprisingly low.

Home Planners, Inc
23761 Reseach Drive
Farmington Hills, Michigan 48024, USA.

Design Number 83265

Area (inc. garage)	3200 sq.ft.	297 sq. m.
Dimensions overall	72'6'' x 38'5''	22.1 x 11.6
Living	22'0'' x 13'0''	6.70 x 3.96
Library	13'0'' x 13'0''	3.96 x 3.96
Dining	13'0'' x 13'0''	3.96 x 3.96
Family	20'0'' x 13'6''	6.09 x 4.11
Beds from	18'0'' x 14'0''	5.48 x 4.26
to	12'0'' x 10'0''	3.65 x 3.04

COTSWOLD

This design takes its name from the part of the country where it will be most at home, but it is in a style that is part of the tradition of all the English countryside. The original was built by a client of D & M Limited in 1982, in the Cotswolds, and was relatively cost effective in spite of the complex front elevation. One reason is that the span of 22ft 10'' is relatively modest, although the Architect did have to arrange for all the first floor walls between the bedrooms to be built in solid blockwork as this was part of the client's brief. Incidentally, the Planners were most enthusiastic about it.

There was a spiral staircase in the original design, although we have shown more conventional stairs in the plan on these pages. Whether you prefer this, or think winding stairs would be more fun, the staircase will certainly be a key feature and merits a great deal of thought. The hall is large enough to hold a number of pieces of furniture, and choice of staircase should really be made after considering how you intend to furnish the hall. An oak staircase to match a small oak refectory table would be a very appropriate combination.

The first floor arrangement is quite conventional, although some would wish to turn the en suite shower room into a larger bathroom at the expense of the fourth bedroom. A bigger cylinder cupboard may also be required by some, and there is room for this if the bathroom door is moved to the right.

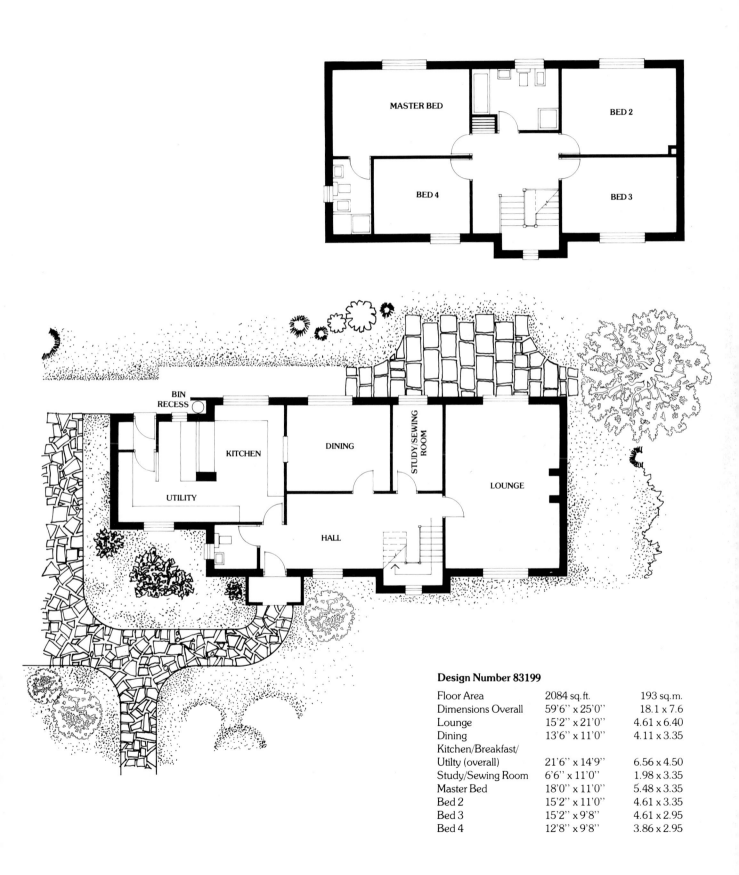

MASTER BED

BED 2

BED 4

BED 3

BIN
RECESS

KITCHEN

DINING

STUDY/SEWING ROOM

UTILITY

LOUNGE

HALL

Design Number 83199

Floor Area	2084 sq.ft.	193 sq.m.
Dimensions Overall	59'6'' x 25'0''	18.1 x 7.6
Lounge	15'2'' x 21'0''	4.61 x 6.40
Dining	13'6'' x 11'0''	4.11 x 3.35
Kitchen/Breakfast/		
Utilty (overall)	21'6'' x 14'9''	6.56 x 4.50
Study/Sewing Room	6'6'' x 11'0''	1.98 x 3.35
Master Bed	18'0'' x 11'0''	5.48 x 3.35
Bed 2	15'2'' x 11'0''	4.61 x 3.35
Bed 3	15'2'' x 9'8''	4.61 x 2.95
Bed 4	12'8'' x 9'8''	3.86 x 2.95

CHATSWORTH

The Chatsworth house suits a site with all-round views, and is a design that affords the housewife the same view from the kitchen sink that she gets from the lounge and dining room. Many clients specifically ask for this, saying that they spend so much of their lives in the kitchen that the view from the kitchen window should be as good as any other.

The arrangement of the master bedroom suite can be changed to give a view to the rear if this is appropriate: if you do this then some re-arrangement of the shower room is necessary so that the windows line up with the lounge windows below.

Drawings are available for a variation of this design with the ground floor layout rearranged so that the utility room is adjacent to the garage, and connects with it. This is the Hardwick design, reference 82266.

Design Number 83266

Floor Area		
(exc. garage)	2052 sq.ft.	190 sq.m.
Dimensions overall	60'6'' x 41'8½''	18.4 x 12.7
Lounge	20'0'' x 13'5½''	6.10 x 4.10
Dining	11'10'' x 11'2''	3.60 x 3.40
Kitchen	13'7½'' x 11'2''	4.15 x 3.40
Study	9'2'' x 8'10''	2.80 x 2.70
Utility	10'10'' x 8'6½''	3.30 x 2.60
Garage	23'11½'' x 17'1''	7.30 x 5.20
Master Bed	13'9'' x 13'5''	4.20 x 4.10
Bed 2	17'1'' x 11'6''	5.20 x 3.50
Bed 3	12'0'' x 11'2''	3.65 x 3.40
Bed 4	11'10'' x 9'2''	3.60 x 2.80

BATHAMPTON

This is a well laid out example of the classic Neo-Georgian house which has always been popular and which can be relied on to appreciate in value ahead of the market. Ideally it should be built with sash windows, but if this is not possible it will still maintain its elegance from the proportions, and from the way in which the front entrance is a focal point.

The choice of walling and roofing material is critical if one is building this house, particularly the balance between the two colours. Often this is a matter of local practice, and before choosing bricks and tiles one has to see whether the original Georgian houses in the area have roofs that are darker than the walls, or lighter — and by how much. You won't want to match the original materials, but stonewold tiles can replace slate, and modern wire-cut bricks will look every bit as well as handmades if the balance between their colours is right.

Design Number 83269

Floor Area (inc. garage)	2475 sq.ft.	230 sq.m.
Lounge	25'3" x 14'0"	7.70 x 4.26
Dining	13'9" x 14'0"	4.19 x 4.26
Breakfast/Kitchen		
(overall)	15'9" x 19'0"	4.80 x 5.80
Study	9'0" x 11'0"	2.74 x 3.35
Utility	8'0" x 12'3"	2.43 x 3.74
Garage	16'0" x 18'0"	4.87 x 5.48
Master Bed	12'0" x 15'3"	3.65 x 4.65
Bed 2	9'8" x 12'0"	2.95 x 3.65
Bed 3	15'8" x 10'5"	4.79 x 3.17
Bed 4	9'0" x 10'5"	2.74 x 3.17

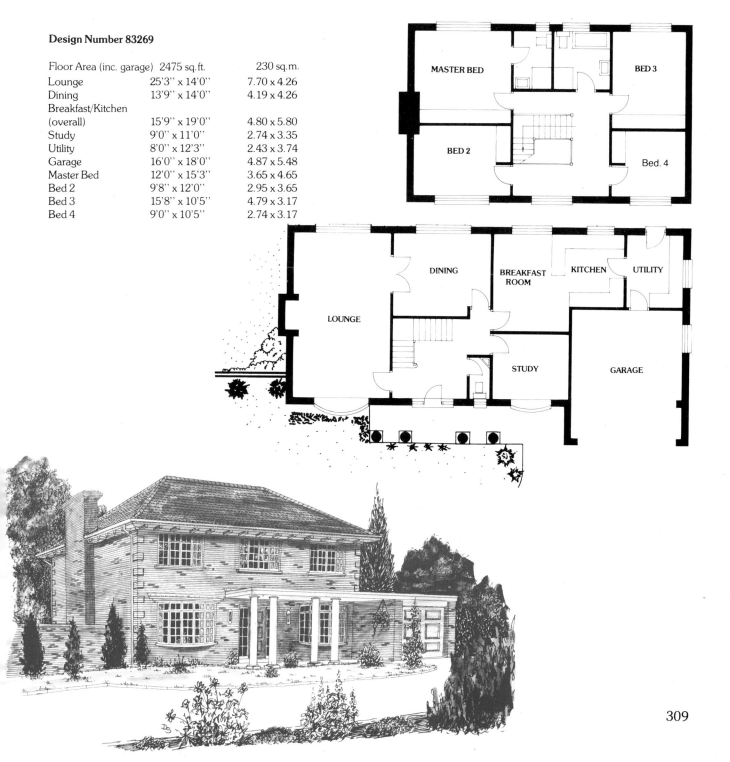

309

YORK

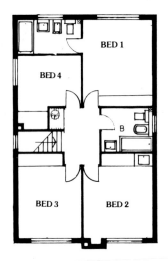

This is a big house, and needs a site with plenty of room. As shown it suits a situation where the main views are to the front. The chimney is a key feature in the building, but if it is not required it can be built internally, giving an opportunity for an angled fireplace at the corner of the inside wall of the lounge. If this alteration is made, the arrangement of windows on the gable end elevation will then have to be considered with care, and the decision must take the landscaping proposals into account.

If the roof pitch has to be increased above 35° to suit the planners, the window to the fourth bedroom may be affected.

The workshop or garden store at the back of the garage is a popular feature of the design.

Design Number 83270

Area (inc. garage)	2600 sq. ft.	240 sq. m.
Overall	53'10'' x 38'4''	16.41 x 11.69
Lounge	23'5'' x 14'1''	7.14 x 4.30
Dining	14'1'' x 11'11''	4.30 x 3.64
Study	11'11'' x 7'10''	3.64 x 2.39
Kitchen	18'5'' x 11'2''	5.60 x 3.40
Bed 1	14'1'' x 11'11''	4.30 x 3.64
Bed 2	12'2'' x 11'11''	3.70 x 3.64
Bed 3	12'2'' x 11'2''	3.70 x 3.40
Bed 4	11'2'' x 9'6''	3.40 x 2.90

A version of this design with a farm office at the rear of the garage (but with its own separate access) is the Pickering, reference 82270.

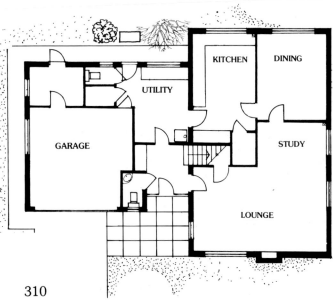

BUXTON

This large house meets a planning requirement in many rural areas that a building of this size should have a complex roof arrangement. To achieve this with an attractive internal layout while arranging for a loadbearing wall below the point at which a roof changes direction is not easy, but it is essential if costs are to be kept down. We think that we have achieved this very well in this new design, and we are sure it will become justly popular.

The huge lounge/dining/living arrangement can be adapted to suit a clients own requirements — and also to suit the view — and if necessary the kitchen can be extended to take in the living room to give a traditional farmhouse kitchen. The storm porch with its cloakroom between 2 sets of doors is a useful feature.

Design Number 83271

Area	2378 sq.ft.	221 sq.m.
Overall	45'9'' x 44'3''	13.94 x 13.49
Lounge	19'0'' x 18'4½''	5.79 x 5.60
Dining	23'5'' x 14'9''	7.14 x 4.50
Kitchen	15'0'' x 11'8''	4.56 x 3.55
Study	10'10'' x 8'11''	3.30 x 2.72
Bed 1	23'5'' x 14'9''	7.14 x 4.50
Bed 2	15'0'' x 11'8''	4.56 x 3.55
Bed 3	18'4½'' x 9'10''	5.60 x 3.00
Bed 4	14'9'' x 8'10''	4.50 x 2.69

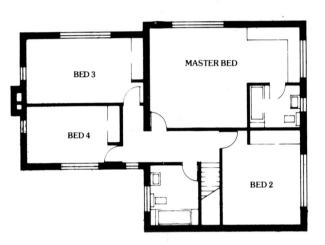

The study/utility room area of the Buxton can be used for a self contained flat. Drawings for this are available as the Matlock design, reference 82271.

BLYTH

The Blyth house is our most popular 4 bedroomed house design, and has been built in one style or another in well over a hundred times. It always looks well, whether built with landscape windows with a generous eaves overhang or with casement windows and a roof to a steeper pitch to suit a planning requirement in a rural area.

The plan shows a large patio window in the lounge rear wall. This can be moved into the side wall if appropriate, and the chimney can be moved to suit. This house is frequently built with the chimney as a feature built out from the lounge gable wall. Either of the screens to the storm porch can be omitted if required, thus giving a larger hall, or a recessed doorway.

The double garage is often reduced to a single garage, or given an extra 2 feet of width to suit a pair of 7 foot garage doors. The utility room behind can be built with a WC at the far end, while on farms it sometimes becomes a porch with a farm office.

A version of the Blyth design with the garage redesigned as a self-contained flat is called the Letwell, reference 82240.

Design Number 83240

Area (exc. garage)	1695 sq.ft.	157 sq.m.
Overall	53'0" x 25'0"	16.15 x 7.64
Lounge	23'5" x 13'10"	7.14 x 4.21
Dining	13'10" x 10'10"	4.22 x 3.31
Kitchen	13'0" x 10'10"	3.94 x 3.31
Bed 1	13'10" x 11'10"	4.21 x 3.60
Bed 2	10'11" x 10'9"	3.32 x 3.27
Bed 3	10'9" x 10'1"	3.27 x 3.07
Bed 4	10'3" x 9'2"	3.12 x 2.79
Garage	18'4" x 17'7"	5.60 x 5.37
Utility	15'1" x 7'4"	4.60 x 2.22

LOUNGE

KITCHEN

UTILITY

DINING

GARAGE

BED 4

BED 2

BED 1

BED 3

ANSTON

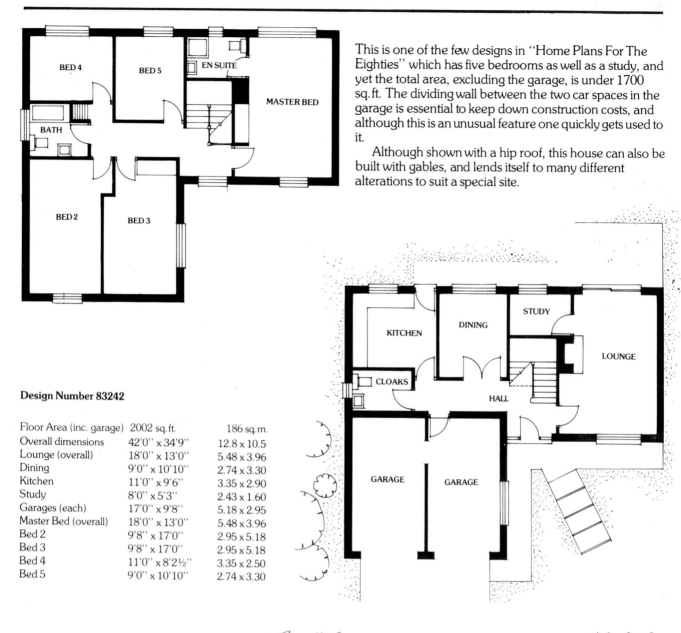

This is one of the few designs in "Home Plans For The Eighties" which has five bedrooms as well as a study, and yet the total area, excluding the garage, is under 1700 sq.ft. The dividing wall between the two car spaces in the garage is essential to keep down construction costs, and although this is an unusual feature one quickly gets used to it.

Although shown with a hip roof, this house can also be built with gables, and lends itself to many different alterations to suit a special site.

Design Number 83242

Floor Area (inc. garage)	2002 sq.ft.	186 sq.m.
Overall dimensions	42'0'' x 34'9''	12.8 x 10.5
Lounge (overall)	18'0'' x 13'0''	5.48 x 3.96
Dining	9'0'' x 10'10''	2.74 x 3.30
Kitchen	11'0'' x 9'6''	3.35 x 2.90
Study	8'0'' x 5'3''	2.43 x 1.60
Garages (each)	17'0'' x 9'8''	5.18 x 2.95
Master Bed (overall)	18'0'' x 13'0''	5.48 x 3.96
Bed 2	9'8'' x 17'0''	2.95 x 5.18
Bed 3	9'8'' x 17'0''	2.95 x 5.18
Bed 4	11'0'' x 8'2½''	3.35 x 2.50
Bed 5	9'0'' x 10'10''	2.74 x 3.30

MINSTER

The Minster developed from our York design, with the same structure adapted to suit a site where the views are to the rear. One result is to separate the kitchen from the utility room: some housewives find it a disadvantage, but others like the idea.

The garage wing has the same popular garden store as the York, and if required the garage door can be moved into the side wall to suit a different drive layout.

As with all designs where the front entrance is in the angle between two wings of the house, care should be taken to give it appropriate emphasis, with projecting steps and an angled approach path. This is so important.

Design Number 83267

Area (inc. garage)	2600 sq.ft.	240 sq.m.
Overall	53'10'' x 38'4''	16.41 x 11.69
Lounge	23'5'' x 14'1''	7.14 x 4.30
Dining	14'1'' x 11'11''	4.30 x 3.64
Study	11'11'' x 7'10''	3.64 x 2.39
Kitchen	14'5'' x 11'2''	4.40 x 3.40
Bed 1	11'11'' x 11'2''	3.64 x 3.39
Bed 2	12'2'' x 11'11''	3.70 x 3.64
Bed 3	12'2'' x 11'2''	3.70 x 3.40
Bed 4	8'10'' x 8'10''	2.70 x 2.70

315

REGENCY

This very large five bedroomed house is a splendid design for a prestige site. The key feature — the portico, stairs, and the two huge round bay windows — must be to a very high standard, and we have detailed drawings and specifications for them.

An unusual feature is that the bathroom to the Master Suite is very large with every luxury, at the expense of the bathroom which serves the other bedrooms. And why not — who is paying for it all anyway! Another factor is that there will probably be washbasins in bedrooms 2 and 3 in a house of this size anyway.

The arrangement of stores, workshop and laundry room in the garage wing was drawn to suit the requirements of a client who particularly wanted this layout, and we anticipate that those wanting a home of this size will have the plan modified to suit their own individual requirements.

Design Number 83268

Floor Area (exc. garage) 2484 sq.ft.		230 sq.m.
Dimensions Overall		
(approx.)	84'6½'' x 32'8''	25.77 x 9.95
Drawing Room	16'0'' x 24'0''	4.87 x 7.31
Dining	17'0'' x 11'0''	5.18 x 3.35
Kitchen/		
Breakfast (overall)	23'10'' x 12'8''	7.26 x 3.86
Workshop	11'3'' x 7'6''	3.42 x 2.28
Store	7'6'' x 8'3''	2.28 x 2.51
Garage	18'0'' x 20'0''	5.48 x 6.09
Laundry	8'9'' x 7'3''	2.66 x 2.21
Master Bed	12'8'' x 16'0''	3.86 x 4.87
Bed 2	16'0'' x 11'0''	4.87 x 3.35
Bed 3	11'0'' x 12'8''	3.35 x 3.86
Bed 4	10'0'' x 11'0''	3.05 x 3.35
Bed 5/Study	8'0'' x 9'0''	2.43 x 2.74

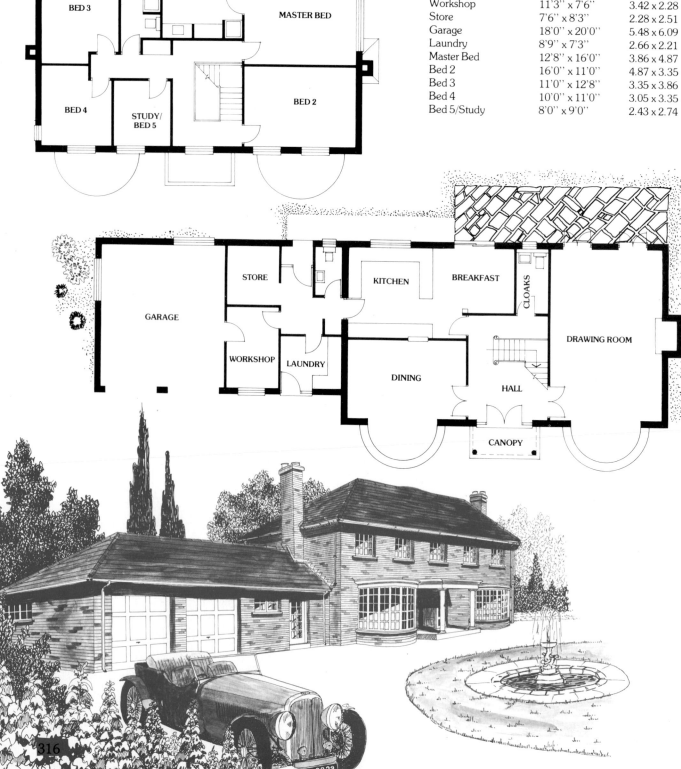

LINCOLN

The Lincoln house is a D & M design which has been built in many parts of the country over the last 10 years, and is invariably built at a low unit cost because of the simplicity of the basic shell design. Look how the internal walls to the first floor rise from corresponding walls on the ground floor, at how the drainage is grouped into two soil pipes, and how the two separate parts of the roof are the same span. These are the sort of features which make for cost effective construction.

The Lincoln is illustrated here in a rural setting in an area where traditional stone construction is required, but it looks just as well when built in brick under a pantile roof. The windows in the lounge can be moved around to suit the view, and a great deal of character is given to the room by the load bearing walls which separate it from both the hall and the lounge. Double doors or a feature arch look well when set in a deep reveal, and most clients building the Lincoln house have exploited this potential to the full.

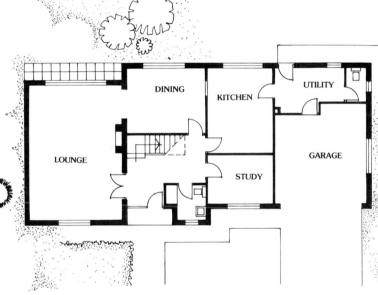

Design Number 83263

Area (inc. garage)	2350 sq. ft.	218 sq.m.
Overall	62'0'' x 27'1''	20.00 x 9.64
Lounge	23'5'' x 16'9''	7.14 x 5.11
Dining	13'11'' x 11'6''	4.25 x 3.50
Study	11'10'' x 8'4''	3.60 x 2.54
Kitchen	14'9'' x 11'10''	4.50 x 3.60
Bed 1	16'2'' x 15'1''	4.94 x 4.60
Bed 2	13'11'' x 11'6''	4.25 x 3.50
Bed 3	13'11'' x 8'6''	4.25 x 2.59
Bed 4	11'10'' x 8'0''	3.60 x 2.44

BAKEWELL

The Bakewell design was first drawn for a client who insisted on a large cloakroom by the front door where he could keep his golf clubs. He also wanted easy access from the hall through the lounge and dining room back to the hall again for the frequent occasions when he was entertaining on some scale. The Bakewell design resulted.

This home is best suited to a large site with views to the rear. It is usually built with patio windows leading outside from both the lounge and the dining room. If this is done, it is essential that the patio on to which they open should be large enough: a generous paved area gives an additional dimension to the feel of any house, while a cramped terrace gives a cramped feel to all about it.

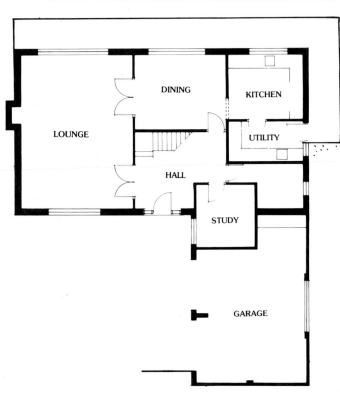

Design Number 83264

Area (inc. garage)	2465 sq. ft.	229 sq. m.
Overall	50'11'' x 45'2½''	15.51 x 13.77
Lounge	23'5'' x 16'11''	7.14 x 5.15
Dining	13'11'' x 11'5½''	4.25 x 3.49
Kitchen	11'10½'' x 10'0''	3.61 x 3.05
Study	9'2'' x 9'0''	2.79 x 2.74
Bed 1	23'5'' x 16'11''	7.14 x 5.15
Bed 2	13'11'' x 8'2''	4.25 x 2.49
Bed 3	11'10½'' x 11'5½''	3.61 x 3.49
Bed 4	11'10½'' x 11'8''	3.61 x 3.55

DUNHOLME

This tile hung house in the Essex style will take its character from the tiles that are chosen for it. Whether both walls and roof are clad with plain tiles, as illustrated, or whether the roof tiles should be a contrasting colour and profile, is something to be considered on site. In doing this it is always important to give careful consideration to the style of adjacent properties.

The ground floor guest room is a popular feature, and is put to many other uses besides accommodating visitors.

There are two variants of this design, both with the study used as the dining room. The Somersham design, reference 82261 dispenses with the rear projection, saving 230 sq. ft. in the total area, while the Buckland design, reference 81261, uses this part of the house for a granny flat.

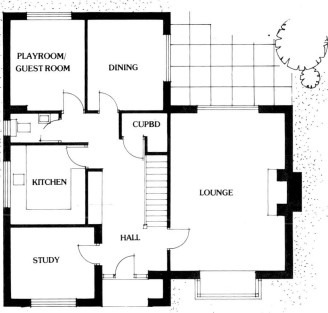

Design Number 83261

Floor Area	1796 sq. ft.	167 sq. m.
Overall size	25'6'' x 39'7''	7.7 x 12.0
Lounge	20'0'' x 15'0''	6.10 x 4.57
Dining	11'6'' x 10'0''	3.50 x 3.05
Kitchen	9'8'' x 10'0''	2.95 x 3.05
Study	11'0'' x 9'0''	3.35 x 2.74
Playroom/		
Guest Room	11'6'' x 9'8''	3.50 x 2.95
Master Bed	15'0'' x 13'2''	4.57 x 4.02
Bed 2	11'0'' x 9'0''	3.35 x 2.74
Bed 3	7'4½'' x 13'7½''	2.25 x 4.15
Bed 4	8'8'' x 9'0''	2.64 x 2.74

HOLBROOK

This large detached house with the garage linked to it by the utility room can be built in two stages: house first, the garage and utility room later. The lounge has an unusual shape and the arrangement of the windows in it can be altered as required to suit the views, or your own ideas on the decor that you require. There are five bedrooms and two bathrooms above, and a great deal of cupboard space. A big home that needs to be set in a big garden.

Design Number 83262

Floor Area		
(exc. garage)	2345 sq. ft.	218 sq.m.
Dimensions overall	76'3½'' x 34'1½''	23.2 x 10.4
Lounge	23'5'' x 21'4''	7.14 x 6.50
Dining	12'6'' x 12'0''	3.81 x 3.65
Kitchen	17'5½'' x 12'0''	5.32 x 3.65
Study	12'0'' x 11'1''	3.65 x 3.38
Utility	12'5'' x 10'4''	3.80 x 3.14
Garage	22'1'' x 19'11''	6.74 x 6.06
Master Bed	17'2½'' x 12'0''	5.24 x 3.65
Bed 2	15'5½'' x 12'0''	4.71 x 3.65
Bed 3	14'6'' x 12'0''	4.41 x 3.65
Bed 4	13'5'' x 10'2½''	4.08 x 3.11
Bed 5	11'1'' x 10'8½''	3.38 x 3.26

WENTBRIDGE

This large 4 bedroomed house was originally designed for a 50 foot wide plot in a very up-market suburb, but it will look equally well on a far larger site which would give an opportunity for some of the windows to be moved into the side walls. The porch roof which continues over the bay window is supported on a gallows bracket: it is always important that these should be really massive and well finished with plenty of detail.

The garage door is a key feature in the appearance of this house, and it is most important that it should be chosen with care. It is illustrated here as a panel door, but there are many other attractive designs available from specialist suppliers, and in most situations one should try to avoid the standard horizontally ribbed doors, which clash with the vertical emphasis of the casement joinery.

The generous hall with its feature staircase is lit by the large first floor landing window, and gives a welcoming feel to the whole house when you step inside the front door.

Design Number 83253

Area (exc. garage)	1770 sq.ft.	164 sq.m.
Overall dimensions	46'11'' x 39'0''	14.3 x 11.8
Lounge	23'5'' x 14'6''	7.14 x 4.42
Dining	11'0'' x 12'3''	3.35 x 3.73
Kitchen	11'0'' x 16'9''	3.35 x 5.10
Utility	6'6'' x 13'5''	1.98 x 4.10
Garage	20'9'' x 18'3½''	6.32 x 5.57
Master Bed	12'6'' x 12'1''	3.81 x 3.68
Bed 2	14'6'' x 9'0''	4.42 x 2.75
Bed 3	11'0'' x 11'0''	3.35 x 3.35
Bed 4	10'0'' x 12'1''	3.05 x 3.68

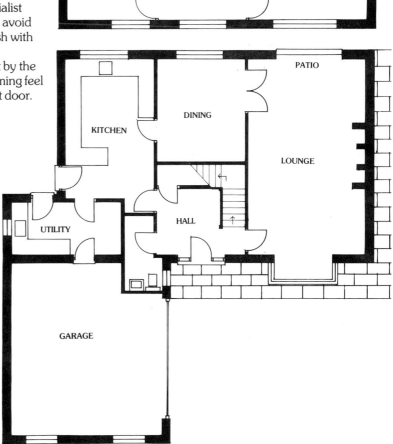

DARTMOUTH

This is an interesting home: we show two sketches to
demonstrate how it is designed to be built into a steep
bank, so that it is seen to be a bungalow from the back, and
a house from the front. Two bedrooms are on the ground
floor, which only extends halfway back under the upper
floor, which has all the living accommodation and two
more bedrooms. This takes some getting used to, but
when you get the hang of the plans you will quickly see
what a clever arrangment this is.

A most successful design, originally built on a site in
Surrey.

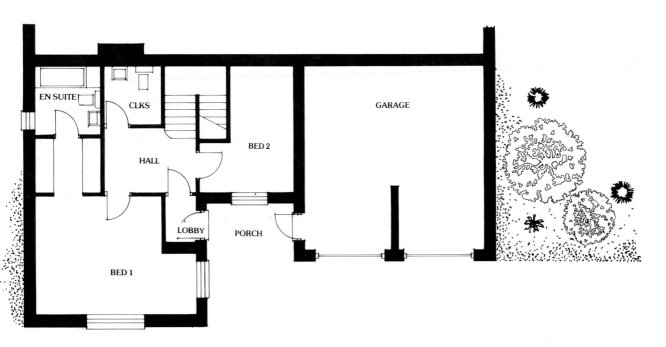

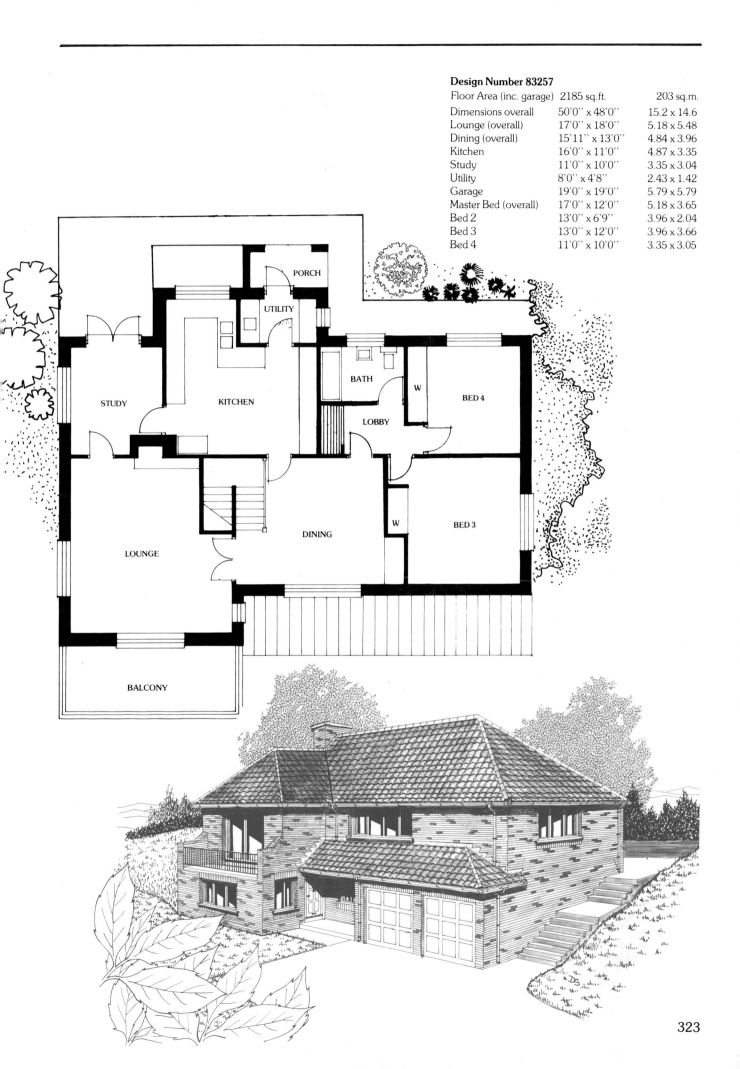

Design Number 83257

Floor Area (inc. garage)	2185 sq.ft.	203 sq.m.
Dimensions overall	50'0'' x 48'0''	15.2 x 14.6
Lounge (overall)	17'0'' x 18'0''	5.18 x 5.48
Dining (overall)	15'11'' x 13'0''	4.84 x 3.96
Kitchen	16'0'' x 11'0''	4.87 x 3.35
Study	11'0'' x 10'0''	3.35 x 3.04
Utility	8'0'' x 4'8''	2.43 x 1.42
Garage	19'0'' x 19'0''	5.79 x 5.79
Master Bed (overall)	17'0'' x 12'0''	5.18 x 3.65
Bed 2	13'0'' x 6'9''	3.96 x 2.04
Bed 3	13'0'' x 12'0''	3.96 x 3.66
Bed 4	11'0'' x 10'0''	3.35 x 3.05

PORCH

UTILITY

STUDY

KITCHEN

BATH

W

BED 4

LOBBY

LOUNGE

DINING

W

BED 3

BALCONY

GREENWOOD

The Greenwood design is the most popular of our
genuinely five bedroom designs, having a study as well as
the fifth bedroom. It is shown here as it might be built in
two different areas — the brick with tile hanging to suit
Kent or Sussex, and stone with render above is typical of
the houses our clients build in Wales.

Design Number 83258

Floor Area (inc. garage)	2422 sq. ft.	225 sq. m.
Dimensions overall	54'11'' x 31'6½''	16.7 x 9.6
Lounge (overall)	26'9'' x 16'0½''	8.15 x 4.88
Dining	10'0'' x 11'0''	3.05 x 3.35
Kitchen	14'9'' x 11'0''	4.50 x 3.35
Study	9'6'' x 8'0''	2.90 x 2.43
Utility	11'0'' x 8'0''	3.35 x 2.43
Garage	19'10½'' x 18'0''	6.06 x 5.48
Master Bed	11'6'' x 12'6''	3.50 x 3.80
Bed 2	14'5'' x 14'0''	4.39 x 4.26
Bed 3	12'0'' x 13'0''	3.65 x 3.96
Bed 4	11'9'' x 8'10''	3.58 x 2.70
Bed 5	8'0'' x 9'10''	2.43 x 3.00

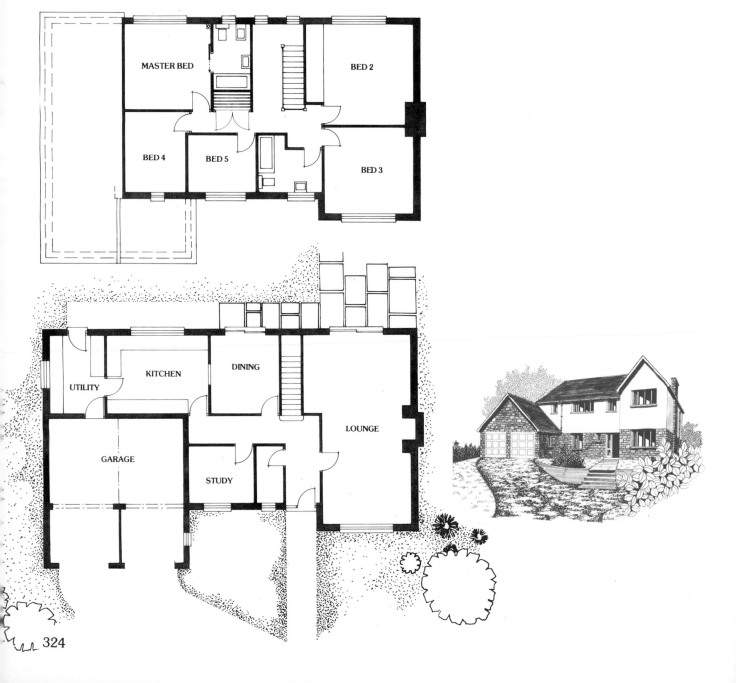

LEAMINGTON

This is the traditional layout for a Tudor home — two gables to the front, an impressive entrance hall lit by a large first floor window, and larger-than-usual bedrooms. The wall between the garage and the house is illustrated with a solid door, and this helps to spread the appearance of the house and garage together, and makes everything seem even larger and more imposing.

Design Number 83251

Floor Area	1570 sq. ft.	146 sq. m.
Overall dimensions	25'3" x 36'6"	7.7 x 11.1
Lounge	23'5" x 12'0"	7.14 x 3.65
Dining	12'0" x 10'0"	3.65 x 3.05
Kitchen	13'1" x 12'0"	3.99 x 3.65
Study	10'0" x 8'10"	3.05 x 2.70
Garage	18'0" x 11'2½"	5.48 x 3.41
Master Bed (overall)	12'0" x 13'1"	3.65 x 3.99
Bed 2	12'0" x 11'0"	3.65 x 3.35
Bed 3	12'0" x 10'0"	3.65 x 3.05
Bed 4	8'0" x 12'1"	2.43 x 3.68

NEWMARKET

BED 2

BED 4

MASTER BED

BED 3

The Newmarket design meets the requirements of those who entertain, and who want a large hall and reception rooms. It has often been built as a farmhouse, with an additional door provided to give access to the study from the back door, so that the study can be used as the farm office. The large kitchen also suits rural living.

Upstairs the en suite bathroom is shown with a shower, basin and WC, but it can easily be rearranged to include a bath and a bidet as well. The main bathroom is also unusually large, and there is an enormous walk-in airing cupboard.

The fourth bedroom is small, and if necessary we can rearrange the whole of the first floor to give more room in the bedrooms at the expense of the large bathrooms, the choice lies with our clients.

A ground floor accommodation for an elderly relative can be provided in this design at the expense of the study and utility room. The modified design is called the Chippenham, reference number 82252.

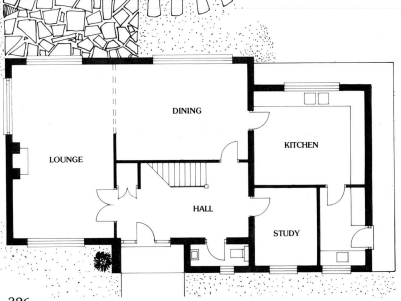

DINING

KITCHEN

LOUNGE

HALL

STUDY

Design Number 83252

Area	1905 sq. ft.	177 sq. m.
Overall	50'2'' x 28'9''	15.29 x 8.76
Lounge	23'5'' x 14'1''	7.14 x 4.30
Dining	17'10'' x 12'11''	5.44 x 3.94
Kitchen	15'5½'' x 13'1½''	4.70 x 4.00
Study	10'0'' x 9'6''	3.04 x 2.90
Hall	17'10'' x 10'2''	5.44 x 3.10
Bed 1	13'1½'' x 12'11''	4.00 x 3.94
Bed 2	12'11'' x 11'0''	3.94 x 3.35
Bed 3	10'2'' x 11'0''	3.10 x 3.35
Bed 4	9'10'' x 7'6''	2.99 x 2.29

This large home was designed as a farmhouse for a client who farms in the North Yorks National Park, and has the massive look and stone features that the Park Planning Board requires.

As far as layout is concerned, it has just about every feature which we have learned that farmers want: somewhere at the back door for the dog to sleep, room for a table and chairs just inside a very large kitchen, a very large hall where two or three large men can linger over their farewells, a study or farm office near the front door, and a lounge as far away from the mud at the back door as possible!

The original was built with an oak open tread staircase and the stairwell was big enough for an antique candelabra, but if this is beyond your pocket, don't despair: ask that the drawings show a pine staircase that is fastened to the walls but structurally independant of them, and know that when you want your luxury staircase you will be able to have it fitted with the minimum of disruption. This idea of making provision for changes in the future is always important with a new home.

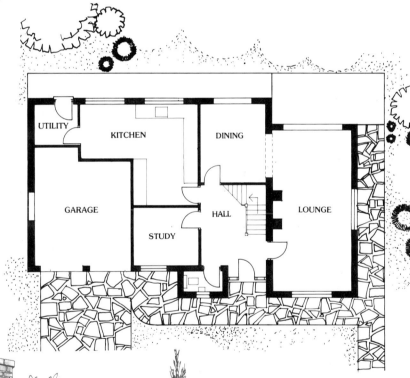

Design Number 83245

Floor Area (exc. garage)	1738 sq.ft.	161 sq.m.
Dimensions overall	49'3" x 27'3½"	15.0 x 8.3
Lounge	23'5" x 12'0"	7.14 x 3.65
Dining	9'11" x 11'6"	3.02 x 3.50
Kitchen (overall)	17'6" x 14'9"	5.32 x 4.50
Study	8'4" x 9'10"	2.54 x 2.99
Utility	6'7" x 5'11"	2.00 x 1.80
Garage (overall)	17'2" x 14'2"	5.24 x 4.32
Master Bed	14'2" x 15'1"	4.32 x 4.60
Bed 2	9'11" x 11'6"	3.02 x 3.50
Bed 3	9'10" x 8'0"	2.99 x 2.44
Bed 4	8'0" x 7'11"	2.44 x 2.42

A five bedroom version of the Thirsk is the Skipton, reference 82245.

KENILWORTH

This large Georgian home has an imposing front entrance which leads into a hall that is lit by a window to the landing in the traditional way. It is illustrated here with a large inglenook fireplace in the lounge and a corner fireplace in the dining room. This is unusual: it is simply how it was built by the client who originally commissioned this design, and of course these features can be changed.

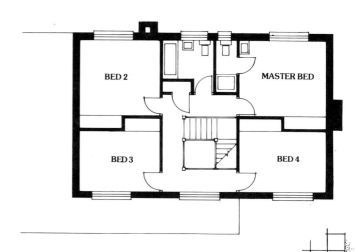

Design Number 83246

Floor Area (exc. garage)	1782 sq.ft.	165 sq.m.
Dimensions overall	58'2'' x 30'4½''	17.7 x 9.2
Lounge	13'0'' x 22'0''	3.96 x 6.70
Dining	15'0'' x 11'0''	4.56 x 3.35
Kitchen (overall)	22'6'' x 10'9''	6.85 x 3.27
Study	8'8'' x 9'8½''	2.65 x 2.95
Utility	6'10'' x 7'8''	2.09 x 2.32
Garage	16'1'' x 17'10''	4.90 x 5.44
Master Bed	13'0'' x 11'0''	3.96 x 3.35
Bed 2	12'0'' x 11'0''	3.66 x 3.35
Bed 3	8'8'' x 12'0''	2.65 x 3.66
Bed 4	8'8'' x 13'0''	2.65 x 3.96

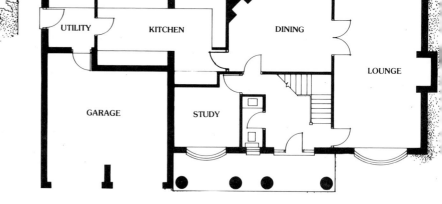

FORDCOMBE

This large house of nearly 2,000 sq. ft. has larger-than-average rooms downstairs and four double bedrooms on the first floor. The arrangement of the study and cloakroom enable it to be used as an extra ground floor bedroom with its own bathroom if required.

This is a home to build in a formal setting, and the terrace shown in the sketch suits it perfectly. A good design for a prestige suburban site.

Design Number 83247

Floor Area	1998 sq. ft.	185 sq.m.
Dimensions overall	38'3" x 31'4½"	11.6 x 9.5
Lounge/Dining		
(overall, exc. bay)	25'10½" x 18'2½"	7.88 x 5.55
Kitchen	12'0" x 13'0"	3.65 x 3.96
Study (overall)	13'6" x 11'4"	4.11 x 3.45
Utility	6'6" x 6'8"	1.98 x 2.03
Master Bed	17'4½" x 12'6½"	5.30 x 3.82
Bed 2	10'0" x 13'0"	3.05 x 3.96
Bed 3	10'0" x 12'6½"	3.05 x 3.82
Bed 4 (overall)	11'0" x 13'0"	3.35 x 3.96

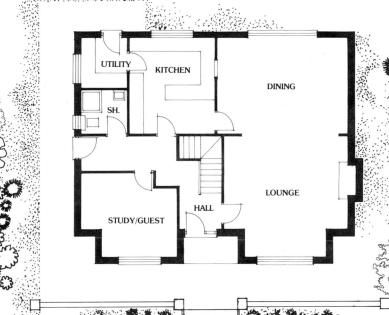

SHERBORNE

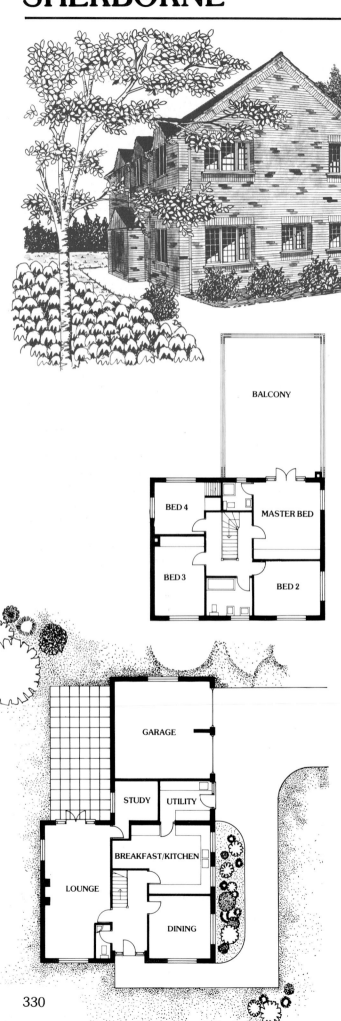

This impressive house was originally built by a lady client of D & M Ltd, as her own new home. When it was completed, circumstances had changed and she did not want to move in, so she sold it, and made a huge profit This started her off on a career as a successful one-woman development company!

The prototype "Sherborne" was built in Butterley Grey Minster bricks, but it would also look well in stone. The leaded lights are double glazed and there are two ways of doing this. One is to have traditional lead strips bonded to the outside of sealed double glazing units, and the other is to have spacers simulating lead in the cavity between the two panes of glass. If you are interested in having leaded lights, then do make a decision between these two systems after seeing them actually installed in a house, and not from sample panes. In a house they look quite different.

The balcony is a major feature of this design, and the decision on the balustrading is most important. There are many choices, and they must be considered in relation to the site, to the use to be made of the balcony, and to the design of any garden furniture to be left up there.

Design Number 83248

Floor Area (exc. garage)	1836 sq.ft.	170 sq.m.
Overall dimensions	34'9'' x 55'2''	10.6 x 16.8
Lounge	25'8'' x 13'1''	7.81 x 3.99
Dining	12'4'' x 12'0''	3.77 x 3.65
Kitchen/Breakfast		
(overall)	13'4'' x 19'6''	4.05 x 5.95
Study	9'0'' x 8'0''	2.74 x 2.43
Utility	10'0'' x 8'0''	3.05 x 2.43
Garage	19'0'' x 18'2''	5.80 x 5.52
Master Bed	15'0'' x 13'0''	4.58 x 3.96
Bed 2	13'0'' x 10'3½''	3.96 x 3.13
Bed 3	13'4'' x 9'10''	4.06 x 2.99
Bed 4	10'0'' x 10'0''	3.05 x 3.05

GRANCHESTER

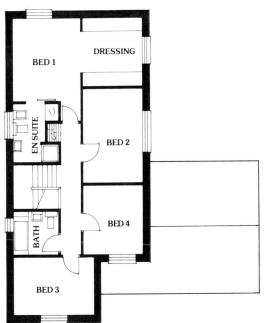

This original and imposing house was designed by D & M for a site near Cambridge and in spite of the complex roof line it was remarkably economical to build. This comes from all the separate elements in the roof being independent of each other: the result looks involved but is very easy to build.

The huge open plan kitchen/breakfast room/dining area, with stairs set in one corner, may not suit everyone and if it is not your taste then dividing walls can be built between the different rooms. However, it was first built exactly as it is drawn here, and is much admired: open plan arrangements where the lounge is at the centre of things are common enough, but the idea of a private lounge and a separate open plan living area elsewhere is unusual.

The dressing area in the main bedroom, with its double row of wardrobes, is another feature that attracts much favourable comment.

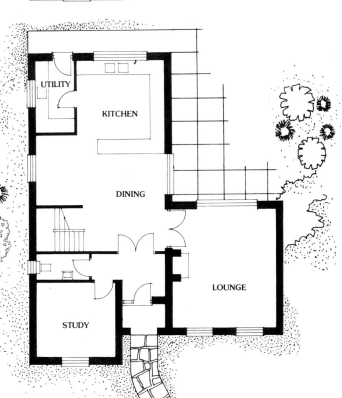

Design Number 83233

Floor Area	1825 sq.ft.	169 sq.m.
Dimensions overall	45'0'' x 37'7''	13.7 x 11.4
Lounge	17'4'' x 15'3½''	5.28 x 4.66
Dining/Kitchen (overall)	27'9'' x 13'3½''	8.46 x 4.05
Study	11'0'' x 12'2''	3.35 x 3.70
Utility	10'4'' x 5'11''	3.15 x 1.80
Master Bed	12'0'' x 10'3'	3.65 x 3.12
Bed 2	13'8'' x 9'0''	4.16 x 2.73
Bed 3	12'2'' x 8'6''	3.70 x 2.59
Bed 4	10'0'' x 9'0''	3.04 x 2.73

SUNNINGDALE

The Sunningdale house follows a very popular design concept that you will find in every book of plans. There are only a limited number of ways in which four bedroomed accommodation with an integral double garage can be offered in a total of only 1560 square feet, and this is certainly the most popular.

Within the design concept we have aimed for the most practical layout for a no-frills family house, with lots of storage space, a large bathroom, a good kitchen, and a really cost-effective design.

The double garage can be reduced in size if required, and the WC behind it need not be built if it is not appropriate. The storm porch can also be omitted, or left to a later stage.

The Sunningdale suits a site with views to the front. Where the principal view is to the rear, or where there are views in all directions, see the Wentworth design which is a variant of the Sunningdale.

Design Number 83234

Area (inc. garage)	1560 sq.ft.	145 sq.m.
Overall	47'11" x 28'9"	14.16 x 8.75
Lounge	18'5" x 12'4"	5.61 x 3.76
Dining	10'9" x 10'6"	3.27 x 3.20
Kitchen	14'10" x 10'9"	4.51 x 3.27
Bed 1	14'1" x 11'0"	4.30 x 3.35
Bed 2	12'1" x 8'8"	3.69 x 2.63
Bed 3	9'0" x 8'6"	2.74 x 2.59
Bed 4	11'0" x 7'11"	3.35 x 2.41

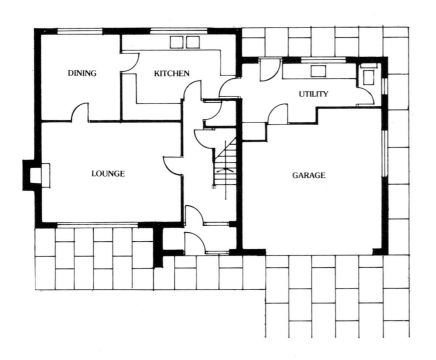

BEVERLEY

This is another design with the projecting bedroom wall which is so popular in the South of the country. There are no significant windows in the side walls, so it can be built on a plot of restricted width if required, although this is a style of home that certainly looks at its best in a large garden.

The study need not be built if it is not required, or alternatively it can be left until a later stage. Another option is to extend it as a granny flat

Design Number 83236

Floor Area	1614 sq.ft.	150 sq.m.
Overall dimensions	36'7½'' x 30'11''	11.16 x 9.4
Lounge (overall)	22'0'' x 14'0''	6.70 x 4.26
Dining	11'10'' x 10'6''	3.60 x 3.20
Kitchen	11'0'' x 10'6''	3.35 x 3.20
Utility	7'0'' x 10'6''	2.13 x 3.20
Study	10'6'' x 8'0''	3.20 x 2.43
Master Bed	13'9'' x 13'2''	4.20 x 4.01
Bed 2 (overall)	12'6'' x 14'0''	3.80 x 4.26
Bed 3	8'6'' x 10'9''	2.59 x 3.27
Bed 4	9'0'' x 11'9½''	2.75 x 3.59
Granny Annexe:		
Bedsitting	13'0'' x 10'6''	3.96 x 3.20
Kitchen	6'0'' x 7'0''	1.83 x 2.13

WESTBURTON

This interesting house has French windows opening from the first floor landing onto a large balcony. It is shown here with a garage and workshop annexe at the rear and a large utility room, but the whole of this area can be re-designed to give a separate family room if required. Upstairs there is a very large bathroom with room for a corner bath and all the other luxury fittings that you can imagine.

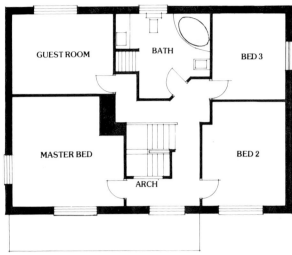

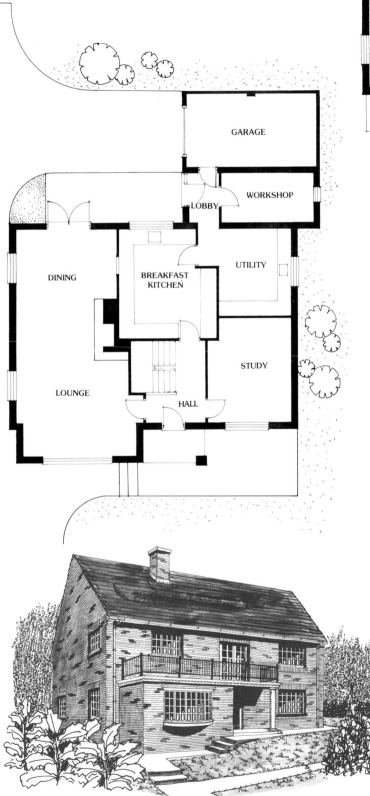

Design Number 83249

Floor Area (exc. garage)	2152 sq. ft.	200 sq.m.
Dimensions overall	52'0'' x 42'11''	15.8 x 13.0
Lounge/Dining (overall)	32'0'' x 15'6''	9.75 x 4.72
Breakfast/Kitchen	14'9'' x 13'6''	4.49 x 4.11
Study	14'0'' x 11'6''	4.26 x 3.50
Utility	11'8'' x 10'0''	3.55 x 3.05
Garage	18'0'' x 10'0''	5.48 x 3.05
Workshop	7'0'' x 12'9''	2.13 x 3.88
Master Bed (overall)	15'6'' x 14'8''	4.72 x 4.47
Bed 2	14'0'' x 11'6''	4.26 x 3.50
Bed 3	11'8'' x 10'0'''	3.55 x 3.05
Bed 4	14'0'' x 11'0''	4.26 x 3.35

WINDSOR

Another traditional house which was designed with the Home Counties in mind, but which has been just as popular in other parts of the country. Our illustration shows contrasting tile hanging above ground floor brickwork, but it can also be built in many other materials.

Note the generous covered porch at the back door. If required, a door can be put in the garage wall to open into this covered area.

Design Number 83250

Floor Area (exc. garage)	1872 sq.ft.	174 sq.m.
Overall dimensions	53'8½'' x 30'5''	16.3 x 9.2
Lounge	23'5'' x 13'0''	7.14 x 3.96
Dining	11'0'' x 9'0''	3.35 x 2.74
Kitchen	11'0'' x 9'0''	3.35 x 2.74
Study	13'9'' x 10'0''	4.20 x 3.05
Utility	6'0'' x 8'6''	1.83 x 2.60
Garage (overall)	17'0'' x 10'5½''	5.18 x 3.19
Master Bed	13'3'' x 13'9''	4.03 x 4.20
Bed 2	11'0½'' x 14'3''	3.36 x 4.34
Bed 3	8'10'' x 11'0½''	2.69 x 3.36
Bed 4	11'0'' x 9'0''	3.35 x 2.74

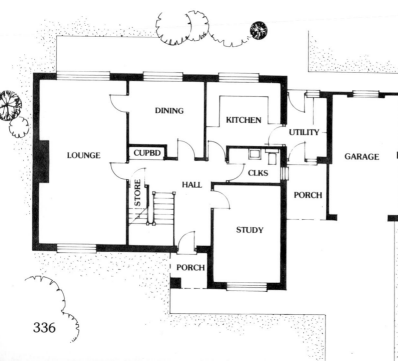

EASTGATE

An interesting design with a half hip roof. The roof above the kitchen and utility room is an extension of the rear slope of the garage roof: an unusual arrangement which gives a lot of character to the back of the house.

The fourth bedroom is small for a house of this size and would probably be used as a box room or sewing room. Alternatively, bedrooms 3 and 4 can be combined to make one very large and interestingly shaped room with two windows in one wall.

Design Number 83243

Floor Area (exc. garage)	1750 sq. ft.	162 sq.m.
Dimensions overall	44'1½'' x 48'0''	13.4 x 14.6
Lounge	23'5'' x 12'4''	7.14 x 3.76
Dining	14'4'' x 10'0''	4.37 x 3.04
Kitchen/Breakfast	14'11'' x 13'2''	4.55 x 4.00
Study	10'0'' x 8'1''	3.04 x 2.47
Utility	10'7'' x 9'0''	3.21 x 2.75
Garage (overall)	21'10'' x 18'0''	6.66 x 5.50
Master Bed	16'2'' x 12'4''	4.94 x 3.76
Bed 2	10'10'' x 10'0''	3.30 x 3.04
Bed 3	10'3½'' x 10'0''	3.14 x 3.04
Bed 4	9'4'' x 6'11''	2.84 x 2.10

MEADOWFIELD

In many ways this is the ideal farmhouse. It not only looks the part, but it has a practical layout that is relevant to the lifestyle of today's working farmers — and their wives!

There are various different versions of this design. One of the most popular is to extend the garage to provide a utility room and W.C. at the kitchen door and this is shown in the inset diagram.

Provision has been made for an Aga or similar solid fuel cooker in the kitchen. If this is not required then the chimney at the left of the building need not be built.

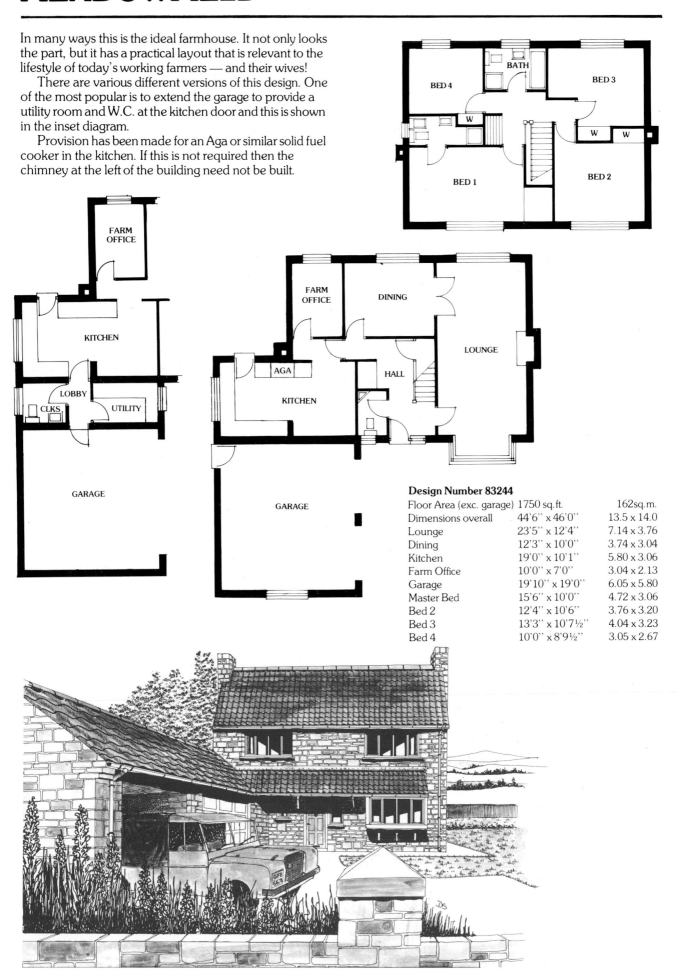

Design Number 83244

Floor Area (exc. garage)	1750 sq. ft.	162 sq. m.
Dimensions overall	44'6'' x 46'0''	13.5 x 14.0
Lounge	23'5'' x 12'4''	7.14 x 3.76
Dining	12'3'' x 10'0''	3.74 x 3.04
Kitchen	19'0'' x 10'1''	5.80 x 3.06
Farm Office	10'0'' x 7'0''	3.04 x 2.13
Garage	19'10'' x 19'0''	6.05 x 5.80
Master Bed	15'6'' x 10'0''	4.72 x 3.06
Bed 2	12'4'' x 10'6''	3.76 x 3.20
Bed 3	13'3'' x 10'7½''	4.04 x 3.23
Bed 4	10'0'' x 8'9½''	3.05 x 2.67

RUSHDEN

This useful design originated in a Bedfordshire village where the planners required gables above all first floor windows — there are three more gable windows on the rear elevation — with a complex roof line to fit in with neighbouring Victorian buildings.

The layout is particularly roomy for a three bedroomed design of only 1140 sq. ft. and has the feel of a much larger property. The hall is lit from a window on the half landing so the front door does not need a glazed screen — something that is often inescapable in compact designs, but which does not have the period feel of the Rushden house.

A shower or bidet can be fitted into the bathroom with only the minimum of alteration, and provided that the drains can be taken around the right hand side of the house, the drainage arrangements are economically grouped together. There are no significant windows in either side walls as far as the building regulations are concerned, and either wall can be built within three feet of a boundary.

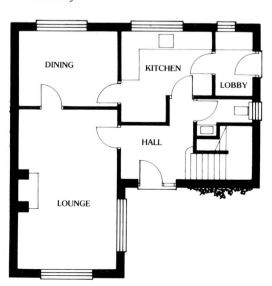

Design Number 83195

Floor Area	1130 sq. ft.	105 sq.m.
Dimensions overall	29'0'' x 28'7½''	8.82 x 8.72
Lounge	18'1½'' x 11'7''	5.52 x 3.54
Dining	11'7'' x 8'4''	3.54 x 2.54
Kitchen (overall)	10'3'' x 10'3½''	3.11 x 3.12
Master Bed	16'3'' x 11'7''	4.95 x 3.54
Bed 2	9'3'' x 10'3''	2.82 x 3.11
Bed 3	11'7'' x 10'3''	3.54 x 3.11

MALVERN

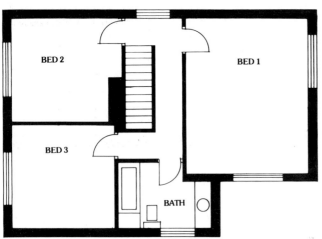

This interesting design is shown in a large garden, but is also very well suited to a narrow site. If necessary it can fit on a plot only 30ft. wide, in which case the bathroom window would be moved from the side wall to a position above the vanity unit. This sort of minor alteration is made to our plans as a matter of routine.

The layout dictates a small hall and landing, which permits an unusually large master bedroom for a house of this size.

A four bedroom version of this design is the Bromyard, reference 82206.

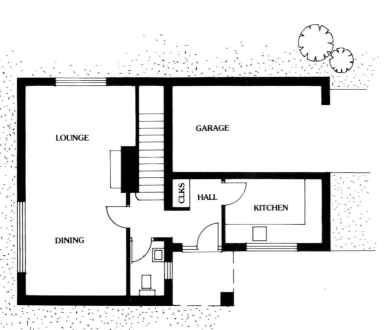

Design Number 83206

Floor Area (inc. garage)	1431 sq.ft.	113 sq.m.
Overall dimensions	24'10'' x 35'5''	7.5 x 10.8
Lounge/Dining (overall)	23'0'' x 12'6''	7.01 x 3.80
Kitchen	7'0'' x 11'2''	2.13 x 3.40
Garage	17'0'' x 9'6''	5.18 x 2.89
Bed 1	17'4'' x 14'0''	5.27 x 4.25
Bed 2	11'4'' x 12'6''	3.45 x 3.80
Bed 3	11'4'' x 11'6''	3.45 x 3.50

PETERBOROUGH

The Peterborough house is a good example of a design concept that is useful on sites where the important views are to the sides and rear, and not to the front. With only two bedrooms in 1150 sq.ft. it has many features of a much larger home, with a very large 'L' shaped living area and a hall that is lit from a gallery window above.

The storage arrangements are very generous, with a cloakroom that has plenty of room for golf bags and the other things usually forgotten by those who design houses. There is also a big walk-in cylinder cupboard, large fitted wardrobes, and plenty of space in the utility room.

The bathroom has plenty of room for any combination of fittings.

Design Number 83200

Floor Area	1156 sq.ft.	107 sq.m.
Dimensions Overall	31'11'' x 25'3½''	9.73 x 7.70
Lounge	18'0'' x 11'0''	5.48 x 3.35
Dining	9'2'' x 12'1''	2.79 x 3.68
Kitchen/Breakfast	12'2'' x 12'1''	3.69 x 3.68
Utility	10'5'' x 7'7''	3.18 x 2.30
Master Bed	13'5'' x 11'5''	4.09 x 3.48
Bed 2	8'0'' x 9'9''	2.43 x 2.96

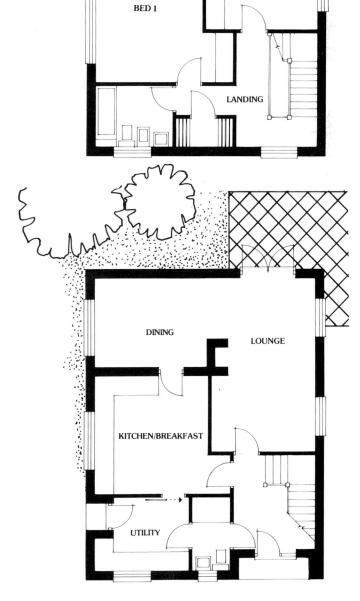

HARTFIELD

This two storey house has the look of a dormer bungalow, but it has a trussed rafter roof which keeps down costs. If it is to be built on a site of restricted width a dormer window may have to be put in the roof to light the third bedroom, but it can fit under the wallplate and avoids purlin construction.

The high window in the hall which extends up to the landing is a striking feature.

Design Number 83197

Floor Area (inc. garage)	1485 sq.ft.	138 sq.m.
Overall dimensions	32'8'' x 34'6''	9.95 x 10.52
Lounge	12'0'' x 19'0''	3.65 x 5.79
Dining	10'0'' x 8'8½''	3.05 x 2.65
Kitchen	12'0'' x 10'0''	3.65 x 3.05
Garage	18'0'' x 10'0''	5.48 x 3.05
Bed 1	12'0'' x 8'6''	3.65 x 2.59
Bed 2	12'0'' x 8'6''	3.65 x 2.59
Bed 3	10'6'' x 9'10''	3.20 x 3.00
Bed 4	12'0'' x 8'0''	3.65 x 2.43

OAKHILL

This is a design for a sloping site where there is at least 8ft. of difference in height between the garage floor level and the front door step.

In our illustration and the plan we have not shown any access onto the flat garage roof, which permits a much cheaper specification than is the case if it were to be used as a balcony. This is something that has to be cleared when a building regulation application is made, and an early decision has to be made whether or not you want french windows opening out onto the garage roof.

If you are building this house it is most important to make sure that the steps to the main entrance are really impressive so that the garage door does not dominate the front of the building. This is easily arranged, and can be quite economical.

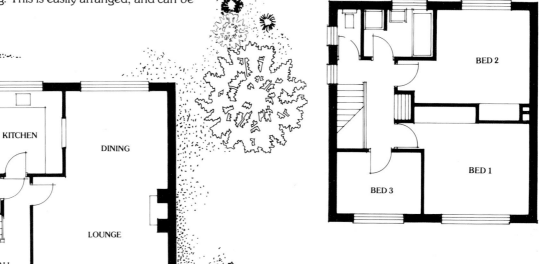

Design Number 83202

Floor Area (exc. garage)	1188 sq.ft.	110 sq.m.
Dimensions overall	50'2½'' x 33'0''	15.3 x 10.0
Lounge/Dining (overall)	15'9½'' x 23'5''	4.81 x 7.14
Kitchen	10'4½'' x 9'4''	3.15 x 2.90
Utility	7'3'' x 8'6''	2.21 x 2.59
Garage	19'0'' x 15'5½''	5.79 x 4.71
Master Bed	12'4½'' x 10'4''	3.76 x 3.14
Bed 2	11'1½'' x 10'10''	3.39 x 3.30
Bed 3	10'0'' x 7'0½''	3.04 x 2.15

WETHERBY

Design Number 83201

Floor Area (inc. garage)	2234 sq.ft.	208 sq.m.
Dimensions Overall	54'4'' x 35'8''	16.55 x 10.87
Lounge	23'4'' x 16'0''	7.11 x 4.90
Dining Hall	19'8'' x 11'6''	6.00 x 3.50
Kitchen/Breakfast	10'6'' x 23'4''	3.20 x 7.11
Utility	10'6'' x 7'8''	3.20 x 2.35
Garage (overall)	19'8'' x 23'4''	6.01 x 7.11
Master Bed	13'6'' x 11'5''	4.15 x 3.50
Bed 2	11'5'' x 11'6''	3.50 x 3.51
Bed 3	10'6'' x 15'5''	3.20 x 4.66

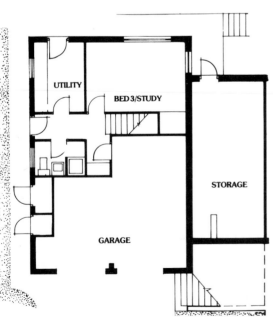

This design for a sloping site has a flight of steps leading up to the front door. It is most important that these should be as generous in width as possible, with the quarter landing carefully integrated into the landscaping.

The front door leads straight into a dining hall — a feature which is gaining popularity. There are two bedrooms on the upper floor, and a complete self contained study/bedroom, utility/kitchen and shower below. As originally designed this was accommodation for an au pair, but it can be put to many uses, including a granny flat if granny can manage the stairs.

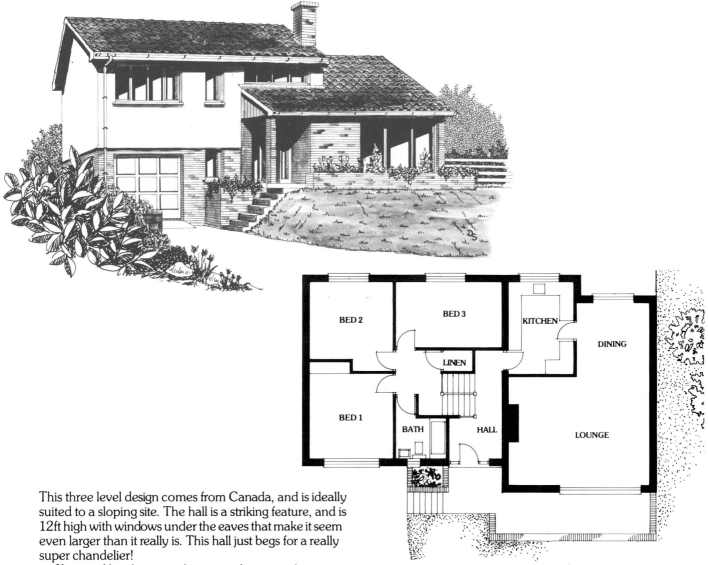

This three level design comes from Canada, and is ideally suited to a sloping site. The hall is a striking feature, and is 12ft high with windows under the eaves that make it seem even larger than it really is. This hall just begs for a really super chandelier!

If ground levels permit the store adjacent to the garage can have its own window and even become an extra bedroom, perhaps with the workshop as a second bathroom. This would be under the main bathroom, which gives an economical drainage arrangement. If you want to do this, it is important to discuss it all with us first, as some re-arrangement is necessary to meet fire regulations.

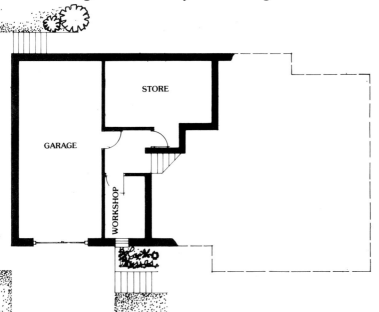

Design Number 83203

Floor Area (exc. garage)	1560 sq.ft.	145 sq.m.
Dimensions overall	50'5'' x 30'3''	15.3 x 9.2
Lounge/Dining (overall)	19'10'' x 25'6''	6.04 x 7.77
Kitchen	13'0'' x 9'6''	3.96 x 2.89
Playroom/Storage (overall)	15'6'' x 9'4''	4.72 x 2.85
Garage	25'3½'' x 12'0''	7.71 x 3.65
Workshop	6'0'' x 8'8''	1.83 x 2.65
Master Bed	12'0'' x 12'0''	3.65 x 3.65
Bed 2	12'0'' x 11'0''	3.65 x 3.35
Bed 3	15'6'' x 9'4''	4.72 x 2.85

QUEENSGATE

Some of the leading Development Companies claim that it was they who pioneered the return to traditional cottage styles, and that Architects followed where they had shown the way. True or not, this attractive cottage design was commissioned by Queensgate Homes of Maidenhead for their Boyn Hill development in 1978, and was a tremendous success.

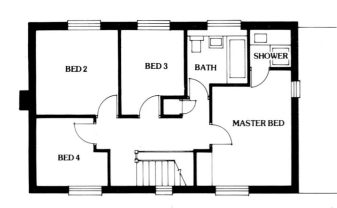

Design Number 83204

Floor Area (exc. garage)	1184 sq.ft.	110 sq.m.
Overall dimensions	54'4" x 19'9½"	16.5 x 6.0
Lounge	11'6" x 17'11"	3.50 x 5.47
Dining	8'9" x 10'10"	2.67 x 3.30
Kitchen	9'4" x 10'10"	2.85 x 3.30
Utility	5'11" x 8'5"	1.80 x 2.57
Workshop	5'11" x 8'9"	1.80 x 2.67
Garage	17'10" x 16'2½"	5.43 x 4.94
Master Bed (overall)	9'5" x 13'4"	2.87 x 4.07
Bed 2	9'10" x 9'10"	3.00 x 3.00
Bed 3	7'6" x 7'6"	2.29 x 2.30
Bed 4	7'10" x 8'6"	2.39 x 2.60

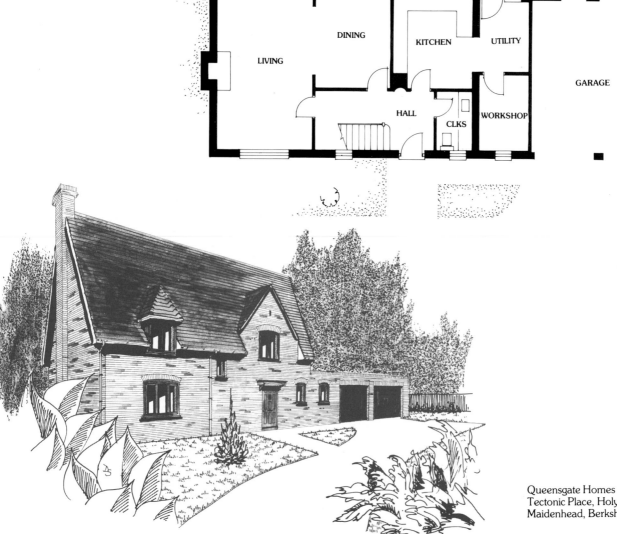

Queensgate Homes
Tectonic Place, Holyport Rd
Maidenhead, Berkshire SL6 3EZ.

STAFFORD

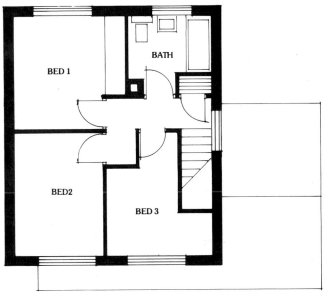

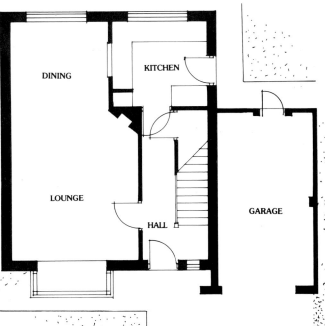

This compact Tudor style house has a lot of character and many features of a far larger home, with the corner fireplace and the bay window providing the potential for a really attractive period lounge decor. The half timbering suits either roughcast render or herringbone brick infill to the first floor walls, and there are many other options available to give this home exactly the regional style that suits a particular site.

Design Number 83191

Floor Area (exc. garage) 925 sq. ft.		86 sq. m.
Overall dimensions		
(inc. garage)	27'7" x 31'8"	8.4 x 9.6
Lounge/Dining	23'5" x 13'0"	7.14 x 3.96
Kitchen	9'6" x 8'3"	2.89 x 2.51
Garage	17'0" x 9'4"	5.18 x 2.85
Bed 1	11'2" x 9'4"	3.40 x 2.85
Bed 2	9'0" x 11'11½"	2.75 x 3.64
Bed 3 (overall)	10'6" x 11'11½"	3.19 x 3.64

HUNTINGDON

This detached family house is particularly popular in country areas, and the porches at the doors, the corbelling under the eaves, and the pointed verges to the gables are features often called for by planners in rural situations, especially if there are older adjacent properties. As drawn here the Huntingdon requires a plot width of at least forty feet, but if the utility room is built at the back of the house, with the kitchen window in the side wall, it can be accommodated on a thirty-foot plot.

As with virtually all square designs with simple roofs, the roof can be turned so that there is a gable to the front, and in some infill situations this is very useful.

The internal layout is straightforward and practical, with a small hall that is lit from a window above the stairs which helps it to feel larger than it really is.

The Huntingdon is a particularly economical design, and has often been built at very low costs per square foot although there is nothing "budget" about it at all.

Design Number 83192

Area (exc. porch and utility which can be varied)	1036 sq.ft.	96 sq.m.
Overall (as illustrated)	33'11" x 25'0"	10.34 x 7.64
Lounge	14'5" x 11'6"	4.40 x 3.51
Dining	10'1" x 11'6"	3.07 x 3.50
Kitchen	12'0" x 11'6"	3.60 x 3.50
Bed 1	13'5" x 12'4"	4.08 x 3.75
Bed 2	12'4" x 10'8"	3.75 x 3.26
Bed 3	8'6" x 9'0"	2.59 x 2.75

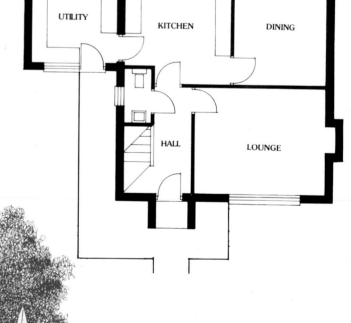

348

GRAFHAM

This is a very popular design in rural areas and combines a practical layout with low construction costs and a cottage appearance that goes down well with the Planners. It is shown here together with our garage type G.28, which is in the same style.

Design Number 83193

Floor Area	1011 sq.ft.	94 sq.m.
Overall dimensions	25'3'' x 30'2''	7.7 x 9.1
Lounge	12'6½'' x 11'7½''	3.82 x 3.54
Dining	9'0'' x 11'6''	2.74 x 3.50
Kitchen	11'0'' x 11'6''	3.35 x 3.50
Bed 1	11'5'' x 12'4''	3.48 x 3.75
Bed 2	10'4'' x 10'9½''	3.15 x 3.29
Bed 3	8'7'' x 8'6''	2.61 x 2.58

SHARNBROOK

Dormer bungalows are not nearly as popular now as they were twenty years ago, but the Sharnbrook is really more of a traditional Bedfordshire cottage than a bungalow. No cottage with a purlin roof and four gable windows is going to be built at a low unit cost, but this design does give a very effective way of getting less than 1100 sq.ft. of compact living accommodation on a minimum site width of only 32 feet.

The first floor landing is lit by a side window, which always has the effect of helping the home to look larger than it is. This is particularly true when the stairs are a feature of an interestingly shaped hall as in this case.

The Sharnbrook has been built as a farm cottage on occasion, with the utility room reduced in size to just a porch, giving the living room of a kitchen that suits people who work on the land. Another option would be to build an external utility room porch at the back door; we have never done this, but it would not present any problems.

Design Number 83194

Floor Area	1004 sq.ft.	93 sq.m.
Dimensions overall	26'0'' x 29'2½''	7.92 x 8.90
Lounge		5.40 x 3.63
Dining		3.63 x 2.54
Kitchen		3.63 x 3.97
Master Bed		5.50 x 3.03
Bed 2		3.03 x 2.70

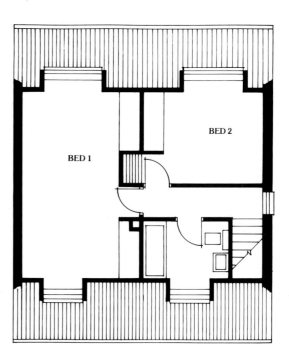

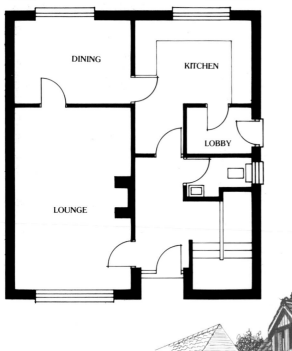

A three bedroom cottage with the same appearance and overall dimensions as the Sharnbrook is the Buckingham, reference 82194.

HALSTEAD

This three bedroom house has a square ground floor plan and can be built with an integral garage at either side. It is illustrated here with a window in the gable end to give light in the loft, and to add character to the design. This particular feature suits a house with a roof at a fairly steep pitch. If the roof pitch is dropped it is practicable to put the garage on the other side, as the garage roof ridge is then below the level of the landing window.

Design Number 83207

Floor Area (exc. garage)	1000 sq. ft.	93 sq. m.
Overall size		
(inc. garage)	43'6'' x 25'3''	13.2 x 7.7
Lounge/Dining	23'5'' x 12'1''	7.14 x 3.68
Kitchen	11'6'' x 7'10''	3.50 x 2.38
Garage	17'0'' x 18'6½''	5.18 x 5.65
Bed 1	11'6'' x 12'1''	3.50 x 3.68
Bed 2	9'11½'' x 11'0''	3.03 x 3.35
Bed 3	11'6'' x 7'10''	3.50 x 2.38

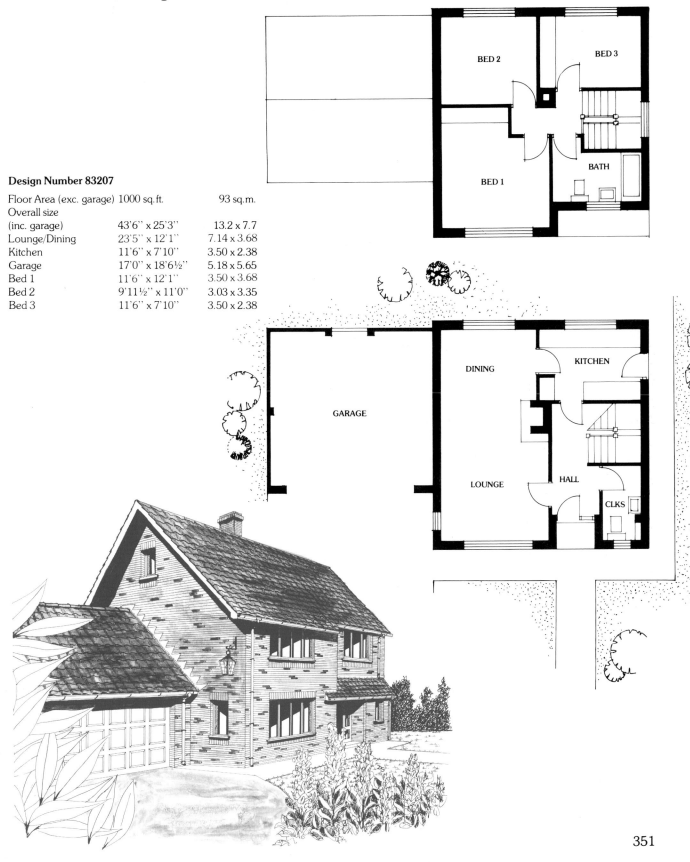

VENTNOR

It is surprising how often our clients insist that a new home should be designed with a large downstairs bedroom for an invalid or elderly parent. This design was drawn to meet this requirement and is shown with a bay window in the room in question. Alternatively, windows can be put in either of the side walls, and the whole of this bedroom accommodation can be re-arranged to suit particular requirements.

Design Number 83208

Floor Area	1345 sq.ft.	125 sq.m.
Overall dimensions	28'6½'' x 34'9''	8.7 x 10.6
Lounge	14'5'' x 12'11½''	4.40 x 3.95
Dining	11'11½'' x 9'8''	3.64 x 2.95
Kitchen	13'5'' x 9'2''	4.10 x 2.80
Ground Floor Bed	11'10'' x 12'9½''	3.61 x 3.90
Bed 1	14'9'' x 10'9''	4.50 x 3.29
Bed 2	13'5'' x 9'2''	4.10 x 2.80
Bed 3	9'8'' x 10'11½''	2.94 x 3.34
Bed 4	9'8''.x 8'0''	2.94 x 2.45

WHITTINGTON

The Whittington house can be built on a site with a frontage of only thirty feet, although it would completely fill the plot and this may not be acceptable to the planners. It is a particularly valuable design where the actual plot is wider, but only a thirty foot strip of it can be built on.

The design is illustrated here with a flat roof and porch, and in most situations this is acceptable. If it is not, drawings are available for it to be built with a tiled garage roof.

The large lounge lends itself to many window arrangements, and if required it can be linked with the kitchen by an arch to give open-plan living. Fitting four sensibly sized bedrooms into this modest overall area means using a glazed area over a door to light the upstairs landing, and a storey height door casing is usually specified for the bathroom door for this purpose.

Design Number 83209

Area (inc. garage)	1200 sq.ft.	111 sq.m.
Overall	34'8'' x 25'1''	10.56 x 7.64
Lounge	23'5'' x 13'0''	7.14 x 3.96
Kitchen	13'5'' x 9'2''	4.10 x 2.80
Bed 1	11'6'' x 10'9''	3.50 x 3.29
Bed 2	13'5'' x 9'2''	4.10 x 2.80
Bed 3	9'8'' x 7'8''	2.94 x 2.34
Bed 4	9'8'' x 8'0''	2.94 x 2.45

FAIRFORD & CHEVINGTON

FAIRFORD

A neat compact house which looks equally well on a narrow site or when set in a large garden. The three different roof lines give it the appearance of a much larger property, and this is the sort of design which is always a very good investment in terms of the building cost/market value ratio.

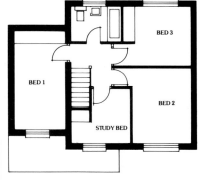

Design Number 83196

Floor Area (exc. garage)	1054 sq. ft.	98 sq. m.
Overall dimensions	31'4'' x 27'6''	9.55 x 8.38
Lounge/Dining (overall)	22'0'' x 13'6''	6.70 x 4.10
Kitchen	10'0'' x 9'8''	3.05 x 2.94
Lobby	4'1'' x 8'9''	1.24 x 2.67
Garage	17'0'' x 8'9''	5.18 x 2.67
Bed 1	15'10½'' x 8'9''	4.84 x 2.67
Bed 2	9'10'' x 12'0''	3.00 x 3.66
Bed 3	11'6'' x 9'8''	3.5 x 2.95
Study Bed (overall)	9'10'' x 8'9''	3.00 x 2.66

CHEVINGTON

This interesting detached house was designed by architect Mike Wigmore of Kevin Neary Associates for the Pimblett Self-Build Housing Association in Hertfordshire, and has some very interesting features. The Housing Association members built their homes with provision in the roof for either one or two more bedrooms to be added at a later date. Roof lights, gable windows and appropriate floor joists were all built in ready for another staircase to be installed and the third floor fitted out whenever the owner wished.

Design Number 83205

Floor Area	936 sq. ft.	87 sq. m.
Dimensions overall	27'9'' x 28'6½''	8.45 x 8.7
Lounge/Dining (overall)	11'4'' x 25'11''	3.45 x 7.90
Kitchen	7'10½'' x 11'10''	2.40 x 3.60
Garage	17'11'' x 8'6''	5.46 x 2.60
Bed 1	9'0'' x 12'10''	2.74 x 3.90
Bed 2	9'0'' x 12'10''	2.74 x 3.90
Bed 3	8'2½'' x 8'6''	2.50 x 2.60

KENMORE

Most detached houses of 1200 sq.ft. have four bedrooms, but there is a steady demand for three bedroomed houses of this size with larger-than-average rooms and generous bathrooms. The Kenmore design is one answer to this requirement. The layout provides a particularly large first floor landing, with room for a desk or sewing table at the landing window.

Design Number 83210

Floor Area (exc. garage)	1215 sq.ft.	113 sq.m.
Dimensions overall	48'11'' x 26'9''	14.9 x 8.1
Lounge	20'6'' x 11'4½''	6.24 x 3.47
Dining	11'1½'' x 9'0''	3.39 x 2.74
Kitchen	12'1½'' x 9'0''	3.69 x 2.75
Utility	7'0½'' x 5'11''	2.15 x 1.80
Garage	16'9½'' x 16'2''	5.11 x 4.92
Master Bed	13'1'' x 11'4½''	3.99 x 3.47
Bed 2	12'0'' x 9'0''	3.65 x 2.74
Bed 3	9'5'' x 7'0½''	2.87 x 2.15

WESTBURY

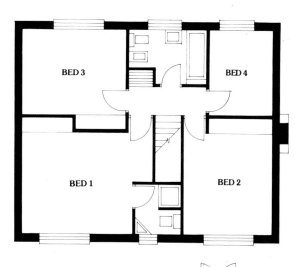

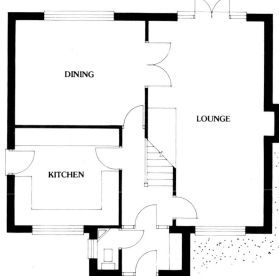

The Westbury design with its prominent gable features will suit many sites where the planners are looking for a strong traditional theme. Inside the house the layout is conventional, with an L-shaped lounge with double doors leading through to the large dining room. On the first floor there is a conventional four bedroom layout with a fully equipped bathroom as well as a small shower room which serves the master bedroom.

The gables can be roofed with either small plain tiles or with any of the flat interlocking tiles, but are not well suited to pantiles. However, in traditional pantile areas it would be normal practice to use pantiles on the main roof, with small plain tiles on the gables and vertical tile hanging above the gable windows.

This design would normally be built in brick, and in the right situation it will look well with plenty of traditional brick features. This sort of thing is illustrated over the front door in the sketch, and one of the joys of having a new house built for yourself is the fun of deciding the details of this sort of feature. In recent years it has become popular to build a discrete plaque with ones initials and the date into the walling above a gable end, and this is always a particularly happy feature of a new home.

Design Number 83215

Area	1410 sq.ft.	131 sq.m.
Overall dimensions	31'2'' x 30'2½''	9.5 x 9.2
Lounge	13'7½'' x 23'5''	4.15 x 7.14
Dining	15'4½'' x 12'0''	4.69 x 3.65
Kitchen	11'1'' x 12'5''	3.38 x 3.79
Master Bed	11'7½'' x 13'1''	3.54 x 3.99
Bed 2	10'4'' x 11'7½''	3.15 x 3.54
Bed 3	12'3'' x 9'10''	3.74 x 3.00
Bed 4	7'3'' x 9'10''	2.20 x 3.00

MEDWAY

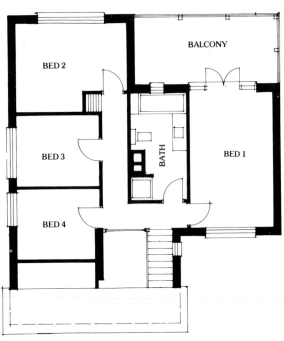

This design was originally built on the Kent coast, with the balcony looking out over the Medway estuary. It is built in local stock bricks under a roof of plain tiles, and looks splendid. The big roof coming down to the front door is typical of the area.

The chimney-breast above the Inglenook fireplace can also take a flue from a solid fuel cooker in the kitchen. It carries through to the bathroom where it serves to box in the shower recess, or, if a shower is not required, to locate a large airing cupboard.

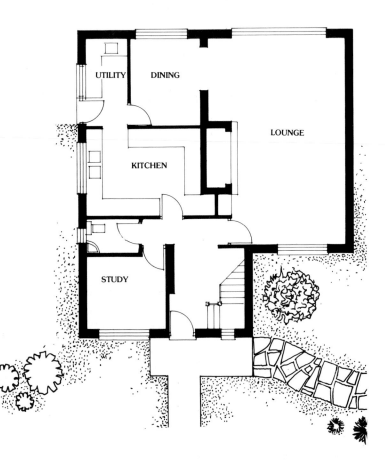

Design Number 83216

Floor Area	1300 sq.ft.	120 sq.m.
Dimensions overall	34'10'' x 31'11''	10.6 x 9.7
Lounge	23'5'' x 16'1½''	7.14 x 4.91
Dining	10'0½'' x 8'0''	3.06 x 2.43
Kitchen	13'1½'' x 9'9''	4.00 x 2.97
Study	9'2'' x 8'3½''	2.80 x 2.52
Utility	10'0½'' x 4'10''	3.06 x 1.46
Master Bed	15'4'' x 9'9''	4.67 x 2.96
Bed 2	13'2'' x 10'0½''	4.00 x 3.06
Bed 3	9'10'' x 8'0''	3.00 x 2.43
Bed 4	9'10'' x 8'0''	3.00 x 2.43

STORRINGTON

This design has the complex roof line and contrasting levels of roof so popular with the planners for infill sites in villages and on farms, and yet is only 1300 sq. ft.

The master bedroom suite is isolated from the rest of the first floor accommodation by an 11" wall, and this is a feature which is deservedly popular. In our plan we show the back door right at the back of the house, but it can easily be moved to the side, or even into the front elevation where it would open into the utility room.

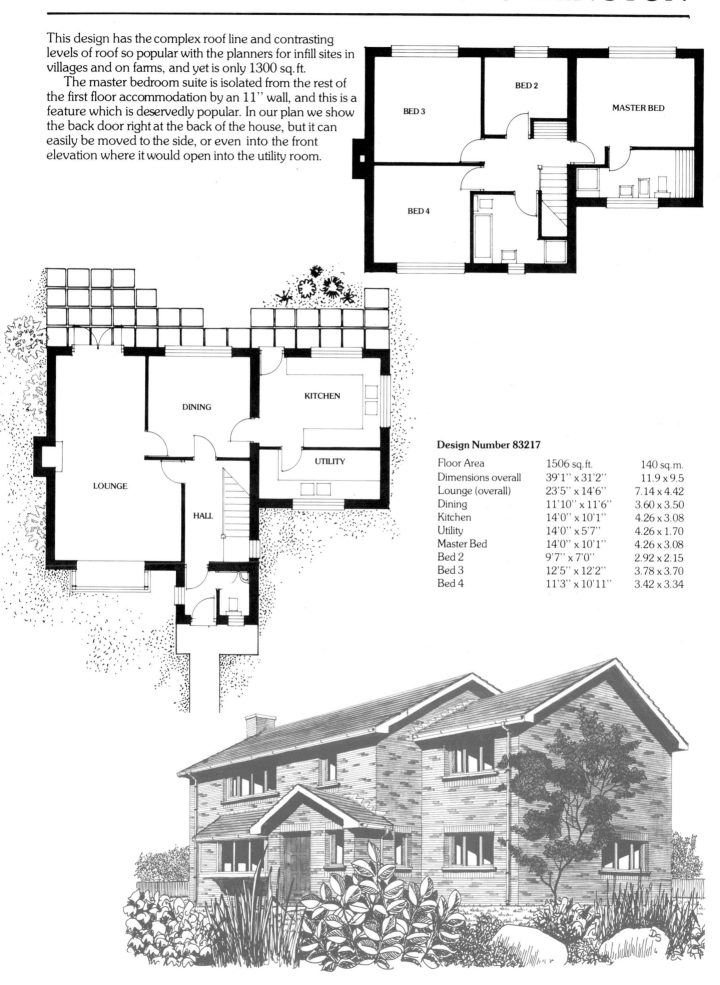

Design Number 83217

Floor Area	1506 sq. ft.	140 sq. m.
Dimensions overall	39'1" x 31'2"	11.9 x 9.5
Lounge (overall)	23'5" x 14'6"	7.14 x 4.42
Dining	11'10" x 11'6"	3.60 x 3.50
Kitchen	14'0" x 10'1"	4.26 x 3.08
Utility	14'0" x 5'7"	4.26 x 1.70
Master Bed	14'0" x 10'1"	4.26 x 3.08
Bed 2	9'7" x 7'0"	2.92 x 2.15
Bed 3	12'5" x 12'2"	3.78 x 3.70
Bed 4	11'3" x 10'11"	3.42 x 3.34

CHELTENHAM

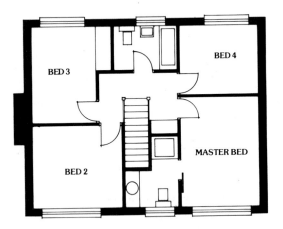

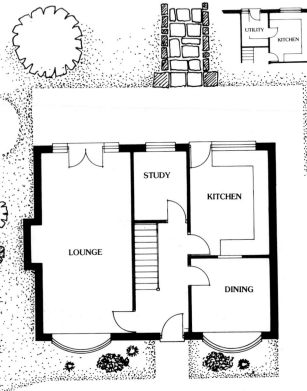

This simple straight forward Georgian style design is as simple and effective as its nineteenth century predecessor, and although the hip roof is not as cost effective as a gable roof, it is cheap to build and will always appreciate ahead of the market.

If required the study can become a utility room as shown on the inset plan. All the drainage is very economically grouped at the back, except for the en suite bathroom. If saving had to be made this bathroom can be fitted out later, being used as a sewing room or study before it is turned into a bathroom. If this is done remember that the drainage stack pipe must be built in when the house is built, as it will be troublesome to put this in later. Everything else is easy, as the water connections can be taken from the cylinder cupboard.

The portico illustrated is typical of the many prefabricated timber and fibreglass porticos on the market. These are usually available with matching bay window heads — which must be constructed so they do not sound like a drum in heavy rain. Some fibreglass window heads used to do that; most have now got this problem sorted out. Incidentally, do not think you are doing anything non-traditional by buying ready made porticos and window heads; in the eighteen twenties the builders merchants catalogues were full of them, and are studied carefully by todays manufacturers who use the original designs.

Design Number 83218

Floor Area	1415 sq. ft.	131 sq.m.
Dimensions overall	25'3'' x 32'0''	7.7 x 9.7
Lounge	23'5'' x 12'0''	7.14 x 3.65
Dining	9'6'' x 10'6''	2.89 x 3.20
Kitchen	10'6'' x 13'7''	3.20 x 4.14
Study	7'0'' x 8'6''	2.13 x 2.60
Master Bed	10'6'' x 14'3''	3.20 x 4.34
Bed 2	12'0'' x 10'6''	3.65 x 3.20
Bed 3	12'7'' x 8'8½''	3.84 x 2.65
Bed 4	10'6'' x 8'10''	3.20 x 2.70

JERSEY

A Granny Flat as an annexe to a large four bedroom home is a design requirement that we meet all the time. The problem comes when the whole lot has to fit on a narrow site: one answer is the Jersey design, which is only 34ft overall and will meet the building regulations requirements to fit on a 40ft width plot. Possibly the Planners would consider this over development, (ie. too much house on too little plot), but it has proved a very useful design on plots with many different frontages.

Note that the flat has its own separate front door: our experience is that this is something which the occupants value very highly.

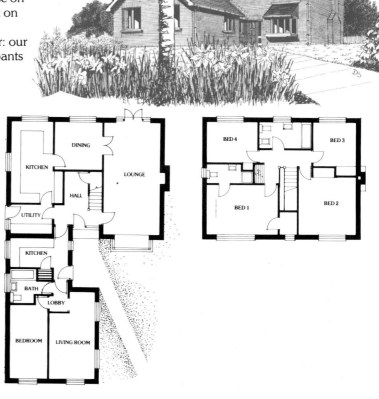

Design Number 83254

Floor Area		
(inc. annexe)	1922 sq.ft.	178 sq.m.
Dimensions overall		
(inc. annexe)	55'7½'' x 34'1½''	16.9 x 10.4
Lounge	23'5'' x 12'4''	7.14 x 3.76
Dining	10'0'' x 10'3½''	3.04 x 3.13
Kitchen	17'3'' x 9'0''	5.26 x 2.74
Utility	9'0'' x 5'10''	2.74 x 1.77
Master Bed	15'6'' x 10'2''	4.72 x 3.10
Bed 2	12'4'' x 11'11½''	3.76 x 3.64
Bed 3	9'3'' x 9'2½''	2.81 x 2.80
Bed 4	10'10½'' x 8'7½''	3.31 x 2.62
Granny Annexe:		
Living Room (overall)	9'8'' x 18'0''	2.95 x 5.48
Bedroom	8'0'' x 15'1''	2.43 x 4.60
Kitchen	6'0'' x 12'3½''	1.83 x 3.75

MANSFIELD

This is one of four designs from the architectural practice of Scattergood & Woodhams of Nottinghamshire. Working from one of the old Dukeries Estate Offices on the edge of Sherwood Forest, they design homes to suit the wooded sites in the local area. The distinctive gable return of the fascia is their unmistakable trademark!

The Mansfield design has an interesting projecting tower which is both distinctive and practical, providing a lobby on the ground floor and an en suite bathroom above.

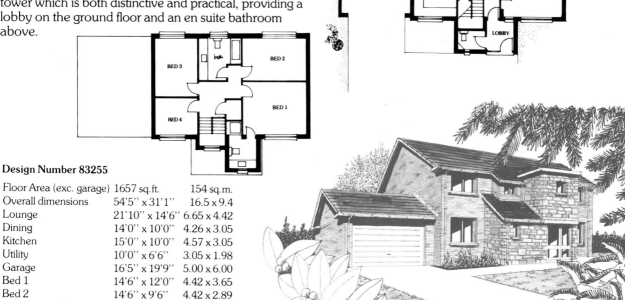

Design Number 83255

Floor Area (exc. garage)	1657 sq.ft.	154 sq.m.
Overall dimensions	54'5'' x 31'1''	16.5 x 9.4
Lounge	21'10'' x 14'6''	6.65 x 4.42
Dining	14'0'' x 10'0''	4.26 x 3.05
Kitchen	15'0'' x 10'0''	4.57 x 3.05
Utility	10'0'' x 6'6''	3.05 x 1.98
Garage	16'5'' x 19'9''	5.00 x 6.00
Bed 1	14'6'' x 12'0''	4.42 x 3.65
Bed 2	14'6'' x 9'6''	4.42 x 2.89
Bed 3	13'0'' x 10'0''	3.96 x 3.05
Bed 4	10'0'' x 8'6''	3.05 x 2.59

HINDHEAD

A classic four bedroom house of 1400 sq.feet, the Hindhead design can be built with Tudor half timbering as shown, or with plain brick or stone walls and masonry pillars to the porch.

The garage need not be built if it is not required, and without it the overall width is under 40ft, which makes this a useful design for suburban infill sites.

A very cost effective design, with the feel of a much larger property.

Design Number 83220

Floor Area		
(exc. garage)	1400 sq.ft.	130 sq.m.
Overall dimensions	48'3½'' x 22'10''	14.7 x 6.9
Lounge	21'0'' x 13'6''	6.40 x 4.11
Dining	11'6'' x 9'6''	3.50 x 2.89
Kitchen	10'0'' x 9'6''	3.05 x 2.89
Study	6'8'' x 9'0''	2.03 x 2.73
Garage	19'6½'' x 10'5½''	5.97 x 3.19
Bed 1	13'6'' x 11'2''	4.11 x 3.40
Bed 2	13'6'' x 9'6''	4.11 x 2.89
Bed 3	10'0'' x 9'0''	3.05 x 2.73
Bed 4	9'4'' x 6'3''	2.85 x 1.89

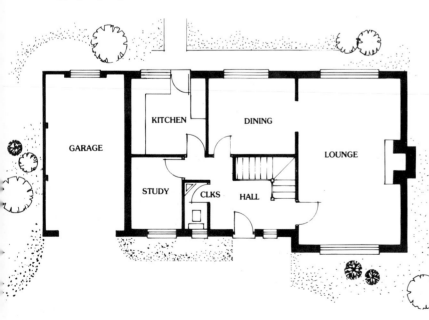

KNEBWORTH

This straight-forward Tudor style home meets the requirements of those who want three large bedrooms in a house of just over 1100 sq. ft. instead of the four bedrooms which are more usual in a property of this size. The layout is simple and cost effective, and without any windows to the side it can be fitted easily into a fairly narrow suburban plot. If it is to be built in the country then all sorts of re-arrangements of the windows are possible.

The winding stairs with a window half way up are a period feature to suit the style of the Knebworth, and if possible the stairs should be made in hardwood. The windows in this design are well suited to leaded lights, and of course, these should be double glazed sealed units.

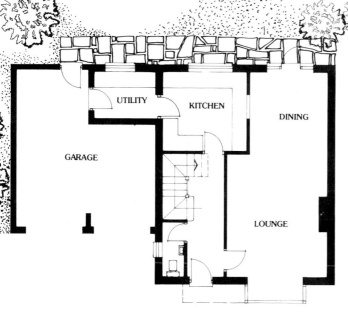

Design Number 83221

Floor Area (exc. garage)	1134 sq.ft.	105 sq.m.
Overall dimensions	42'1'' x 29'11''	12.83 x 9.13
Lounge	13'0'' x 15'6''	3.96 x 4.73
Dining	10'4'' x 10'0''	3.15 x 3.05
Kitchen	10'0'' x 11'0''	3.05 x 3.35
Utility	8'0'' x 6'0''	2.43 x 1.83
Garage (overall)	20'0'' x 18'0''	6.10 x 5.48
Master Bed	11'6'' x 13'0''	3.50 x 3.96
Bed 2	12'6'' x 11'6''	3.81 x 3.50
Bed 3	9'6'' x 9'2''	2.90 x 2.80

APPLETON

The Appleton is another design with a complex shape and roof line in today's cottage style, carefully arranged in a way to keep down unit costs. Note how all the changes of roof lines are above load bearing walls, without any valleys or other expensive features. It is a D & M design that has been built in a number of different parts of the country, and which looks best with a fairly steep roof pitch.

The illustration shows a double garage door: if funds and the site allow, it would be preferable to stretch the garage by another two feet and have two single doors. In some situations these would look best as old fashioned side hung doors with strap hinges.

Inside the room arrangement is simple and logical, and the way in which the master bedroom is away from the rest of the first floor accommodation is always very popular.

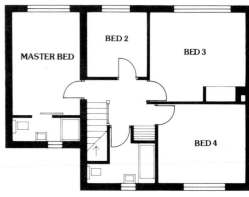

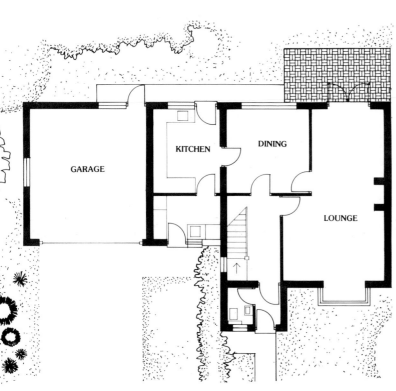

Design Number 83222

Floor Area (exc. garage)	1404 sq.ft.	130 sq.m.
Dimensions Overall	51'5'' x 31'1½''	15.67 x 9.49
Lounge (overall)	14'6'' x 23'5''	4.42 x 7.14
Dining	12'0'' x 11'6''	3.60 x 3.50
Kitchen	9'6'' x 11'6''	2.90 x 3.50
Utility	5'9'' x 9'6''	1.74 x 2.90
Garage	16'7'' x 17'6''	5.06 x 5.34
Master Bed		
(exc. shower room)	9'6'' x 13'11''	2.90 x 4.24
Bed 2	8'7'' x 9'0''	2.61 x 2.75
Bed 3	13'5'' x 12'4''	4.08 x 3.75
Bed 4	10'10'' x 12'4''	3.29 x 3.75

FOSSEBRIDGE

This interesting design of 1570 sq.ft. requires only 40ft. of plot width to meet building regulations, although it is certainly too large for a site with a total width of this size. However, where only a 40ft. width of a larger plot can be used for a building, because of some limitation to the use of the rest of the site, this design comes into its own.

The bedroom layout is unusual as the shower room is en suite with the guest room. This is very convenient when this room is occupied by an older person living with the family.

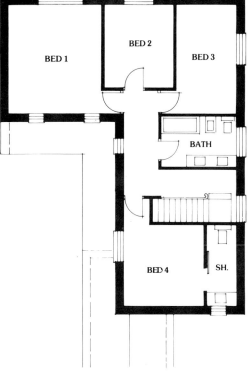

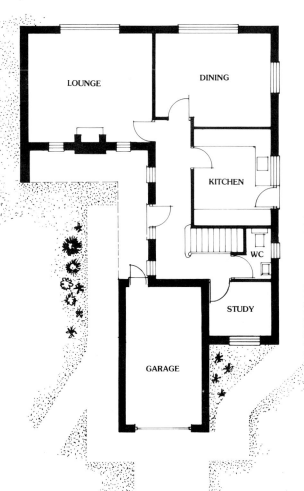

Design Number 83223

Floor Area (inc. garage)	1744 sq. ft.	162 sq.m.
Dimensions overall	33'7'' x 51'3''	10.2 x 15.6
Lounge	16'5'' x 14'0''	5.00 x 4.26
Dining	15'0'' x 12'0''	4.57 x 3.65
Kitchen	12'0'' x 10'0''	3.65 x 3.05
Study	7'0'' x 8'0''	2.13 x 2.43
Garage	17'6'' x 10'0''	5.33 x 3.05
Master Bed	14'1'' x 14'0''	4.29 x 4.26
Bed 2	10'8'' x 9'0''	3.26 x 2.74
Bed 3	14'0'' x 8'0''	4.26 x 2.43
Bed 4	10'9'' x 10'4''	3.27 x 3.15

TWYFORD

Another thirties style home with a lounge and dining room that are virtually square, and three larger-than-average bedrooms. The hall with its prominent winding staircase is a key feature of the lay-out, and with windows to both the hall and the landing it is very light and airy. A straight-forward design with many period features that are very popular again.

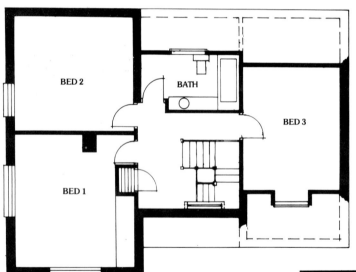

Design Number 83224

Floor Area (inc. garage)	1722 sq.ft.	160 sq.m.
Dimensions overall	39'0'' x 30'2''	11.8 x 9.1
Lounge	14'0'' x 15'0''	4.26 x 4.57
Dining	14'0'' x 13'0''	4.26 x 3.96
Kitchen		
(inc. breakfast area)	11'6'' x 13'7½''	3.50 x 4.15
Garage	10'6'' x 17'0''	3.20 x 5.18
Bed 1	12'0'' x 15'0''	3.66 x 4.57
Bed 2	14'0'' x 13'0''	4.26 x 3.96
Bed 3	11'0'' x 13'10''	3.35 x 4.20

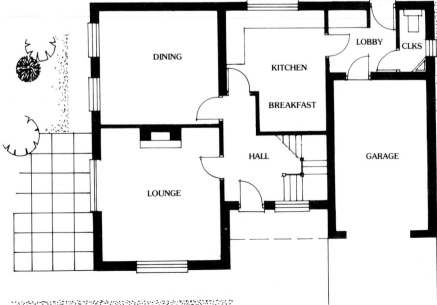

BROCKENHURST

The Brockenhurst design was originally drawn to meet the planners requirements in a conservation area where a new house had to have a complex shape and roof line to conform to the local architectural idiom, and it has since been used on a number of other sites. There is very little waste space in this layout, and it has the advantage of a kitchen with views in all directions.

The complex roof and the unusual shape do not help with building costs, but it is a remarkably attractive house and looks particularly well when built in rustic brick under a pantile roof.

Remember that both the appearance of the house and the feel of the individual rooms can be altered by moving windows.

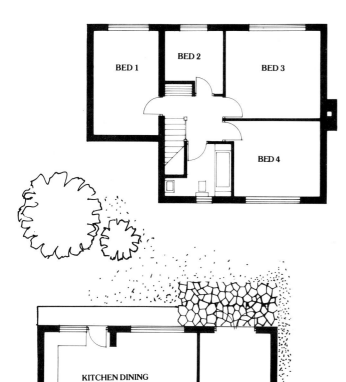

Design Number 83225

Area	1357 sq.ft.	126 sq.m.
Overall	34'3'' x 31'0''	10.45 x 9.44
Lounge	23'5'' x 14'6''	7.14 x 4.42
Kitchen	14'7'' x 9'6''	4.44 x 2.90
Dining	12'0'' x 11'6''	3.60 x 3.50
Bed 1	14'7'' x 9'6''	4.44 x 2.90
Bed 2	8'7'' x 7'0''	2.61 x 2.15
Bed 3	13'5'' x 12'4''	4.08 x 3.75
Bed 4	12'4'' x 10'9''	3.75 x 3.29

A three bedroom version of this design is available and is called the Northwich. The reference number is 82225

LONGFORD

A square, solid traditional house for people who are square, and solid in their outlook, and proud of it! All the rooms are generous, and the straightforward layout enables many features to be altered to suit individual requirements. In particular, the garage can be extended to the side to make room for a second car if required.

The front door has a deep porch, but a window to the first floor landing ensures that the hall is light and cheerful. There is room for a desk or table at this window, and the end of the landing can be used as a study or workroom.

Design Number 83226

Floor Area (inc. garage)	1776 sq.ft.	165 sq.m.
Dimensions overall	35'5'' x 33'0''	10.79 x 10.06
Lounge	13'0'' x 18'0''	3962 x 5486
Dining	12'0'' x 10'0''	3658 x 3048
Breakfast Kitchen	17'10'' x 10'0''	5436 x 3048
Utility	10'7'' x 5'11''	3235 x 1800
Garage	10'0'' x 16'5''	3055 x 5004
Master Bed	10'7'' x 11'7''	3235 x 3528
Bed 2	13'0'' x 11'0''	3962 x 3353
Bed 3	13'0'' x 11'4''	3962 x 3466
Bed 4	10'7'' x 8'6''	3235 x 2591

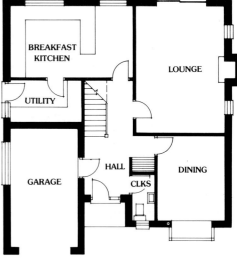

WENTWORTH

This attractive family house has both the lounge and kitchen windows to the rear, suiting a North aspect site. The dining room can either be completey separate from the lounge, or it can be connected to it with an arch as shown, giving scope for imaginative decor. There is a large utility room, and we have shown a WC at the far end of it. This need not be built if it is not required.

The cloakroom area can be rearranged with access off the porch to give a larger hall at the expense of storage room in the cloakroom. Alternatively, the outer door and screen to the storm porch need not be built at all, or can be put in at a later date.

The Wentworth can be built with a single garage replacing the double garage illustrated. Note that the pergola shown on our drawing is a suggested landscaping feature, and is not part of the structural design.

Design Number 83227

Area (inc. garage)	1560 sq.ft.	145 sq.m.
Overall	47'11'' x 28'9''	14.16 x 8.75
Lounge	14'5'' x 14'5''	4.39 x 4.39
Dining	13'2'' x 9'0''	4.02 x 2.74
Kitchen	11'5'' x 10'11''	3.49 x 3.31
Bed 1	14'1'' x 11'0''	4.30 x 3.35
Bed 2	12'1'' x 8'8''	3.69 x 2.63
Bed 3	9'0'' x 8'6''	2.74 x 2.59
Bed 4	11'0'' x 7'11''	3.35 x 2.41

Plans are available for this home with a self-contained flat in place of the garage, with the option of turning the flat into a garage at a later date. This design is called the Corsham, reference 82227.

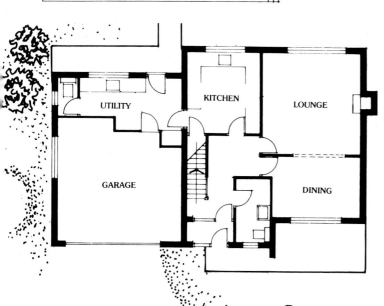

STAMFORD

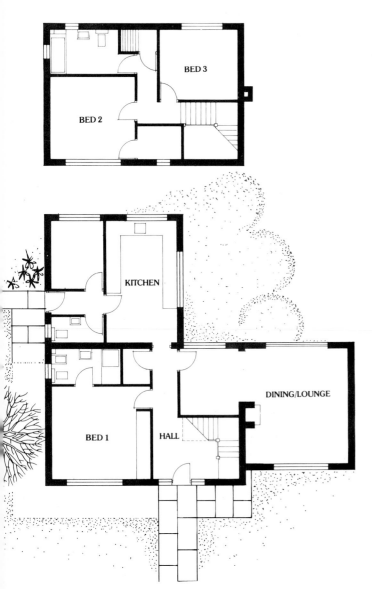

This design was drawn to meet a situation where a bedroom is required on the ground floor of a 3 bedroomed house, and by designing two separate single storey wings this has been achieved in a way that avoids the structure looking like a bungalow with a first floor extension. It is particularly useful in situations where the planners are insisting on a house rather than a bungalow, but where our clients must have a ground floor bedroom.

The hall is particularly well laid out and the stairs with two quarter landings gives the feel of a much larger property once one enters the front door. In the sketch it is drawn as built in a cottage style to meet the typical planning requirements for a farmhouse, but the same basic layout can be modified to give the executive look appropriate to a pery-urban situation.

The "spare" room at the back door has been built as a farm office, as a shower room and WC on a stock farm, and simply as a hobbies room. Alternatively the whole of this wing can be redesigned to meet a clients own special requirements.

Design Number 83228

Area	1523 sq.ft.	141 sq.m.
Overall dimensions	37'10"x 44'6½"	11.5 x 13.5
Lounge	16'1" x 14'8"	4.90 x 4.47
Dining	9'10" x 8'6"	3.00 x 2.60
Kitchen	10'5" x 16'11"	3.16 x 5.15
Utility	6'6" x 7'7"	1.97 x 2.30
Master Bed	14'8" x 13'0"	4.46 x 3.96
Bed 2	12'2" x 11'8"	3.70 x 3.56
Bed 3	11'4" x 9'10"	3.46 x 3.00

STOWMARKET

This 3 bedroomed house of just under 1600 square feet was originally designed as a farmhouse, and the accommodation is laid out to suit the working farmer. In many ways it reflects traditional ideas — a large hall, lit from above with winding stairs: a square lounge: solid masonry walls to the master bedroom to give total sound insulation and all rooms of a generous size.

The front door is tight in the angle between the two wings of the house, and when this is an inescapable feature of the layout — as it is in this case — it is essential that it is given a strong character to identify it as a focal point. In this case this is achieved by a really massive gallows bracket to the porch roof, and this should be backed up with very careful landscaping.

Design Number 83229

Area	1555 sq.ft.	144 sq.m.
Overall dimensions	32'10'' x 39'9''	10.0 x 12.1
Lounge	16'0'' x 15'11''	4.88 x 4.84
Dining	10'0'' x 10'0''	3.04 x 3.04
Kitchen	16'2'' x 10'8''	4.93 x 3.25
Study	10'0'' x 8'0''	3.04 x 2.43
Utility	7'0'' x 10'8''	2.13 x 3.25
Master Bed	13'1'' x 10'8''	3.97 x 3.25
Bed 2	11'1'' x 10'8''	3.38 x 3.25
Bed 3	10'0'' x 11'1''	3.04 x 3.38

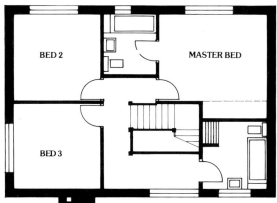

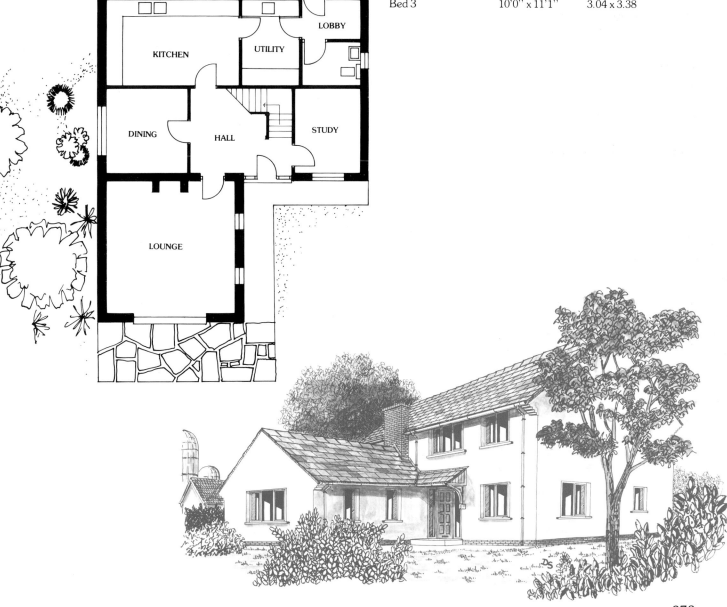

SOUTHWELL

The Southwell house has an unusual layout with a large study: it was originally built for a Doctor who wanted a study door adjacent to the front door. Note the box room on the first floor: a Victorian design feature that can be very useful in today's busy world.

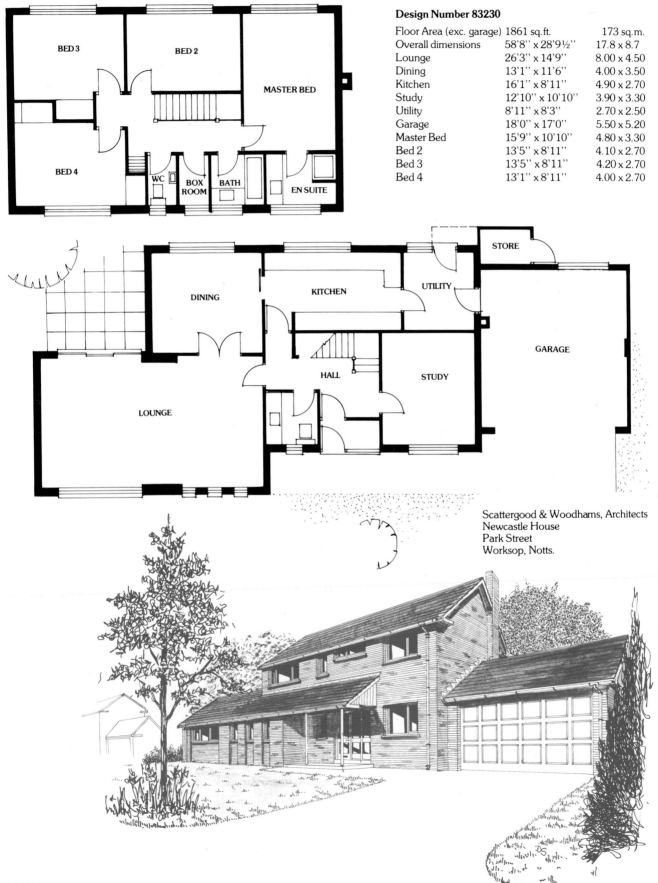

Design Number 83230

Floor Area (exc. garage)	1861 sq.ft.	173 sq.m.
Overall dimensions	58'8'' x 28'9½''	17.8 x 8.7
Lounge	26'3'' x 14'9''	8.00 x 4.50
Dining	13'1'' x 11'6''	4.00 x 3.50
Kitchen	16'1'' x 8'11''	4.90 x 2.70
Study	12'10'' x 10'10''	3.90 x 3.30
Utility	8'11'' x 8'3''	2.70 x 2.50
Garage	18'0'' x 17'0''	5.50 x 5.20
Master Bed	15'9'' x 10'10''	4.80 x 3.30
Bed 2	13'5'' x 8'11''	4.10 x 2.70
Bed 3	13'5'' x 8'11''	4.20 x 2.70
Bed 4	13'1'' x 8'11''	4.00 x 2.70

BED 3

BED 2

MASTER BED

BED 4

WC

BOX ROOM

BATH

EN SUITE

DINING

KITCHEN

UTILITY

STORE

GARAGE

LOUNGE

HALL

STUDY

Scattergood & Woodhams, Architects
Newcastle House
Park Street
Worksop, Notts.

EASTWOOD

Another Scattergood & Woodhams design, this one originally drawn for a prestige site in a South Yorkshire village. The large hall and landing were very popular features of the Eastwood when it was built speculatively, and it is sure to be just as much a favourite with those choosing a design for a site of their own.

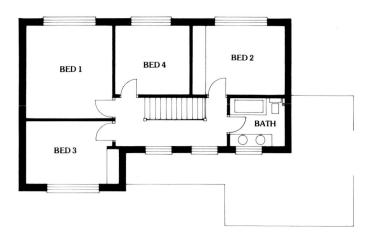

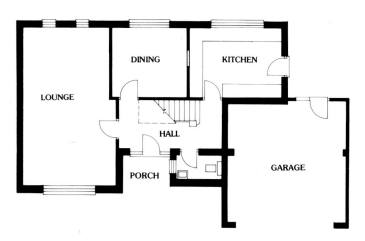

Design Number 83231

Floor Area (inc. garage)	1711 sq.ft.	159 sq.m.
Overall dimensions	47'9½'' x 29'6''	14.5 x 8.9
Lounge	23'0'' x 15'0''	7.01 x 4.57
Dining	11'0'' x 10'0''	3.35 x 3.05
Kitchen	13'9'' x 10'0''	4.19 x 3.05
Garage	15'9'' x 17'0''	4.80 x 5.18
Bed 1	13'3'' x 13'0''	4.03 x 3.96
Bed 2	13'9'' x 10'0''	4.19 x 3.05
Bed 3	13'3'' x 10'0''	4.03 x 3.05
Bed 4	11'0'' x 10'0''	3.35 x 3.05

Scattergood & Woodhams, Architects
Newcastle House
Park Street
Worksop, Notts.

LUDLOW

The Ludlow design with its gable roof and solid appearance suits a rural site, and is popular in Wales and the Midlands. It has a very traditional layout with two separate bathrooms instead of the more modern en suite arrangement, and the two larger bedrooms are well above average size. Essentially a design for a site with views at the back of the house.

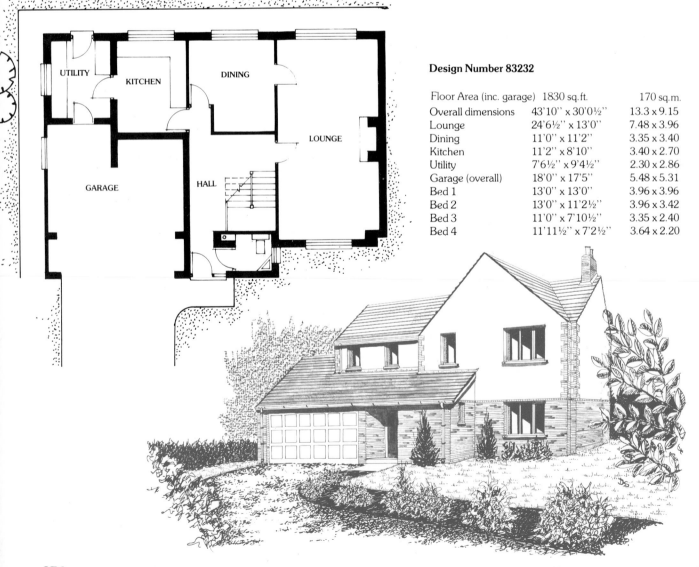

Design Number 83232

Floor Area (inc. garage) 1830 sq.ft.		170 sq.m.
Overall dimensions	43'10'' x 30'0½''	13.3 x 9.15
Lounge	24'6½'' x 13'0''	7.48 x 3.96
Dining	11'0'' x 11'2''	3.35 x 3.40
Kitchen	11'2'' x 8'10''	3.40 x 2.70
Utility	7'6½'' x 9'4½''	2.30 x 2.86
Garage (overall)	18'0'' x 17'5''	5.48 x 5.31
Bed 1	13'0'' x 13'0''	3.96 x 3.96
Bed 2	13'0'' x 11'2½''	3.96 x 3.42
Bed 3	11'0'' x 7'10½''	3.35 x 2.40
Bed 4	11'11½'' x 7'2½''	3.64 x 2.20

FOXWOOD

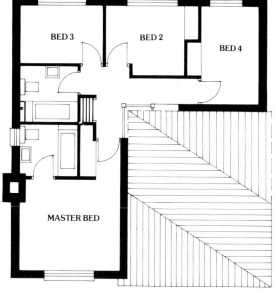

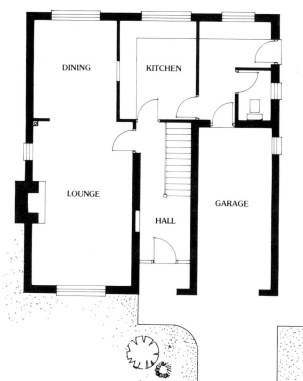

The complex shape of the roof of this large four bedroom home is typical of Surrey, Kent, and Sussex, where the tile hanging would also be in character. However, it is not an expensive house and can be built on a site of restricted width as none of the side windows are the principal windows of what the Building Regulations call "habitable rooms".

The ground floor layout is straight-forward, while upstairs the master bedroom is well separated from the other three bedrooms. This is always a popular feature.

Design Number 83259

Floor Area (garage)	1776 sq.ft.	165 sq.m.
Dimensions overall	33'0'' x 30'0''	10.0 x 9.1
Lounge	12'0'' x 19'0''	3.65 x 5.75
Dining	10'0'' x 12'0''	3.05 x 3.65
Kitchen	9'0'' x 12'0''	2.74 x 3.65
Utility (overall)	8'6'' x 12'0''	2.59 x 3.65
Garage	18'6'' x 8'10''	5.63 x 2.70
Master Bed	12'0'' x 10'6''	3.65 x 3.20
Bed 2	9'0'' x 8'8''	2.74 x 2.65
Bed 3	10'0'' x 6'9''	3.05 x 2.05
Bed 4	8'2'' x 12'0''	2.49 x 3.65

HORNCASTLE

Three hips and one projecting gable was a feature of homes built in the thirties, and in this design it serves to make a large house look even larger. The storey height window to the stairs serves the same purpose, and the whole feel of this house is of a home that is even larger than its 2100 sq. ft. All the rooms are generous in size, particularly the master bedroom suite. An impressive house for a prestige site.

Design Number 83260

Floor Area (inc. garage)	2368 sq. ft.	220 sq.m.
Overall dimensions	29'3" x 58'2"	8.9 x 17.7
Lounge	14'0" x 27'0"	4.26 x 8.24
Dining	11'6" x 13'0"	3.50 x 3.96
Kitchen	12'0" x 11'6"	3.65 x 3.50
Breakfast	8'0" x 9'10"	2.43 x 3.00
Study	8'8½" x 11'7"	2.65 x 3.53
Garage	17'0" x 16'4½"	5.18 x 4.98
Utility	7'5" x 9'10"	2.26 x 3.00
Master Bed	12'0" x 11'6"	3.65 x 3.50
Bed 2	14'0" x 15'2"	4.26 x 4.63
Bed 3	11'6" x 13'0"	3.50 x 3.96
Bed 4	14'0" x 11'6"	4.26 x 3.50

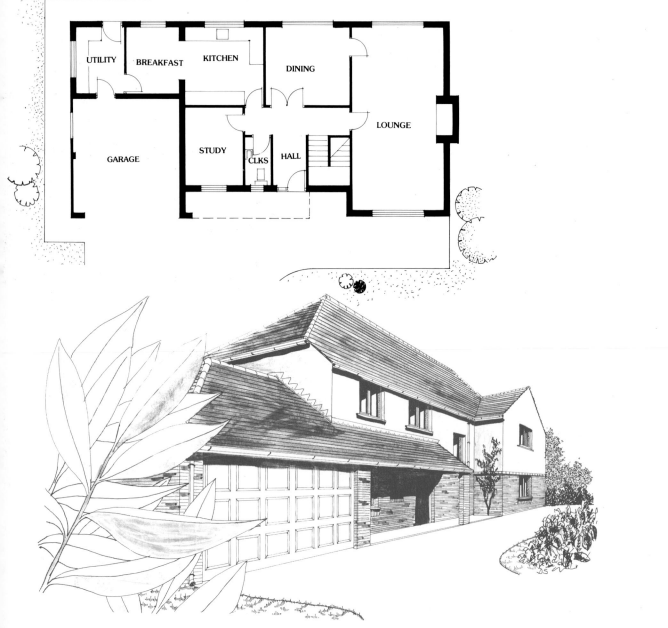

DEREHAM

This is another 1700 sq.ft. house with three large bedrooms instead of four smaller ones. Some of the space saved has gone into an impressive hall, the dining room is much larger than usual and will accommodate a table for a dozen diners.

The study can have its door moved to open into the kitchen, and becomes a utility room or laundry if required.

Design Number 83237

Floor Area (exc. garage)	1700 sq.ft.	158 sq.m.
Dimensions overall	38'9'' x 30'11''	11.8 x 9.4
Lounge	20'0'' x 13'0''	6.10 x 3.96
Dining	11'0'' x 15'9''	3.35 x 4.80
Kitchen	13'0'' x 14'3½''	3.96 x 4.35
Study	9'0'' x 8'0''	2.74 x 2.43
Master Bed	14'6'' x 13'0''	4.42 x 3.96
Bed 2	14'3½'' x 13'0''	4.35 x 3.96
Bed 3	14'3½'' x 10'6''	4.35 x 3.20

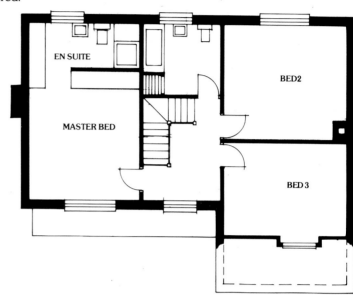

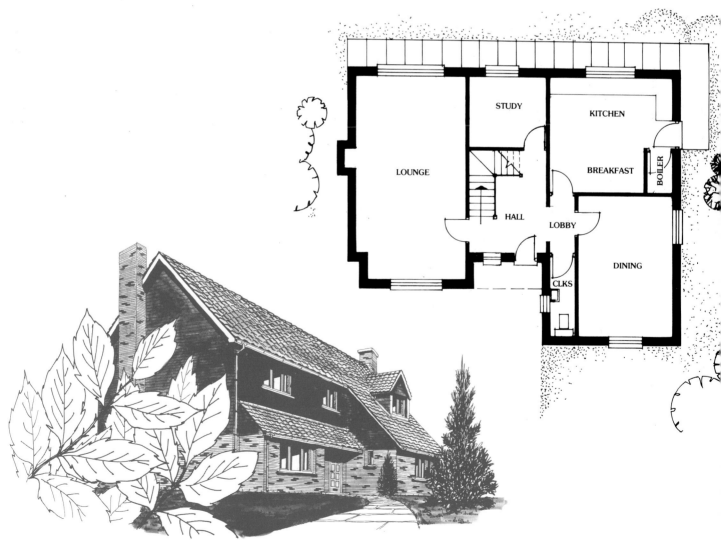

WINCHELSEA

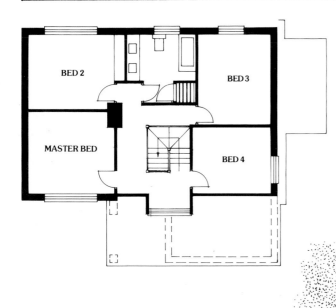

Design Number 83238

Floor Area (inc. garage)	1851 sq.ft.	172 sq.m.
Dimensions overall	45'5'' x 34'4''	13.8 x 10.4
Lounge	23'5'' x 13'0''	7.14 x 3.96
Dining	12'0'' x 10'0''	3.65 x 3.05
Kitchen	13'3½'' x 11'0''	4.05 x 3.35
Utility (overall)	11'1'' x 6'0''	3.38 x 1.83
Garage	18'6'' x 11'7''	5.63 x 3.53
Master Bed	12'0'' x 13'0''	3.65 x 3.96
Bed 2	11'1'' x 13'0''	3.38 x 3.96
Bed 3	13'3½'' x 11'0''	4.05 x 3.35
Bed 4	12'1'' x 9'10''	3.68 x 2.99

This unusual house was originally designed for a site in Kent, but will be equally at home anywhere in the south of the country. The character is all in the external appearance, with two windows under tiled eyebrows and a third set deep behind the eaves. Inside the house the layout is wholly conventional and very convenient.

A roof of this sort will almost certainly have to be clad with traditional small plain tiles, which are expensive, but a home like this will certainly have a premium value. Leaded lights to the windows will further add to the cost — and to the value.

PETERSFIELD

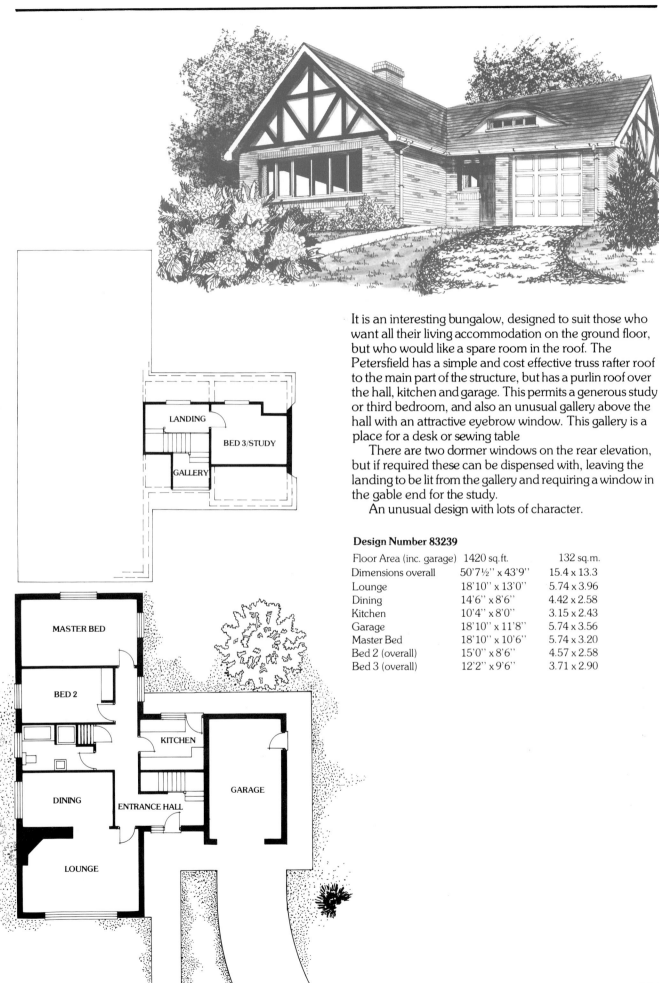

It is an interesting bungalow, designed to suit those who want all their living accommodation on the ground floor, but who would like a spare room in the roof. The Petersfield has a simple and cost effective truss rafter roof to the main part of the structure, but has a purlin roof over the hall, kitchen and garage. This permits a generous study or third bedroom, and also an unusual gallery above the hall with an attractive eyebrow window. This gallery is a place for a desk or sewing table

There are two dormer windows on the rear elevation, but if required these can be dispensed with, leaving the landing to be lit from the gallery and requiring a window in the gable end for the study.

An unusual design with lots of character.

Design Number 83239

Floor Area (inc. garage)	1420 sq.ft.	132 sq.m.
Dimensions overall	50'7½'' x 43'9''	15.4 x 13.3
Lounge	18'10'' x 13'0''	5.74 x 3.96
Dining	14'6'' x 8'6''	4.42 x 2.58
Kitchen	10'4'' x 8'0''	3.15 x 2.43
Garage	18'10'' x 11'8''	5.74 x 3.56
Master Bed	18'10'' x 10'6''	5.74 x 3.20
Bed 2 (overall)	15'0'' x 8'6''	4.57 x 2.58
Bed 3 (overall)	12'2'' x 9'6''	3.71 x 2.90

HORNDEAN

This boathouse and holiday home is designed for the familiar situation where a yachtsman wants to let the living accommodation on a commercial basis for part of the year, but does not want the tenants to have the use of his boathouse. To meet this requirement there are no internal stairs, and the two parts of the building are quite separate. The whole structure is designed to be built economically, and the first floor is supported on a prefabricated concrete decking which can be positioned by the crane on the lorry that delivers it. There are further savings to be made if some pillars are acceptable in the boathouse, but a clear span is quite practicable.

Design Number 83272

Floor Area
(exc. boathouse)	840 sq. ft.	79 sq.m.
Lounge	19'0'' x 11'0''	5.79 x 3.36
Dining	12'4'' x 8'2''	3.78 x 2.50
Kitchen	12'0'' x 10'6''	3.68 x 3.19
Bed 1	11'7'' x 10'6''	3.54 x 3.21
Bed 2	10'7'' x 9'0''	3.23 x 2.75

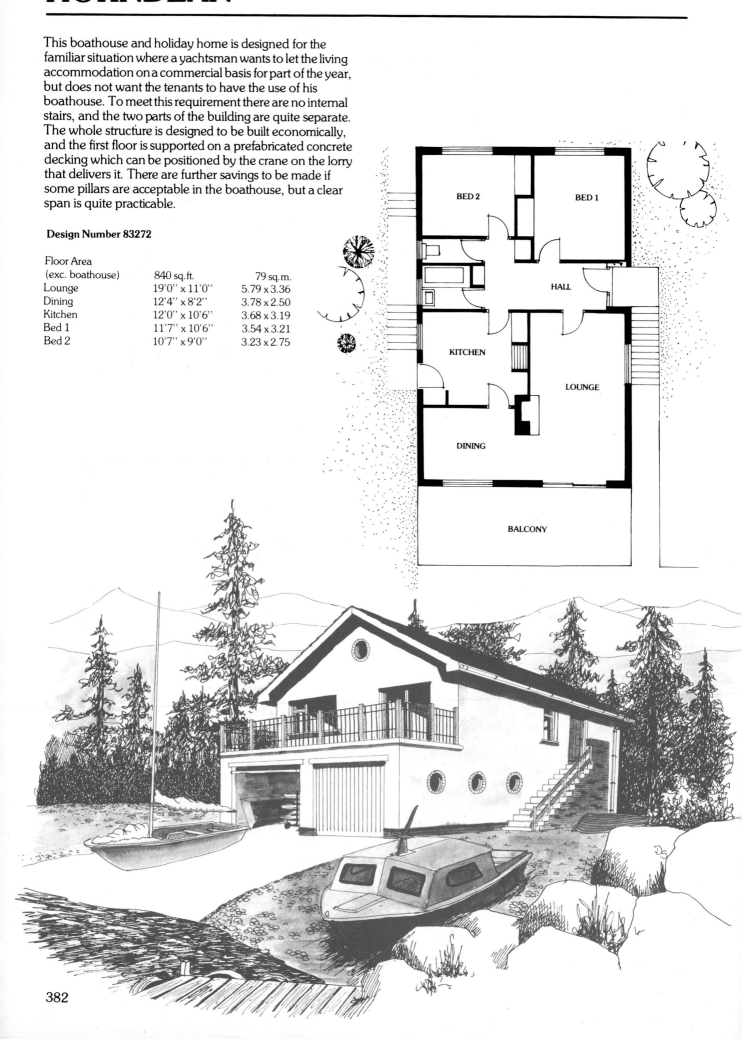

LEANDER

There are still sites for the classic waterside home for the boating enthusiast. Planning considerations will almost certainly require that the design should be traditional, and practical considerations will dictate a generous "wet oil skins" area by the door, a first floor lounge, and a balcony.

This design from the USA is the classic answer to these requirements. The master bedroom suite is on the ground floor with bedroom 2, whilst a further guest room is above. The layout is as practical for the soaking wet crew coming in from a gale as it is for the party they will give when they hear that they have won the race on handicap. Above all the structure is very cost-effective and avoids the money-no-object features often found in this sort of building.

Design Number 83273

Floor Area
(exc. covered area)	1469 sq.ft.	136 sq.m.
Lounge	15'0" x 23'4"	4.57 x 7.11
Dining	9'11" x 9'0"	3.02 x 2.74
Kitchen	9'0" x 11'1"	2.74 x 3.36
Utility	7'2" x 7'8"	2.20 x 2.35
Master Bed	14'0" x 9'0"	4.26 x 2.74
Bed 2	10'9" x 11'0"	3.26 x 3.35
Bed 3	10'9" x 13'0"	3.26 x 3.96

Home Planners, Inc
23761 Reseach Drive
Farmington Hills, Michigan 48024, USA.

CARSHOLME

The Carsholme garage/flat was originally built in a Notts orchard where the planners insisted on a 40% pitch roof. It seemed a pity to waste the space in the roof and so provision was made for a small flat above. The whole arrangement works very well, and the design has been used many times. Sometimes the flat has been built as a games room, but usually it is used for overflow accommodation or as a staff flat

This garage can be built without fitting out the first floor, and provided that this space is shown as a loft in the planning application it should escape rating as domestic accommodation. It can always be completed as a flat at a later date.

The two illustrations shew alternative arrangements for the side windows in the flat.

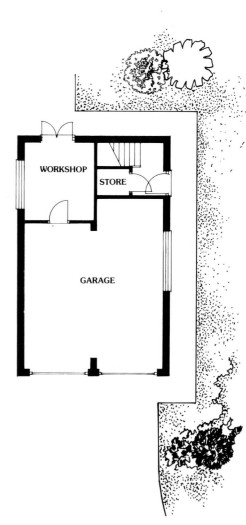

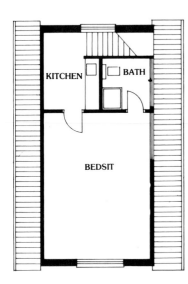

Design Number 83274

Every garage for a new home should be considered in relation to the house or bungalow itself, so that the smaller building enhances the appearance of the larger, and is related to it in a way which is both practical and attractive. The garage may not be built until a later stage, but the planning application for a new home invariably shows it on the site plan. Remember that the Local Authority may insist on the garage being sited where there is room for a vehicle to turn round on the plot, without having to back out into the road.

All the garages shown are intended to illustrate styles, and practicable sizes. Drawings are available for all of them with garage doors in any style and with any arrangement of side doors, garden stores, workshops or outside W.C.'s that may be required. The dimensions can also be varied within fairly wide limits, but remember that the minimum internal width for a single garage is eight feet, for a double garage with double door is sixteen feet, and for a double garage with twin doors is seventeen feet six.

Standard garage doors are either 6ft.6'' or 7ft. high. We are often asked for drawings for garages with increased headroom for caravans. This can be arranged, but it is rarely a success. A high garage usually manages to make the adjacent house or bungalow look small, and it is difficult to get the proportions right. If this is what you want please discuss the problem with us — there are ways around it.

GARAGE G.21

This large double garage has two separate doors in a gable end, with a garden store and optional W.C. behind. The doors are deeply set in the brick reveals, which gives a very substantial feel to the building. It is important that the roof pitch should match the pitch of the roof to the house or bungalow — the two illustrations show how important this is.

Floor Area (total)	460 sq. ft.	42.7 sq.m.
Overall external	21'6'' x 23'5''	6.5 x 7.1
Garage	18'0'' x 20'10½''	5.48 x 6.36
Store	4'0'' x 14'6½''	1.22 x 4.43
W.C.	4'0'' x 6'0''	1.22 x 1.83

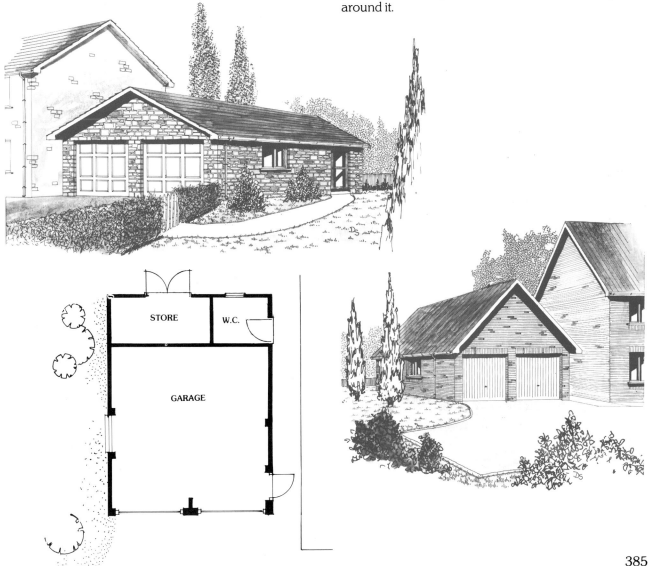

STORE W.C.

GARAGE

GARAGES

GARAGE G.22

This unusual roof arrangement keeps down the overall height to the building while retaining a tiled front elevation. It also keeps down construction costs. Drawings are available for a version of this garage with two separate 7ft. doors.

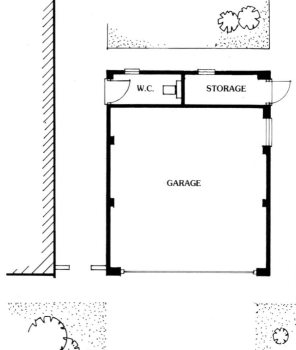

Total Floor Area	387 sq.ft.	36 sq.m.
Overall external dimensions	22'11'' x 18'10''	6.9 x 5.7
Garage (internal)	18'2½'' x 18'0''	5.55 x 5.48
W.C. (internal)	8'11'' x 3'6''	2.72 x 1.06
Store	8'11'' x 3'6''	2.72 x 1.06

GARAGE G.23

A hip roof may be appropriate to a garage built beside a new house where this roof style is a feature. It is shown here with a double door, but drawings are available for this garage with two doors separated by a substantial pillar.

GARAGES

GARAGE G.24

This flat roofed garage has room for a workbench in front of one car, and a garden store in front of the other. The double doors into the store are necessary if a ride-on mower has to be garaged as well as the cars: few of these will go through a standard doorway.

Total Floor Area	396 sq.ft.	36.8 sq.m.
Overall dimensions	21'6½'' x 20'1''	6.5 x 6.1
Garage (internal overall)	19'0'' x 20'10½''	5.79 x 6.36
Garden Store	10'4'' x 5'0''	3.13 x 1.52

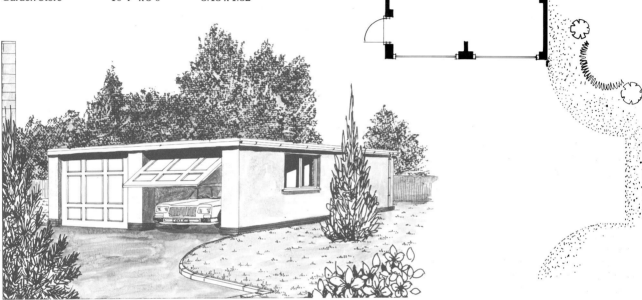

GARAGE G.25

When choosing a design for a garage it is important to consider how it will look in relation to the house which it serves. Sometimes this means that the doors of the garage should be under the eaves and not in the gable end, and this design meets this requirement. Drawings are available for a version with two separate doors.

Floor Area	327 sq.ft.	30.4 sq.m.
Internal dimensions	18'0'' x 18'2½''	5.4 x 5.5
External dimensions	18'10'' x 19'0''	5.7 x 5.8

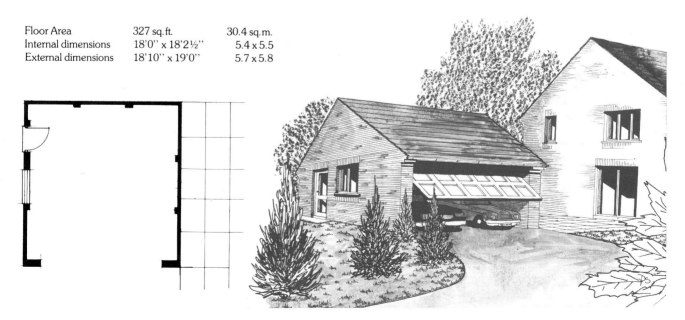

387

GARAGES

GARAGE G.26

This garage has a parapet roof with a coping. It is an extremely useful design in some areas, particularly when built in stone to match existing stone buildings.

Floor Area	392 sq. ft.	36.4 sq.m.
Internal	18'0" x 21'9"	5.4 x 6.6
Overall dimensions	23'9" x 20'0"	7.2 x 6.0

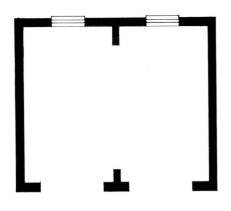

GARAGE G.27

This straight-forward single garage with a pitched roof is shown with traditional side-hung doors. In spite of the convenience of up-and-over doors there are many who like wooden doors of this sort, and all our garage drawings can be altered to show this feature.

Floor Area	207 sq. ft.	19.2 sq.m.
Internal dimensions	11'2" x 18'0"	3.4 x 5.4
External dimensions	11'10" x 19'0"	3.6 x 5.8

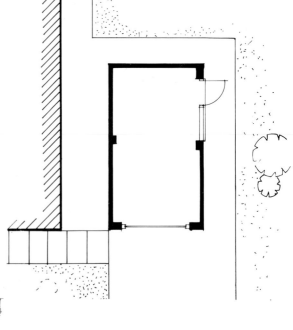

GARAGE G.28

This is a very useful design for a village site where small outbuildings are the rule, and a rectangular garage would seem too modern. The workshop is a useful size, and can, of course, be used for many other purposes, including being a farm office.

Overall dimensions	17'2½'' x 17'8''	5.2 x 5.3
Workshop Floor Area	84 sq. ft.	7.8 sq.m.
Workshop Internal	7'0'' x 12'0''	2.13 x 3.66
Garage Floor Area	150 sq. ft.	14 sq.m.
Garage Internal	9'0'' x 16'8''	2.74 x 5.07

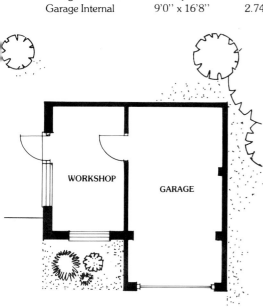

GARAGE G.29

A simple straight-forward garage of the minimum width for a modern car, making it suitable for sites where space is at a premium.

Floor Area	140 sq. ft.	13.0 sq.m.
Overall dimensions	9'9'' x 18'6''	2.9 x 5.6
Internal dimensions	8'3'' x 17'0''	2.5 x 5.1

GARAGES

GARAGE G.30

A single garage with the up-and-over door under the eaves. This is the minimum size for a modern car, but of course, it can be extended to your own requirements.

Floor Area	140 sq. ft.	13 sq.m.
Overall dimensions	9'9'' x 18'6''	2.9 x 5.6
Internal dimensions	8'3'' x 17'0''	2.5 x 5.1

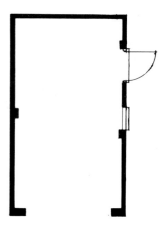

GARAGE G.31

This flat roofed garage attached to one wall of a bungalow requires very careful consideration of floor heights if it is to look right. It is important that the fascia continues from the bungalow right around the garage at the same depth.

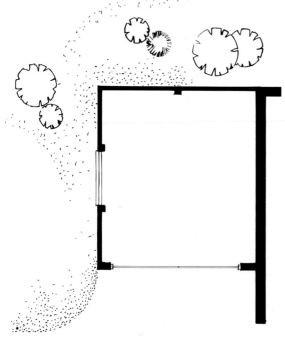

Floor Area	333 sq. ft.	31 sq.m.
Internal dimensions	18'6'' x 18'0''	5.6 x 5.4
Overall dimensions	18'4'' x 19'0''	5.7 x 5.8

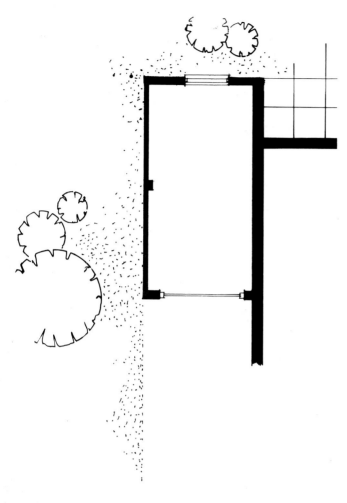

GARAGE G.32

This is a single garage version of Garage G.31 showing it projecting behind the rear wall of the bungalow. This is often arranged to give a sheltered patio area.

Floor Area	207 sq.ft.	19.2 sq.m.
Internal dimensions	11'6'' x 18'0''	3.5 x 5.4
External dimensions	11'10'' x 19'0''	3.6 x 5.8

GARAGE G.33

It is far easier to build a garage against the side of a house than against the side of a bungalow, as the relationship between the floor levels is not critical.

Floor Area	207 sq.ft.	19.2 sq.m.
Internal dimensions	11'6'' x 18'0''	3.5 x 5.4
External dimensions	11'10'' x 19'0''	3.6 x 5.8

The P.S.S. Service

P.S.S. PLANS

Plans Sales Services Ltd is a specialist company within the D & M Group which handles sales of plans for houses and bungalows in the style of the designs in this book. The service which is offered covers the supply of plans and specification notes as detailed on page 394.

To provide these plans P.S.S. require specific information regarding the site and other details for the proposed building, and this is most conveniently provided by completing the order form on page 397.

ALTERATIONS TO PLANS

Many of the designs illustrated are standard plans for which drawings are immediately available. Such standard plans can be altered provided that the design concept is not changed. The cost of such alterations is quoted as an extra to the basic cost of the plans, and the procedure for preparing altered plans is for an order form to be sent to P.S.S. with the appropriate remittance for the cost of the standard plans. Two prints of the floor plans and elevation for the standard plans will be sent to the client, one copy of which should be returned marked up with the alterations required.

If the alterations are practicable the extra fee required for the altered drawings will be quoted, and if accepted the special drawings will be prepared to an agreed timescale.

SITE PLANS AND LOCATION PLANS

Planning applications require a site plan and a location plan. These are normally reproduced on a single sheet. The standard P.S.S. service can include drawing these plans from data supplied by clients, and responsibility for the accuracy of this data rests with the client.

Location plans are prepared from either any location plan which accompanied an application for an existing outline consent, or from a 1:2500 or similar large scale Ordnance Survey map, or from a deed plan or other map available. The original or photostats of such plan should be sent with the order and should have the boundary of the client's land clearly marked. The company holds a licence to reproduce Ordnance Survey plans in this way.

Site plans are best drawn from sketches prepared by clients, which must include adequate dimensions to allow them to be drawn to scale, and sufficient detail with regard to such features as existing drainage, trees on the site and other details required by the local authority. Delay will be unavoidable if these points are not covered.

We recognise that some clients prepare their own site and location plans.

Plans are normally prepared from master data, and are normally captioned with a general description such as 'Proposed bungalow for Mr. H. Smith at High Lane, Sutton.' They carry the client's name and address in the bottom right-hand corner. Except for a reference number they do not carry a P.S.S. or any other logo or name, except when they are timber frame plans for which the design calculations are available from Prestoplan Homes Ltd.

Purchase of the plans conveys an automatic licence to build the dwelling to which they refer. They may not be used for the construction of further dwellings unless arrangements for this have been specially recognised and confirmed in correspondence. Enquiries from builders and others for the use of designs on a repeat basis are welcomed.

FOUNDATION DETAILS

Most of our plans are drawn assuming a level site, but designs specifically advertised as suitable for sloping sites show standard details for notional slopes. All plans are normally supplied for solid ground floor construction with strip foundations, unless otherwise requested. Where a reinforced concrete raft is required, notional details will be shown, and further details may have to be provided by a Civil Engineer as explained below.

If the ground conditions are unusual, or if you are building on a steep slope, the Local Authority may require a site investigation and that foundations or retaining walls are specially designed. This information is only required to support Building Regulation applications, not Planning Applications. If an application to build on such sites is made using our standard drawings the Local Authority will reply advising whether any special data is required. Although we do not undertake the necessary site investigations and foundation design work for this ourselves, we can put clients in touch with Civil Engineers able to do this work.

If in doubt about this please telephone us and discuss you situation.

ALTERATION TO PLANS FOLLOWING NEGOTIATIONS WITH PLANNING AUTHORITIES

Negotiations with planners sometimes result in a request from the local authority for a new set of plans incorporating design changes. In this case the planning officer concerned should be invite to overdraw one of his original prints with his required alterations, and this should be sent to us. We will quote for preparing the revised drawings and supplying prints as appropriate.

QUERIES RAISED IN CONNECTION WITH BUILDING REGULATION APPLICATION

Queries relating to site conditions must be dealt with by the client. P.S.S. will deal with all queries which relate to the structure of the building raised by the local authority arising from building regulation applications. This is handled by sending P.S.S. the original or a photostat of the letter from the authority setting out the additional information required, and P.S.S. will return to the client three copies of amended drawings providing the relevant information or calculations — one for the client to retain and two to be sent to the authority. There is no charge for this if standard designs are involved.

If building regulation queries relate to an altered design, and arise from the alteration to the design, as

The P.S.S. Service

when roof design calculations are required after the span of a standard design has been increased, or special steelwork or timber joists are introduced, the cost of providing this information and any revised drawing will be quoted.

Information that is required regarding proprietary materials or products may have to be obtained from manufacturers. We advise on how this information is best obtained.

For obvious reasons it is preferable that clients check that no alterations are required by planning officers before dealing with building regulation queries.

Additional copies of plans required are avaible at a nominal charge to cover printing and postage.

P.S.S. are able to handle a limited number of planning and building regulation applications on behalf of clients. Fees for this are quoted individually. This work may be carried out by other companies within the D & M Group, or by associates. The number of applications handled in this way is limited as all require individual attention. Normally, 95% of clients make their own submissions to the local authority.

TIMBER FRAME CONSTRUCTION

Clients who wish to build in the style of any of the designs in this book in timber frame can do so using the services of Prestoplan Homes Ltd. All the types of home shown in this book can be built using a timber frame and not just those from the Prestoplan standard range.

Plans can be supplied through P.S.S. if desired but it is preferable to contact Prestoplan direct if you wish to build in timber frame.

Prestoplan Homes Limited
Four Oaks Road
Walton Summit Centre
PRESTON PR5 8AS.

DESIGN AND MATERIALS LTD.

P.S.S. is part of the same group of companies as Design & Materials Ltd., and if requested D & M will provide other services for those wishing to build to designs in styles shown in this book.

D & M offer an integrated architectural and material supply service for any house or bungalow in a style illustrated, and this will include a wide range of ancillary services including assistance in placing a contract with a builder. Other special services are provided for those who wish to manage the construction work themselves as self-builders. All D & M services are for traditional construction.

Clients who have purchased plans from P.S.S. can obtain a quotations from D & M for the supply of materials for the building entirely free of obligation.

Design & Materials Limited
Carlton Industrial Estate
Worksop
Notts S81 9LB.
Phone (0909) 730333

FEES FOR P.S.S. PLANS

Prices are quoted according to work involved. As a guide, 1992 average prices were as follows. If a set of P.S.S. drawings leads to using the D & M service the cost of the drawings is refunded.

Plans for homes to 1001 sq.ft.
£275.00 + £48.12 VAT = £323.12

Plans from 1002 to 1399 sq.ft.
£300.00 + £52.50 VAT = £352.50

Plans from 1400 to 1699 sq.ft.
£350.00 + £61.25 VAT = £411.25

Plans from 1400 to 2001 sq.ft.
£400 + £70.00 VAT = £470.00

Plans over 2001 sq.ft.
from £425.00 + £74.37 VAT = £499.37

Standard garages with plans
£30.00 + £5.25 VAT = £35.25

Standard garages without plans
£120.00 + £21.00 VAT = £141.00

Carsholme garage/flat
£200.00 + £35.00 VAT = £235.00

The arrangements for altering plans and the fees involved are detailed elsewhere.

Extra copies of drawings required at any time are available at £1 per print.

All fees are subject to VAT.

Preliminary enquiries by telephone are welcome.

Plan Sales Services Ltd.,
Lawn Road, Carlton-in-Lindrick,
Worksop, Notts S81 9LB.
Phone Worksop (0909) 733927

Company Reg. No. 1625297

The P.S.S. Service — Drawings

A SET OF P.S.S. DRAWINGS COMPRISES:
* 12 copies of 1:50 floor plans, 1:100 elevations and 1:20 sections with full notes indicating compliance with Building Regulation Standards.
* 4 copies of a foundation plan.
* 4 copies of a floor joist plan
* 12 copies of a site plan and location plan.

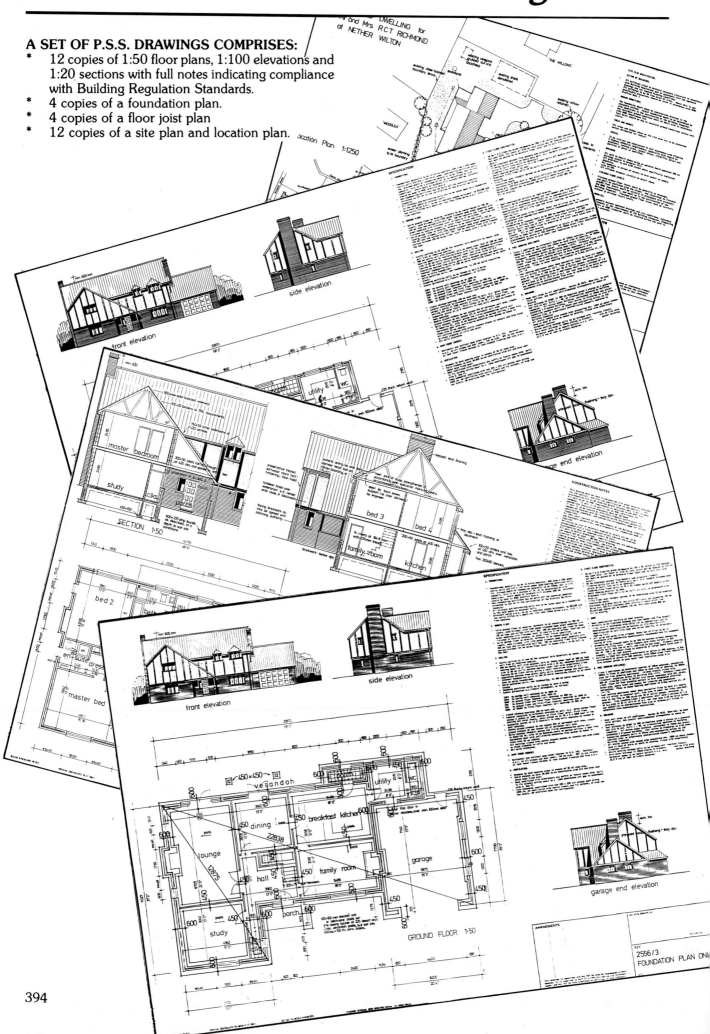

The P.S.S. Service — Ordering Plans

The P.S.S. Service is a **service**, and the company relies on its reputation for its continuing success. They aim to make ordering a set of plans as easy as possible, and are always ready to give advice to prospective purchasers before they commit themselves. The easiest way to get this advice is to telephone on 0909 733927 during office hours. One of the senior staff is usually on hand to discuss your requirements with you, but if the right person for you to speak to is not immediately available then someone will arrange to phone you back. If you prefer to write to P.S.S., they will send a reply back to you on the day that they get your letter.

The full details of the service are set out on pages 392 and 393, and explains how P.S.S. prepares drawings to your own requirements. They will draw your site plan, will provide a specification for the building, and much more. Please read these pages carefully, and if you have any queries telephone 0909 733927.

An order form is on page 397. If possible please complete the part asking for your phone number, as we would like to be able to telephone you if there is any point regarding your order which we would like to check with you.

Addresses

Plans for designs in this book.
Plan Sales Services Ltd, Lawn Road, Carlton-in-Lindrick, Worksop, Notts S81 9LB. Tel: 0909 733927.

A special service for building designs in this book using traditional construction.
Design and Materials Limited, Carlton Industrial Estate, Worksop, Notts S81 9LB. Tel: 0909 730333.

A service for timber frame construction.
Prestoplan Homes Limited, Four Oaks Road, Walton Summit Centre, Preston, Lancs PR5 8AS. Tel: 0772 627373

Choosing bricks or pavers.
Butterley Brick Limited, Wellington Street, Ripley, Derby. Tel: 0773 570570

Choosing stone.
E.C.C. Quarries Limited, Okus, Swindon, Wilts. Tel: 0793 528131.

Choosing tiles.
Redland Roof Tiles Limited, Redland House, Reigate, Surrey. Tel: 0737 242488.

Choosing joinery.
Malden Timber, Malden House, Radlett Road, Park Street, St. Albans, Herts. Tel: 0727 73337 or any of their branches.

Choosing doors.
Malden Timber, Malden House, Radlett Road, Park Street, St. Albans, Herts. Tel: 0727 73337 or any of their branches.

Choosing staircases.
Bolton and Paul (Joinery) Ltd, Riverside Works, Norwich NR1 1EB. Tel: 0603 660133.

Choosing staircase fittings.
Richard Burbidge & Sons Ltd., Whittington Road, Oswestry, Shropshire SY11 1HZ. Tel: 0691 655131

Choosing garage doors.
P.C. Henderson Limited, Romford, Essex RM3 8UL. Tel: 0402 34555.

Choosing roofs.
Hy Arnold Ltd., Holton Heath Trading Park, Poole, Dorset. Tel: 0202 623777 or Hy Arnold Ltd, Carr Wood Road, Glasshoughton, Castleford, W. Yorks. Tel: 0977 554220.

Choosing a bathroom.
Ideal Standard Limited, P.O. Box 60, Hull HU5 4JE.

Choosing a kitchen.
Spring Ram Contracts plc, Springbank Industrial Estate, Sowerby Bridge, W. Yorks HX6 3JE. Tel: 0422 839955.

Choosing heating.
Solid Fuel Advisory Service at the address in your local telephone directory.

NHBC publications available to non-members from:
NHBC, 58 Portland Place, London W1.

Building on your own, using sub-contractors or your own labour?
Read *Building Your Own Home*, £10.50 post paid from Ryton Books, Ryton Street, Worksop, Notts, who send it with the current month's list of councils with plots for sale to self-builders.

Self build groups.
General leaflets from the National Federation of Housing Associations, 30/32 Southampton Street, London WC2 7AE.

Insurance for those building on their own.
A special insurance policy for those building on their own land is available with Norwich Union and is offered by D.M.S. Services Limited, at Orchard House, Blyth, Worksop, Notts S81 8HF. Tel: 0909 591652 for proposal forms.

Management services for individual homes.
Shire Country Homes, 'Imagine', The Bungalows, Rolvenden Hill, Cranbrook, Kent TN17 4JN. Tel: 0580 240448

Plans Order Form

P.S.S. Ltd.

Please supply a set of plans as in Home Plans. A cheque to cover fees is enclosed.

I understand the basis on which plans are supplied, and am available to deal with queries by phone, when the most convenient time to ring is

a.m./p.m.

Are you placing this order following previous contact with P.S.S.? If so, please give some reference (eg. date of telephone call, or details of correspondence).

Yes/No

Do you require plans for a design generally as shown in the book? ☐ tick

Or with alterations? ☐ tick

Or an original design? ☐ tick

Many plans in this book are of standard designs for which standard drawings are available. Others illustrate design styles in which new drawings can be prepared.

Which is the design that meets, or most nearly meets you requirements? (Give page number or design number)

Site Address . . . .

. . . .

To which hand (ie. as illustrated, or in mirror image)?

In what materials will you build?

Roofing . . . .

External Walling . . . .

Please indicate appropriate roof pitch (tick).

22½°   30°   35°

40°   other — please state

Name . . . .

Address . . . .

. . . .

. . . .

Daytime phone number . . . .

Evening phone number . . . .

Prices are quoted according to work involved. As a guide, 1992 average prices were as follows. If a set of P.S.S. drawings leads to using the D & M service the cost of the drawings is refunded.

Plans for homes to 1001 sq.ft.
£275.00 + £48.12 VAT = £323.12

Plans from 1002 to 1399 sq.ft.
£300.00 + £52.50 VAT = £352.50

Plans from 1400 to 1699 sq.ft.
£350.00 + £61.25 VAT = £411.25

Plans from 1400 to 2001 sq.ft.
£400 + £70.00 VAT = £470.00

Plans over 2001 sq.ft.
from £425.00 + £74.37 VAT = £499.37

Standard garages with plans
£30.00 + £5.25 VAT = £35.25

Standard garages without plans
£120.00 + £21.00 VAT = £141.00

Carsholme garage/flat
£200.00 + £35.00 VAT = £235.00

The arrangements for altering plans and the fees involved are detailed elsewhere.

Plan Sales Services Ltd., Lawn Road, Carlton-in-Lindrick, Worksop, Notts S81 9LB.
Phone Worksop (0909) 733927

Is the roof to be shown with barge boards and fascia, or with pointed verge and corbells? Please tick appropriate sketch.

BARGE BOARD AND FASCIA   POINTED VERGE AND CORBELLS

Advise whether any french windows or patio doors should be shown as french windows or as sliding patio doors (this does not count as an alteration to a standard design).

Should any fireplace and chimney shown in the drawings be retained or deleted? This does not count as an alteration.

Do you require the drawings to show a solid concrete ground floor, or a suspended timber ground floor or concrete beam and block construction?

The attention of clients is drawn to the terms and conditions of sale printed on the reverse of this order form.

Terms and Conditions

TERMS AND CONDITIONS OF SALE

1. These terms and conditions are concerned with the sale by Plan Sales Services Ltd. of plans as advertised in the book *Home Plans*. All sales of plans by the company unless expressly stated otherwise are in accordance with these terms and conditions of sale, and clients placing an order for these plans are deemed to do so under these conditions.

2. All contracts are for the sale of plans only, and do not imply the provision of an architectural service, advice on the use of plans or the construction of buildings or other services of any sort except where specifically arranged in writing.

3. All plans offered are fully detailed in accordance with current architectural practice, but no liability is accepted for any loss of any sort or additional expense incurred consequent on any failure, real or alleged, of the plans to meet the requirements of any body, statutory or otherwise, or of any loss of any sort or additional expense incurred due to any failure to submit the plans as and when required to any body, statutory or otherwise. All dimensions on drawings which relate to site dimensions, drainage, access, or other features of a development are deemed to have been checked and approved by clients. Clients purchasing plans are advised in writing to check all dimensions shown on drawings and to satisfy themselves that they are in every way correct. No responsibility can be accepted for any loss consequent on failure to do this.

4. All plans are supplied as being adequate to enable competent craftsmen, properly directed and working to the published recommendations of the National Housebuilders Registration Council to erect the building to which they relate, but no liability whatsoever is accepted for the building so erected. Contracts are established on the understanding that all plans and drawings supplied will be used by persons competent and experienced in the use of building plans and drawings, and no liability will be incurred due to the failure of such persons to relate plans and drawings to site conditions, materials delivered, or other circumstances, or to take immediate action on discovering any anomaly in the drawings.

5. The company will alter drawings as detailed in the book *Home Plans*, and in other advertising literature, but such alterations will only be made in accordance with specific and precise instructions.

6. The company will deal with technical queries dealing with application of the Building Regulations and N.H.B.C. requirements to the structures shown in the drawings, but can only do this if provided with an original or a photostat of the query on the letterhead of the authority requiring this information. Information required regarding proprietary materials or components to be used may have to be obtained from manufacturers. We advise on how this information is best obtained.

7. The company is unable to deal with queries from statutory authorities relating to site conditions.

8. All orders for plans are dealt with immediately they are received. If plans are required urgently, as when drawings have to be submitted to a planning authority within a deadline, this should be advised to the company in writing and the work will be given every priority. However, no responsibility can be accepted for the consequences of any delay in delivery of plans.

9. Proof of posting of plans shall be proof of delivery. Any plans lost in the post will be replaced at 'copy plan' cost.

10. Master negatives of plans supplied will be kept for a period of three years only.

11. No refunds can be made in respect of plans returned as no longer required, whether or not they have received Planning Consent or Building Regulation Approval.

12. Where clients are referred to Design and Materials Ltd., or any other company for special services beyond the scope of the P.S.S. service, any new contract is between the client and the company concerned, and P.S.S. Ltd. will not be a party to any such contract.

13. The copyright of all plans is held by the company, and remains with the company on the supply of plans. The supply of a set of plans as advertised conveys a licence to build one dwelling to the plans supplied, and the erection of further dwellings is a breach of copyright unless this has been the subject of a separate written contract.

14. These terms and conditions define the nature of the contract, and attention is drawn to them in the book *Home Plans* and other publications. They do not detract from the statutory rights of the client in the contract.

15. The description of the P.S.S. service as published in this edition of *Home Plans*, replaces all previous descriptions, and all contracts made from the date of the publication of this edition are on these terms.

Also by Murray Armor —

Two Essential Books

BUILDING YOUR OWN HOME

Now in its thirteenth edition, it deals with every aspect of building a house or bungalow from finding a site and obtaining planning consent all the way to obtaining the final VAT refunds. The standard handbook for the thousands who build a new home each year.

PLANS FOR DREAM HOMES

Plans for Dream Homes complements Home Plans with a further 460 plans of recently completed new homes, with text that discusses their design features in relation to their sites and the homebuilders requirements.

A wealth of advice and design information for anyone contemplating a new home. Working drawings are available for all the designs illustrated.

THE RYTON BOOKS LIST OF SELF BUILD OPPORTUNITIES

A list of serviced plots for sale in all parts of the country is sent with all orders for these books received by Ryton Books.

From all booksellers or by post from Ryton Books, 29 Ryton Street, Worksop, Notts. (Tel. 0909 591652)

 CREDIT CARD ORDERS
— Phone 0909 591652 **VISA**
(Books despatched within 24 hours)

BUILDERS RISKS INSURANCES
FOR THOSE BUILDING ON THEIR OWN LAND

The Norwich Union is able to offer an insurance package for those who are building for their own occupation private dwellings of traditional construction with the help of labour only sub-contractors. It does not apply to the extension, alteration, repair or renovation of existing buildings. This affords Contract Works, Public Liability and Employers' Liability cover and automatically includes the interest of any Mortgagee. Cover will be provided in one policy document, summarised as follows. This description of insurance must be regarded only as an outline. The policy is a legal document and as such defines the insurance in precise terms. A specimen copy of the policy form is available on request.

CONTRACT WORKS

Cover	"All Risks" of loss or damage to:
	(a) the new building whilst under construction and materials for incorporation therein
	(b) plant, tools, equipment and temporary buildings (other than residential caravans).
Sum insured	The full rebuilding cost of the property, excluding the value of the land.
including	(a) your own and hired plant, tools and equipment used in connection with the work up to a total sum insured of £2000 (can be increased if required).
	(b) Employees personal effects and tools whilst on the site up to a sum insured of £250 any one employee.
	(c) Architects, Surveyors and other fees necessarily incurred in rebuilding following loss or damage.
	(d) the cost of removing debris following any claim.
Excluding	(a) the first £50 of each and every claim for loss or damage to employees personal effects or tools.
	(b) the first £250 of each and every other loss.

EMPLOYERS LIABILITY (compulsory by law)

Cover	Your legal liability for death or bodily injury to employees, including labour only sub-contractors, arising out of the building work.
Limit	Unlimited.
Including	Legal costs and expenses in defending any claim.
Note	A Certificate of Insurance will be provided, and must by law be displayed on site.

PUBLIC LIABILITY

Cover	Your legal liability to members of the public for death, bodily injury or damage to property, arising out of the building work.
Limit	£1,000,000 any one loss.
Including	Legal costs and expenses in defending any claim.
Excluding	The first £100 of any claim for damage to property.

PERIOD	From the commencement date you specify (which should be no earlier than the date you complete the proposal form) up to completion of the building work, subject to a maximum of 24 months. Extensions to this period are available on payment of an additional premium. There is no refund for early completion.
THE POLICY	Will be sent direct to you by the Insurance Company.
THE PREMIUM	£4.90 per 1,000 on the rebuilding cost of the property. (Minimum £60,000). This is a total rate for all the cover set out above, subject to submission of the completed proposal form overleaf.

Rebuilding Cost Up to £	Premium £	Rebuilding Cost Up to £	Premium £	Rebuilding Cost Up to £	Premium £
60,000	294.00	90,000	441.00	140,000	686.00
65,000	318.50	95,000	465.50	150,000	735.00
70,000	343.00	100,000	490.00	160,000	784.00
75,000	367.50	110,000	539.00	170,000	833.00
80,000	392.00	120,000	588.00	180,000	882.00
85,000	416.50	130,000	637.00	190,000	931.00

Over 190,000 @
£4.90 per £1000

IMPORTANT

The above terms only apply:
(a) up to 31st December 1992. Phone to confirm rates for proposal forms completed after that date.
(b) to risks in Mainland Great Britain only. Proposals from N. Ireland are quoted individually. Phone 0909 591652 for a quotation.
(c) where there is no history of flooding in the area.

THE AGENCY

The Agency is DMS Services Ltd., a company which provides specialised insurance services to those building on their own. The proposal form overleaf should be completed and sent to the agency with a cheque for the premium payable to the Norwich Union Fire Insurance Society Limited.

D.M.S. Services Ltd., Orchard House, Blyth, Worksop, Notts. S81 8HF. Phone 0909 591652

Proposal - BUILDING OWN PRIVATE DWELLING
The Insurer: Norwich Union Fire Insurance Society Limited

Name of Proposer	Phone No.

Full Postal Address

....

Postcode

Address of property to be erected

....

Commencing date of insurance

Important - Please give a definite answer to each question (block letters) and tick appropriate boxes

	Yes	No	If "Yes" please give details
1. Have you made any other proposal for insurance in respect of the risk proposed?	☐	☐	
2. Has any company or underwriter declined your proposal?	☐	☐	
3. Have you ever been convicted of (or charged but not yet tried with) arson or any offence involving dishonesty of any kind (eg fraud, theft, handling stolen goods)?	☐	☐	

4. Will the property be

(a) of standard brick, stone or concrete construction, roofed with slates, tiles, asphalt, concrete or metal? ☐ ☐

(b) of timber frame construction? ☐ ☐

(c) occupied as your permanent residence on completion? ☐ ☐ (If "No" please refer to DMS Services Ltd.) Phone 0909 591652

5. (a) Will the total value of plant, tools, equipment and temporary buildings used exceed £2,000 on site at any one time? ☐ ☐

Contractors plant hired in with operators, such as excavators, need not be included if proposers are wholly satisfied the hirers insurances cover all risks. However if cover is required on such machines phone DMS Services on 0909 591652

(b) Will plant be hired-in for which you are responsible to insure? ☐ ☐

6. Is there any history of flooding in the area? ☐ ☐

7. Will all work be in accordance with drawings approved by the Local Authority and the instructions of their Building Inspector? ☐ ☐

8. State estimated value of building work on completion at builder price for reinstatement. £ ____

N.B. This will be the limit of indemnity for item (a) of the Contract Works Section.

9. Material facts — state any other material facts here. Failure to do so could invalidate the policy. A material fact is one which is likely to influence an insurer in the assessment and acceptance of the proposal. If you are in any doubt as to whether a fact is material it should be disclosed to the insurer.

Note: 1. You should keep a record (including copies of letters) of all information supplied to the insurer for the purpose of entering into the contract.
2. A copy of this proposal form will be supplied by the Insurer on request within three months of completion.
3. Please note that the details you are asked to supply may be used to provide you with information about other products and services which the Norwich Union Group can offer.

Declaration To be completed in all cases:
I desire to insure with the Insurer in the terms of the Policy used in this class of Insurance. I warrant that the above statements and particulars are true to the best of my knowledge and belief and that I have not witheld any material information. I agree to give immediate notice to the insurer of any alteration to the circumstances described herein and that this proposal shall form the basis of the contract between us.

Proposer's signature	Date

Send completed form to DMS Services Ltd., Orchard House, Blyth, Worksop, Notts. S81 8HF, together with a cheque made payable to the Norwich Union Fire Insurance Society Limited. Any queries to DMS Services, Phone 0909 591652.

Norwich Union Fire Insurance Society Limited. Registered in England No. 99122. Registered Office: Surrey Street, Norwich NR1 3NS. Member of the Association of British Insurers. Member of the Insurance Ombudsman Bureau.

HOME PLUS COVER
On completion cover for the building and contents is available under a Norwich Union Home Plus policy. For details tick this box — ☐

NOTES

NOTES